OXFORD HISTORICAL MONOGRAPHS

Editors

M. H. KEEN   P. LANGFORD
H. M. MAYR-HARTING   H. C. G. MATTHEW
A. J. NICHOLLS   SIR KEITH THOMAS

D1100519

The Evolution
of the
Labour Party

1910-1924

BY

ROSS McKIBBIN

CLARENDON PRESS · OXFORD

Oxford University Press, Walton Street, Oxford OX2 6DP

Oxford New York Toronto
Delhi Bombay Calcutta Madras Karachi
Petaling Jaya Singapore Hong Kong Tokyo
Nairobi Dar es Salaam Cape Town
Melbourne Auckland

and associated companies in
Berlin Ibadan

ISBN –19–821899–0

Oxford is a trade mark of Oxford University Press

Published in the United States
by Oxford University Press, New York

First published 1974
Reprinted in Paperback 1983, 1986, 1991

© Oxford University Press 1974

British Library Cataloguing in Publication Data
McKibbin, Ross
The evolution of the Labour Party 1910–1924.—
(Oxford historical monographs)
1. Labour Party—Great Britain—History
I. Title
324.24107'09   JN1129.L32
ISBN 0–19–821899–0

Printed in Great Britain by
Antony Rowe Ltd
Chippenham

TO MY PARENTS

FOREWORD TO THE 1991 IMPRESSION

THIS book was first published in hardback fifteen years ago and was based upon a thesis completed twenty years ago. It thus rests on many of the assumptions that were common in the late 1960s and early 1970s and these are, to some extent, apparent in the argument. It was also written under the powerful influence of a school of labour history associated with Oxford University whose members included my own supervisor, A. F. Thompson. This 'school' (if it can be properly called that) has always emphasized the institutional character of the British trade unions and their ideological ambiguity, as well as their predominance in the wider labour movement. Its influence had several effects on my thesis. One was my emphasis upon the authority of the unions and the decisive way they shaped the Labour Party. This in turn meant a preoccupation with the Liberal Party and the Liberalism to which the unions (and the early Labour Party) were intimately related. The result was that the thesis was less internal to the working class than it would have been had I done it elsewhere.

This book was also the first to draw heavily on the archives of the Labour Party—then at Transport House, now in Manchester. Frank Bealey and Henry Pelling had made significant use of the pre-1906 correspondence,[1] but thereafter the very large (though incomplete) archive had apparently become inaccessible. Due to some luck and the benevolence of the then librarian of the Labour Party, Irene Wagner, I was given admittance to it. This was for a doctoral student immensely good fortune and it produced what was then (and still is) unusual in the historiography of British political parties: a study based to a considerable degree upon the 'official' records of a major party. This had, however, dangers as well as attractions. It undoubtedly gave the thesis a strong empirical base which has pretty well stood the test of time; even in retrospect I would not wish to change much of the argument which developed from that evidence, either for the national or the local Labour parties. On the other hand, it unquestionably cast the thesis in an administrative mould and I was obliged to get around that by the introduction of arguments that were themselves problematical—as several reviewers pointed out.

The thesis rested upon one other assumption that was never made explicit. Insofar as I had a model of a social-democratic party in mind when I began it, it was the Australian Labor Party. This precocious and

[1] F. Bealey and H. Pelling, *Labour and Politics, 1900—1906* (London, 1958).

politically formidable organization, which in its consistent capacity to maximize its electorate is probably without equal, is in its structure and political culture very similar to the British Labour Party. It was, and is, institutionally tied to and dependent on the trade unions, a number of which were originally merely colonies of the British unions which founded them. It was, and perhaps still is, the classic 'labourist' party. In fact, this model turned out to be as misleading as helpful: I assumed that the similarities between the two—rather than the differences—were of first importance, whereas the reverse was probably true.

Put simply, the book has three main arguments: that the Labour Party's supersession of the Liberal Party as the principal party of the 'left' was probably inevitable; that the First World War was comparatively unimportant in this process; and that the Labour Party's success had little to do with any large-scale ideological conversion to socialism as a formal doctrine but much to do with a diffuse form of 'labourist' class consciousness whose organizational embodiment was the trade union. These arguments are not in practice presented as baldly as that but this summary in no way parodies them. How do they stand today?

The first two obviously hang together—if the one then almost certainly the other. At the time the contrary position had been persuasively argued by Trevor Wilson, Neal Blewett, and Peter Clarke.[2] All three concluded that the war was decisive in the 'downfall' of the Liberal Party, that there was, therefore, an accidental element in the Labour Party's emergence. I was sceptical of this conclusion both on a priori and 'evidential' grounds. I believed (and still do) that the political culture of Britain was more like that of Western Europe or Australasia than it was that of the United States: in which case the containment of the industrial working class within the traditional party system would almost have been impossible—except in the event of the Liberal Party turning itself into something like the Labour Party.[3] It was thus class and not war which brought down the Liberal Party. The other reason for scepticism was the plain fact that the Labour Party *had* been founded before 1914 and as an organization was not in retreat but expanding steadily. That was something the Labour Party archives did seem to establish. In which case the war could not itself be decisive: it clearly could influence the timing of events but not the events themselves.

[2] T. Wilson, *The Downfall of the Liberal Party* (London, 1966); P. F. Clarke, *Lancashire and the New Liberalism* (Cambridge, 1971); N. Blewett, *The Peers, The Parties and the People* (London, 1972).
[3] I argued this case more specifically in conjunction with Colin Matthew and John Kay, 'The Franchise Factor in the Rise of the Labour Party', *English Historical Review*, 91 (Oct. 1976).

At the time of publication this argument was criticized both for being a negative one—a hypothesis rather than an argument, since what happened in the war was not examined historically— and for explaining the changes in terms of a concept, a particular form of class consciousness, which itself needed explaining. J. M. Winter, for example, argued that even at the level of the leadership of the organized labour movement the programme and the institutional reforms of the 1918 Labour Party can be accounted for only as consequences of the First World War.[4] More recently, Bernard Waites has suggested that the structure of British society was indeed profoundly affected by the war—very much more than I had been prepared to concede—and that (by implication) the emergence of the Labour Party as one of the two major parties was a result of this.[5]

These arguments now seem to me to have considerable force, particularly as I have argued elsewhere that the Second World War was absolutely decisive in the Labour victory of 1945.[6] I plainly underrated the immediate consequences of the war on both the Liberal and Labour parties, particularly its effect on the political loyalties of the trade unionized working class. (Although I also believe that its effect on much of the middle class was probably even more important.[7]) Yet I could not go as far as Dr Winter or Dr Waites. The a priori presumption for the rise of the Labour Party still, I think, to a considerable extent holds true. What the war did was to put beyond doubt what certainly was in doubt in 1914—the future political behaviour of the *organized* working class. But that it was in doubt is what is important. Furthermore, the negative argument remains a powerful one: the Labour Party may well have been contained in the Edwardian period, but it was not going to go away. Nor were the social and political structures which produced it.

The Evolution of the Labour Party argues that the real structural explanation for the rise of Labour was an intense working-class consciousness which was not revolutionary or even socialist but which would only be exploited by a party whose first loyalties were to the organized working class. Those who criticized this proposition did so for two reasons. The first was an historical one: that—as Peter Clarke pointed out—there was no evidence that the kind of trade-union consciousness which, in fact, I was deploying was actually synonymous with 'working-class consciousness'. On the contrary, it was suggested,

---

[4] See J. M. Winter, *Socialism and the Challenge of War* (London, 1974).
[5] B. Waites, *A Class Society at War* (Leamington Spa, 1987). This is an excellent book which argues its case very attractively.
[6] See Ross McKibbin, *The Ideologies of Class* (Oxford, 1990), 286–93.
[7] Ibid. 268–75.

the Labour advance was very incomplete—as its record in the interwar years demonstrates.[8] This objection, therefore, would emphasize how limited was the Labour Party's relationship to a wider working-class consciousness. I would now accept much of this objection. It was not until the 1940s that the Labour Party broke out of its traditional territory, and it was only the Second World War which permitted it to do so. It was here that the Australian model was probably a hindrance. The Australian Labor Party early on established itself as the ordinary man's party and (with ups and downs) has maintained itself as the ordinary man's party ever since then. Despite its best efforts, however, the British Labour Party has been much less successful in doing that—in part because the ideological environment in which the two Parties grew was different in comparatively small but crucial ways. In any case, the assumption that 'class'—that is, the working class broadly defined—was on the side of Labour was more easily and commonly accepted in the 1960s and 1970s than it is today.

None the less, the substance of the argument in *The Evolution of the Labour Party* has not, I think, been fundamentally upset by this objection. The book consistently emphasizes that the attempts of the Labour Party leadership to free itself from financial, ideological, and electoral dependence on the trade unions never succeeded and in the circumstances of the time probably never could. In the ideological conditions of the interwar years this made an appeal to working men and women (and particularly women) outside the unions difficult to sustain. And even more difficult with occupation groups, such as farmers, who did not even think of themselves as working men. Nevertheless, those whose votes it had *already* gained it was unlikely to lose.

Several reviewers—some more crushingly than others[9]—made the point that the class consciousness I had invoked to explain these changes was not itself described; that, furthermore, such a description should precede any examination of the Labour Party. This was both a fair and an unfair criticism. As I freely concede in the book the Labour Party did not and could not stand outside the political culture of the working class. That culture was fundamental. But to have worked from culture to Party would have rendered any study of the Labour Party itself impracticable; indeed, almost impossible. I have, however, tried to make up for this in *The Ideologies of Class* which follows directly, if not logically, from *The Evolution of the Labour Party*. It might have been better had it been written first; but that it was written second does not undermine the conclusion of *The Evolution of the Labour*

[8] *English Historical Review*, 91 (Jan. 1976), 159.
[9] See, for example, Peter Linebaugh in *Victorian Studies* (Autumn 1976).

Party. On the contrary, it seems to me that the kind of class consciousness I have described here confirms it.[10]

Finally, this book argues that 'socialism' as a more or less consistent body of principles was of little importance either in converting people to the Labour Party or in determining the attitudes of those responsible for the great changes of 1917—18. What was decisive was the much narrower labourism of the trade unions. In retrospect, I think this the most unsatisfactory argument of the book: not in its 'rightness' or 'wrongness'—since I still think it basically 'right'—but in its formulation. There is little evidence that those who voted Labour either before or after 1914 were much influenced by a specific form of socialism or even by any driving dissatisfaction with the *status quo*. But many had grievances perpetuated by experience and folklore, and in a number of the later publicly owned industries (like the coalmines) they long survived nationalization.[11] Furthermore, these grievances were effectively mobilized by the Labour Party via a socialist vocabulary. Therefore, the distinction, 'socialism' or 'not-socialism', or 'socialism' or trade union 'reformism', now seems to me too crude.

In a thoughtful critique of *The Evolution of the Labour Party*, Stuart Macintyre argued that there was not in fact any agreed trade-union 'view'; rather there was a sort of moral spectrum within the non-Marxist labour movement which ranged from labourism to what he calls 'Labour Socialism'. He also notes (which is certainly true) that most Labour leaders of any significance were by the early 1920s, if not before, calling themselves socialists.[12] Something like a modified version of Dr Macintyre's argument I would now accept. It does not demonstrate that most Labour voters also called themselves socialists—that would be much more surprising—but it does suggest that there had developed a particular Labour rhetoric which both implied a moral critique of capitalism and an ideological validation of Labour politics. How far individuals thought this rhetoric imperative upon them varied very widely, as did its consequences. For some it provided a kind of ideological justification for the piecemeal reformist legislation they always intended; for some it created an often paralysing tension between what they felt they ought to do and what they could do; for others it represented a measure against which all Labour governments must fail. This is how I think the argument should be formulated: socialism as a system was not of major significance either to most

[10] See McKibbin, *Ideologies of Class*, 294—7.
[11] A theme which, for example, runs throughout N. Dennis, F. Henriques, and C. Slaughter, *Coal is Our Life* (London, 1956).
[12] S. Macintyre, 'Socialism, the Unions and the Labour Party after 1918', Society for the Study of Labour History, *Bulletin* (Autumn 1975).

Labour voters or to most Labour leaders; but socialism as a rhetoric of political action helped to determine the way in which many of them viewed the world. It was, therefore, but in no precise way, as much ideological as instrumental.

St John's College, Oxford   R. I. McK.
September, 1990

ACKNOWLEDGEMENTS

In preparing this book I must thank Mr. K. Tite and Dr. H. M. Pelling, who examined it in thesis form and commented valuably both on style and content, Mr. Richard Shackleton, Mrs. Betsy Morgan, Dr. Cameron Hazlehurst, Mr. Chris Cook, Dr. Neal Blewett, and Dr. J. M. Winter. I must mention separately Dr. Peter Pulzer, Dr. Colin Matthew, and Dr. Boyd Hilton who read the manuscript in whole or in part, and the Dean and Students of Christ Church who gave me both time and congenial company in which to write it. I am especially grateful to Mrs. Irene Wagner and the staff of the Labour Party library, without whose assistance in the early days this book literally would not have been possible, and, above all, to Mr. A. F. Thompson for the kind of help no graduate student has a right to expect.

St. John's College, Oxford   Ross McKibbin
December 1973

CONTENTS

ABBREVIATIONS

1. Abbreviations used in the text:

A.E.U.	Amalgamated Engineering Union
C.W.S.	Co-operative Wholesale Society
D.L.P.	Divisional Labour Party
F.R.D.	Fabian Research Department
I.L.P.	Independent Labour Party
L.R.C.	Labour Representation Committee
L.R.D.	Labour Research Department
N.U.J.	National Union of Journalists
P.T.F.	Printing Trades Federation
S.A.C.	Scottish Advisory Council
T.U.C.	Trades Union Congress
N.A.C.	National Administrative Council

2. Abbreviations used in the footnotes:

'DHF'	*Daily Herald* Files
'FHD'	Fabian Historical Documents
'GC'	Minutes of the General Council of the T.U.C.
'LPLF'	Labour Party Letter Files
'NEC'	Minutes of the National Executive of the Labour Party
'PC'	Minutes of the Parliamentary Committee of the T.U.C.
'SEC'	Minutes of the Scottish Executive of the Labour Party

INTRODUCTION

THIS is a study of the Labour Party in its formative years. It is an examination of Labour's evolution over nearly two decades: from the mid-Edwardian period to the end of the first Labour government in 1924. By that time it was recognizably today's Labour Party, though with one crucial difference—it was then at all levels a working-class organization, and this is the study of a truly proletarian party.

Political action is the result of social and cultural attitudes which are not primarily political, and for most people politics play only a subordinate and inarticulate part in their lives. To capture this culture is a task impossible in the limited space available to me, and I have been selective in the treatment of my subject. This book has three aims: I have tried to illustrate the character of the Labour Party by an analysis of its mass organization, to suggests reasons why it replaced the Liberal Party as the principal party of the left, and, finally, I have tried to show that the attempt of the Labour leadership to create a 'global' working-class movement (as the Germans were supposed to have done) was very largely a failure.

Two of the victims of confined space are any sustained discussion of Westminster politics on the one hand, and any lengthy account of Labour in the First World War on the other. But neither of these, I think, is necessary for the purposes of this book. There are two reasons why I have largely—though not entirely—excluded parliamentary politics. Firstly, anything I had to say about the parliamentary disintegration of the Liberal Party would be supererogatory: it has been done elsewhere and with more detail than I could provide. Secondly, it seems to me that the emergence of the Labour Party as an increasingly large parliamentary force was not anyway a function of Westminster politics but of broad social and economic changes whose political consequences were apparent initially in the country and only later in parliament. The emphasis of the book, therefore, is on these changes and on 'mass' politics. Furthermore, the Labour Party's centre of gravity, at least until 1922, was extra-parliamentary. The parliamentary party was small and comparatively ineffective; decisions about the national Party's growth were made by the national executive and conference, both dominated by the trade unions.

Omission of a lengthy discussion of the war is, prima facie, more difficult to justify. But there are obvious difficulties. I have looked at it in terms which are of importance to my argument, but a general analysis of the war's impact upon the British working classes is something that I could not hope to do within the boundaries of this book. Such an analysis is, in any case, hedged with methodological difficulties. If it could be demonstrated that, as compared with 1914, the war significantly modified working-class life and political attitudes, and that there was a relationship between this and the changes in the Labour Party, it would clearly be valuable. I do not know that it can be demonstrated, and I admit that I have not tried to do this.

I have divided the book into three. In the first part, which ends with the outbreak of war, I have looked at the national and local structure of the Labour Party, at its relations with other working-class organizations and with the Liberal Party. I have argued here that the Labour Party cannot be seen as a declining force before 1914, but that, on the contrary, it was already successfully mobilizing working-class support at the expense of the Liberals, and that this was happening almost regardless of what went on in parliament.

In the second part, a single chapter, I have discussed the origins of the 1918 constitution of the Labour Party, and the place of the socialist objective, clause IV, in it. I have concluded that to focus attention upon the socialist objective is to misunderstand the events of 1918, which must be seen in other and less specific terms. I have also argued that the Party was more an agent of the unions at the end of the war than it was at its beginning, and that the war itself probably strengthened the 'right' rather than the 'left' within the Labour movement.

In the final part of the book, which I take from 1918 to the end of 1924, I have returned to some of the themes of the first part. I have examined the development of a mass party, and its position within a wider working-class movement. I have argued that the 1918 reorganization did not work as it was expected to, that the attempt of the Labour Party to shift itself from a more or less exclusive working-class base was almost certainly and inevitably a failure, and that one result of this failure was irresistible trade-union pressure upon the structure and institutions of the Labour Party.

The book has a general thesis. The rise of the Labour Party and the slow attrition of the Liberal Party, I have suggested, both came from an acutely developed working-class consciousness. To see this, however, in terms of the dissemination of 'socialism' is to see only the surface of what happened: there were many socialists in the Labour Party, and possibly an even larger number of anti-socialists, but in practice these were irrelevant categories. Voting Labour implied allegiance to certain working-class traditions and not necessarily to any political ideology. Thus the class-consciousness which produced the Labour Party at the same time deprived it of any ideological exactness and excluded it from many areas of working-class life.

This thesis itself rests partly upon a proposition argued implicitly in the book: that the 1918 Representation of the People Act, by which almost 80 per cent of the new voting population was enfranchised for the first time, transformed the conditions under which Labour grew. So long as the Labour Party's appeal was necessarily confined to the largely lower middle and artisan class enfranchised in 1867 and 1884 its progress was slow and difficult. Though it did make inroads into these classes before 1914, it was this same limited electorate that gave Edwardian 'progressivism' its vigour, and sustained the Liberal government from 1906 on. But the 1918 Act, all at once, gave Britain for the first time an electorate in which the industrial working class was now unquestionably predominant. The 'Liberal' vote, indeed, may even have survived more or less intact, but after 1918 was overwhelmed by voters who could not be enrolled by official Liberalism. Much of this new electorate voted Labour in 1918; but had it been enfranchised it probably would have done so in 1914 as well.

The history of the Labour Party is a long one, and I have not begun at the beginning. It might be helpful, therefore, to outline briefly the history of the organization which took the name Labour Party in 1906. It postdated the Independent Labour Party (the I.L.P.), founded in 1893, by seven years. There were differences other than just years. Whereas the I.L.P. had a more or less coherent critique of capitalism, corporatively the Labour Party had none. The reasons for its establishment were more prudential.

The I.L.P.'s objective, as its name implied, was Labour parliamentary representation independent of all other parties, together with a commitment to some kind of socialism. But the unions took up independent representation more ambiguously. Further, they were divided in what they wanted. The 'new unions' of 1889–90, the unions of general and unskilled workers, were to some degree outside the hierarchy of Victorian industry and politics, and, at a theoretical level, considerably influenced by socialism. But the leadership of the older craft unions had scarcely, if at all, moved beyond traditional radicalism and adherence to the Liberal Party. However, the industrial world of the craft unions was much less secure than their political loyalties. Structural and technological changes in industry, and an apparently co-ordinated offensive by employers through the courts and 'free' (non-union) labour associations, threatened the unions institutionally and their members occupationally. They were thus torn between conventional Liberal political loyalties on the one hand, and on the other, a growing dissatisfaction with a social system which the Liberals in fact represented. Where the industrial position of organized workers still seemed sure, as, for example, it did to most miners, political and industrial attitudes continued to go hand in hand. The Miners' Federation of Great Britain was absent from the inaugural conference of the Labour Party, and even after it affiliated in 1909 the old harmony between the miners' unions and the Liberal Party in some coal-fields remained intact.

Had the Liberals shown much vigour in the late 1890s, the proponents of independent Labour representation might still have been defeated. But it was argued that the Liberals had not only been ineffective in defending working-class interests but also deplorably weak in their opposition to imperialism. It was the apparent inability of the Liberal Party to defend conventional Liberalism as much as anything else that led to the foundation of the Labour Party. Despite, therefore, the absence of the more radical trades councils from the T.U.C.—excluded in 1895 precisely because of their radicalism—the 1899 congress of the T.U.C. voted narrowly to join in the formation of an independent political party.

Effectively, the conference which met at the Memorial Hall, Faringdon Street, in February 1900, was agreed upon independent Labour representation, but upon little else. It was assumed that the new party would defend the 'interests' of the working class in parliament and protect the threatened privileges of the unions, but it had no 'objective' other than the negative one that it renounced support for all other parties. The modesty of the programme was declared in the organization's name: not (as Keir Hardie wanted) United Labour Party, but Labour Representation Committee, commonly known as the L.R.C. The Committee's formal structure did little to resolve the tensions that otherwise accompanied its foundation. Unlike the I.L.P., it had no well-defined organization; it was merely the sum of its affiliated societies. 'Members' of the L.R.C. were members only by right of belonging to a body which had affiliated to the Committee. The national executive of the L.R.C. was elected on a strictly sectional basis, and this remained so until 1917. Societies in no way lost their identity by affiliating to the Committee. The I.L.P., for example, continued unchanged, a vigorous and, to a large degree, self-sufficient body, and it is clear that many members of the I.L.P. gave their first loyalties to the I.L.P.

In the constituencies the L.R.C. was represented by trades councils, which could affiliate, or by local L.R.C.s, which were, like the national body, organizations composed of affiliated societies. The constitution of the L.R.C. did not allow individual membership as we know it; in practice, this was a rule not applied and frequently violated. But so long as the societies which gave birth to the Labour Party were so divided politically, and while the I.L.P. was still able to act as counter to the numerically much larger unions, it was impossible for the L.R.C. to conceive a programme, or to encourage formally individual membership.

The Committee was founded in time to fight the 1900 elections, and two of its candidates were elected: Keir Hardie (I.L.P.) for Merthyr Tydfil, and Richard Bell, secretary of the Amalgamated Society of Railway Servants, for Derby. It was a spacious conception of unity that brought these two together—Hardie, a socialist, and Bell, a Liberal in everything but name. Bell was to leave the L.R.C. altogether, but a parliamentary party of these two was no accident: it was a situation inherent in the L.R.C.'s formation. Between 1900 and the general election of 1906 this pair were joined by three more M.P.s. Richard Shackleton won Clitheroe with the acquiescence of the Liberals (1902), while Will Crooks (Woolwich) and Arthur Henderson (Barnard Castle) were both elected in 1903.

Despite the efforts of the L.R.C.'s first secretary, James Ramsay MacDonald, the number of trade unionists affiliated remained below 400,000 until the Taff Vale decision of 1901. Taff Vale, the culmination of a long series of legal judgements against the unions, was a major defeat for them. It apparently made unions liable for the actions of their members, opened their funds to judicial plunder, and even presaged an attack upon the right to strike itself. The feelings of insecurity that had marked the 1890s were intensified, and in two years affiliated membership increased by half a million.

Given the past decrepitude of the Liberal Party, a determination to reverse the course of judicial and governmental policy towards the unions might have led to independent Labour activity on a wide front. But the L.R.C.'s development was at once helped and complicated by a Liberal revival. Joseph Chamberlain's decision to take up tariff reform à outrance immediately divided the Conservatives and united the Liberals. Furthermore, both the unions and the I.L.P. rallied to free trade as enthusiastically as the Liberal Party—a good example of how politically united the British left was in practice. In these circumstances, and following Labour's success in the by-elections already mentioned, MacDonald and the Liberal Chief Whip, Herbert Gladstone, concluded an agreement (September 1903) allowing the L.R.C. free runs in a number of constituencies. As a result, twenty-nine candidates endorsed by the Committee were elected to parliament at the 1906 elections. When the 1906 parliament met, the L.R.C. took the name Labour Party, elected a parliamentary chairman, Keir Hardie, and appointed its own whips.

Politically, this agreement between the Liberal and Labour Parties was a sensible one, since, politically, they disagreed on so little. In the short run, it was valuable for both sides; in the long run, it perhaps only exacerbated differences within the new Party. Those Labour M.P.s who were elected by agreement with the Liberals, and frequently with their assistance, were independent only in some senses of the word, and however much the Labour and Liberal parties had in common politically, socially they were a world apart.

I

THE LABOUR PARTY IN 1910

1. *Head Office*

J. BRUCE GLASIER, speaking to delegates at its 1912 conference, said that the Labour Party 'had no confession of faith, no means of giving testimony to a whole-hearted support of the principles of the Party'. It was a 'federation of national organizations', a loose and ill-defined alliance rather than a coherent party with specific policies.[1] With this description few at the conference would have disagreed. Nevertheless, the Labour Party did have an 'object'—in 1910 it was to 'secure the election of Candidates to Parliament and organize and maintain a Parliamentary Labour Party, with its own whips and policy'. It was not a programme, but it was generally understood to mean the *independent* representation of labour, and by 1914 the way to make such representation effective was almost obsessively debated within the movement. In 1910, however, its preservation was problem enough.

By the end of 1909 the 'federation' had built up a parliamentary party of forty-five ill-assorted members. Twenty-nine had been elected in 1906; another one, J. W. Taylor (Chester-le-Street) had joined immediately after the election; two more, Joseph Pointer (Attercliffe), and Pete Curran (Jarrow), were the result of by-electoral gains; a further thirteen were miners who joined when the Miners' Federation adhered to the Party in 1909. The 'federation' itself is not easily described. Of the 1,430,539 members affiliated in 1910, all but 35,377 were trade unionists. Of the unionists no less than 550,000 were miners. The I.L.P. and the Fabian Society affiliated on 35,377 members; the Women's Labour League had 4,000 members.[2] The 'federation' allowed both the unions and the socialist societies considerable autonomy. While most affiliated bodies worked within the constitution, several of the member unions of the Miners' Federation occasionally operated in obvious defiance of it.

Affiliated to the Party were 148 trades councils and local Labour parties.[3] Not all of them served purely political functions. Most, indeed, were weighted towards the industrial side of the movement, and some trades councils were probably quite apolitical. The importance

---

[1] *Conference Report*, 1912, pp. 92-4.   [3] *Conference Report*, 1911, p. 7.
[2] *Conference Report*, 1911, p. 7.

of trade-union branches to the local parties was made clear when national unions were enjoined after the Osborne Judgement; a number of parties collapsed and most found themselves in difficulty.[4] Furthermore, the idea that the Labour Party ought to be represented in the constituencies by purely political organizations was a relatively new one. It was not until 1905 that local parties had been permitted to affiliate to the national Party, and then only in constituencies without trades councils. Not until September 1910 were political organizations encouraged to affiliate to the national Party.[5] Likewise, with the exception of a few constituencies, local parties did not permit fee-paying individual membership. Individuals who wished to join the Party and who were not trade-unionists had to do so either through the I.L.P. or the Fabian Society. While the importance of formal individual membership has certainly been exaggerated, the lack of a uniform system of local parties and the existence of competition between trades councils and branches of the I.L.P. caused problems both in the country and for Head Office in London.

'Head Office' meant the national executive of the Party and its bureaucracy. The national executive was the overseer of all organization. In 1910 it had sixteen members, eleven from the unions, three from the socialist societies, one from the trades councils and local Labour parties, and one from the women's organizations; after 1912 the Party treasurer was elected by conference. The three sections at conference—unions, socialist societies, local organizations, and women—elected their members to the national executive separately. After 1918 all members of the executive were elected by the whole conference.

The day-to-day administration of the Party was left to the secretary, Ramsay MacDonald, who was elected by conference, the assistant secretary, J. S. Middleton (appointed 1903), the national agent, Arthur Peters (appointed 1908), and the treasurer, Arthur Henderson. The secretary was much the most important officer of the Party and had no equivalent in either of the older parties.[6] Though directly responsible to the national executive (which normally met every month), in practice the execution of the Party's affairs was in his hands. Furthermore, he could summon the executive's subcommittees at discretion, as, indeed, he could the full executive if he thought the occasion required it. Since he was also responsible for the agenda of

<hr/>

[4] See below, pp. 20–1.

[5] See below, pp. 33–9.

[6] For an interesting comparison with Sir Robert Hudson when he was secretary both of the National Liberal Federation and the Liberal Central Association, see N. Blewett, *The Peers, The Parties and the People: The General Elections of 1910* (London, 1972), pp. 276–7.

executive meetings his power to determine the direction of its policies
was reinforced.

MacDonald (secretary, 1900–11) and Henderson (secretary, 1911–
1934) were a unique partnership in modern British politics. Together
they dominated the Labour Party until the 1930s. They, and they
alone, held all the offices which the Labour Party had to offer:
secretary, treasurer, chairman, and leader of the parliamentary party.
Even before 1931 their personal relations were often strained. In 1908
MacDonald called Henderson a 'bloody liar' before a couple of
witnesses, including Middleton;[7] in 1910 Henderson resigned from
the national executive over a remark MacDonald was alleged to have
made about him and was only with difficulty induced to return;[8]
their wartime disputes are well known; and in 1931 they parted
company without regret on either side. As types they could not have
been more different, and they disliked each other personally. Yet, for
the most part, they worked well together precisely because their
differences were personal and only marginally political.

In 1910 MacDonald was forty-three. He was an 'I.L.P.er', a
graduate of various ethical societies, a journalist and clerk who had
found his way into the intellectual and slightly faddish world of genteel
London radicalism. A littérateur with an overcharged and emotional
style he was probably more a Continental than a British phenomenon,
but he had a well-to-do wife, a fluent secretarial pen, a clear if narrow
mind, was a good committee man and a very effective platform speaker.
After his election to parliament in 1906 he had increasingly turned to
wider political interests. It was no secret that he coveted the chairmanship of the parliamentary party or that he hoped to turn the position
into one of real leadership. In any case he was having difficulty in
combining the secretaryship with his growing parliamentary duties.
MacDonald was a highly political secretary, one who gave much
thought to strategy and the electoral problems of a third party, but he
had initiated few organizational changes since 1906. By 1910 a more
professional manager was needed. Wider questions could be left to
MacDonald acting in a different capacity.

The man who aspired to MacDonald's position had been chairman
of the parliamentary party in 1908–9 and was now treasurer and chief
whip. Henderson was four years older than MacDonald and his path
through the Labour movement was marked by milestones quite different

---

[7] J. S. Middleton, 'Unpublished Memoir'. (I am grateful to Mrs. Lucy Middleton for
giving me access to this.) The occasion was a conference on wages boards.

[8] MacDonald was supposed by Henderson to have described his appointment as acting
secretary in 1909 as 'an insult.' The incident was smoothed over by W. C. Robinson and
Keir Hardie. (See 'NEC', 11 Feb. 1910, and Henderson to Robinson, 15 Feb. 1910, 'LPLF:
Uncat.').

from those that guided MacDonald. Moulded by the politics and religion of the north-east, he had made his reputation as an organizer of the Ironfounders and as a workers' representative on the North-East Coast Conciliation Board. He was elected as a Liberal to the Newcastle and Darlington councils and became Liberal agent in Barnard Castle. His conversion to independent Labour representation was due not to his own political development, but to the decision of his union to nominate candidates under the auspices of the Labour Representation Committee. He was duly elected L.R.C. member for Barnard Castle in 1903. That he became a Labour candidate in deference to his union was an act characteristic of his whole career. The unequalled authority he came to possess in the Labour movement was perhaps less a result of his ability to lead it in the direction he wanted than of his sensitivity to its wishes.

The assistant secretary of the Party, J. S. Middleton, was, like MacDonald, a journalist and an I.L.P.er. He was conscientious and relentlessly hard-working—in 1924 he described his recreations as 'office drudgery for the cause'—devoted to MacDonald and skilful at mending any fences broken by his more temperamental chiefs. Arthur Peters, the national agent, was a diligent, if uninspired, officer. He had made his name as organizing secretary of Charles Duncan's efficient party in Barrow and was popular with constituency workers. Like Henderson he was both Wesleyan and teetotal, and rather over-subscribed to that fund of piety at Head Office which those who were neither Wesleyan nor teetotal found irritating.[9] Middleton was in charge of the office at 28 Victoria Street, cluttered rooms used for storing Party propaganda as well as for business, and had five assistants, including Scott Lindsay, who was attached to the parliamentary party and was later its first secretary. Head Office operated on a low budget: in 1909–10 £553 10s. 0d. was paid in salaries and there was an outlay of £1,896 6s. 4½d. on what might be called national executive expenses—literature, meetings, deputations, etc.[10]

2. Organization in the Country

Contrary to what is usually alleged, the organization of the Labour Party in the country was broadly similar to that after 1918. A number of large cities had central Labour parties; many boroughs and industrial county divisions had some kind of constituency party. But in 1910 the Party's coverage was still limited and its structure far from

[9] See, for example, M. Cole (ed.), *Beatrice Webb's Diaries, 1912–1924* (London, 1952), pp. 116–17, 20 Mar. 1918.
[10] For details see, R. I. McKibbin, 'The Evolution of a National Party: Labour's Political Organisation, 1910–1924' (Univ. of Oxford D.Phil. thesis), p. 6.

complete.[11] For example, neither London nor Glasgow had central parties. In London political rivalries had continuously prevented the formation of such a body even though the London Trades Council had given up serious political work.[12] In Glasgow there was a sort of united body, the Registration Committee, which attempted to co-ordinate the electoral activities of the five constituency parties. But the Committee did not work and its functions were all assumed by the Glasgow central party when it was established in 1912.[13]

Probably the most effective central party was the Manchester Labour Representation Committee. It supervised virtually all electioneering and did so with some success. All divisional parties were affiliated to the central party and were expected to report to the secretary regularly. The general committee, composed of delegates of affiliated unions and socialist societies, elected an executive committee which co-ordinated activities throughout Manchester and Salford. In 1910 the central party affiliated to the national Party on a membership of 17,959.[14]

The Liverpool Labour Representation Committee was inevitably *sui generis*. Given the political and religious peculiarities of Merseyside, it was impossible to establish efficient organization. There were no constituency parties, but some wards had associations which were formed by the central party organizer. However, they existed only for as long as he thought necessary. National elections were conducted by hastily formed divisional councils, half of whose eight members were from the central party and half from the I.L.P. They do not seem to have been very satisfactory.[15] The party was, furthermore, chronically short of funds: between 1910 and 1914 total cash in hand did not exceed £6 0s. 0d. Largely for sectarian reasons the central party was demoralized by the 1910 elections: by James Sexton's campaign in West Toxteth[16]—Sexton was very obviously Roman Catholic—and then by the decision of the Carpenters and Joiners to transfer the popular A. G. Cameron (an Ulster Presbyterian) from Kirkdale to Jarrow.[17]

---

[11] For the regional distribution of local Labour parties and trades councils, see G. D. H. Cole, *A History of the Labour Party since 1914* (London, 1947), pp. 9–13.
[12] P. Thompson, *Socialists, Liberals and Labour: the Struggle for London, 1885–1914* (London, 1967), pp. 265–85.
[13] See below, pp. 30–1.
[14] Manchester and Salford Labour Representation Committee, *Annual Report*, 31 Dec. 1909, p. 3.
[15] Liverpool Labour Representation Committee, 'Minutes', 25 Nov. 1910.
[16] Ibid., 22 Feb. 1910.
[17] For the consequences of this, see Secretary Bootle I.L.P. to Middleton, 2 Nov. 1910, 'LPLF: Affiliations 1910'; Middleton to Secretary Bootle I.L.P., 3 Nov. 1910, 'LPLF: Affiliations 1910'.

The Birmingham central party worked as well as could be expected in unfavourable circumstances, although its performance was criticized by MacDonald.[18] The Newcastle borough party was a lively body—a bit too lively for Head Office—but its effectiveness was impaired by a partisan intervention in Tyneside union disputes.[19] In Coventry, a city of growing importance, politics were dominated by the I.L.P.,[20] as they were in Bradford.[21] The Sheffield Trades Council, though it actively concerned itself with the affairs of neighbouring mining constituencies, was less than industrious in the city; organization was dependent very much upon the divisional parties.

In Scotland generally organization was weaker than in England. The Edinburgh central party had just taken up municipal organization and had yet to make the leap into a parliamentary candidature. Like similar bodies in Aberdeen and Dundee, the Edinburgh party had both insufficient funds and insufficient membership.[22]

The main burden of electoral organization was thus borne by the individual constituency parties. Nearly all of them were delegate parties: that is to say, local parties or trades councils made up of delegates elected by trade unions and socialist societies on an agreed basis. In the nature of things much was left to the discretion of the local secretary, who was frequently able to run a party single-handed and not always to the benefit of the national Party. A determined secretary had an arena of independent action less and less available to him after 1918. If Labour were strong enough to contest the municipal elections, then the organization of such elections was often in the hands of the secretary alone. He compiled registration lists, drummed up canvassers, planned meetings, and supervised the distribution of propaganda. If the Party contested a parliamentary election in the constituency, then it was almost certain that the national agent would assist, though he was dependent, once again, on the local secretary for the mobilization of supporters.

But the powers of the secretary are easily exaggerated. They were almost certainly modified by a kind of 'individual membership' which many parties tacitly allowed. Apart from the handful of local parties well known for accepting individual members on a formal basis,[23] the evidence suggests that a large number of local parties in practice 'admitted' individuals if for no other reason than that they could not

[18] See below, p. 14.
[19] See below, pp. 36–7.
[20] J. A. Yates, *Pioneers to Power* (Coventry, 1950), pp. 20–51.
[21] A. F. Brockway, *Socialism over Sixty Years* (London, 1946), pp. 39–44.
[22] Edinburgh Labour Party, *Report* (1911), pp. 6–7; also Dundee Labour Representation Committee, *Annual Report* (1916), p. 2.
[23] See below, pp. 7–9.

work without them. Most local parties empowered themselves to establish ward committees. The Ince Parliamentary Division Labour Party permitted the executive committee

... to form Committees of sympathisers and workers in various districts ... with a view to more effective preparation for, and action in, elections; also to take such measures as may be deemed advisable for the promotion of Labour principles among the people.[24]

The Edinburgh Labour Party established a few ward associations for the municipal elections of 1911, and found their success such as to provoke special comment.

[The] result of the elections brings into prominence one outstanding fact, the great value of having Labour Committees for some time before it decided to contest the Wards. The formation of some of these Committees in some of the older Wards in the city should be one of the principal duties of your new Executive.[25]

In 1912, Fred Bourton, secretary of the Mid-Derbyshire Labour Party, described his organization as one 'composed of Trade Unions and Socialist Societies and associate members'.[26] Furthermore, the Mid-Derby party had been formed under the auspices of Head Office in an attempt to wrest organization away from the constituency's Lib–Labs.[27] Whatever the 'official' view of individual membership, therefore, apparently Head Office had no objection to local parties introducing it *ad hoc*.

In practice, the average local party or trades council with reasonable union support and with its fair share of I.L.P.ers and individual sympathizers probably differed little from the so-called 'model' parties. On examination it becomes clear—despite the received opinion[28]—that the electoral successes of the 'model' parties were not in the first instance due to the excellence of their organization. Henderson's party in Barnard Castle, often seen as the prototype of the post-1918 parties, had a paying individual membership, permanent ward committees, and a strong women's section. It had as well a distinct corporate and evangelical style, so that enthusiasm for the movement was easily and effectively organized. Support for Henderson was underpinned by his popularity as a parliamentary member, his roots in the constituency, and, not least, his fame as a local nonconformist preacher. Yet the Barnard Castle party was formed after his election to parliament in 1903; there was not even a political organization to nominate

[24] Ince Parliamentary Division Labour Party, *Rules*, no. 17 (1910).
[25] Edinburgh Labour Party, *Report* (1911–12), p. 3.
[26] *Derbyshire Times*, 9 Nov. 1912.
[27] See below, pp. 27–8.
[28] For the received opinion, see S. Webb, *The New Constitution of the Labour Party* (London, 1918), *passim*.

him—that was put together (in rather slapdash fashion) on MacDonald's instructions and was in no way a constituency party. The real strength of his candidature was his industrial support, the well-organized miners, foundry workers, and quarrymen in this huge constituency.[29]

What was true of Barnard Castle was true also, *mutatis mutandis*, of the other 'model' constituencies. Even that most formidable of local parties, the Woolwich Labour Representation Association was founded only after Will Crooks's election as M.P. for Woolwich in 1903, though both the victory and the Association so soon passed into Labour mythology that the two became inseparable. But the Woolwich organization was remarkable none the less.[30] It affiliated trade unions, working-men's clubs, and socialist societies, all of which sent delegates to a general council, together with 'associate members' paying individual subscriptions and grouped in ward committees which also sent delegates to the general council. The committees were an 'immediate success'[31] and by 1909 there were no less than 3,000 associate members. Through the ward committees and led by 'street captains' canvassing was made a continuous process. Aside from electoral activities, the party established a sociological group, a cricket section, a choir, and a band. There were frequent bazaars and tea meetings. The structure was crowned by Crooks's personality and that of his redoubtable agent, Will Barefoot, secretary of the Party until 1941 and editor of its paper, the *Woolwich Pioneer*.

But, as Thompson points out, Labour was rather lucky in Woolwich.[32] It was an area whose workers were more or less dependent on one industry, its unions were strong, and it had a social homogeneity akin to some of the mining divisions. The Royal Arsenal Co-operative Society further helped to develop political consciousness in the district. Comparable factors were at work in Clitheroe, Shackleton's constituency, where the local party was patterned, as Bealey points out,[33] on the federal structure of the Weavers' unions. While Clitheroe had an able agent, Fred Constantine,[34] Shackleton's strength lay in the Weavers and in their secretary, A. B. Newall, a man of unusual political drive. Similarly, in Barrow it is not clear which was more important, Charles Duncan's well-oiled organization or the strength of the Engineers in this essentially one-industry town. The local machinery had been created

[29] P.P. Poirier, *The Advent of the Labour Party* (London, 1958), p. 198.
[30] Thompson, *Socialists, Liberals and Labour*, pp. 253–62.
[31] Ibid., p. 256.
[32] Ibid., pp. 260–2.
[33] F. Bealey and H. M. Pelling, *Labour and Politics, 1900–1906* (London, 1958), p. 237.
[34] Clitheroe Labour Party, *Agent's Annual Report* (1915), pp. 3–4, 7.

by Arthur Peters and maintained by Egerton Wake, who, having succeeded Peters as secretary of the Barrow party, later succeeded him as national agent. The party was based upon ward committees (which were 'greatly strengthened' after the 1906 election)[35] membership of which was open to all on payment of a small fee. Like Woolwich and Clitheroe, however, Barrow was a self-contained constituency, and not yet divided by those inter-union disputes which caused so much trouble during and after the war.

There were two technical differences between the 'model' parties and the rest. In the first, individual members paid fees; in the second, they did not. The 'model' parties were also more competent at registration than most other local parties and trades councils. The compilation of voting lists was then both more important and more difficult than now, not only because the franchise was restricted, but because it was restricted in so many obscure ways. Adequate registration lists, compiled by someone who knew the electoral laws, were regarded as an essential of good organization: hence the first product of Henderson's and MacDonald's partnership, a manual on registration and electoral law.[36] Hence, too, one part of the criticism of Labour M.P.s who relied on Liberal organization: the vital registration lists were thereby in the possession of the Liberal Party. Furthermore, it was not possible to assemble lists at speed. Henderson, an old hand at this, wrote to MacDonald:

... take a constituency with 11,000 electors (not a large one). You get the various lists on August 1st, now every name, address, qualification and description is to compare with the current Register. The new entries on the list are to be marked and enquiry has to be made you have to enquire how long they have been in their present house, if not the full qualifying time, then you want to know where they came from, if you satisfy yourself that they are qualified, you must see they are properly described. ... Then there is the old entries on the current Register you find when you examine your marked copy some of those have gone who were your supporters, the question arises why are they not on the new list—are they dead, have they removed, each name must be specially marked for enquiry ... This is to be done right through the eleven thousand voters, and your claims and objections must be completed and into the post by the 19th.

'In my humble judgement,' he concluded, 'it cannot be done by the voluntary worker.'[37]

Yet what most obviously distinguished the 'model' parties was the degree and consistency of union support. No amount of technical skill

[35] Barrow-in-Furness Labour Representation Committee, *Report* (1905–6), p. 13.
[36] Poirier, p. 206.
[37] Henderson to MacDonald, 6 June 1903, 'LPLF: LRC 9/11'.

could overcome a lack of that. Thus, even in overwhelmingly working-class constituencies, the absence of sympathetic or effective unions made contests impossible. In January 1911 Peters reported to the national executive on such a situation in West Ham North.

I have had to resort to personal enquiries, the constituency having no representative Labour Party. Six wards of the borough form the Division and notwithstanding repeated efforts not a single representative of the Party was sent to the Town Council last year. In the southern part of the borough [West Ham South, Will Thorne's constituency] the remaining six wards elect eighteen [Labour] councillors and now form the working majority of the Council . . . The Division contains about 10,000 electors, the Trade Unions are weak, the Railway Workers at Stratford being the strongest, but not by any means inclined towards our platform at present . . . it would appear quite impossible to convene a representative gathering of the Movement of the Division, which under the circumstances, makes even the possibility of a decent show remote.[38]

The best example of what happened to Labour organization when the unions were indifferent or hostile was to be found in constituencies held by Miners' Federation candidates, and those few other seats where Labour candidates might be expected to stand against sitting Liberals.[39] Though these seats were potentially, and indeed became, the safest of all for Labour, and though nowhere else were the unions or their members more politically conscious, nowhere else, paradoxically, was Labour's political organization less effective.[40] In Chesterfield (James Haslam), Mid-Derbyshire (J. G. Hancock), N.-E. Derbyshire (W. E. Harvey), Hallamshire (J. Wadsworth), Hanley (Enoch Edwards), West Monmouth (T. Richards), Normanton (Fred Hall), Nuneaton (William Johnson), South Glamorgan (W. Brace), Rhondda (W. Abraham, 'Mabon') and N.-W. Staffordshire (Albert Stanley), seats held by the general staff of Lib–Labism, there was no independent Labour electoral machinery of any kind, apart from sullen I.L.P. branches and a few dubious trades councils.

In a number of these divisions, not only was the creation of Labour organizations resisted, but Liberal machinery was well oiled and even extended. In both Chesterfield and N.-E. Derbyshire Haslam and Harvey continued to use the Liberal agent, S. E. Short, and showed

---

[38] 'NEC', 17 Jan. 1911.

[39] In Jan. 1910: Bishop Auckland, Mid-Lanark, Cockermouth, Whitehaven, Holmfirth, N.-E. Lanarkshire, N.-W. Lanarkshire, and Morley.

[40] There is a full discussion of electoral organization in the mining constituencies in Roy Gregory, 'The Miners and Politics in England and Wales, 1906–1914' (Univ. of Oxford D.Phil. thesis, 1964), pp. 50–7, since published (in truncated form) as *The Miners and British Politics, 1906–1914* (Oxford, 1968). All references are to the thesis, to which I have found myself greatly indebted.

no signs of wanting another.[41] In Mid-Derbyshire, though Hancock claimed that he paid his Liberal sub-agents personally, in all likelihood the money came from the Derbyshire Miners' Association. Some of the dirty linen was put out in April 1914: if the testimony of the Derbyshire Miners is to be believed they gave £6,742 to local Liberal funds between 1907 and 1914.[42] Similarly, as House, Smillie, Hartshorn, and others found to their cost, no machinery was to be available to Labour candidates who stood against sitting Liberals. Occasionally a Labour candidate could draw upon independent support: the railwaymen in N.-E. Derbyshire, the engineers and iron and steel founders in Lancashire, or the I.L.P. in Merthyr. For the most part, however, and particularly in the Midlands, miners' M.P.s were elected as they wanted to be, with Liberal organization, Liberal agents and Liberal policies.

This machinery would be Liberal so long as the miners wanted it to be, just as these constituencies would remain Liberal only so long as the miners continued to vote Liberal. Conversely, Labour political organization in the mining areas would become effective only when the miners' political sympathies were engaged, when Labour organizers could count on the same kind of industrial support in the mining areas as they could in Woolwich or Barrow. There was a general lesson to be learnt from this. Though Labour's organization was probably more dependent on the unions in the mining constituencies than elsewhere, the difference was only one of degree. While the trades councils and local parties were not as politically divided—except perhaps in Lancashire—as John Burnett found them in the 1890s,[43] political indifference or active political opposition to Labour within them and within the unions affiliated to them was a more formidable obstacle to Labour representation than mere organizational incompetence.

3. The General Elections of 1910

The dissolution of Parliament in December 1909 caught the Party by surprise.[44] In the circumstances, whatever plans there were for an

[41] Gregory, p. 271.

[42] Ibid., p. 341.

[43] S. and B. Webb, *A History of Trade Unionism, 1660–1920* (London, 1920), pp. 454–6.

[44] There were two general elections in 1910. The first, in January, followed the rejection of the 1909 budget (the 'People's Budget') by the House of Lords. The general election left the Liberals dependent upon the Irish—though not upon Labour. Partly because of this, partly because of the Lords' action the year before, the Liberal government introduced legislation to limit the constitutional powers of the Lords. This was also effectively rejected by the Lords, and King Edward VII insisted upon another election before agreeing to a creation of peers. A second election was thus held in December 1910, with a result almost identical with that of January. The legislation, the Parliament Act, was passed the following year.

*is closer to lib
Than soc?*

V

ambitious campaign were abandoned; only seventy-eight candidates were nominated. MacDonald, just back from India, favoured even more radical excisions, but Henderson, acting secretary, did not stand in the way of a larger number. Main considerations seem to have been the state of local organization and likely financial support for the candidate. All seats contested were those where Labour considered itself actually or potentially strong. They were, despite the apparently disappointing results, the type of constituency that had to be fought if Labour were to make its long-heralded second advance.

In addition, candidates were selected with an eye to the Liberal Party. It was assumed that the reasonably effective working of some kind of understanding with the Liberals was essential to the maintenance of the Party as a substantial parliamentary body. Despite ructions from both sides, the 'arrangements' in the double-member constituencies worked well; there were no wild-cat or unofficial candidatures. Liberal threats of intervention in Gower and South Glamorgan successfully confined the South Wales Miners to those seats they already held. On the other hand, rumours of Labour candidates in West and South Leeds were partly designed to secure a free run for James O'Grady in the East division. This aside, as Blewett points out, Labour had little room for manœuvre.[45] The Liberals accepted the results of 1906 (and even these imperfectly)[46] but would permit no further advance, not even from by-electoral gains—Joseph Pointer was unopposed in Attercliffe, but the Liberals fought hard and successfully to wrest Jarrow from Pete Curran.

There were twenty-four constituencies where Liberal and Labour candidates fought each other.[47] In none of these twenty-four was Labour successful and in all but four they finished at the bottom of the poll.[48] Of the seventy-eight candidates forty were successful. There was some turnover of seats, with gains outweighed by losses. Richard Bell's seat in Derby was won by J. H. Thomas, and Manchester East and Wigan were also won; but Summerbell was defeated in Sunderland, as were Crooks in Woolwich, Curran in Jarrow, Jenkins in Chatham, T. F. Richards in West Wolverhampton, MacPherson in

[45] Blewett, p. 239.

[46] For example in Chatham, where J. H. Jenkins, the former Labour M.P., having lost the seat to a Conservative in January, finished bottom of the poll to a Conservative and a Liberal in December.

[47] The constituencies were: Bow and Bromley, Bishop Auckland, Huddersfield, Jarrow, East Bristol, Cockermouth, Crewe, Eccles, Gateshead, Holmfirth, Hyde, Leigh, S.-W. Manchester, Middlesbrough, Morley, Portsmouth, Spen Valley, Tewkesbury, West Fife. Glasgow Camlachie, Mid-Lanark, North Ayrshire, N.-E. Lanark, and Govan.

[48] The four were: Bow and Bromley (Liberal in third place), Huddersfield (Conservative in third place), Jarrow (Conservative in third place) and Fife West (Conservative in third place).

Preston, and MacLachlan in S.-W. Manchester. In the seventy-eight constituencies Labour polled 505,690 votes or 36·6 per cent of all votes cast.[49]

There is little doubt that the results were disappointing, even if some were expected. Losses to the Conservatives were considered inevitable, but the Party's apparently poor showing against Liberal candidates was disquieting and made doubtful any further parliamentary advance. It seemed true also that the Party's organization had overreached itself. MacDonald soon made known his dissatisfaction. He wrote that constituencies have 'no right to ask for a candidate until they are prepared to do justice to one; and, on the other hand, candidates have no business to turn candidatures into propaganda demonstrations . . . The Party had paid dear for the Pyrrhic victory in Colne Valley.'[50] He asserted that as soon as the Lords had become an issue three-cornered fights were 'foredoomed' and that 'half a dozen seats' could have been won by their elimination had not 'the suspicion of the comrades spread like measles, and we had to go into the fight with battalions which we knew would never stand the shock'. In consultation with Peters he had prepared for the national executive a detailed report on the election.

The report[51] was divided into four : 'seats held', 'defeated members', 'unsuccessful candidates', and 'new constituencies'. Of 'seats held' MacDonald reserved most of his fire for the mining divisions. Many of the Miners' M.P.s had flagrantly not run under the terms of the constitution. MacDonald commented :

I think immediate steps should be taken to rectify this for the next election. Labour Parties should be formed in their constituencies, and the Agents they have appointed, or are about to appoint, should be clearly understood to be the Agents of these Parties.

Of the constituencies lost ('defeated members') MacDonald was more cautious than Peters. The national agent favoured the husbanding of Chatham. MacDonald was not so sure. 'In my opinion much depends upon what Jenkins proposes to do. If he is willing to continue, good and well : if not, Chatham is not a first rate constituency.'[52] Peters recommended that T. F. Richards be renominated for West Wolverhampton, but again MacDonald was sceptical. Richards, he

[49] For a detailed examination of the results, see Blewett, pp. 134–41.
[50] *Labour Leader*, 4 Feb. 1910. For Colne Valley, see below, pp. 49–51.
[51] Memorandum filed as 'NEC', 13 Apr. 1910.
[52] MacDonald was right. The results in 1906 and Jan. 1910 were:

	1906	1910
Labour	6692	6130
Conservative	4020	7411

hoped, might be shunted to Northampton where 'he would have a safe seat for life'. Nothing was said of Woolwich other than that Crooks felt bound to it. Sunderland, both agreed, was in a delicate condition: only the selection of a candidate immediately could prevent a second Liberal candidature. 'In the possible absence,' Peters wrote, 'of a strong local man it might be desirable to suggest a Trade Union nominee whose society would be willing to look after the necessary and important work of Registration and organisation generally.'[53] Though MacDonald thought that one of the local unions would provide a candidate, in December it was fought and won, to the surprise of some, by Goldstone of the Teachers.[54] As for Preston, MacDonald, unlike Peters, was happy to let it go. 'A Textile candidate', MacDonald wrote,

undoubtedly would be the strongest, but even then I think he would require to be a Catholic, and from the national point of view M.P.s with special qualifications and pledges are a source of weakness. Moreover, if the Textile Operatives will only add one candidate to their list I think Burnley would be the better constituency for us to fight . . .

In Jarrow, a conference had to be called at once (Curran had died shortly after the January election). To MacDonald the best sort of candidate seemed to be one who 'whilst retaining the votes of the Miners, would have special claims upon the iron trade electors'.

Of the unsuccessful candidatures (heading three) MacDonald was enthusiastic about Bow and Bromley. Birmingham East, Crewe, and Belfast East were dropped without regret. Huddersfield and Kirkdale he was just prepared to approve, although 'owing to the conduct of the Huddersfield Labour Party, the Liberals have been able to get a firm grip on the constituency and the prospects of success are not at all bright'.[55] Kirkdale would never be won 'until our organisation is sufficiently good to make "personation" on the part of the other side impossible . . . Liverpool is rotten and we had better recognise it'.

---

[53] This was a good example of organizational dependence on the unions and the success of a big union, in this case the Shipwrights, in conducting a campaign.

[54] Even Hardie, never one to throw cold water on a Labour candidature, wrote: 'I think first of all it is a pity that the Sunderland men should have rushed the candidature. He may be all that his friends claim for him but at the same time past experience makes one very doubtful about accepting the statements of local enthusiasts in a matter of this kind.' (Hardie to Edward Pease, 23 June 1910, 'FHD, Box 3'.)

[55] This was a view of events he did not always take. When it appeared that the Fabian Society was going to drop the Huddersfield candidature, MacDonald wrote that 'this is open to considerable objection. You committed yourselves to a contest in Huddersfield for the last election; your candidate [H. Snell] did remarkably well and left a good impression behind in the constituency. The general feeling is that it would be a mistake to let the constituency go without a contest at the coming election' (MacDonald to Edward Pease, 14 Mar. 1910, 'FHD, Box 5'). The Fabians did not abandon the candidature. (Fabian Society Executive, 'Minutes', 14 Apr. 1910.)

He came out strongly against further contests in Holmfirth, Middlesbrough, Wakefield, West Toxteth, Hyde, Leigh, Eccles, Morley,
and Spen Valley. Energies should be concentrated on Huddersfield
and S.-W. Manchester; either Whitehaven or Cockermouth ought
to be contested, but not both simultaneously. In Scotland he advocated
the abandonment of the Lanarkshire candidatures, but the retention
of Camlachie and Fife West.

MacDonald did, however, consider the possibility of contests in
hitherto uncontested seats. Northampton and Burnley, both Social
Democrat strongholds, were, he thought, good material. South
Nottingham, Houghton-le-Spring, Devonport, Oldham, Rotherham,
East Northants., Forest of Dean, West Hull, and the Hartlepools
were possibilities for the future. However, he urged that the situation
in Leeds 'be allowed to drift a little . . . if we arrange a conference a
resolution committing us to two, if not three, candidates . . . will be
carried'—caution designed to avoid a Liberal challenge to James
O'Grady in East Leeds as well as to keep the Leeds Trades Council in
check.[56]

The memorandum was completed by three general recommendations from the national agent and several appended comments from
MacDonald. First, Peters suggested,

that all local conferences where the selection of a candidate is the chief
business, in addition to the National Executive being represented . . . I
suggest that the National Agent should also be in attendance . . . The delegation should be brought to recognise the necessity for and the advantages of
sound organisation.

Second:

that candidates should be encouraged to make the appointment of an Agent
through the Head Office . . . In not a few of the Divisions recently contested
I am confident our success was considerably injured by incompetent men
serving as agents . . .

And finally:

that more care and discretion should be exercised in the selection of speakers
during the election. To have persons upon our platform attacking the policy
of the Party under the cover of supporting a particular Candidate is not the
best method of winning elections. In cases where this persisted, headquarters
should be empowered to withdraw its official speakers.

MacDonald endorsed all suggestions with emphasis and added a
couple of general conclusions of his own. 'The alternative before us',
he told the national executive,

[56] See below, p. 16.

2

is a much shorter list of Candidates with a much bigger proportion of wins; or, a slightly shorter list of Candidates (I do not believe that if an election came this year we could possibly put as many Candidates in the field as we did last January) with a proportion of failures pretty much as we did then.

In considering these alternatives ... I would strongly urge upon it the necessity of

(a) considering the financial situation;

(b) the equally great necessity of increasing our representation in the House of Commons.

MacDonald succeeded in his immediate aims: the Party went to the country in December with fifty-six candidates, twenty-two fewer than in January, and elected forty-two. Five seats were gained— Bow and Bromley, Fife West, Sunderland, Whitehaven, and Woolwich, and three lost—St. Helens, Wigan, and Newton. All the seats written off by MacDonald were, with the exception of Mid-Lanark, uncontested. There were only three new candidatures— South Leeds, East Glamorgan, and Mid-Glamorgan. Of the five gains, two were the result of private agreements with the Liberals, Bow and Bromley and Whitehaven, where three-cornered contests had given the Conservatives victory in January. In Fife West Will Adamson defeated the sitting Liberal in a considerably reduced poll and after the withdrawal of the Conservative. The other two victories were fortuitous.

In fact, of course, the more far-reaching of Peters's suggestions had scarcely any immediate effect upon the efficiency of Party organization. But then neither did MacDonald's supposedly beneficent concentration of energies. Labour's percentage of the votes cast in contested seats did rise, from 36·6 to 40·88, but more as the result of the abandonment of weaker candidatures than of anything else. Three of the five gains followed Liberal or Conservative withdrawals and in all but Fife West the outcome was almost mathematically certain. Crooks's victory in Woolwich was largely accidental, as was his defeat in January, and Goldstone's victory in Sunderland was also just good luck. The distinct movement of opinion to the Conservatives in December in Lancashire was a more likely explanation for the three losses there than any organizational weaknesses—though these were noticeable.[57]

The Party's electoral organization was fairly similar in both elections; there was too little time between them for any obvious improvements to take place. The type remained unique to Labour: at one end enthusiastic success, at the other outright incompetence— an average level of muddling through.

[57] Gregory, p. 521; Blewett, p. 286.

Constituency organization varied, as it did at the best of times. Woolwich and Barnard Castle managed pretty well, both being based on workmen's clubs and a developed organization with adequate committee rooms.[58] But in few constituencies were there permanent committee rooms and the usual practice was for agents to hire unused buildings—'derelict tobacco shops', as James Griffiths put it[59]—for the duration of the contest, or to take over the front rooms of a conveniently placed enthusiast's house, however humble. The *Labour Leader* correspondent has left a memorable description of Clynes's headquarters in the Manchester constituency of Miles Platting: 'the committee room in E— Street is a cottage kitchen, area about eight feet square, low, dim, dreary'.[60]

Only in a few places was there any form of standing organization. Usually workers were recruited from the unions and the I.L.P. or just from sympathizers. Despite grumbles from Labour organizers this was not an ineffective method. At Huddersfield in January Snell claimed to have found organization 'contemptible'[61] and wrote of the constituency's lack 'of a well prepared electoral machine, steady discipline, and drudging canvassers'. In reality, he polled 5,686 votes, put the Conservatives into third place, and was beaten by only 1,470—not a bad performance, as MacDonald recognized.[62]

Labour depended heavily on public meetings, and they were one medium where the Party could match all comers. Labour candidates could count on addressing eight or nine meetings a day and would hope for an address by one 'star' speaker, such as MacDonald, Hardie, Snowden, Henderson, R. C. Wallhead, W. C. Anderson, or Bruce Glasier. With the possible exception of Henderson, all of them were notable platform performers, and Henderson made up in portentousness anything lost in style. The I.L.P.ers, particularly, could be relied on. Snowden had made his reputation as an itinerant speaker in the 1890s and his mastery of dialect was more than a bonus.[63] Wallhead, with his 'stage tragedian's voice' and dramatic gestures, also excited great enthusiasm.[64]

Similarly, Labour's pictorial propaganda helped to make up for

[58] Furthermore, there was something about Crooks that attracted the polite classes. Not only did he have the assistance of the middle-class ladies of the London Women's Labour League (Central London Branch 'Executive Committee Minutes', 29 Nov. 1910), but he had the use of the Countess of Warwick's automobile, and many others besides, at a time when Labour candidates regarded cars as an exotic luxury (Blewett, p. 294).

[59] To the author, 10 Nov. 1966.

[60] *Labour Leader*, 21 Jan. 1910.

[61] H. Snell, *Men, Movements and Myself* (London, 1936), p. 187.

[62] See above, p. 14n.

[63] C. Cross, *Philip Snowden* (London, 1966), pp. 35–6, 69.

[64] A. F. Brockway, *Inside the Left* (London, 1942), p. 30.

other defects of organization. Boldly drawn and highly coloured, these inspirational posters were good enough to do service for the next twenty years. The great pre-vorticist posters, 'Forward, the Day is Breaking', 'To-day Unemployed', etc., together with those of Will Dyson's caricatures issued as posters, have now become something of cult objects. In addition to these, manifestoes were generally provided free of charge to local parties.[65]

'Star' speakers and striking propaganda made up for much, but reliance on prominent figures who were themselves M.P.s and often Party administrators further strained national organization. Mac-Donald was clearly harried throughout both elections, and he fought Leicester under difficult circumstances. Apart from having to run Head Office from Leicester, there were the usual and maddening irritatoins of electioneering.[66]

Despite the effects of the Osborne Judgement, the Party's electoral finances were, on the whole, sufficient. Each endorsed candidate was assured of adequate funds. In January 1910 the Party was able to lend the Railway Servants £850 for the candidatures of Hudson and Wardle and in December £1,450 was lent to five candidates—£750 going to Wardle, Hudson, and Thomas, £500 to G. H. Roberts of the Typographical Association, and £200 to G. W. Bowerman (acting secretary of the T.U.C.) of the London Compositors. There were further grants from the Special Appeal Fund to Joseph Pointer (£200), the I.L.P. (£200) and smaller grants to Whitehaven and Kirkdale.[67] In January, Blewett has calculated, each Labour candidate spent an average of £881; in December it fell to £736. This tended to be £150 to £200 lower than the corresponding figures for the Conservative and Liberal candidates.[68] The total cost of the elections to the Party in January and December was £68,996 and £41,306 respectively.

One final word needs to be said about the conduct of the 1910 elections. It is an open question how many successful Labour candidates owed their election to Liberal organization. The campaigns of the majority of the Miners' M.P.s were certainly run by the Liberal Party. Only in South Glamorgan, Ince, Merthyr, and St. Helens was there any substantial Labour organization. It seems true that a number of the eleven M.P.s who sat for double-member constituencies owed their election partly to Liberal efforts. MacDonald himself was

[65] McKibbin, 'Evolution of a National Party', pp. 29–30.
[66] For examples, MacDonald to Middleton, Middleton to MacDonald, Nov.–Dec. 1910, 'LPLF: Uncat.'.
[67] For details, see below, pp. 20–21.
[68] Blewett, p. 290.

actually embarrassed by the Liberal campaign on his behalf,[69] and the Liberals made sure that their supporters did not plump or split votes with Conservative candidates in the other boroughs. Liberal assistance was not confined to the two-member divisions: in Deptford, Gorton, and even the two Manchester seats it was difficult to disentangle the Labour campaign from the Liberal.[70] At Bow and Bromley, R. C. K. Ensor feared that Lansbury might be 'court martialled and shot as a traitor' for accepting Liberal help in December;[71] Joseph Pointer received extensive Liberal assistance in Sheffield Attercliffe.[72] Even in Clitheroe in January, some, at least, of the enthusiasm for Shackleton was generated by Liberals. It was recorded that he 'addressed an enthusiastic meeting of his constituents at Nelson . . . and he had the support of the Mayor and prominent local Liberals'. At Barrowford the 'audience was composed of Mr. Shackleton's supporters and the "Land Song" was sung'.[73] The 'Land Song' was indisputably the song of the Radical single-taxers, and these displays were probably as embarrassing to Shackleton as similar ones were to other Labour leaders.

Labour was disappointed by the results of 1910 and it appeared as if the task facing the Party was a threefold one. First, the organization of local parties had to be made more uniform. Second, it was necessary to make affiliated bodies take their political duties more seriously, even if this meant transferring affiliation from an 'industrial' to a purely 'political' party. Finally, Labour had to rally the trade unions, and particularly the Miners, behind local parties, for the organization of the Labour Party rested, in the last resort, on union officers, union members, and union money.

[69] D. Cox, 'The Rise of the Labour Party in Leicester' (Univ. of Leicester M.A. thesis, 1959), p. 63.
[70] For Deptford, Thompson, p. 429; for the Manchester area, P. F. Clarke, *Lancashire and the New Liberalism* (Cambridge, 1971), pp. 311–39.
[71] Ensor to Lansbury, 7 Dec. 1910, 'L.S.E. MS. Lansbury', IV, p. 449.
[72] For details of Sheffield from MS. Wilson (Univ. of Sheffield) I am grateful to Dr. N. Blewett of Flinders University.
[73] *Labour Leader*, 7 Jan. 1910.

II

PARTY AND RANK-AND-FILE
1910–1914

To the growth of the Labour Party between the election of December 1910 and the outbreak of war there were few strictly technical obstacles; most of them were, in the broadest sense, political. However, it was argued at the time[1] that the Osborne Judgement of 1909,[2] by making illegal the political levy—trade-union contributions to Labour Party finances—genuinely hampered Labour in its attempts to expand after 1910.

Though both W. B. Gwyn and Clegg, Fox, and Thompson have pointed out that the worst fears of the Labour leadership were not realized,[3] these fears were plausible, and Gwyn, for example, has almost certainly underestimated the financial losses to the Party between 1909 and 1915. It is clear, in fact, that direct losses to the Party's income in those six years were at least £20,000. Furthermore, the Judgement prevented the Labour Party tapping the immense growth in the same years of the membership of the general workers' unions: thus to that figure must be added another £7,000 or £8,000. As a loss to the Party's revenues this estimate must be reckoned a cautious one, and the real loss may have been a good deal higher.[4]

This fall in possible income came at a time when the Party was beginning potentially expensive organizational developments.[5] But the effects of the Judgement went beyond just the national Party. It worsened relations between the Party and a number of affiliated unions, since such unions both had to abandon parliamentary candidatures and resented being badgered by the Party for voluntary subscriptions. It was also a perceptible dampener on the electoral efforts of L.R.C.s and trades councils. Of the local party records that survive, virtually every one shows that the Judgement led to a steady fall in affiliated membership and thus in revenue. Even the strongest parties, like Manchester and Leeds, were badly hit, while for tender flowers, like the Liverpool

---

[1] See *Conference Report*, 1911, p. 24.

[2] For the Judgement see W. M. Geldart, *The Osborne Judgement and After* (London, 1910), and H. H. Schloesser and W. S. Clark, *The Legal Position of Trade Unions* (London, 1912).

[3] W. B. Gwyn, *Democracy and the Cost of Politics* (London, 1962), p. 197; Clegg, Fox, and Thompson, p. 419.

[4] For a full discussion of the Osborne Judgement and the Party, see McKibbin, 'Evolution of a National Party', pp. 34–54.

[5] See below, pp. 31–3.

L.R.C., the Judgement was almost fatal. A surprisingly large number of L.R.C.s collapsed completely or disaffiliated—how many cannot be discovered exactly—and the Judgement ensured that there was effectively no rise at all in the number of L.R.C.s or trades councils affiliated to the national Party between 1910 and 1913.[6] Finally, it should be noted that the enjoining of unions under the Judgement made them determined to keep their levies to the Party artificially low when Party finances were reorganized in 1912.

Gwyn is, on the whole, right when he concludes that the Party got around Osborne. But it did so only because there was a reduction in the number of parliamentary candidates between the January and December 1910 elections,[7] and because there was no general election in 1914 or 1915. It is, therefore, possible to conceive of circumstances when the effects of the Judgement would have been serious indeed. That being said, however, it is clear that the Party was not judicially pauperized. There was, after all, no 1915 election; Labour organization was always cheap to run and largely voluntary; and the disputes over Party expenditure before 1914 were almost always political—not, that is to say, a question of how much money could be afforded, but whether it was politically prudent to spend it at all.

1. Head Office and Local Parties

Before the reorganization of the Party in 1918, Head Office was a frequent participant in the activities of the local parties. It was not, indeed, different in kind from post-war intervention: but it was more frequent, partly because of the genuinely hampering effect of the Osborne Judgement at local level, and partly because some of the unions were not prepared to undertake constituency work anyway.

Head Office was enlivened by the succession of Henderson to the secretaryship in 1911. This was a change long in the air. In his letter of resignation MacDonald noted that only the Osborne Case and 'the fact that there was some considerable amount of unsettlement in the Party' kept him on. Now that the Judgement was being remedied by legislation and some 'modifications' ('new departures' in his first draft) were under way, he felt it time to go, particularly as 'other work has been pressed upon me'.[8]

---

[6] The number of local bodies affiliated to the Party was:

1909	155
1910	148
1911	149
1912	146
1913	158

[7] See above, p. 16.

[8] MacDonald to the chairman of the national executive, (?) July 1911, 'LPLF: Uncat.'. The other work was, of course, the chairmanship of the parliamentary party.

Henderson was an energetic and mobile secretary, and for much of 1912 and 1913 he was on tour. These tours were the normal means of contact between London and the constituencies. The secretary, often accompanied by the national agent and regional union officials—even before the war Henderson tended to travel *en grande tenue*—met L.R.C., trades council, and union representatives, teaching them organizational techniques, broadcasting Westminster political gossip, and generally encouraging local efforts. About two days were spent in each place: in October 1913 Henderson's weekly itinerary for Durham was 'Saturday, till Monday, Newcastle; Monday night Durham; Tuesday–Wednesday St. John's Chapel Durham; Wednesday–Friday Stanhope Durham; Saturday till Tuesday, Darlington'.[9] It meant extensive travelling, and the itineraries could be complicated if by-elections intervened.

I agree to your suggestion as to Hardie and self going to Lanark [for the prospective by-election]. I shall go either on Friday November 21 or on the 24th . . . If I could change a meeting I have with the Crook Trades Council from Thursday 20th November to Saturday November 22 I could give Thursday and Friday next week . . . If I did not go till next week commencing Monday November 24 I could give about four nights . . . I shall be at Stanhope till about noon tomorrow. I then go to speak at [Tow Law?] on the fringe of my constituency . . . I travel to York to sleep at the Station Hotel leaving for Sheffield at 7.30 on Saturday morning for a conference with employers at Royal Victoria Hotel. I return from Sheffield on Monday to Bishop Auckland to speak for the Gas Workers Union.[10]

These tours were tiring—'it is very stiff night after night speaking from two to three hours'—and the perambulation from one station hotel to another lowering to the spirits. One consequence, in Henderson's case, was an almost neurotic obsession with the weather and with the 'foulness' of the atmosphere.

The burden on Henderson and Peters was such that it became necessary to delegate one or two members of the national executive to attend meetings at which some sort of Head Office presence was required, and this was the practice by 1914.[11] But by 1913 when the Party had the additional task of securing favourable results from the Trade Union Act ballots, it was already apparent that the work was too much for the secretary and the national agent even with assistance from the national executive. In 1913, therefore, two 'national organizers' were appointed: Sam Higenbottam of Nottingham (and

[9] Henderson to Middleton, 24 Oct. 1913, 'LPLF: Uncat.'.
[10] Henderson to Middleton, 13 Nov. 1913, 'LPLF: JSM Uncat.'.
[11] See, for example, 'NEC', 21 Jan. 1914.

A. G. Cameron's agent in Kirkdale), and William Holmes, a former I.L.P. organizer, and a future general secretary of the Agricultural Labourers' Union. To these was added, at first in a voluntary capacity, Egerton Wake, later national agent, whose highly strung life and premature death gave him a special place in the history of the Labour Party. He had been chairman and secretary of the Chatham Labour Party (conducting Jenkins's victorious campaign in 1906) until he succeeded Peters as Charles Duncan's organizing secretary (Barrow) in 1908. He was on the national administrative council of the I.L.P. in 1915 and 1916 and on the national executive from 1914 to 1918. His abilities quickly came to be valued by Henderson and he was a semi-permanent roving organizer until his official appointment as organizing secretary for Scotland and Wales in 1918.

Head Office was charged with the establishment of new parties, the rejuvenation of languishing ones, and the conduct of by-elections. By-election candidatures were usually improvised, and since, despite MacDonald's publicly expressed disapproval of propagandist campaigns, many of them were in fact propagandist, organization had sometimes to be developed from nothing.[12] The formula for by-elections was simple and universal: there was a maximum number of public meetings, of imported M.P.s, and of imported agents. In July 1912 at Crewe, Henderson, Wake, and Peters were active. Even so, Henderson was 'far from satisfied with the arrangements and advised Wake to send for several new agents . . . I have suggested that [Peters] should devote all his time going around keeping them up to the mark'.[13] Thus there is perhaps some truth in the uncharitable comments of the *Holmfirth Express* that the Labour Party in Holmfirth 'has more agents than canvassers . . . and more speakers than voters'.[14]

The N.-E. Derbyshire by-election of May 1914, where imported agents often were the canvassers, showed how necessary they could be. The *Derby Daily Express* notes that James Martin would have to rely upon 'the voluntary efforts of the miners' lodges and the check-weighmen, many of whom are Radicals of the Harvey and Kenyon type'.[15] Such 'types', it seems, were not forthcoming. Fred Constantine, agent for Clitheroe, who acted in N.-E. Derbyshire, wrote later that 'the people, generally speaking, had no idea what Labour politics meant, and the wonder was that under the circumstances the Labour candidate polled as well as he did'.[16] Imported

---

[12] For the political background of the by-elections, see chapter IV, *passim*.
[13] Henderson to Middleton, 17 July 1912, 'LPLF: Affiliations 1912'.
[14] *Holmfirth Express*, 4 June 1912.
[15] *Derby Daily Express*, 9 May 1914.
[16] Clitheroe Labour Party, *Agent's Annual Report*, 1915, p. 3.

M.P.s were, of course, obliged to speak. At Houghton-le-Spring in March 1913 Henderson had 'eight M.P.s for Monday and 30 meetings. We could have done with two or three more, but I think we shall manage'.[17] *The Times* correspondent in N.-E. Derbyshire was sure that Labour would try to make good other defects 'by a brilliant campaign of oratory'.[18]

Speakers were, therefore, something that Head Office could be relied upon to provide and 'star' speakers were much prized by local parties. The secretary of the newly formed South Shields Labour Party wrote to Peters in March 1912 that

a splendid opportunity is . . . afforded of having a prominent Labour M.P. sent down to give us some encouragement and a lift up . . . Now if arrangements could be made say before the end of April to get some front ranker such as Ramsay MacDonald or Snowden or Hardie good work could be accomplished.[19]

2. *Local Parties and the Miners' Unions*

The groundwork for the formation of new L.R.C.s was normally done during organizational tours and in most industrial areas this was straightforward enough. However, the establishment of organization in the coal-fields was nowhere so easy. Yet the mining constituencies were peculiarly important to Labour: in theory they were the safest single reservoir of working-class seats in the country. The parliamentary existence of the Labour Party before 1918, and indeed thereafter, to a large extent depended upon the successful organization of the coal-fields. However in 1914 only three mining constituencies with Labour members—Mid-Derbyshire, Nuneaton, and Normanton —had *independent* Labour electoral machinery.[20]

Following MacDonald's report on the January 1910 elections,[21] a deputation from the Party saw the Miners' Federation, with no apparent result.[22] It seems that requests for drastic improvements in mining organization were largely ignored, though such requests had some surprising advocates. In November 1910, Fred Hall, M.P. for Normanton, told a meeting of trade unionists that 'a Labour Representation Committee should be formed in the Normanton Division, which should meet regularly for the purpose of keeping our hold on the Division and also for making all political arrangements'. The L.R.C.

[17] Henderson to Middleton, 14 Mar. 1913, 'LPLF: JSM Uncat.'.
[18] *The Times*, 3 May 1914.
[19] Secretary, South Shields Labour Party, to Peters, 5 Mar. 1912, 'LPLF: Affiliations 1912'.
[20] See below, p. 27.
[21] See above, p. 13.
[22] 'NEC', 13 Apr. 1910; 30 Jan. 1911; also Gregory, p. 586.

was formed the next year,[23] but there is no evidence that any other party was formed at the same time.

Much depended, of course, on the attitude of the miners' unions. Although the executive of the Miners' Federation was not positively obstructive before 1912, neither was it helpful, while several of the regional societies did their best to prevent the development of local organizations. The Derbyshire Miners' Association refused to be represented at organizational conferences in Chesterfield and N.-E. Derbyshire in 1911, and some of its officers, notably Frank Hall, actively resisted organizational change.[24] In such circumstances Head Office was inclined to hand the problem back to the localities. Peters could only suggest that

if the lodges in the two Divisions [Chesterfield and N.-E. Derbyshire] can by resolutions bring all their pressure to bear on their Executive the thing is comparatively easy ... Carefully organise a plan of campaign in the direction and I am most confident it will have beneficial results.[25]

Yet the lodges, even if they were not Lib–Lab, would hardly take such action unless more pressure was put on them than Peters evidently thought necessary.

Until 1912 the Labour Party had little real co-operation from any section of the Miners' Federation. In February 1911, MacDonald rather pompously announced to the secretary of the Miners' Federation, Thomas Ashton, that he had been

requested to state to you that ... the time has now come (in fact, is overdue) for the formation of definite Labour parties in the constituencies where you have Members or where you propose to run Candidates ... I will be glad to hear from you at your earliest convenience as to whether you will co-operate.[26]

The Federation gave no reply.

By the end of the following year, however, the position had moved, decisively as it now appears, in the Labour Party's direction. In the first place Head Office concluded that its relative passivity in 1910–11 had been ineffective. There was a limit, also, to Henderson's patience in the face of scarcely concealed insults from the 'old warhorses'[27] of the Federation. Secondly, the experience of three by-elections in 1912—Holmfirth, Hanley, and Midlothian—convinced Head Office that direct intervention was immediately necessary. Finally, by 1912 it was clear that the political complexion of the Miners' Federation,

[23] Normanton Division Labour Party, *Annual Report*, 1911, pp. 4–5.
[24] See below, pp. 56–9.
[25] Quoted in Gregory, p. 284.
[26] MacDonald to Ashton, 8 Feb. 1911, 'LPLF: LP/MF/11/655'.
[27] Henderson's (rather surprising) phrase to Middleton, 6 Mar. 1912, 'LPLF: Uncat.'.

at all levels, was beginning to favour the Labour Party: an obvious example was the election in July 1912 of Robert Smillie, an I.L.P.er, to succeed Edwards as president of the Federation.

The new 'direction' began in May when Henderson went to Nuneaton, William Johnson's tiresome constituency, to assist in the establishment of a divisional L.R.C. This was followed by a propaganda campaign conducted by Thomas Richards M.P. and Arthur Peters, which lasted a month. Head Office had acted thus because Johnson, one of the more shameless Lib–Lab M.P.s, had persistently breached the Party's constitution. But his union, the Warwickshire Miners' Association, refused to affiliate to the new L.R.C. and until it did little could come of Henderson's intervention.

The results of the by-elections—Hanley in particular—probably did more than the efforts of the Labour Party.[28] The refusal of the Liberal Party to accept miners' candidates was a salutary lesson for the county unions. Soon after Hanley the North Staffordshire Miners resolved that 'in future . . . we cease to finance any alliance between Liberalism and Labour and that we take immediate steps to set up machinery for the formation of a Labour Association for political purposes'.[29] Similarly, the result in Holmfirth, though by no means as bad as that in Hanley, led at the end of 1912 to the formation of a divisional L.R.C. which did include amongst its affiliated societies the local miners' lodges.

At the same time as the by-elections were making the miners more enthusiastic about independent Labour representation, changes in the leadership of the Federation increased its readiness to put pressure on its affiliated unions. On 21 May another deputation from the Labour Party met the Federation to discuss what were politely called 'irregularities' in coal-fields constituencies. In 1910 Ashton had dismissed similar complaints as 'trifling in their nature, untrue or not proven'.[30] In 1912 they were at least taken seriously. By August Henderson felt able to put three questions to Ashton, and imperatively rather than interrogatively.

I shall esteem it a favour if your Federation could give categorical answers to the following questions: —

1. What steps, if any, does your Federation propose to take to secure the formation of local Labour Parties in all the constituencies now held by Miners' Representatives and for which the nomination of Miners' Candidates at the next General Election is contemplated?

2. Is it possible for your Federation to amend its Standing Orders which

---

[28] For Hanley, see below, pp. 53–6.
[29] Quoted in Gregory, p. 564.
[30] Quoted in Gregory, pp. 58, 280.

limits the choice of candidates to the district where a vacancy occurs?[31]

3. Does your Federation propose to appoint full-time agents in the constituencies now held by Miners' Representatives and in constituencies which the Federation proposes to contest at the next Election?[32]

Ashton replied affirmatively to the first and second questions, but hedged on the third.[33] Nothing, he said,

> was done in the matter of appointing full time Agents in the Constituencies now held by Miners' Representatives, but it is, of course, open to any District to appoint such Agents, as you are aware the Lancashire and Cheshire Miners' Federation are doing at the present time.

However, in October 1912, the executive of the Federation formally instructed its affiliates to undertake the establishment of 'Political Labour Parties' in all constituencies they controlled and the locality rule was abolished.

Progress thereafter was patchy rather than slow. Some constituencies, mostly in the Midlands, continued to resist therapy. In November 1913 the agenda of a joint meeting of the executives of the Party and the Federation included items on Chester-le-Street, Houghton-le-Spring, Morley, Mid-Lanark, South Lanark, Hanley, N.-W. Staffordshire, Chesterfield, Mid-Derbyshire, and Hallamshire. By the outbreak of the war, the Durham divisions had 'become regular' (as the saying went) and the Scottish constituencies were at least in hand. But the remainder, in an area stretching from Stoke to Sheffield, were almost intractably 'irregular'.

The reasons for this are not hard to find. The Midland divisions were still prosperous, and, unlike constituencies dependent upon the export trade, there were yet few tensions between owners and men. At the same time, furthermore, it is likely that the sudden increase in Labour activity after 1912 stiffened resistance from the otherwise easy-going sitting members. This was most noticeable in those divisions within easy oversight of the Sheffield Trades Council which in 1912 had come under control of a coalition of socialists and anti-Lib–Lab trade unionists. Its habit of despatching socialist outriders to neighbouring constituencies as both prophets and observers had the effect, for example, of forcing J. G. Hancock (Mid-Derbyshire) to concede the principle of independent Labour organization while redoubling his efforts to avoid the reality. Hancock's tactic was to retreat into a kind of inspired lunacy. After overwhelming pressure

---

[31] This was the widely criticized 'locality rule' which, it was believed, prevented effective candidates from being chosen, as well as those less ambiguous in their attitude to the Liberal Party.

[32] Henderson to Ashton, 6 Aug. 1912, 'LPLF: LP/MF/11/666'.

[33] Ashton to Henderson, 12 Oct. 1912, 'LPLF: LP/MF/11/669'.

had been exerted by local officials and by the Sheffield Trades Council, he agreed to meet delegates from the national executive and the Federation at Alfreton on 15 March 1913. But the conference was not held since Hancock could not be found. The delegation set out to catch him; he skipped from one town to another, with Henderson, Smillie, and the rest trailing about half an hour behind. He was eventually tracked down in Nottingham, claimed that he had been told that the conference was cancelled, and left the exhausted and scattered delegation to make their way home.[34]

But however many old Lib–Labs were prepared to die in the last ditch, they had already lost the hunt. In a body such as the Miners' Federation quick results could not be expected. Most important was that the Federation should have agreed to the establishment of 'Political Labour Parties' and that everybody, even people like Hancock, should have accepted them, at least *pro forma*. From then on, it was a matter of time. But the results were not seen until after 1914.

3. *London and Glasgow*

The absence of central parties in the two principal cities of the United Kingdom was one of the more surprising aspects of Party organization. It was at the same time a cause and a result of the political weakness of Labour in London and Glasgow. In neither were there any obvious hindrances to Labour: the religious differences of Liverpool were much attenuated (though a factor) and the Chamberlainism that dominated Birmingham was almost non-existent. Yet in County London Labour held only three seats—Woolwich, Bow and Bromley, and Deptford,[35] and in Glasgow only one, Blackfriars. It was usually assumed that, unlike the situation in Liverpool and Birmingham, superior organization alone would largely overcome these deficiencies. By the end of 1914, with mixed success, central parties had been founded in both cities.

Paul Thompson has provided a full account of the evolution of the London Labour Party.[36] As he points out, London was more a case of aborted growth than none at all. Up to 1910 there had been several attempts to unite the Labour forces of the city, all unsuccessful. Thompson sees two reasons for this. The first was the position of the trade unions. The number of London unions affiliated to the Labour Party fell from seventy in 1904 to fifty in 1913. Chances of recovery

---

[34] For an account of this comic episode, see Henderson to Ashton, 20 Mar. 1913, 'LPLF: LP/MF/11/455'.
[35] In Greater London Labour held one other seat, West Ham South.
[36] Thompson, pp. 418–96.

were seriously hampered by the Osborne Judgement and the lapsing of several important unions, notably the Compositors.[37] It was not until 1912 that affiliated trade-union membership reached the 1904 figure. Secondly, the very size and social complexity of London made for an unusual variety of political organizations. It gave, for example, the Social Democratic Federation a strength it did not have elsewhere: only in London was it as strong as the I.L.P., while both faced competition from traditional London radicalism. Successive attempts to secure united action foundered on the rivalry of these three. Where the Labour Party was traditionally strong the Social Democrats worked loyally enough for it; elsewhere they opposed co-operation and encouraged unions to disaffiliate.[38] The industrial militancy of 1911–1913 and the decision of the Social Democratic Federation (now the British Socialist Party) to apply for affiliation to the Labour Party transformed this situation.

By 1913, therefore, it was considered that another attempt was worth making. In October a large meeting of union delegates was addressed by MacDonald, Henderson, and Bowerman, but its chances were affected by the refusal of the I.L.P. to attend. On the other hand, the London Trades Council had now softened its attitude to fusion. The simultaneous death of Harry Quelch and retirement of James MacDonald, both members of the British Socialist Party and unfriendly to the Labour Party, gave the Trades Council a less intransigent leadership. In March 1914, the new chairman, John Stokes of the London Gasworkers, proposed a conference to establish 'a united working class party on the L.C.C. at the 1916 election',[39] and it met on 22 May 1914. The conference, on Stokes's urging, was quite unusually tolerant. A constitution modelled on the national Labour Party was approved and the executive elected represented fairly evenly the balance of forces. Of the eighteen officers, five were from the British Socialist Party, eight from the I.L.P., and there were five non-socialist trade unionists.[40]

One reason for the success of the conference was that the delegates were presented with definite rather than casual proposals. The change of heart of the British Socialist Party, the growing willingness of the I.L.P. to co-operate, and the gradual dissolution of organized London radicalism were equally important. Like the political evolution of the coal-fields, this success was also to some extent a function of age. It did appear as if younger officials were less wedded to the

---

[37] See below, pp. 20–21.

[38] Thompson claims that they were partly responsible for the lapsing of the London Carmen, Bargebuilders, Fawcett Association, Coal Porters, and Navvies (p. 469).

[39] Thompson, p. 492.

[40] Several of the socialist members were, of course, also unionists.

different ideologies of the socialist societies or to that unique brand of Lib–Labism which had achieved so much in London before 1906.

The Glasgow Labour Party was founded at its first attempt, but the result was less satisfactory. At the beginning of 1911 there were five L.R.C.s in Glasgow—Hutchestown (Blackfriars), Central, Camlachie, Govan, and Partick—in addition to the elections committee of the Trades Council, the Co-operative Society Defence Association, and a joint body, the Registration Committee, which was supposed to co-ordinate electoral registration in the city.[41] The Glasgow I.L.P. Federation, the strongest of the socialist societies in the city, itself had twenty branch affiliates.[42] It was a complicated and unsatisfactory situation. The national executive, therefore, summoned (18 May 1911) a gathering of unions and socialist societies to consider the formation of a central Labour Party whose task, Peters said, would be 'to unify and control all election work in the District'.[43] It was agreed that such a party was indeed 'desirable' and a constituent committee was appointed to organize one.

The committee established the form of representation fairly easily,[44] but there was virtually no agreement as to the basis of finance.[45] The Govan Trades Council then refused to affiliate and the Social Democrats also withdrew on the grounds that the proposed party was ideologically suspect.[46] When the inaugural conference of the new Party met on 21 March 1912 it had been weakened financially and politically to the point of premature extinction. The inaugural conference was then told that the Co-operative Defence Association, one of the Party's great props, had seceded.[47] The presence of the co-operators had always been too good to be true. At the second meeting of the committee the Association had bluntly suggested that the new party should be called the Progressive Party—perhaps by analogy with the old London Progressive Party—(and the suggestion was not rejected immediately) 'as it might be possible that other bodies than those eligible for affiliation to the Labour Party might be admitted'.[48] Such Lib–Labism was unacceptable to the Labour

[41] 'Minutes of a Conference to consider the Formation of a Central Party in Glasgow', 18 May 1911.

[42] Secretary, Glasgow Labour Party, to Middleton, 6 July 1914, 'LPLF: Affiliations 1914'.

[43] 'Minutes etc.', 18 May 1911.

[44] 'Minutes of a Constituent Committee', 13 June 1911. There were to be five delegates from the Co-operative Defence Association, three each from the Trades Council, the I.L.P., and the Social Democrats, and two each from the Fabians, Women's Labour League, Govan Trades Council, and every L.R.C.

[45] 'Minutes', 13 June 1911; 1 Aug. 1911.

[46] 'Minutes', 1 Aug. 1911.

[47] Glasgow Labour Party, 'Minutes', 21 Mar. 1912.

[48] 'Minutes', 13 June 1911.

forces, while anything else than a 'progressive' party was apparently unacceptable to the Association. In practice, it was unlikely that the co-operators would have ever joined on suitable terms, and it is surprising, even though relations between the two were better in Scotland than elsewhere, that the Labour groups thought they would.

Nevertheless, the new Party got under way, and was conceivably better off without the Social Democrats and the co-operators. It was able to supervise electoral activity more energetically than the old Registration Committee and was lucky in its first secretary, Ben Shaw, though he left shortly afterwards (and with great relief) to become secretary of the Scottish Advisory Council.[49] But the Party did not meet expectations: it did little to toughen those transient phenomena, the divisional L.R.C.s; it displayed a perplexing attitude to parliamentary candidatures, and was totally resistant to Head Office direction and advice. But the social and political foundations for a 'standard' Labour party did not exist in Glasgow: the unions were untypically weak and the socialist societies untypically strong. The foundation was certainly there for a working-class party, but when it emerged after 1918 it was one whose character was unique to the west of Scotland. Glasgow was already an 'independent principality', and it was so because those unifying filaments, the national trade unions, were less effective in Glasgow than in any other major industrial city. When in 1917 Henderson said that the Glasgow Labour Party 'totally failed to meet the requirements of so large an area', he was not referring to organizational requirements alone.[50]

4. *Assistance to Local Parties*

It was clear that once the dust of the 1910 elections had settled the national executive would turn to the strengthening of Party organization on the lines of MacDonald's recommendations.[51] It was assumed that some form of new assistance would be given to the L.R.C.s, and that this aid should include in its provisions the appointment of agents. Henderson put a scheme together in almost his first act as secretary. He decided to make use of the rearrangement of finances that payment of M.P.s made necessary to divert to the local parties some of the money that would normally have gone to the parliamentary fund. This scheme was not inherited from MacDonald, and if MacDonald had detailed thoughts about assistance—he had as it turned out—Henderson made no use of them. He proposed a flat increase in Head

---

[49] See below, p. 42.
[50] For Scotland generally, see below, pp. 39–43.
[51] See above, p. 15.

Office's contribution to Returning Officers' expenses—from 25 per cent to 50 per cent of the total.[52]

MacDonald, who was at Lossiemouth when the national executive received Henderson's proposition, was appalled. He was becoming more and more obsessed with the consequences of Labour candidatures,[53] and he unerringly picked the political implications of Henderson's hand-out. He doubted, he said, the wisdom of this plan.[54]

I would hold out the bait in other directions. For instance I should agree with the local parties who appoint full-time agents to pay them 25% of these agents' *salaries*, provided we approve of the agents and are satisfied with his [sic] work ... If we increase our share of the Returning Officers' expenses, I should favour some discrimination. I should provide that a Candidate ought to record a certain percentage of votes before he gets his full share unless the Executive *before* the election agrees that the candidature is necessary irrespective of the votes cast and accepts responsibility beforehand. We shall have to very carefully safeguard ourselves against wild-cat candidatures and so I do not think that the mere fact that we are to give half the Returning Officers' expenses instead of a quarter will help us much in that direction. It will only increase our difficulties with the local bodies which will find greater facilities than ever for committing themselves to candidatures, and then telling us as they do that the Movement expects a fight, and would be seriously damaged if it does not get it.

He was glad, however,

that the Committee considered the question of the Party's control of candidates as apart from the particular organisations which bring them forward first of all. That is going to be a difficult problem for us in the future if certain things which are now happening are a forecast of what is to continue to happen. I do not think, however, that an extra quarter of the Returning Officers' expenses will enable us to face that question.

Political motives prompted this letter, but MacDonald had raised important matters of organization which were, in principle, correct. Henderson's scheme was ill-considered. Given the deficiencies of local organization little would have been done by an unselective grant to the constituencies. Apart from being ultimately more generous, MacDonald's suggestions had the merit of placing emphasis upon the appointment of full-time agents and making these appointments dependent upon Head Office approval. At any rate, MacDonald convinced the national executive, which presented conference with his scheme rather than Henderson's.[55] It was decided that applications for

[52] 'NEC', 30 Sept. 1911.
[53] See below, pp. 77–81.
[54] MacDonald to Middleton, 6 Oct. 1911, 'LPLF: JSM Uncat.'.
[55] *Conference Report*, 1912, pp. 14–15.

financial assistance 'must be accompanied by a complete statement showing the affiliated local party's composition and details of its organization'—a requirement palpably inserted to diminish the political autonomy of local parties—as well as a half-yearly report indicating work done and 'the state of organisation'.[56]

The introduction of the grants-in-aid (May 1912) was an important step. The number of full-time agents increased fairly rapidly, from seventeen in 1912 to about eighty in 1918. There is no evidence, however, that the form of grant made much difference one way or the other to local parties: they showed themselves as ready to put up candidates without agents as with them. Rather unexpectedly, this decision to tie the right to contest to organizational efficiency limited the power of the national executive to refuse endorsement to a candidate for political reasons. The appointment of a full-time agent immediately removed any objections the national executive could decently raise, even if the candidature were otherwise thought undesirable.

5. Trades Councils and L.R.C.s

Until 1918, and for some time thereafter, the characteristic local organ of the Labour Party was the trades council, acting either in that name or nominally disguised as 'Trades Council and Labour Party'. For a Party whose organized social basis was overwhelmingly a trade-union one this was not surprising. But the aims of the trades councils were always primarily industrial and they frequently behaved as if politics were an irritating distraction from their real business. At the same time, however, they were jealous of their political rights. Disappointment with the 1910 elections encouraged the view that political bodies should alone represent the Party in the constituencies. Middleton noted

that in the early days of the Labour Movement it was necessary and desirable that the existing Trades Councils should form an essential part of the L.R.C. [i.e. pre-1906 Labour Party]. And we at Head Office realise to the full what excellent service the Councils were able to render us in the early years. As the political side of the Movement has developed however, it is extremely desirable that these bodies [local L.R.C.s] should be our points of local contact.[57]

There were many L.R.C.s more than willing to be such 'points'. In September 1910, as a result of disputes in Plymouth and Manchester, MacDonald had been obliged to formulate a rule of thumb by

[56] 'NEC', Undated Memorandum, 1912.
[57] Middleton to Secretary, Portsmouth Trades Council, 4 Nov. 1913, 'LPLF: Affiliations 1913'.

which affiliation could be transferred to L.R.C.s with as much tact as possible. The Plymouth L.R.C., 'the Plymouth Co-operative and Labour Party', which appears to have been a front for the local co-operative society, had applied for affiliation to the Party. The application was bitterly contested by the local trades council.[58] The Manchester L.R.C., a perfectly orthodox party which did most of the electoral work in the city, had also asked the trades council to surrender its affiliation. The council declined, claiming that it was more representative of the unions in the area, while the L.R.C. was composed merely of the 'socialist element'.[59] After a fruitless attempt to amalgamate the two bodies MacDonald decided to take a hand and recommended to the national executive that it

lay down no hard or fast rule as local circumstances vary so much, but I think that when L.R.C.s and trades councils cannot agree themselves the Executive should have power to arbitrate between them and give a decision which will be binding. The decision need not be the same in every case because the Executive should take into consideration all the local circumstances and its experience of them.[60]

The 1911 conference, therefore, more or less gave Head Office a free hand to deal with local bodies. Yet it is clear that the national executive was reluctant to use this power, not because it did not wish to use it, but because the balance of power in the constituencies often made it impossible to do so. Moreover, the well-publicized opposition of many trades councils made Head Office unwilling to annoy them— at least any more than was necessary to compel them to do their electoral duty. Rarely was a transfer of affiliation arranged amicably or easily, and in several cases it could not be arranged at all. Only the Portsmouth Trades Council volunteered to give up its affiliation. North Staffordshire surrendered with good grace—though the secretary added a crushing rider: 'I might add for your information that the Trades Council will be the dominating party with 15 delegates.'[61]

In the large divided boroughs the councils usually had to be bullied into even contemplating a transfer of affiliation. In two cases at least the councils were so obstructive that the solution was virtually unconstitutional. In Manchester, after the failure of long negotiations, a form of dual affiliation was accepted: the Council was satisfied with

---

[58] 'NEC', 29 Nov. 1910.
[59] Leslie Bather, 'A History of the Manchester and Salford Trades Council' (Univ. of Manchester Ph.D. thesis), pp. 171-2.
[60] 'NEC', 29 Sept. 1910.
[61] Secretary, North Staffordshire Trades Council, to Henderson, 25 Aug. 1913, 'LPLF: Affiliations 1913'.

nominal affiliation, while the L.R.C. was able to achieve the direct contact with Head Office it had always sought.[62] In Leeds an even more curious arrangement was reached. The Council and the L.R.C. affiliated as one body, paying double fees and having a divided delegation at conference. All official correspondence was sent to the Trades Council, which would 'remit to the Secretary of the local Labour Party such communications as were of a political character'.[63]

In London, Glasgow, and Newcastle affiliation was transferred with much ill will or only after prolonged and difficult negotiations. The London Labour Party decided to seek affiliation in January 1917, and the formal application expressed a readiness to meet the Trades Council, and such a meeting was proposed by Middleton.[64] The secretary of the Council, Charles Stokes, replied that his executive 'agreed that we raise no objection, in accordance with the terms of [the London Labour Party's] resolution. There is now no need for the conference as suggested.'[65] Stokes soon felt obliged to elaborate on this cryptic intelligence.

You say that we can leave the Labour Party to make suitable arrangements, by this I presume 'we' to be the London Trades Council.

The London Trades Council as such does not accept any responsibility for any arrangement on this matter. If the Labour Party accepts the affiliation, the responsibility is theirs and we see no reason why we should depart from the terms of the resolution that only asked us not to raise any objections to the application for affiliation.[66]

Head Office was taken aback at this turn of events. Middleton 'rather gathered' that a conference 'would have been an exceedingly useful preliminary' to the national executive's 'consideration of the whole subject'.[67] He told Morrison that 'a preliminary conference of representatives would have been most advisable'.[68]

Most appear to have been surprised by the Trades Council's reaction. Morrison dismissed it as typical of the Council's refusal to take political organization seriously, but it was obviously more than that. The Council, so long the only focus for Labour in the capital, resented losing status and power to a newcomer. Perhaps residual resentments at the way the London Labour Party had been formed

[62] Bather, p. 173.
[63] 'NEC', 15 Sept. 1915.
[64] Middleton to Stokes, 17 Mar. 1917, 'LPLF Affiliations 1917'. See also, *London Labour Party Circular*, May 1917.
[65] Stokes to Middleton, 13 Apr. 1917, 'LPLF: Affiliations 1917'.
[66] The same, 16 Apr. 1917.
[67] Middleton to Stokes, 21 Apr. 1917, 'LPLF: Affiliations 1917'.
[68] Middleton to Morrison, 21 Apr. 1917, 'LPLF: Affiliations 1917'.

played some part, while Morrison, unsurprisingly, had made enemies.[69] The hostility of the Council to the transfer of affiliation did show how attached councils were to their privileges, and how reluctant they were to abandon them, particularly as they were ineligible for affiliation to the T.U.C. Furthermore, the hostility of the Council was not confined to verbal expressions. It refused to contribute to the finances of the London Labour Party and without the tempering that trades councils provided for shorn lambs elsewhere, Morrison's party remained severely straitened, and without Trades Council assistance, for the next seven years.[70]

In Newcastle the transfer was effected in even more unpleasant circumstances. The L.R.C. applied for affiliation in September 1913, the secretary reminding Henderson that they had long sought it and that 'there never had been any living connection between the national party and [the Trades Council]'. Since their last application the number of societies affiliated to the L.R.C. had increased from twenty-seven to fifty-six.

The fact of our submitting a half yearly and Annual Report to you makes quite clear that identity of interest and need for closer connection between the local Committee and the National Party. Mr. MacDonald, Mr. Hudson [M.P. for Newcastle] yourself and Mr. Peters are bound to feel in view of the known facts that our repeated claim for affiliation is more than justified.[71]

The national executive agreed that his argument was 'cogent and reasonable'; they hoped, however, that a conference would reach a mutually satisfactory settlement. Henderson himself would be prepared to attend.[72] But the proposed conference was never held.

On 13 November the Trades Council decided to abandon its affiliation

and thus to allow the L.R.C. to have the position they have so long coveted and so long 'intrigued' for. Any Joint Representation with the L.R.C. is absolutely out of the question. Recent happenings in connection with them . . . have greatly increased the bitter feelings already existing so that any Conference such as you suggest would probably do more harm than good.[73]

At the same time the Council issued a statement to the press complaining that it had been coerced by the national executive into disaffiliation.[74] This was a blow to Head Office, particularly to Henderson

[69] See Morrison's correspondence to Middleton, London Labour Party File, 'LPLF: Affiliations 1917'.
[70] See below, pp. 170–3.
[71] Secretary, Newcastle L.R.C., to Henderson, 15 Sept. 1913, 'LPLF: Affiliations 1913'.
[72] Middleton to Secretary Newcastle L.R.C., 10 Oct. 1913, 'LPLF: Affiliations 1913'.
[73] Secretary, Newcastle Trades Council, to Middleton, 14 Nov. 1913, 'LPLF: Affiliations 1913'.
[74] *Newcastle Daily Journal*, 14 Nov. 1913.

whose fief the North-East was, and where things were usually ordered better. There was, however, probably little that could have been done. By taking the side of the National Amalgamated Union of Labour against the Steel Smelters in a peculiarly bitter dispute over organization in the heavy engineering industry, the L.R.C. had earned the disapproval of a Trades Council still dominated by craft unions. Middleton regretted the Council's decision and noted that 'in other centres, as the result of friendly and frank discussion, better feelings have prevailed'.[75]

In Glasgow the Trades Council agreed to surrender their affiliation, but conducted such a successful retreat that negotiations took well over a year. The Glasgow Party formally requested affiliation as early as April 1912; the Trades Council formally refused to relinquish it in July. After a year of dogged resistance from the Council, the Party at last asked Head Office to intervene.[76] In August 1912, while in Glasgow for a union conference, Henderson took the opportunity to persuade the Council to abandon affiliation. On the other hand, to do so he appears to have given them scarcely constitutional guarantees as to consultation and right of access.[77] In this way an 'amicable agreement' was reached, affiliation was transferred, but only after the Council had extracted concessions from Head Office of a kind not foreseen by MacDonald in 1910.

Occasionally, Head Office itself would take the initiative, though only when there was no alternative and no powerful groups involved. Thus, for example, Head Office intervened in Islington after the Trades Council's decision to endorse Horatio Bottomley for Hackney South in January 1910 led to demands for its disaffiliation. This affair, as with anything that involved Bottomley, was not easily plumbed, but it was MacDonald who took the first step in disaffiliating the Trades Council. 'We think the matter very unsatisfactory,' he wrote, '. . . I think it would be a very good thing if you tried to get your body [the Islington L.R.C.] affiliated; you could raise the point that the existing Council is not in reality a Trades Council at all.'[78] The L.R.C. was easily coached and their application was replete with charges against the Trades Council.

(1) The Islington Trades Council who are at present affiliated, do not under their constitution take any political action, this was one of their strong points when they changed their name from the Islington Labour Party.

[75] Middleton to Secretary, Newcastle Trades Council, 16 Nov. 1913, 'LPLF: Affiliations 1913'.
[76] Ben Shaw to Middleton, 25 July 1913, 'LPLF: Affiliations 1913'; Glasgow Labour Party, 'Minutes', 14 Apr., 4 July 1912.
[77] 'NEC', 8 Oct. 1913.
[78] MacDonald to Secretary, Islington L.R.C., 20 Mar. 1911, 'LPLF: Uncat.'.

(2) They have by their actions forfeited all right to speak for the voice of Labour . . . the crowning point being reached when they issued the Manifesto describing Bottomley as 'the true and tried friend of Labour'. . . .
(3) Owing to their constitution, the I.L.P., the W.L.L. [Women's Labour League] etc. are denied affiliation, in fact the I.L.P. were told point blank they could not be affiliated.[79]

The result of this exchange was the immediate affiliation of the L.R.C., though the arrangement lasted less than a year.

It is clear from these proceedings that Head Office had been given powers often more impressive on paper than in their discharge. As was to be the case after 1918, the national executive did its best to encourage change, but was prepared to withdraw in face of local opposition or the realities of trade-union strength. Even when trades councils were on the defensive, their powers of obstruction were formidable, if under-used : the London Trades Council threw away its chances in a fit of pique and its behaviour towards the London Party—on financial matters particularly—tended to be destructive. Nevertheless, in two of the cases examined here trades councils were actually able to recover lost ground. In 1917 the North Staffordshire Trades Council successfully reclaimed its affiliation, and, significantly, because the L.R.C. was now objectionably dominated by the 'I.L.P.–pacifist element'.[80] Despite its uncertain status, the Islington Trades Council proved so determined to hold its affiliation that the national executive was obliged to patch together an amalgamation of the L.R.C. and the Council.

This is not to say, of course, that the executive was without influence. By 1914 affiliation to the national Party was held by 'political' parties in London, Glasgow, Manchester, Leeds, and Newcastle. In 1910 in none of these was this so. Thus organizations whose function was purely political and largely electoral represented the national Party and this was probably an advance. Nevertheless in Manchester, Leeds, and Glasgow the national executive was forced to concede to trades councils rights which were theoretically those of L.R.C.s, and everywhere else councils refused or were reluctant to surrender affiliation. But this was not necessarily a source of weakness to the Labour Party. Arguably, a more debilitating one would have been readiness of the councils to disaffiliate. So long as they wished to remain affiliated to the Party they were interested in it; so long as that was the case, the Party was sure of at least a minimum of activity and enthusiasm. The Labour Party recognized this : all it could do was to

---

[79] Secretary, Islington L.R.C., to MacDonald, 24 Apr. 1911, 'LPLF: Uncat.'. For the original incident, see *Islington Daily Gazette and North London Tribune*, 27 June 1910.
[80] 'NEC', 16 May 1917.

insist that the councils should take their political duties seriously. This it attempted to do.

6. Regional Organization until 1915

Before 1918, and certainly before 1915, regional questions in practice meant Scotland. In July 1911 the national executive rejected a proposed conference on Welsh organization. Elsewhere, important regional bodies existed only in Lancashire and Cheshire, but rivalry between the old-established Lancashire and Cheshire Federation of Trades Councils and the newly founded Federation of Labour Parties reduced the effectiveness of both. It was, furthermore, the kind of rivalry unlikely to bring intervention from a Head Office which was unwilling to offend either party.[81] Anyway, both Federations only met irregularly and indecisively.

Scotland was in a different category. For many reasons Scotland could claim some measure of independence. Apart from its national history, the traditions and problems of the Labour movement in Scotland were in many ways different from those in England, and in the recent past it had possessed at least three independent Labour representation associations.[82] Additionally, Scotland was a useful and acceptable administrative unit. From a national point of view, therefore, the problem was to concede Scottish demands for autonomy, while at the same time ensuring organizational efficiency and continued control over wider questions of strategy.

As early as 1910 MacDonald had suggested taking Scotland in hand. After some dawdling a conference of Scottish delegates was held in Edinburgh in August 1911 and the national executive was represented by MacDonald and Ben Turner.[83] They concluded that the

political organisation of Scotland is not quite as good as it might be . . . The steady and persistent work of local Labour parties is not so marked as in England. For this, to some extent there is an inclination to blame the Central Executive, but we do not think our Scottish friends quite appreciate how much this form of excellence depends upon local workers.

The contests in Scotland, it was alleged, have been too much kept within certain Trade Union areas, as for instance, Lanarkshire . . . It was also pointed out that an unfortunate sectarian bitterness is prevalent in some districts where the Trade Union movement is strongest [Clydeside, Lanarkshire], and that this weakens political Trade Unionism. With this in mind

---

[81] For this, see above, p. 38.

[82] See H. M. Pelling, *The Origins of the Labour Party, 1880–1900* (Oxford, 1965), pp. 69–71, 149, 204.

[83] Characteristically, it met on the same day as the Annual Demonstration of the Lanarkshire Miners, so no representative of the Scottish miners was present. (*Scotsman*, 6 Aug. 1911.)

some of the delegates blamed the Party ... We are of opinion that if it were possible to create [a Scottish advisory committee] it might prevent a good deal of the resentment which some of the older workers of the Movement in Scotland undoubtedly feel ... [84]

This committee was to be a skeletal one: it should have a permanent secretary and an annual conference, but no paid organizer and few powers. The narrowness of this recommendation was based upon a most dubious political assumption: that Scotland had been 'but slightly affected by the tub-thumping appeals to sentimentality and drastic action in Parliament, which has given us so much trouble in other places'. The idea of a patient Scotland was disproven by events.

The MacDonald–Turner proposals were not acted upon, and exactly a year later Henderson arranged conferences in Glasgow, Aberdeen, Dundee, and Edinburgh to discuss Scottish organization. Though they seem to have been reasonably friendly, they were by no means a triumph for the secretary; the 'spirit of enthusiasm and unanimity' he detected at Edinburgh meaning only that there was less opposition there to Head Office than elsewhere.[85] All the conferences grumbled at London's supposed lack of zeal in promoting Labour candidates and all laid plans for new contests. Three of them, Aberdeen, Dundee, and Edinburgh, prepared draft schemes for Scottish organization, and in only one, Aberdeen, were the unions guaranteed equal representation with other societies either in a conference or in a putative Scottish executive. These drafts were a tribute not only to the strength of the socialists in Scotland, but also to the paradoxes of Scottish Labour: Aberdeen was a socialist stronghold, whereas Dundee, whose draft was explicitly designed to diminish union influence, had in the Jute Workers a most effective and powerful trade union.

Dundee proposed a Scottish council to consist of one delegate from each parliamentary constituency with an L.R.C. or trades council affiliated to the Party.

The [Dundee] Committee had two main things in view when discussing their scheme. First, they understood that the National Party wanted to get into closer touch with Scottish constituencies rather than with the Trade Unions, and, secondly, they recognised that whatever machinery is set up, it must be subject to the National Party.

... they are of opinion that the representatives sent by the organisations in the various constituencies would be more likely to reflect public opinion and give a better insight into the Scottish Political Movement than delegates sent by Trade Societies ...

[84] Report filed as 'NEC', (?) Sept. 1911.
[85] Report of the Conferences filed as 'NEC', 4 Nov. 1912.

... to invite delegates sent by the various Trade Societies as a basis of organisation would, in our opinion, result in another meeting of the Scottish T.U.C. under another name, and this, in our judgement, would be a calamity ...

Likewise, the Edinburgh draft excluded the unions from guaranteed representation, though not as boldly as Dundee. The formulation of these drafts suggests I.L.P. influence, and I.L.P.ers would certainly have been active at the conferences. On the other hand, the convenor of the Dundee conference was G. R. Shepherd, the future national agent,[86] and his reasons for signing the Dundee draft were doubtless as much organizational as political.

Henderson did not literally follow the line of these drafts, and considering their provisions this is not surprising. As amended in January 1913, his scheme for a Scottish Advisory Council (S.A.C.) was a rather simple-minded compromise: as compared with the constitution of the national Party the unions were over-represented in its annual conference but under-represented on its executive.[87] This juggling did not meet union requirements. When it was presented to the 1913 conference of the Party it was opposed by the Scottish unions (particularly the Miners) on the grounds that they were grossly under-represented,[88] and by some of the national unions on the grounds that there was no need for a Scottish committee at all. Tom Shaw of the Textile Workers could not see

any earthly reason for setting up an organisation in an organisation ... If a separate organisation of this character was to be set up for Scotland, should one be set up for Ireland, one for Wales, one for the individual districts of England, and one for the agricultural districts? ... If there were any problems ... there were sufficient Scotsmen on the Executive to deal with them ... Scotland was no worse situated than any other part of the country.[89]

Henderson's scheme was defeated by 225 to 105.

When the 1914 conference met, the national executive had prepared a second plan more favourable to the Scottish unions. Both the proposed conference and the executive were modified to increase union representation.[90] The revised S.A.C. was to have its own secretary, although his salary was to be paid by London, ensuring that he would, in effect, be an agent of Head Office and not of the S.A.C. Though

---

[86] Shepherd was then registration agent in Dundee. He became assistant national agent in 1924 and succeeded Wake as national agent in 1929. He was ennobled by the Attlee government: the only Party functionary qua functionary to go to the Lords.

[87] For details, see McKibbin, 'Evolution of a National Party,' p. 94.

[88] See particularly the speeches of Smillie and John Robertson (both of the Miners), *Conference Report*, 1913, pp. 77, 79.

[89] *Conference Report*, 1913, p. 78.

[90] *Conference Report*, 1914, pp. 99–100; for the Scottish constitution, pp. 27–8.

the Textile Workers continued to oppose any form of Scottish autonomy, the new plan, now acceptable to the Scottish unions, was approved by conference, and Head Office was instructed to proceed with the inaugural conference.

This was by no means easy. Arrangements were bedevilled by problems of representation and affiliation—and these were largely the making of the Glasgow Labour Party. Persistent rivalry between this body and the Glasgow Trades Council[91] led to disputes about representation at conference, and an agreement was made almost impossible by the wild inaccuracy of the published membership figures of both organizations, and the difficulty of discovering how many of the nine nominal Glasgow L.R.C.s ever actually existed simultaneously. The Glasgow row inflamed similar tensions in Edinburgh and both thereby precluded an inaugural conference before the outbreak of war.[92]

Like those European governments who were supposed to have rushed into war as a way of suppressing insoluble social problems, the national executive used the war as an excuse for postponing the inaugural conference of the S.A.C. indefinitely. However, when it was plain that the war was not coming to a swift conclusion, the executive agreed to allow the conference to take place, but nervously specified that the agenda could 'deal only with organisation matters'.[93] The problem of the Glasgow Labour Party was capriciously solved by allowing it thirteen delegates while not examining too closely the basis of their representation. The conference finally met on 21 August 1915 with MacDonald tactfully chosen to represent the national executive. The most remarkable thing about the conference was that it was held at all; an executive was elected with Robert Smillie as chairman and a secretariat under Ben Shaw established. But the scheduled eve-of-conference organization meeting was a fiasco, because, apart from MacDonald and Shaw, no one turned up. The chairman made no attempt to exclude 'political matters' from the agenda, and the conference was indeed about little else. 'Political matters', in practice, meant the Labour movement's attitude to the war and the coalition government.[94]

In his report to the national executive MacDonald sensibly did not make anything of this.[95] It was wishful thinking to imagine that an assembly of the Scottish Labour movement would talk only about organization after one year of war. In any case, MacDonald was not

---

[91] See above, p. 37.
[92] For details, see McKibbin, 'Evolution of a National Party', pp. 96–7.
[93] 'NEC', 14 Apr. 1915.
[94] See Inaugural Conference of the Scottish Advisory Council, *Report and Proceedings*, *passim*.
[95] MacDonald to Middleton, 25 Aug. 1915, 'LPLF: Uncat. Scotland'.

himself in a position to criticize this. But he did emphasize that 'something much greater should be made of these Conferences. In particular I think that Friday afternoon and evening should be devoted to Conferences of M.P.s, candidates and agents with the Scottish Executive. Scotland needs a lot of stirring up'. The establishment of the S.A.C. illustrated both particular and general problems of regional devolution in the Labour Party. In the particular, Scotland differed perceptibly in degree from most of England in the balance of its working-class organizations: the unions relatively were weaker and the socialist societies relatively more influential. On the other hand, the unions were strong enough to ensure that the socialists could not be predominant. The result was that Party organization in Scotland was both more ineffective than in England, and more politically divided.

Furthermore, the problematical history of the S.A.C. had general lessons. The attempt to improve electoral organization by extending local autonomy while at the same time increasing central over-all direction was everywhere as much likely to fail as to succeed, and in the conditions of Scotland more likely to fail. Finally, it was obvious that a number of the great national unions were opposed in principle to 'federalizing' the Party, and this in turn created conflicts which Head Office found it difficult to settle. Experience of regional devolution after 1918, rather than solving these problems, merely showed how intractable they were.

7. The Labour Party and the Co-operative Union

Long before the foundation of the Co-operative Party at the end of the First World War[96] Labour attempted to form some kind of alliance with the Co-operative Union. There were both tactical and ideological reasons for this. Tactically, it was argued, Labour stood to gain much from the co-operators: electoral support and financial assistance for the Labour Party and for trade unions. Ideologically, it was assumed that the co-operatives represented the third element in working-class organizations, with the Party and the unions as the other two. They were an intrinsic part of working-class life, an institutional alternative to capitalism, and it could be maintained, as Sidney Pollard has done, that even 'those of their active members who voted Liberal and Conservative were committed to the "Co-operative Commonwealth", a concept which was comfortably nebulous yet clearly implied some kind of socialism'.[97] Thus negotiations with the

---

[96] See above, p. 181.
[97] S. Pollard in A. Briggs and J. Saville (eds.), *Essays in Labour History, 1886–1923* (London, 1971), p. 190.

Co-operative Union were undertaken not only for short-term electoral reasons, but also in order to advance that unified and political working-class-consciousness which was always the aim of the Labour leadership. Before 1914 neither of these desiderata was achieved.

There seem to have been friendly relations between a number of L.R.C.s and co-operative associations. MacDonald's own party at Leicester affiliated the local co-operative society, as did Clitheroe,[98] while in Plymouth the L.R.C. and the city co-operators were politically united.[99] In Scotland, where co-operatives were an even more significant part of working-class life than in England, such relations were probably even closer, and the conferences of the S.A.C. were testimony to this.[100] But even there this was not always so. The Co-operative Defence Association had been a disruptive force in the foundation of the Glasgow Labour Party,[101] and proselytizing 'Labour' co-operators were even at one time threatened with expulsion from the Kinning Park society, the city's largest.[102]

Nationally, there was no formal contact, friendly or otherwise, between the Labour Party and the Co-operative Union. The Labour Party, realistically, assumed that nothing could be done unless the Union itself took the initiative, although it was more than ready to respond. 'Political Co-operation with other Forces' was often talked about at co-operative congresses.[103] The action of the united board of the Co-operative Union (its national executive) in publicly supporting the government in both 1910 elections led to discussion at the 1911 congress. In 1912, William Maxwell, chairman of the International Alliance (and himself co-operative candidate for Glasgow Tradeston in 1900), apropos the strikes of the previous year, tentatively proposed negotiations with other sections of the Labour movement.[104] This speech, and others like it at the 1912 congress, was used by the united board as an excuse to open negotiations with the Labour Party. In September therefore, Alfred Whitehead, the secretary of the Union, suggested to Henderson a meeting of the three executives (the Labour Party, the T.U.C., and the Union) 'to consider whether co-operation between the three bodies is possible, and if so, to what extent, and in what manner'.[105] This proposition was understandably the model of

[98] Bealey and Pelling, *Labour and Politics*, p. 257.
[99] See above, p. 34.
[100] See, for example, *Scottish Conference Report*, 1915, p. 23.
[101] See above, pp. 30–31.
[102] P. J. Dollan, *History of the Kinning Park Co-operative Society Limited* (Glasgow, 1923), p. 77.
[103] *Co-operative Congress Report*, 1911, pp. 73, 416–22.
[104] *Co-operative Congress Report*, 1912, p. 454.
[105] Whitehead to Henderson, (?) Sept. 1912, 'LPLF' Uncat.'.

caution. 'It should be understood that if such a conference is arranged it would be of a non-committal character . . .'

The suggestion was received by the Labour Party with surprise and scepticism, but the national executive agreed to attend and named six delegates. Nothing that happened at the conference (8 February 1913) in any way made them more enthusiastic. Tom Fox concluded that 'we might reasonably expect' co-operators to support and work for Labour candidates, but that 'I should be rather backward in suggesting to Co-operators the financial backing of our candidates'.[106] W. C. Robinson could not even hope for that.

I have very little confidence in the men who are leading the Co-operative Movement; I do not consider their sympathies are with the Labour Movement.

The rank and file are in advance of many of their heads and officials. I have little hope of arriving at anything substantial with these joint meetings . . .

I wish it was possible to realise some hope, but personally my experience of these Managers and Committees of Co-operators are of the narrow radical type.[107]

Finally, while W. C. Anderson looked for 'a *closer working relationship* between the three sections of the Labour movement', anything in the 'nature of actual *affiliation*' was out of the question.[108]

A closer working relationship was obviously the most that could be expected. The conference of 8 February resolved merely that 'there should be closer mutual effort—educational and practical',[109] but agreed to reconvene on 30 May : a date all too typically chosen, since it fell eighteen days after the opening of a co-operative congress more than likely to demolish any kind of political alliance.

The congress did exactly this, but over the heads of both its executive bodies. When the central board[110] had its ordinary eve-of-congress meeting, the majority of its members seemed favourable to continuing negotiations.[111] When congress met, the Cambridge and Manchester and Salford societies jointly moved a resolution approving the 'closer union', to which there was an amendment instructing the central board to keep strict neutrality in party politics. There was always much hedging at congress when it came to politics and the mover of the resolution, T. W. Carter, said that he

[106] Fox to Henderson, 12 Feb. 1913, 'LPLF: Uncat.'.
[107] Robinson to Henderson, 10(?) Feb. 1913, 'LPLF: Uncat.'.
[108] Anderson to Henderson, 12 Feb. 1913, 'LPLF: Uncat.'. Italics his.
[109] Memorandum filed as 'NEC', 8 Sept. 1913.
[110] The central board had no Labour equivalent. It was an elected board of seventy-two members responsible for the agenda of congress. Day-to-day functions were delegated to the united board which had fourteen members. See S. and B. Webb, *The Consumers' Co-operative Movement* (London, 1921), p. 139.
[111] *Co-operative Congress Report*, 1913, pp. 21–2.

knew where the crux of the matter lay; it was when they came to introduce into the discussion the Labour Party. He desired to say he held no brief for the Labour Party ... but he recognised the enormous good that party had done in the general upliftment of the people.[112]

The opposition was led on this occasion, as on all others, by Edward Owen Greening. Greening, now in his late seventies, one of the founders of the Union and the International Alliance, had himself, almost unbelievably, been co-operative candidate in Halifax in 1868. Despite his earlier Christian Socialism he was now an old-fashioned radical.[113] He did not, he said, 'want to introduce politics into co-operation but co-operation into politics'. The amendment was carried by 1,346 to 580. 'Narrow radicalism' had a field day.

Despite this vote, the united board rather daringly decided to press ahead. The resumed conference of 30 May produced a draft scheme for joint institutions. It foresaw a United Co-operative and Labour Board with six members from the Union and three each from the T.U.C. and the Party. The first three objects of the board were generalities, but the others were more specific and potentially of value to both movements. They provided for investment, co-operative banking institutions, the distribution of food and benefits to unionists during strikes, and the like.[114] These were exactly the sort of arrangements that were sometimes made after the war, and their inclusion makes it clear that the leaders of both movements were thinking of co-operation on a very wide scale.

But the opponents of any political relationship with the Labour Party regarded this scheme as a deliberate violation of the 1913 congress's decision. Throughout the following June the *Co-operative News* was filled with sustained criticism of the united board, and Greening was encouraged to write a long article attacking the board.[115] The volume of critical comment was such that the united board decided to postpone any action until the 1914 congress.[116] This sensible and almost unavoidable decision rather disgusted the Labour Party, though given their earlier pessimism it is hard to see why.[117]

The draft proposals were then circulated to the full central board, but when the 1914 congress met in Dublin the draft's opponents succeeded in deferring debate for another year on the grounds that the

[112] For the debate, see *Co-operative Congress Report*, 1913, pp. 488–503; also A. Barnes, *The Political Aspect of Co-operation* (Manchester, 1922), pp. 15–17.
[113] Tom Crimes, *Edward Owen Greening* (London, 1924), pp. 83–93.
[114] 'NEC', 8 Oct. 1913.
[115] *Co-operative News*, 14 June 1913.
[116] Whitehead to Henderson, 16 June 1913, 'LPLF: Uncat.'.
[117] See, for example, Middleton to F. S. Button, 30 Oct. 1913, 'LPLF: JSM Uncat.'.

affiliated societies needed more time for consideration: a complaint which was not, on the face of it, unreasonable.

To simplify the process, the united board conducted a referendum on three resolutions. The results are listed below.[118]

Resolution One: That this Conference approves the formation of a Joint Co-operative Labour Board ... For 464; Against 905.

Resolution Two: That this Conference is in favour of a Joint Board as suggested, but to consist only of representatives from the Trade Unions and the Co-operative Movement ... For 477; Against 748.

Resolution Three: That this Conference does not approve of any joint action with any outside organisation ... For 740; Against 668.

In these circumstances the central board could not very well proceed further. The 1915 congress was presented with a resolution from the board itself that no further action be taken, and a Warrington amendment approving the scheme was heavily defeated. Nothing more was done until the end of the war.[119]

It is true that there was by 1914 a substantial minority of co-operators favourable to political relations with the Labour Party. But since the co-operative societies were predominantly working-class organizations anyway this is surely not surprising. It was, however, clear that the large majority of co-operators who cared one way or the other was not ready for joint action with the Labour Party. To write this off, as Professor Pollard does, as merely a setback (if that) to the flowering of co-operative political consciousness,[120] is to underrate the strength of non-Labour feeling in the Union before the war and to overrate the success of co-operative political action after it. Like most of the trade-union leaders, the members of the united board worked hard to convert their followers to Labour politics. But, on the whole, co-operators as *consumers*, or even as co-operators (which might have implied some kind of political belief), were not going to be recruited into the political Labour movement; this was to be almost as true after the war as before. That in turn was a sign that 'active' working-class consciousness in this country was more fragmented and inarticulate than Labour leaders cared to admit.

[118] *Co-operative Congress Report*, 1915, pp. 137–43.
[119] See above, pp. 178–191.
[120] Pollard in Briggs and Saville, p. 195.

III

LABOUR CANDIDATES AND THE LIBERAL PARTY, 1910–1914

1. *The Situation Before 1910*

CHANGES in the Party's structure assumed that it was a growing organization which would attempt to increase its parliamentary representation whenever possible. It was doubtful, however, whether this was possible in practice. For Labour was tied in a variety of ways to the Liberal Party—by the Liberal sympathies of so many of its members, by a broad concurrence on a number of important issues, by electoral agreements, and by the shared emotions of a common ancestry. Furthermore, Labour and Liberals were competing largely for the same territory: only in a few great urban areas, London, Birmingham, and Merseyside, did the Conservatives stand to lose more from Labour competition. Therefore, only when Labour had disentangled itself from Liberalism would its organization be free to develop without constriction.

From the very beginning it was tacitly understood that the Party would win its parliamentary spurs by agreement with the Liberals. Neither MacDonald nor, later, Henderson needed persuasion that this was so. Though the initiator of Shackleton's candidature at Clitheroe in 1902, A. B. Newall, secretary of the Colne Weavers, was ready to fight a three-cornered contest, MacDonald carefully negotiated Shackleton's triumph with the Liberals.[1] Henderson almost gave up his candidature in Barnard Castle (1903) when he found himself opposed by a Liberal as well as a Tory. (Only pressure from the local trade unions pressed him on: 'I see no other course than that of going full steam ahead. The delegates will hear of nothing else.'[2]) Soon after Henderson's election MacDonald and Herbert Gladstone, the Liberal chief whip, put together an agreement designed to give each party free runs in certain constituencies and to avoid difficulties in double-member boroughs.[3]

After the successes of 1906 the leadership of the Party (including Hardie) was convinced that the agreement had been necessary for

---

[1] Bealey and Pelling, pp. 98–124; but they underestimate Newall's part in the by-election. See his letters to MacDonald, 24 Nov. 1901, 30 Nov. 1901, 'LPLF: Uncat. Misc.'.

[2] Henderson to MacDonald, 25 May 1903, 'LPLF: LRC 9/181'.

[3] For details of the agreement see Bealey and Pelling, pp. 143–59, 298–9.

Labour's parliamentary advance. But its effectiveness was always uncertain. On the one hand, it had not excluded all three-cornered contests; on the other, it was likely to affront those who regarded the Party's function as the establishment of *independent* working-class representation. The leadership therefore usually denied that any agreement existed,[4] and decided its electoral tactics as circumstances dictated. Consequently by-elections often forced crises in the Party and these crises seemed to get worse and more frequent as time passed.

The conflicts that were perhaps inherent in these tactics were strikingly revealed by the Colne Valley by-election (July 1907) and Victor Grayson's victory there.[5] Colne Valley was not the only three-cornered contest fought in the life of the 1906 parliament, but Grayson's candidature, and the refusal of the national executive to endorse it, caused disagreements in the Labour movement unique to by-elections in that parliament. Furthermore, though MacDonald was more sympathetic to Grayson than many others on the executive, he was alarmed at what he took to be the implications of Grayson's election, and this alarm informed his attitude to three-cornered contests until the outbreak of war.

MacDonald did his best to find some way to endorse Grayson, but his candidature was unconstitutional and there was no getting over that. He put the position to Grayson as tactfully as he could. The I.L.P.

are working in alliance with the Labour Party. That alliance occasionally hampers us, but in the vast majority of instances it helps us ... I have a feeling that neither you nor your promoters in Colne Valley have ever fairly met us in the difficult situation we are placed ... I have been unofficially sounding my Trade Union colleagues of the National Labour Party with a view to ascertaining how far they are prepared to meet us but I have not received much encouragement.[6]

So far as he could, MacDonald sorted things out for Grayson: Labour M.P.s were not barred from speaking for him, and several did. At the same time he sniffed demagoguery in the air and that worried him.

I have never been in such an unpleasant fix in all my life as in this Colne Valley business ... If the branches of our Party decline to carry out the resolutions passed at our Conferences we ought to know from them beforehand ... such action ... is most unfair to Members who consider themselves

---

[4] Thus MacDonald wrote that the 'statement that there was any agreement between the Liberals [and Labour] at the last General Election is absolutely untrue'. (MacDonald to Secretary Clapham I.L.P., 26 May 1908, 'LPLF: Uncat. Misc.'.)

[5] For an account of the by-election, see H. M. Pelling, *Popular Politics and Society in Late Victorian Britain* (London, 1968), pp. 136–43.

[6] MacDonald to Grayson, 27 June 1907, 'Private and Confidential', 'LPLF: LP/CAN/-06/2/42'.

bound by these resolutions and whose responsibilities do not allow them to play ducks and drakes with honourable understandings.[7]

MacDonald was immediately suspicious of Grayson's dash and self-drama, the more so, perhaps, as these were qualities he, himself, brought to Labour politics. His marginalia on one of Grayson's letters show how his mind was turning, even if they are lost in the impertinence of the letter itself. 'I must', Grayson announced,

confess myself extremely dissatisfied . . .
    What more could we have done than has been done? My name was, *in proper form*, submitted to the [I.L.P.] as the locally selected candidate. [J.R.M. Not on list. Question unsettled and we had to delay.]
    We had no intention of 'forcing the hands' of the N.A.C. [National Administrative Council of the I.L.P.] being quite assured that they were prepared to clear a way. I understand that the *correct procedure* is for the N.A.C. to submit that candidate to the Labour Party for its adoption. [J.R.M. Not so unless and until properly promoted — wires are cheap — might have been sent.] . . .
    Candidly, my dear MacDonald, if anyone has adequate ground for complaint, I think it is the present writer.
    As things stand, therefore, I gather that in the event of my success at the polls, I shall be a free-lance socialist member, independent of the Labour Group. So be it. By devious ways we shall arrive. [J.R.M. Regrettable revelation of what you have in mind.][8]

Grayson did indeed become a 'free-lance socialist member'. His parliamentary demonstrations on behalf of the unemployed, crowned by his expulsion from the House in October 1908, excited sections of the Labour movement, and were contrasted with the apparent passivity of the parliamentary party. MacDonald was angered by what he considered ingratitude—particularly in the light of his own 'right to work'[9] bill—and amazed at the credulity of those who were inspirited by Grayson's 'stunts'. To one critical correspondent, whose party had resolved itself in favour of Grayson's 'noble and determined stand', MacDonald replied that the 'resolution is sheer rubbish from beginning to end'.[10] MacDonald's outbursts became so unrestrained that Middleton induced him to write a reasoned reply to James Phipps, secretary of the Ormskirk branch of the Railway Servants and one of his romantic admirers—'Poor Scotch Friendless Lad when alone in London deprived himself of such necessities as tea and sugar and drank hot

[7] MacDonald to Edgar Whiteley, 10 July 1907, 'LPLF: LP/CAN/06/2/63'.
[8] Grayson to MacDonald, 3 July 1907, LPLF: LP/CAN/06/2/53'.
[9] For this, see Clegg, Fox, and Thompson, p. 397.
[10] MacDonald to Secretary, North Islington I.L.P., 20 Oct. 1908, 'LPLF: LP/CAN/-06/2/79'.

water to enable him to pay for his education' he once apostrophized MacDonald—a reply composed with a view to publication in the *Labour Leader*, though not, apparently, published by it.[11]

The whole affair had profoundly depressed MacDonald: partly because the movement's attitude to a cocksparrow like Grayson seemed saddeningly immature, and partly because the bulging correspondence file was an intimation that the 'tub-thumpers',[12] and worse, the syndicalists, had the ear of the movement—that the crude abuse of Tillett's *Is the Parliamentary Labour Party a Failure?* (1908) was more effective than he had imagined.

The matter of three-cornered contests led to scenes at both I.L.P. and Labour Party Conferences in 1909; at both the policy of the leadership was approved, but only grudgingly.[13] MacDonald, who had detected 'a spirit of reckless irresponsibility' which was 'heading the whole Movement straight upon the rocks', was confident that the conferences would 'ultimately settle things'.[14] But there was no obvious solution to the conflict between the development of Labour as an independent political party and a recognition that in practice the contemporary causes of the Liberal Party were also its causes. In 1914 this antagonism between working-class-consciousness and the needs of parliamentary politics still remained unresolved.

2. *The 1910 Elections*

The elections of 1910 came in the midst of these difficulties. Circumstances were unfavourable to Labour which appeared more as an adjunct to the Liberal Party than its competitor. How was the 'second advance' to be achieved? All Labour leaders were agreed that the Party should increase its representation, but less sure how to do this. Having intended to put up about 110 candidates, the Party went to the country with seventy-eight.[15] The smaller number was due to the suddenness of the election and to the fear that the larger number would harm the Party's chances. In any case the national executive no more wanted to see the government defeated than did the government itself.

As the campaign progressed it was plain that the Party was aware that three-cornered contests might appear merely 'wrecking'. At the same time its leaders were having trouble in showing how they differed from the government. On 14 December Henderson endeavoured to explain Party policy:

[11] MacDonald to Phipps, 6 Nov. 1908, 'LPLF: LP/CAN/06/2/122'.
[12] MacDonald to Sam Hague, 20 Oct. 1908, 'LPLF: LP/CAN/06/2/93'.
[13] Clegg, Fox, and Thompson, pp. 411–12.
[14] MacDonald to W. Brown, 1 May 1908, 'LPLF: LP/MAC/09/1/2'.
[15] See above, p. 12.

In some cases where the Labour Party had decided that there was no prospect of winning a constituency, they had honourably withdrawn from the fight. In the other cases where they had found it necessary to proceed with the candidature, they had only done so feeling assured that they could win. He was strongly desirous of seeing as few three-cornered contests as possible on this occasion. (A voice: there should be none.) That was exactly what they were trying to get at, but it was difficult. Having regard to what he said, if the Liberal Party did likewise, there would not be many three-cornered contests.[16]

This suggests that three-cornered contests occurred more in sorrow than in anger. More than this, Henderson was conceding that the issues of the election were those decided by the Liberal Party and that Labour had to adjust itself to them as best it could.

Privately, MacDonald agreed. In April 1910 he told the national executive that the initiative, in effect, lay with the Liberals. Only if they came 'out in disgrace' might Labour 'do slightly better in three-cornered fights than last January'. But if the government 'worked up the same enthusiasm as it did at the last election by convincing the democratic electorate that it means business . . . we will probably do worse . . . because our weakness was then revealed and the relative position of the parties is now perfectly well known'.[17]

In any case, the Liberals made it clear that they would permit no expansion. The Liberal chief whip, J. A. Pease, said so not too delicately in a letter to his Party's candidate at Bishop Auckland, Sir H. H. Allan, who was threatened with an opponent from the Durham Miners.[18] Pease agreed that it was 'the right principle' that Liberals should 'respect the seats which at the last General Election returned Labour Representation candidates and that the L.R.C. organisation should respect other progressive candidates standing for seats held by other Labour representatives or Liberals in 1906'. He produced one *douceur*—the possibility of electoral reform within the life of the new parliament. If the 'L.R.C. party' remained content with their present numerical strength 'they would surely not be prejudiced in the long run'. But 'if an aggressive attitude was persisted in by the Labour Party, Labour could not expect official Liberalism to stand on one side and remain unnominated'. He concluded by reminding Labour of three propositions.

1. That if they now press L.R.C. candidates for seats which were won by Liberals, or Labour members who have not signed the constitution [Lib–Labs] they must expect retaliatory attacks on their own candidates standing

---

[16] *The Times*, 15 Dec. 1909.
[17] 'NEC', 13 Apr. 1910.
[18] Allan was opposed by William House at both elections. He was also Pease's brother-in-law.

for those seats which they now hold. In my opinion ... the Labour Party are more likely to be losers if an uncompromising attitude is adopted ...

2. Liberal legislation has not been in the past, nor in the future is it likely to be, much influenced by members who claim no loyalty to the Government ...

4. That the issues of the next General Election are such that all Liberal, Radical, and Labour members can whole-heartedly unite in supporting.[19]

Despite some local skirmishing Pease was not obliged to carry out his threats and the Labour leaders no doubt took the point of propositions two and four. Thus in both elections the Party more or less maintained its strength at the expense of electoral independence and any increase in parliamentary representation. (At the dissolution of parliament in 1909 Labour held forty-five seats, after the December election forty-two.) Seventy-eight candidates in January, and the even more exiguous fifty-six in December, represented the minimum the national executive could endorse and still satisfy the Party activists and the maximum that would not provoke Liberal retaliation.

Since Labour considered itself more than a working-class adjunct to Liberalism, in the long run this policy had no future. Moreover, it was likely that not all Liberals were happy with a policy that left Labour with seats that could well be won by them. Both parties were bound to some extent by the residual spirit of the MacDonald–Gladstone agreement, and this seemed to imply a code regarding seats held by each. But adherence to this code was not enthusiastic on either side. It is arguable that Liberal headquarters was happy enough with such 'arrangements' as had been reached, but after 1910 many local associations could not accept their permanence. Even the attachment of Liberal headquarters to the pact could be exaggerated: Pease's diaries are dotted with examples of its contingency. 'I told [Asquith] the position of the Labour Party, how broken up they were in faction ... I asked Asquith to take all opportunities to notice [the Lib–Labs] rather than the L.R.C.'[20] More surprising still, 'After Cabinet—told Asquith I proposed to fight Ramsay MacDonald at Leicester, he approved, i.e. Maddison [MacDonald's Lib–Lab colleague] and Sir Edward Wood. I wrote Wood accordingly'.[21] Quite why Wood was put up and then in 1910 abandoned is not clear, but obviously Pease and Asquith did not regard themselves as inhibited by obligation. Indeed, they appear to have been less moved by the needs of progressive unity than was MacDonald himself.

On the Labour side adherence to the pact was always prudential.

[19] *The Times*, 17 Nov. 1909.
[20] 'J. A. Pease Diaries', 1 June 1908. I am grateful to Dr. Cameron Hazlehurst of the Australian National University for allowing me to see these in typescript.
[21] Ibid., 1 July 1908.

MacDonald may have seen in it the basis of a more extensive and durable agreement, but most other members of the Party saw it as a temporary affair, designed to carry Labour over its immediate difficulties. Between 1910 and 1914 the actions of both sides put up many obstacles to any formal renewal of the old agreement. Since the issues that separated them were less those of policy than of class, compromise was made even more difficult.

3. The Liberal and Labour Parties in the Coal-fields

Between 1910 and 1914 the most serious disputes took place in constituencies whose Members were nominated by the Miners' Federation. While these were held by an older generation of miners, whose politics remained Lib–Lab even after they formally joined the Labour Party in 1909, the Liberals were content to leave them unchallenged. However, when it was clear that their successors would be not just nominally bound by the Labour Party constitution local Liberal associations immediately intervened with purely Liberal candidates. These encounters were largely confined to the prosperous Midlands coal-fields—Derbyshire, North Staffordshire, Nottinghamshire, and Warwickshire—where diminishing profitability had not yet divided miners from their masters. Here the social and economic conditions which produced coal-field Liberalism survived longest.[22] Yet though these fields were, in Gregory's words, 'the laggards', they were subject to the same changes as the others. It was these changes that made the Hanley, Chesterfield, and N.-E. Derbyshire by-elections crises in 'progressive' politics.

The Hanley division of Staffordshire was deeply impregnated with Liberalism, though its M.P., Enoch Edwards, was by no means as committed to the Liberal Party as some of his colleagues. As president of the Miners' Federation he had handled relations between the Federation and the Labour Party with tact and goodwill. But Edwards had done nothing to assist the development of Labour organization in the constituency, believing to the end that the local Liberal association would show the same benevolence to his successor as it did to him. When Edwards died in June 1912 it should not have surprised anyone when the Liberals claimed the seat. Yet Labour was shocked and indignant.

In a way both sides were right. Edwards had been a Labour M.P. and on these grounds Hanley was a Labour seat. On the other hand,

---

[22] In the other main coal-fields the break with Liberalism was earlier and more painless. It would be tedious and repetitious to summarize here Gregory's exhaustive work on these regions. See 'Miners and Politics', *passim*; in more brief compass, his book, *Miners and British Politics*, pp. 68–119.

Edwards was a Liberal in most of his beliefs and was indubitably elected by Liberal organization. It was not always certain that the Liberals would put up a candidate. Their headquarters was reluctant, and the *Daily News* wished that the Liberal Party 'had waived its claim to Hanley'.[23] But London's hesitation was swept aside by the local association. After a barnstorming tour of the constituency by J. C. Wedgwood and E. G. Hemmerde, the association chose another single-taxer, R. L. Outhwaite. Outhwaite was a good radical and on the point of being endorsed by the local Labour party when the national executive intervened and requested it to find a candidate of its own.[24] On 2 July, after making certain that any Labour candidate would have to sign the constitution, the Liberals formally endorsed Outhwaite, while the local Labour bodies, after some hesitation, nominated Sam Finney, president of the North Staffs. Miners, and not, as it turned out, a good candidate.[25] Liberal headquarters thereupon rallied loyally to their Party, and the contest was opened by a telegram from Elibank, the chief whip: 'The fight must go on.'[26]

At this stage the situation was complicated by the death of the Liberal Member for Crewe. On 2 July the national executive resolved to contest Crewe as well, though at any other time it was not a seat that Labour would have fought. In January 1910 Frank Rose had polled only 1,380 votes and there appears to have been little organization.[27] Nevertheless, on 14 July James Holmes of the Railway Servants was adopted as Labour candidate. The decision to fight Crewe was obviously a reprisal. As MacDonald put it, 'Hanley is a Labour seat and the Liberals are the aggressors. If they will not allow us to retain our present numbers in Parliament, we must take steps accordingly'.[28] If Hanley were allowed to revert to the Liberals, Labour faced the prospect of losing other seats held by nominally Labour miners' M.P.s. Crewe, it was hoped, would be an added lesson. While for MacDonald and Henderson Crewe was useful only for the limited purposes of revenge, others hoped it meant a new departure— like Snowden, who thought 'it would be war to the knife',[29] the enthusiasts in local organizations, and the professional critics of the parliamentary party: the British Socialist Party, the *Daily Herald*,[30] and the left wing of the I.L.P.

---

[23] *Daily News*, 4 July 1912.
[24] 'NEC', 2 July 1912.
[25] Finney was, however, elected for Burslem in 1918.
[26] *Daily News*, 4 July 1912.
[27] Henderson to Middleton, 17 July 1912, 'LPLF: Uncat. Misc.'.
[28] *Daily Herald*, 4 July 1912.
[29] *Daily Herald*, 3 July 1912.
[30] See, for example, *Daily Herald*, 3 July 1912.

The by-elections were fought with extraordinary virulence.[31] Opponents of the government took new heart; *The Times* noted hopefully that 'it may be in the growing intractability of the Labour Party we are witnessing the beginning of the end of the coalition'.[32] Hanley, however, revealed, as MacDonald feared it would, Labour's weakness in the Midlands. Outhwaite won by 654 and Finney was at the bottom of the poll. In Crewe, though Holmes increased the Labour vote to 2,485, he also finished last. But Labour's intervention was sufficient to let the Conservative in—which was the point.

At the height of battle Hanley did seem a turning-point in Labour–Liberal relations. Finney was supported even by W. E. Harvey and Albert Stanley, a case of union loyalty vanquishing political principles there, for it was surely the first time they had ever opposed a Liberal candidate.[33] The *Labour Leader* claimed that 'the Hanley by-election of 1912 will be noted as a turning point in its fortunes . . . The election does not only mean the death-blow of Liberal–Labourism in Hanley. It means the death-blow of Liberal–Labourism as a national force'.[34] Hanley was not that, but it was of importance none the less.

Hitherto Labour leaders had tended to think that the Liberals would be defensive in face of Labour expansion. They were disconcerted that the Liberals should actually claim seats held by Labour—and do their best to win them. MacDonald in particular was offended and behaved as if his reputation depended on Liberals not acting this way, as to some degree it did. 'For myself,' he wrote, 'I hope we shall lose . . . every seat which we hold under Hanley conditions . . . The Liberals do not love us . . .'[35] But the aim of Hanley and Crewe was to ensure precisely that every seat that Labour held 'under Hanley conditions' was not lost. MacDonald could not have liked what appeared to be close at hand : a political free-for-all which could ruin the Labour Party and return the Conservatives. What was a surprise was the eagerness of the local Liberals to take the seat and the unwillingness or inability of Liberal headquarters to stop them. That they did not necessarily share his view of the electoral understanding shocked MacDonald. Hence his anger.

More humiliating to the Party was the extraordinary Kenyon affair. It is not necessary to recount the full story here,[36] but the Chesterfield by-election of August 1913 was of significance in Labour's relations with the miners' organizations, and indirectly with the Liberal Party itself.

[31] See, for example, *The Times*, 17 July 1912.
[32] *The Times*, 26 July 1912.
[33] *Labour Leader*, 11 July 1912.
[34] *Labour Leader*, 11 July 1912.
[35] *Labour Leader*, 18 July 1912.
[36] See Gregory, pp. 302–34.

In May 1913 Barnet Kenyon, an 'amiable, soft-hearted, easy going'[37] miners' agent with the same impeccable Lib–Lab background as the sitting Member, James Haslam, was nominated by the Derbyshire Miners as prospective candidate for Chesterfield. The nomination was endorsed by the local Labour party. In August 1913 Haslam died and Kenyon came forward as the only Labour candidate. For Head Office and the Miners' Federation Kenyon raised all the old problems: he was a quite unreconstructed Lib–Lab who had begun his campaign in what was, even for Derbyshire, sensational style. To endorse him would make a joke of Labour independence, not to do so was to lose yet another seat to the Liberals. The Labour Party refused to endorse him as did the Miners' Federation. Kenyon was elected as a 'Labour and Progressive' candidate, but was, nevertheless, given the Labour whip at the beginning of 1914 on the grounds that he had unreservedly accepted the constitution. Two weeks after this surprising decision—surprising both of Kenyon and the Labour Party —he resigned from the parliamentary party, deciding, apparently, that it had no future.

In this frequently comic story four things need to be noted: the attitudes of MacDonald and Henderson; Kenyon's acceptance and then resignation of the whip; the action of the Miners' Federation; and, finally, the effect of the affair on the Derbyshire Miners.

MacDonald's behaviour was exactly in character. He had waged the most vigorous campaign at Hanley and had always worked towards the establishment of independent Labour organizations in the mining seats.[38] Among Labour leaders he was most opposed to the endorsement of Kenyon. He told him that

the reports in the newspapers of your speeches and the knowledge I have of what has been done at this end, make it impossible for me to do anything but acquiesce in the resolution which the Executive passed not only unanimously but emphatically — that it could not endorse your candidature . . . if you want to be a Liberal candidate . . . say so quite honestly. If you are to run as a Labour candidate you must accept certain responsibilities. To try to do both is wrong morally and if acquiesced in would make the continued existence of the Party impossible . . . Unless the papers are lying very much more than usual you have not carried out your pledges, and have not observed the conditions you gave Henderson to understand you would observe.[39]

As MacDonald implies, Henderson originally favoured endorsement. What 'conditions' he wrung out of Kenyon are not known, though one can make a good guess at the spirit in which they were

[37] *Yorkshire Post*, 7 May 1914.
[38] See above, p. 13.
[39] MacDonald to Kenyon, 12 Aug. 1913, Gregory, p. 312.

accepted. When the question came before the national executive Henderson was on tour but remained opposed to refusing endorsement. He did not consider 'that such a course is warranted by the circumstances of the case. It is calculated to harm Kenyon's chances, risk the loss of a seat to the Party, and probably be very much misunderstood by many of our Trade Union supporters throughout the country.'[40] Henderson was clearly, if understandably, suppressing his critical functions. As secretary he had a bureaucratic concern with keeping the Party as numerically large as possible. He probably allowed these considerations to override doubts he certainly must have had about Kenyon's campaign; nor does he appear to have expected the executive to act other than as it did—'though I am disappointed I cannot say that it gives me any surprise', he told Middleton.[41]

The reasons for Kenyon's acceptance of the whip are a story in themselves, but it seems as if the financial needs of the Derbyshire Miners made Kenyon and the secretary, Frank Hall, more amenable to Party discipline.[42] Whereas on 14 January 1914 Kenyon announced that he would abide by the constitution only 'as understood and practised by the late Mr. J. Haslam and others',[43] on 9 February he and Hall went to London and agreed to accept its terms without reservation. The decision to give the whip to Kenyon was controversial—Smillie telegraphed his disapproval—and, given the likelihood of rows within the Party, a dubious one. Much embarrassment was avoided by Kenyon's sudden resignation from the parliamentary party on 18 February. He had decided that Labour meant socialist—and that he was not. Talks with some of the older Lib–Labs, like Fenwick, convinced him that his place was, where it always should have been, in the Liberal Party.

Though to contemporaries the Chesterfield by-election was a setback to Labour it was yet another blow to Lib–Labism. It was unlikely that the Party would again try to accommodate itself to a candidate who had already accommodated himself to the Liberal Party. Moreover, it was unlikely that another Kenyon would bother to seek the Labour whip. Apart from Johnson and Hancock (who were bequeathed to the Party when the Miners' Federation affiliated

---

[40] Henderson to Middleton, 9 Aug. 1913, 'LPLF: LP/MF/11/356'.

[41] Henderson to Middleton, 12 Aug. 1913, 'LPLF: LP/MF/11/359'.

[42] When endorsement was refused financial assistance automatically lapsed. Kenyon, therefore, had to find funds elsewhere. They were provided by Sir Arthur Markham, the meddlesome M.P. for Mansfield who lent him £1,700 (Gregory, p. 312). With the refusal of the Miners' Federation to provide the money, Hall certainly hoped that Kenyon's signing the constitution would land the Party with his debts. It says something for Kenyon's honesty, one supposes, that he was prepared to forfeit this happy solution.

[43] 'NEC', 24 Jan. 1914.

and were a different case) this was Labour's last dealing with the Lib–Lab M.P.s.

The affair was also important for the two responsible trade unions, the Miners' Federation and the Derbyshire Miners. Of everyone involved the Federation came out best. It had withdrawn endorsement of Kenyon early in the campaign and thereafter ignored (though with some division) the threats of the Derbyshire Miners to leave the Federation's political fund. The Chesterfield by-election seemed to confirm what had hitherto been an evolving process : that the majority of the Federation's executive were now partisans of independent Labour representation.[44] While this had, no doubt, much to do with the coal dispute in the first half of 1912 and then the Hanley by-election, it was also a reflection of those changes in the unions by which supporters of the Labour Party were gaining control of the county associations and thus of the Federation itself.

Finally, if Kenyon's sudden entry into the parliamentary party was a surprise, so was the sudden capitulation of the Derbyshire Miners. MacDonald's action, Gregory writes, was 'triumphantly justified';[45] but was it? Kenyon, after all, was admitted to the parliamentary party. The triumph was accidental rather than planned. With Kenyon's help the national executive had won a war of attrition. When he resigned the whip the Derbyshire Miners suddenly abandoned resistance. They could not hold out indefinitely against the Federation as well as the Party, and financial dependence on coal-owners like the Markhams was scarcely alluring. The Association had been more deeply divided over Kenyon than its bold front showed and Hall had been irritated by Kenyon's unpredictable behaviour in parliament. The correctness of MacDonald's action lay in the original refusal to endorse Kenyon; that influenced the Federation to do the same thing. Thus, in the end, the Derbyshire Miners promised that there would be no repetition of the affair.

Nor was there. Within a few months of the Chesterfield by-election N.-E. Derbyshire fell vacant. Potentially, this was another Hanley or Chesterfield, but the change in the attitude of the county union ensured that it was not in fact. N.-E. Derbyshire was like Hanley : it had a Lib–Lab M.P., W. E. Harvey, and was distinguished by its utter lack of Labour organization. As early as January 1911 MacDonald had told Harvey that neglect of Labour organization

---

[44] Gregory has calculated that of the twenty members of the Federation Executive, thirteen were Labour and the rest Lib–Lab or Conservative. The doubtful inclusion of Albert Stanley in the thirteen does not alter the fact that the political complexion of the Federation had turned decisively in Labour's favour. (Gregory, pp. 591–2.)

[45] Gregory, p. 316.

perpetuates the Liberal hold which is so strong in the constituency, and it means that if you were to die ... there would not be sufficient strength to keep the seat for us; the Liberal Association would simply step in and fill your shoes by a Liberal candidate whom it would be impossible to fight successfully.[46]

The position had improved slightly since Chesterfield, but N.-E. Derbyshire was still one of those problems to be faced as the Lib–Lab M.P.s retired or died.

When Harvey died, the decencies of mourning scarcely seem to have been observed by anyone. The day after his death (28 April 1914) Frank Hall told MacDonald of his determination that 'this election shall be fought on Labour lines'.[47] Understandably MacDonald was not convinced of Hall's good faith. He reminded him that the Kenyon affair was a 'most deplorable fiasco' and urged him to make up his mind 'quite definitely'. If he could not loyally support a Labour candidate it would be better not 'to stretch our Constitution and methods both of which have been definitely imposed on us by Conference after Conference'.[48]

Though this was a timely warning, there is no evidence to suggest that the Derbyshire Miners were not genuine in their conversion to Labour politics. Henderson had hurried up for Harvey's funeral and there had a mafia-like conclave with Hall during the obsequies; Hall assured him that they intended to go ahead. The Association met on 4 May—'almost before the breath was out of Mr. Harvey's body'[49] —and agreed that any candidate must sign the constitution.[50] With equal speed the local Liberal caucus had met and decided that, though Harvey's successor might be a miner, in effect, he must not sign the constitution with any serious intention of keeping it. If he did, he would face Liberal opposition.[51]

On 5 May, after being closeted with Henderson and Clynes, the miners decided to nominate James Martin, president of the county association. It was a characteristic choice, for Martin had been president of the Staveley Liberal association and was now vice-president of the N.-E. Derbyshire Liberal association. He had 'worked for the Liberal Party, spoken for it and prayed for it'.[52] Martin's name was placed before the Liberal caucus the following day. There were no personal objections to him, but the Liberals could not accept

[46] Ibid., p. 587.
[47] Hall to MacDonald, 29 Apr. 1914, 'LPLF: LP/PA/14/1/58'.
[48] MacDonald to Hall, 30 Apr. 1914, 'LPLF: LP/PA/14/1/59'.
[49] Derbyshire Courier, 9 May 1914.
[50] Yorkshire Post, 5 May 1914.
[51] Derbyshire Courier, 9 May 1914.
[52] Derby Daily Express, 8 May 1914.

a candidate 'bound by the ticket of the Labour Party, who refuses the co-operation and support of the Liberal Party'. They, therefore, nominated J. P. Houfton, managing director of the Staveley Colliery and the perfect choice of a radical, predominantly middle-class Liberal caucus. Houfton claimed that the Liberals 'had done all they could . . . It was not only the question of giving way now . . . but for evermore . . . For members of a great political party that was impossible.' Why, he asked, 'couldn't they send us another Kenyon? We should have accepted him.'[53] They would indeed.

Both nominations were controversial. The local Liberal press immediately worked up a campaign against the endorsement of Martin by the miners' lodges. The *Derbyshire Courier* claimed, probably correctly, that

we have good ground for saying that in a good number of cases, the attendance when the lodge vote was taken was very small, and consisted of little more than a few officials and those extremists who never miss an opportunity of voting towards the capture of their organization by the socialists.[54]

On the other hand, Houfton was not received with much enthusiasm in London. The *Daily Chronicle* felt 'bound to say that Labour had a rightful claim to the seat'.[55] The Liberal campaign was noticeable for the absence of official support, and was fought, as was Hanley, by those who felt themselves most endangered by Labour's assertions of independence: the confident radicals, Markham, Outhwaite, Wedgwood, and Hemmerde.

Martin's truly astonishing campaign tended to be obscured by the general recriminations. 'In all essential things', he announced, 'I am a Liberal, but as the Derbyshire Miners' Association is connected with the M.F.G.B., I, as president of the county association, can take no other stand than to support the Labour principles of the Miners' Federation.'[56] And so he fought his fight. In its way this was, of course, a very significant remark, but more interest was attached to MacDonald's speech at Staveley on 10 May. He noted that the Liberals had 'decided to force' a three-cornered fight. 'They did it at Hanley and won. It is the most expensive victory Liberalism has had within this generation. They have lost five or six seats as a result of their actions[57]. . . What impertinence! . . . We have the seat. The Labour Party', he went on, 'is going to grow. It is not going to accept

[53] *The Times*, 5 May 1914.
[54] *Derbyshire Courier*, 9 May 1914.
[55] *Daily Chronicle*, 7 May 1914.
[56] J. E. Williams, *The Derbyshire Miners* (London, 1962), pp. 511–12.
[57] They had, in fact, lost four.

its present strength as its final strength. It is going to contest constituencies where it has got a hold, and the convenience of no party will deter us . . .' Labour, he said, was prepared to support any necessary alteration in the electoral system which, he was afraid, was being used by the government to prevent 'you voting as you want'. He then turned the tables on the Liberals, using their favourite argument— that in a time of crisis (over Home Rule in this case) the 'progressive vote' ought not to be split. When 'so much depends on unity, your local Liberal leaders have thrown down the gauntlet with such insulting emphasis that we are bound to take it up not only here, but elsewhere'.[58]

This is an ambiguous address. Contemporaries were struck by its militancy, but MacDonald was careful not to commit himself to anything too daring, and its final call for unity considerably softens the earlier tones. But whatever his intentions, the speech further embittered Labour–Liberal relations in Derbyshire, and was an appropriate contribution to a remarkable campaign. There was never much doubt that Martin would finish last; but with no organization and no real Labour tradition behind him he gained a surprisingly good 3,669 votes to Houfton's 6,155. 'Labour Candidate's Large Poll' was *The Times* headline,[59] and Martin's intervention let the Conservative in. Together with the Kenyon affair the by-election had effectively crippled Lib–Labism in Derbyshire. Its complete disintegration was a matter of time. Martin, piqued by his defeat, said that he would stand again—'he had fought the workers' battle but they had not stood by him. The disgrace was not his; it belonged to them'. More important, Hall announced plans for the establishment of independent Labour organizations throughout the county and said that his association would contest as many seats as it could at the next general election.[60]

4. The Leicester and Keighley By-elections, 1913

In Hanley, Chesterfield, and N.-E. Derbyshire the national executive was working for the expansion of the Party. But there was also another side to Labour politics. Outside the mining constituencies, there were many in the rank and file who wanted to move the Party faster than Head Office was ready to go. Thus, while the leadership was encouraging Labour candidatures in mining seats, even at the risk of three-cornered contests, it was trying to avoid them elsewhere. If to MacDonald and Henderson this was an intelligible policy, it was often difficult to explain to the Party as a whole.

'It is just possible that before you return [from India],' Henderson told MacDonald in April 1913, 'Leicester will have elected a new colleague for you.' Crawshay Williams had been cited as a co-respondent; it was 'an unfortunate and nauseous business and a good deal of gossip has taken place in the Lobbies . . .'.[61] Neither of them foresaw that the Carr Gomme–Crawshay Williams divorce suit, one of the society scandals of the year, would cause the most serious dispute within the Labour Party before 1914, and one from which MacDonald's pre-war reputation never really recovered.

On the whole, the Labour and Liberal Parties had been able to sort out between them the double-member constituencies, of which Leicester was one. In December 1910 eleven Labour M.P.s had been elected in tandem with Liberals and both sides had benefited from this arrangement; equally, both stood to lose heavily by competition. No one was more aware of this than MacDonald and it was unlucky that a vacancy should have occurred in his own constituency. From the beginning it was clear that Labour would have difficulty in avoiding a candidature in the by-election and that anyway the consequences would be disagreeable.

Leicester was well known for its militancy and the agitation for a second candidate had been under way long before 1913. In January 1910 there had been some dissatisfaction at Labour–Liberal co-operation, and the local Trades Council, 'usually the most moderate of bodies', passed a resolution deploring it.[62] In December 1910 there were plumpings on both sides.[63] It was not, therefore, surprising that the local Party should have made moves towards a candidature when Crawshay Williams formally resigned his seat.

Together with the local I.L.P. it decided to sound MacDonald first, though only as a matter of form. MacDonald, understandably, was cautious, though what he wanted was clear enough :

I would really prefer [he wrote] to leave it to yourselves. My own personal view is that it would be a mistake to fight. Under the circumstances of the election our vote would drop, and although we could explain that quite satisfactorily locally, it would be impossible to make that clear to the country. The result would be that the party here and in the country would suffer, and no compensating benefit would come of it.[64]

MacDonald's warnings were ignored. On 15 June the local I.L.P.

[61] Henderson to MacDonald, 4 Apr. 1913, 'LPLF: LP/HEN/08/1/78'.
[62] Cox, p. 63.
[63] Ibid., p. 64.
[64] *Labour Leader*, 26 June 1913. To the great embarrassment of Head Office the Leicester Labour Party released from their minute books a summary of all meetings held between 12 June and 19 June. Unless otherwise stated this account is based upon the Leicester Party's précis published in the *Labour Leader*.

resolved to fight, provided that the 'National Party' financed them, and decided to nominate George Banton. The following day the Leicester Labour Party voted by 67 to 8 to support Banton, and to send a deputation to the national executive. At the same time MacDonald's agent, A. H. Reynolds, wrote agitatedly to him: '*You* are the *only* man who can stop it I think.'[65]

The deputation met the national executive on the 17th and, after a long and heated discussion, the latter resolved that it 'was not advisable to fight', but was ready to listen to the advice of the N.A.C. The N.A.C., however, was irresolute. On 16 June it refused to endorse Banton, but the next day, following pressure from the local I.L.P. and a favourable report from the treasurer of the I.L.P., T. D. Benson, it reversed itself. But its reversal carried with it the proviso that the greater part of the expenses should be borne by the national executive. Thereupon the Leicester Labour Party decided by 63 to 9 to go ahead.

On 18 June Henderson, Roberts and Benson went to Leicester to defend the policies of their respective executives. What happened at this extraordinary meeting can be pieced together from the two records of it that survive. The meeting was lively by both accounts.

Mr. Benson [Henderson said] stated the position for the N.A.C. who had decided not to contest the vacancy, largely owing to the financial position of the Party. Mr. Benson was then subjected to a long and determined heckling in which much feeling was displayed . . .

I was then called upon to put before the meeting the position of the N.E.C. . . . I was then subjected to many angry interruptions when giving the reasons against a contest from the National Standpoint.

Delegates were then given the opportunity of stating their views in speeches limited to ten minutes, and there were so many speeches that it was just upon eleven when a resolution was unanimously carried expressing a strong desire to fight, and urging upon the N.A.C. and the N.E.C. the advisability of their giving full assistance.

Henderson concluded that

many of those present appeared to be willing to fight irrespective of the attitude of the N.A.C. or the National Executive, or even the effect upon Mr. MacDonald's position . . . In the absence of a Labour candidate, either official or unofficial, some of the delegates at the meeting would not only vote Tory but would use all their influence with the rank and file to induce them to do the same.[66]

---

[65] D. Marquand, 'Ramsey MacDonald', ch. VIII, p. 45. I am grateful to Mr. David Marquand M.P. for giving me access to the typescript of his forthcoming biography of MacDonald.
[66] Henderson to the national executive, 'NEC', 19 June 1913.

Leicester's report gave more detail. Benson said

that we could not have a contest now because the I.L.P. had no money . . .
   To this it was replied that it was fortunate that the vacancy was due to the resignation of the Liberal member, otherwise we should have lost the seat as the I.L.P. had no money.
   Mr. MacDonald's position in Leicester was much stronger than the deputation, or even Mr. MacDonald knew . . .
   Mr. Henderson spent much time talking of such things as the 1909 Budget, the 1910 election . . . and Home Rule. He repeatedly stated that we must keep this Government in until next January, because of the Trade Union Act, Home Rule etc. . . . [He] anticipated that the Tory would poll at least 9,000 votes on this occasion, and that if the Labour Party put a man into the field the result would be that the Tory would get in, a general election would be brought appreciably nearer, and the Labour Party was not ready for a general election.
   In reply it was admitted that his figures . . . were correct, but they were no guide as on these occasions there was much cross-voting, and the Tory vote was very little over 7,000 . . . It was shown that we count on 8,000 votes and are likely to get more.
   The reason why the Party wanted to fight was that they wanted to take the same independent line in Parliamentary elections, and because they deeply and strongly resented:
   Sir Edward Grey's action over Persia, Miss Malecka . . . [67]
   The action of the Government over the railway strike and the miners' strike.
   The prosecutions of Crowsley, the bros. Buck, Bowman and Tom Mann last year.[68]
   The prosecution of Edgar Whiteley, and the bringing to Leicester of the leading counsel in that prosecution to be the Liberal candidate.[69]
   The rejection by the Government of Mr. Snowden's amendment to the second reading of the Finance Bill etc. etc.

The N.A.C.'s behaviour was unedifying. They refused not to endorse Banton, but effectively scuttled his candidature by declining to finance it. The emergency committee of the national executive

[67] They meant Anglo-Russian intervention in Persia which resulted in the deposition of the Shah and an extension of British influence. Miss Malecka was a Polish socialist charged by the Russian government with being a member of a revolutionary organization. The circumstances of the case made it an international *cause-célèbre*, and Grey was accused of pandering to Tsarism by refusing to receive deputations, petitions etc.
[68] All were charged in 1912 with incitement to mutiny by urging troops not to fire on strikers. Mann was convicted and sentenced to six months' imprisonment, only one month of which he served. The Buck brothers were printers of the *Syndicalist* whose articles formed the basis of the charge.
[69] Edgar Whiteley, manager of the National Labour Press (the I.L.P. press), in company with the Pankhursts, was convicted in May 1912 of incitement to damage property. He was printer of the *Suffragette* whose contents were crown evidence. Chief counsel for the prosecution was Gordon Hewart, Liberal candidate for Leicester.

met on 19 June, but was immediately adjourned by Henderson who had summoned the full executive for the afternoon. It heard Henderson's report and resolved by ten to one to withhold endorsement. A letter from the N.A.C. which 'approved' the candidature was ignored. This news was conveyed to the Leicester Party in a confused telegram from the N.A.C. which attempted to lay final blame on the Leicester I.L.P. for the failure of the candidature. The local Labour party, which met the same day, consequently abandoned the contest, but not without firing a couple of parting shots. They resolved

that in acting as they have done . . . [the national executive and the N.A.C.] have acted to the injury of the working class movement and have helped to hinder unity and progress in our cause.

The final facts to be stated are that this conclusion . . . has given the greatest possible pleasure to the Liberals and roused deep and strong resentment throughout the Leicester Labour Party.

This was not, however, the end of the story. In the absence of a Labour candidate, the British Socialist Party decided to nominate E. R. Hartley, and he had the support of a number of leading local I.L.P.ers. MacDonald, therefore, decided to intervene again. 'What this bye-election is to answer,' he wrote to Banton (who was erroneously suspected of supporting Hartley), 'is whether the movement in Leicester has a mind and will of its own.' If it did, he would stand by it; if it supported Hartley he 'could not be its candidate when the next appeal to the country comes'. Indeed, if Hartley's vote showed that he had significant Labour support, 'without delay you will have to find someone else to fill my shoes'.[70]

It was unlucky that this letter should have found its way to public knowledge, and even unluckier that the gist of a meeting between MacDonald, Henderson, and Roberts and a deputation from Leicester also became public. According to MacDonald he repeated confidentially to them what he had told Banton—'a heavy Hartley vote would have to be regarded as a censure which Mr. MacDonald could not overlook'.[71] On 25 June, the following day, the Leicester Liberal association issued a manifesto whose contents were supposed to have been read 'at a meeting of the Labour Party'.

The action of the Leicester Labour Party [the 'statement' continued] is regarded as such a grave violation of National Party discipline, and such a graceless disregard of Mr. Ramsay MacDonald's position as will inevitably lead to a considerable disruption of the Labour Party forces, and must compel Mr. MacDonald to sever his connection with Leicester . . . Nevertheless,

[70] Marquand, ch. VIII, p. 49.   [71] Ibid., p. 50-1.

every Labour voter who is concerned to preserve Party discipline and under-standings ... should give no encouragement to the candidature of Mr. Hartley, which is not recognised by the official Labour Party.[72]

The publication of this caused an immediate uproar—though garbled, it was clearly based upon accurate information. It had been written by a junior Liberal whip, Sir Maurice Levy, who had been told of MacDonald's attitude by the garrulous George Roberts, Labour chief whip.[73]

Head Office could scarcely have expected the stupefaction with which their decision was received on all sides. Within a few days the national executive had protests from large numbers of organizations, from the British Socialist Party (inevitably) to the Textile Workers (surprisingly and unfairly); there was scarcely an important union or trades council that did not resolve itself as opposed to the executive's action.[74] In the I.L.P. the ructions were even worse. The *Labour Leader* thought the action 'a grave mistake'.[75] Much was made of MacDonald's rash challenge at Hanley in which he invited the Liberals to contest his seat at Leicester. Alfred Salter reported from Bermondsey that 'all work in our branch has come to complete standstill'. It would take a year to recover from the 'blow dealt to us by the N.A.C.'. They would lose half their membership 'at least' and 'all fighting enthusiasm is utterly destroyed'.[76]

The national executive were badly shaken. Henderson was 'quite frankly rocked'; the whole thing had been 'a most dreadful shambles'.[77] MacDonald also appears to have been taken aback and his printed defence of the executive's actions was not as cautious as it might have been.[78] Yet the national executive could claim to be legitimately surprised. There were, after all, good electoral and tactical reasons why Leicester should not have been contested. As Henderson said:

Surely if as Secretary with the knowledge of electioneering that he might possess he tried to estimate what the result of a contest would be, he could be permitted to do so without the charge being thrown at the Executive that they were trying ... to create a situation so that in the interests of Mr. MacDonald the seat should not be fought.[79]

[72] Text in *Conference Report*, 1913, pp. 10–11.
[73] See the criticism of Roberts at the special Party conference in Jan. 1914, *The Times*, 28 Jan. 1914.
[74] See 'NEC', 15 July 1913; also 'LPLF: Affiliations 1913', where there is a large file of critical correspondence.
[75] *Labour Leader*, 26 June 1913.
[76] Salter to Herbert Bryan, 28 June 1913, 'L.S.E. MS. Herbert Bryan. General Correspondence'.
[77] Henderson to Middleton, 3 July 1913, 'LPLF: Uncat. Misc.'.
[78] See below, pp. 77–8.
[79] *Conference Report*, 1914, pp. 85–90. The Socialist candidate, E. R. Hartley, polled 2,580 and Hewart won by 1,584.

He was probably right in believing that an official Labour candidate would have let the Tory in; perhaps also right that local organization was not good enough to make much of a showing. All the short-run arguments favoured the executive. There was no reason why they should have jeopardized MacDonald's position by putting up a candidate. There was, furthermore, the argument that a contest would provoke widespread retaliation that Labour was not ready to face. On the other hand, MacDonald had committed himself to a position that was always controversial. Characteristically, he made it a personal issue, a question of loyalty to himself. There is no doubt, moreover, that his attitude became widely known. Quite apart from the Leicester Party's damaging revelations and Roberts's disclosures, it seems likely, the grape-vine being what it was, that MacDonald's actions were not only known but embellished.

Everyone in the movement seems to have thought that the Leicester decision was more significant than any other by-election in this period. 'No single bye-election', Henderson admitted, 'has engaged the attention of the Executive or the Emergency Committee so much as Leicester did.'[80] It was the most ominous sign yet that the short-term electoral arrangements that MacDonald had managed so skilfully a decade earlier were perhaps no longer acceptable to the people they were designed to benefit.

How MacDonald and Henderson related the Leicester 'shambles' to the future is debatable. It is possible that it made the other members of the executive less inclined to fly in the face of local feeling. It is certainly true that Henderson was overruled by them when he tried to prevent a three-cornered contest in Keighley in November 1913.

Just as Kenyon was leading the Party through the hoops over Chesterfield the elevation of S. O. Buckmaster to the Solicitorship-General made another by-election necessary. Keighley had been contested in the past by W. C. Anderson and was not a double-member seat. To that degree the local party was in a stronger position than its counterpart in Leicester. That there would be a by-election was known by the middle of October and Henderson's position was clear. 'I understand the difficulties about Keighley,' he told Middleton, 'and I hope I can fix up a strong number of the N.E.C. who with Arthur [Peters] will do what they can to avoid a candidature.'[81] He later elaborated his objections:

The I.L.P. have done very little in the constituency since the Anderson fight. [October 1911] The time before the poll is inadequate having regard to the previous neglect and contests on promotion to office invariably go more

---

[80] *Conference Report*, 1914, p. 88.
[81] Henderson to Middleton, 24 Oct. 1913, 'LPLF: Uncat. Misc.'.

strongly with the promoted Member ... In this case I anticipate a considerable falling away of our previous support and this will seriously weaken our position in the constituency and damage us in the country ... [82]

Nevertheless, after some delay, the Keighley Party moved towards a candidature. The local I.L.P. had an enthusiastic meeting on 26 October and decided to nominate William Bland. 'The cheers with which this statement was greeted', reported the *Yorkshire Post*,

substantiate what has previously been stated in this column, namely that whatever view the National Labour Executive take of the situation the feeling among local Labour men is against letting the opportunity go by without making an effort to garner the grain sown by the last contest.[83]

On 28 October W. C. Robinson and Peters from the national executive, together with Bruce Glasier from the I.L.P., met the Keighley Party. After three hours the delegates decided to support Bland and his candidature was endorsed by the national executive two days later. This decision was received at Keighley with 'the utmost satisfaction. Local enthusiasts in the Labour Movement have all along been anxious for a fight.'[84]

Why did the national executive endorse the candidature? Partly because Henderson was not there to bully its members. Above all, however, the executive wished to avoid another Leicester. As Clynes said, a contest at Keighley would be 'a proof of the independence and self-contained position of the Party both in the House of Commons and the country'.[85] The *Yorkshire Post* claimed that the executive have yielded 'to local pressure and they have acted in the interests of ... "Labour solidarity" '.[86] If they had, as seems probable, it was a prudent surrender; but Henderson remained unconvinced.

He was suspicious of local organization on principle and needed, what he apparently did not get at Keighley, impressive evidence of its soundness. Furthermore, he believed that the political climate, local and national, was unfavourable.[87] Finally, he was convinced that the I.L.P. was forcing a candidature at Keighley in order to embarrass Head Office and at the expense of the Party's general welfare. 'I am in no way surprised', he told Middleton,

at the decision with regard to Keighley or what you say as to the *Labour Leader*. I have seen for some time a deliberate attempt to exploit the larger

---

[82] The same, 29 Oct. 1913.
[83] *Yorkshire Post*, 27 Oct. 1913.
[84] *Keighley News*, 1 Nov. 1913.
[85] *Manchester Guardian*, 13 Nov. 1913.
[86] *Yorkshire Post*, 31 Oct. 1913.
[87] Henderson to Middleton, 12 Nov. 1913, 'LPLF: LP/HEN/08/1/98'. He was sure that the effect of the Dublin transport workers' strike would harm Labour.

movement in the interests of the I.L.P. The policy is all the more freely pushed if it can in any way harrass MacDonald or conflict with his position. This vacancy was too good an opportunity for them to miss.[88]

This letter is not to be taken seriously as a factual statement. Whatever the attitude of the *Labour Leader* to Leicester, its treatment of Keighley was less immoderate than Henderson's.[89] Moreover, although the I.L.P. initiated the candidature, as in Leicester, it was the overwhelming support it received from the trade-union delegates that made Bland's nomination possible. In both parties union delegates made up the great majority of the total; in both as high a proportion of union delegates supported a candidate as did those from the socialist societies. Yet the letter is a good reflection of Henderson's state of mind, and probably MacDonald's as well. Both were trying to find a middle way between conflicting pressures: between the requirements of parliamentary politics on the one hand, and the difficulty of explaining these requirements to the rank and file on the other.

As for Keighley itself, Bland conducted a vigorously anti-Liberal campaign ('is not Mr. Bland opposed to the Unionist Party as well?' asked the *Keighley News*)[90] and did slightly better—Henderson's computations were wrong for once—than Anderson did in 1911, the vote rising from 3,452 to 3,646. He did so well, indeed, that his candidature was endorsed without opposition on 27 January 1914.

5. *Summary*

This chapter has examined only the most significant by-elections between 1910 and the war and it is not possible to say that the more or less *ad hoc* understandings and quiet agreements that made up the Liberal–Labour 'alliance' had broken down entirely. But the self-restraint which alone made possible such a working arrangement was disappearing on both sides. The understandings could only have been preserved intact by Labour at the price of deep divisions within the Party, more unofficial candidatures, and the abandonment of each Labour-held constituency as it fell vacant.

There is no reason to suppose that the growing 'intractability' of Labour (to quote *The Times*) was primarily ideological or even connected with specifically objectionable policies of the Liberal government. It is possible, though difficult to prove, that the industrial disturbances of 1911–13 contributed to militancy in the rank and file which, in turn, made local parties less willing to stand aside for Liberal candidates. Yet this was perhaps less fundamental than a growing

[88] Henderson to Middleton, 31 Oct. 1913, 'LPLF: Uncat. Misc.'.
[89] See *Labour Leader*, 23 Oct. 1913.
[90] *Keighley News*, 2 Nov. 1913.

feeling in the country that the Liberal Party was no longer the party of the working classes, but that in some perceived if indefinable way the Labour Party was. Thus the repeatedly criticized failings, or apparent failings, of the parliamentary Labour Party did not make its critics less anxious to promote Labour candidates. Furthermore, there is evidence that in the years immediately before the war there was something of a radical 'counter-attack'. That was so certainly in the mining seats where Liberal campaigns were mounted and led by the radicals. This caused comment even in the cabinet: 'Lloyd George came in for a good deal of abuse . . . on having a private land system enquiry and running a land question campaign through satelites [sic] at the bye-elections.'[91] It is probable that the renegotiation of a Lib–Lab agreement would be no more acceptable to many local Liberals than to local Labour parties.

If things went on as they had gone for the last three years, there seems no reason why Labour should not have contested as many single-member constituencies as it could—the momentum of political and organizational development pointed to that. It is possible that MacDonald might have tried to negotiate a new agreement, conceivably more advantageous to the Party than the last one, and he might have been assisted by Liberal headquarters. But before the outbreak of war there was not much to show that this was practical politics.

[91] 'J. A. Pease Diaries', 8 Aug.–7 Oct. 1912.

IV

LABOUR ON THE EVE, 1914

BETWEEN the first general election of 1910 and the outbreak of the war the Labour Party had not been transformed, but it had, nevertheless, changed significantly. In most of the great cities local Labour parties had taken over the duties of the trades councils, though the latter remained the characteristic organization in the smaller boroughs and county towns. At the same time, if only to defend themselves, the councils were beginning to discharge their political functions more effectively. Since the trade unions remained the sheet anchor of organization this was as important as the establishment of local Labour parties. Likewise, in the mining constituencies Labour was unquestionably stronger in 1914 than it had been in 1910. Despite the genuine difficulties imposed by the Osborne Judgement, Head Office had extended assistance to local parties, both for electoral expenses and the salaries of their agents. Head Office itself had expanded modestly with the appointment of two national organizers and Henderson's succession gave organization much more energetic direction. At the regional level it was a question which was the greater triumph: the agreement in principle to establish a separate Scottish organization or the defeat of attempts to decentralize the Party. Probably the second, but at the same time Labour was probably strengthened by the establishment of the Scottish Advisory Council, whatever its later disappointments.[1]

Thus, in some form or another, nearly all those reforms associated with the 1918 constitution had been anticipated. Furthermore, these organizational changes assumed that the Party was willing and able to expand. Despite the many political difficulties in the selection of candidates and constituencies, Henderson's efforts had already done much to make the Party a national one. At the same time Labour's relationship with the Liberal Party was more liable to rupture than before. Such was by no means deliberate Labour policy, and its leaders observed this development with a mixture of alarm and helplessness. Whatever they did to restrain the local parties[2] they faced the prospect of an irresistible increase in the number of candidatures, particularly in single-member constituencies.

How many seats, then, might Labour have been expected to

[1] See above, pp. 39–43. [2] See above, pp. 32–3.

contest in a general election in 1914 or 1915? If the election came in 1914 it is possible to make a reasonably accurate prediction; a figure for 1915 is more indeterminate. It is not clear when the Liberals would have gone to the country. In the early part of 1914 there was much talk of an election but a heightening of the Irish crisis made a summer one doubtful. A winter election was a possibility, though not one usually favoured by 'progressive' governments. Excluding the sudden fall of the ministry, an election was likely in the spring or summer of 1915. Henderson thought this the government's intention, but had little confidence in their ability to choose a date of their own.

Personally, I have never thought [he told MacDonald] the Government deliberately intended to go to the country. What I have felt is that they will be compelled to do so by sheer force of political circumstance ... Had there been no Amending Bill [to exclude the Six Counties from the Home Rule Bill] I think the Government could have carried out their present intentions, but it appears to me that Carson has only to go on insisting upon an election and the Amending Bill will afford no means of escape for the Government.[3]

At any rate, impressed by election rumours, the national executive had set up a sub-committee 'to consider the general electoral situation of the Party' in February 1914[4] and the executive considered its reports on 8 and 21 April.[5] On 29 June, as a result of these deliberations, the national agent presented to the executive a consolidated report which is useful in assessing the Party's electoral position. Constituencies were classified in four ways: seats held by Labour, those where a candidate had been sanctioned, those where one had been selected but not sanctioned, and those whose position was uncertain.

TABLE 1[6]

Labour Seat	Sanctioned	Selected	Uncertain
Stockport			Crewe
Whitehaven			Cockermouth
Derby			Chesterfield
Mid-Derby			
Sunderland	Bishop Auckland	Darlington	Gateshead
Barnard Castle	Jarrow	South Shields	Chester-le-Street
Chester-le-Street		Houghton-le-Spring	
S. West Ham		N.W. Durham	
	Portsmouth		Southampton
E. Manchester	Oldham	Eccles	Widnes

[3] Henderson to MacDonald, 29 May 1914, 'LPLF: LP/MAC/09/1/73'.
[4] 'NEC', 10 Feb. 1914.
[5] 'NEC', 8–21 Apr. 1914.
[6] 'Table of Prospective Labour Constituencies', 'NEC', 21 Apr. 1914.

Labour Seat	Sanctioned	Selected	Uncertain
N. E. Manchester	Preston	Newton	Accrington
Blackburn	St. Helens		Rossendale
Clitheroe	Leigh		Kirkdale
Barrow	Wigan		West Derby
Westhoughton			
Gorton			
Ince			
[Bolton]*			
Leicester		E. Nottingham	Northampton
Norwich		E. Bristol	E. Northants.
Newcastle			Morpeth
			Wansbeck
N.W. Staffs.	W. Wolverhampton		Hanley
			Wednesbury
			Walsall
	E. Birmingham	W. Birmingham	Nuneaton
	Coventry		
E. Leeds	W. Hull	York	Middlesbrough
Normanton	Sowerby	Keighley	Wakefield
Hallamshire		Barnsley	Colne Valley
W. Bradford		Rotherham	Holmfirth
Halifax		Doncaster	Hallamshire
Attercliffe		Osgoldcross	Pudsey
			Spen Valley
			Huddersfield
			W. Leeds
Deptford	Bermondsey		Limehouse
Woolwich			Poplar
Rhondda		Mid-Glamorgan	S. Glamorgan
W. Monmouth		E. Glamorgan	S. Monmouth
Gower		N. Monmouth	Monmouth City
S. Glamorgan			
Merthyr		W. Monmouth	Camarthen
			Boroughs
Blackfriars	Camlachie	Leith	St. Rollox
Dundee	S. Ayr	Montrose	N. Aberdeen
W. Fife	Midlothian	W. Lothian	W. Lanark
	S.-E. Lanark		S. Edinburgh
			Falkirk
			Greenock

* Omitted in the Table.

There were 37 'Labour Seats', 18 'Sanctioned', 22 'Selected', and 40 'Uncertain'. Hallamshire and Chester-le-Street, where there was doubt about the intentions of the sitting members (J. Wadsworth and J. W. Taylor respectively), occur both in the 'Labour Seat' and 'Uncertain' lists. Though they are classified separately, the position in both Mid-Derby and Nuneaton (held by the recalcitrant Lib–Labs, Hancock and Johnson) was still obscure.

Peters's table was a provisional one, but in the event of a 1914 election only two of the listed constituencies, Crewe and Kirkdale, indisputably would not have been contested.[7] Most of the 'uncertain' seats had candidates in the process of selection, or had already selected candidates, but had not yet settled the question of financial responsibility. Similarly, 'selected' candidates were those where only formal sanction had yet to be given. Allowing for the usual rush of sanctions on the eve of a general election it can be assumed that nearly all Peters's 117 would be fought.

How many others would there be? And how many in 1915? There are a few imponderables. The Miners' Federation was one. On 21 April Henderson reported that, 'should the election take place during the present year', the Miners would limit themselves to twenty-two candidates, including the sitting members, and this figure seems to have been confirmed by the Federation itself.[8] Gregory, however, has concluded that in the event of a 1915 election the Miners could have contested twenty-seven seats.[9] Further still, a memorandum in Lloyd George's papers—internal evidence suggests it was by Vernon Hartshorn—argues that, unless the Liberals were more accommodating, the South Wales Miners would put up an even larger number of candidates than Gregory calculated they would have.[10] At any rate, the figure for putative miners' candidates should clearly be treated as a flexible one.

Understandably, Peters did not include possible candidates from the British Socialist Party. On 23 June 1914 it formally applied to the national executive for affiliation and appended to its application a list of prospective constituencies. There being no 1915 conference due to the war, the application was not approved until 1916. Otherwise, it would probably have been affiliated by a 1915 election. Albert Inkpin, secretary of the British Socialist Party, suggested that they would contest E. Bradford, Burnley, Carlisle, Northampton, Reading, Rochdale, and Southampton, all of them traditional socialist strongholds. Only Southampton had been listed by Peters, and in the 'uncertain' list. In fact, Tom Lewis of the British Socialist Party had been selected, but sanction was withheld due to an inter-union dispute.[11]

[7] 'NEC', 21 Apr. 1914.
[8] In a letter to the national executive, 'NEC', 29 June 1914.
[9] Gregory, *Miners and British Politics*, p. 50.
[10] 'Lloyd George Papers, c/17/4/1', dated Feb. 1914.
[11] Lewis had been nominated by the British Seafarers' Union, one ruled superfluous by the Joint Board, and his nomination was contested by the Ships' Stewards. ('NEC', 21 Apr. 1914.)

It is difficult, furthermore, to estimate how many last-minute candidatures there would have been. It is a safe bet that the majority of such contests would be 'propagandist' and forced on the national executive by determined local parties. One or two can be imagined from Glasgow[12] and a larger number from London.[13] Liverpool was an unlikely starter,[14] but with a little encouragement the Leeds party would have contested another two seats.[15] Similarly, it would be surprising if at least some of the constituencies fought in January 1910, but excluded from Peters's list, were not put forward. They were all of them, with the exception of Tewkesbury (a rather eccentric choice) and North Belfast, considered conceivable Labour victories.[16]

Thus had the general election been held in 1914, Labour might have contested 125 to 140 seats. Without encouragement from Head Office, and this was probably not to be expected, an election in 1915 would have found the Party with not more than an additional ten to twenty candidates: a couple more from the miners, five from the British Socialist Party, several more from London, Glasgow and Manchester, two in Plymouth and Devonport (possibilities even in 1914),[17] and perhaps several more in south Wales and industrial Scotland.[18] There was, however, a distinct quickening in the growth of the Party's electoral organization in 1913 and 1914 and this might have yielded another ten or so candidates. At a 1915 election Labour might have put up 170 candidates, but a more realistic estimate is about 150.

Single-member constituencies would probably have been contested without much regard for the two major parties, although most of them, apart from Labour's own, were, in the nature of things, Liberal-held. In any case, unless there was an agreement to do so, the Liberals showed no real sign of respecting sitting Labour members. Henderson himself was to be opposed in Barnard Castle—'it will not disturb my spirit' he told Middleton[19]—and the great majority of Labour candidates in mining constituencies would have had Liberal

---

[12] See Glasgow Labour Party, 'Minutes', 13 Feb. 1914. The two most likely were Tradeston and Govan.

[13] The result largely of the establishment of the London Labour Party. Even by its own standards, Labour had been under-represented in London.

[14] For some reasons why, see Liverpool L.R.C., 'Minutes', 19 Dec. 1913.

[15] Leeds L.R.C., *Year Book*, 1914, pp. 5–7.

[16] The other constituencies were N. Ayrshire, Hyde, N.-E. Lanarkshire, N.-W. Lanarkshire, and S.W. Manchester.

[17] 'NEC', 21 Apr. 1914.

[18] For Scotland, see *Daily News*, 24 June 1914. It calculated that a 1914 election would have seen only seven Labour candidates in Scotland; but if the election were deferred a year there would be twelve.

[19] Henderson to Middleton, 23 Aug. 1912, 'LPLF: LP/HEN/08/1/64'.

opposition.[20] As to the double-member boroughs, everyone was reticent. It is difficult to say what would have happened with them; but second candidatures, either official or wild-cat, were possibilities in Leicester, Newcastle, Dundee, and Blackburn.

Yet there was always the possibility of a new electoral arrangement with the Liberals, and there is much evidence to suggest that it was one favoured by MacDonald. After all, the Labour Party had, for the most part, emerged as a substantial parliamentary force by arrangement, and the arranger was MacDonald. Furthermore, though he had not ruled out an electoral struggle with the Liberals, his own evolutionary theories seemed to imply a tactic of cautious development according to circumstances; and this tactic did not even exclude the slow conversion of much of the Liberal Party itself to socialism. Finally, an arrangement had the merit of ensuring Labour's parliamentary representation in a system notoriously unfair to third parties.

Is this what MacDonald wanted?[21] He had become increasingly concerned with three-cornered contests before the 1910 elections,[22] and in 1910 he appears to have thought of some formal, if limited, scheme of parliamentary support for the government; 'an agreement to support the present Government in carrying out certain objects, and terminating when these objects have been attained'.[23] This was a clear piece of kite-flying and as such it was not taken up by the Liberals—though it might have made Lloyd George more confident in offering MacDonald a place in a coalition ministry.[24]

While in his dispute with Henderson over the original grants-in-aid scheme he claimed to favour some expansion of candidatures under rather penal conditions,[25] by 1913 it was a question whether he favoured independent candidatures at all. His opposition to a candidate in the Leicester by-election[26] was certainly justifiable, but Leicester could not be treated in isolation.

Are we capable of . . . devising a method of fighting . . . over a series of years? . . . Are we capable of saying . . . 'We will not fight Leicester because we are not ready to take the second seat' or 'We shall use the Parliament Act[27] not

[20] Gregory, *Miners and British Politics*, p. 50.
[21] For a more general discussion, see R. I. McKibbin, 'James Ramsay MacDonald and the Problem of the Independence of the Labour Party, 1910–1914', *Journal of Modern History*, 42, 2 (June 1970), pp. 216–35.
[22] See above, pp. 50–51.
[23] *Labour Leader*, 4 Feb. 1910.
[24] See McKibbin, 'James Ramsay MacDonald', pp. 253–4.
[25] See above, p. 32.
[26] See above, pp. 63–4.
[27] He meant not the Parliament Act of 1911, but the Trade Union Act of 1913, which restored the right of the unions to contribute to the political fund of the Labour Party, and thus largely reversed the Osborne Judgement.

because we accept Mr. Asquith's statement about food taxes, or about Sir Edward Grey's foreign policy, but because, taking in the mass the circumstances which we have to face in 1913 and keeping in view the political conditions which we desire to reach, the best policy which we can adopt now is to secure the effectiveness of the Parliament Act, whilst we attack the details to which we object'... that is going on systematically and intelligently.[28]

The following week he commented more sharply on the notion that a candidature in Leicester would have emphasized the Party's independence. There was 'no substance in it at all'.

We were told that if we fought Crewe we should remove the suspicion. We fought, and before the election was well over the suspicion crawled out again ... 'Fight Midlothian,' they said, 'and it will die.' Midlothian was fought and the suspicion survived. What we have to recognize is that this suspicion will never be allayed but will be fed by such demonstrations ... It is a quack medicine for a serious disease.[29]

He returned to the subject yet again a week later. He asserted that the parliamentary party must use its independence with regard to 'particular circumstances' and clearly this 'did not rule out arrangements with other Parties'. This was done, he said, in the most correct circles; he pointed to arrangements for the second ballot in Germany (and who could be more correct than the S.P.D.?) and to coalitions and alliances in Holland, Sweden, etc.[30]

But this argument does not develop sequentially. Its first part is the evolutionary theory again, written as obliquely as only MacDonald could write, but familiar enough : Labour would have to move slowly, its progress a circumstantial one; good opportunities might be exploited but only after careful thought. The second part of the argument, however, seems to imply something quite new. For one thing, it starts from false analogies. In a country with the second ballot or the alternative vote some form of instruction to the elector was (and is) necessary. That Socialists and Progressives should vote for each other in the second round of German elections was a convenient and inevitable arrangement, though less successful than MacDonald implied.[31] In Britain technical swaps of this sort were impossible; what could be done was a limitation of candidates by each of the arranging parties. MacDonald's readers could scarcely be blamed for assuming that that was what he wanted. In effect, he was now arguing publicly for what had always been denied in the past even when it

[28] *Labour Leader*, 3 July 1913.
[29] *Labour Leader*, 10 July 1913.
[30] *Labour Leader*, 17 July 1913.
[31] See C. E. Schorske, *German Social Democracy, 1905–1917* (New York, 1965), pp. 224–56.

happened—though, to be sure, for an agreement negotiated under different conditions than the one he put together with Herbert Gladstone in 1903. And this is exactly what his critics did assume he wanted. At the Party's special conference to consider electoral policy (27 January 1914) MacDonald was accused of turning the Party into an echo of Liberalism, and by some, like W. C. Anderson, who were not among his traditional critics. In reply, MacDonald more or less repeated what he had written in the *Labour Leader*.[32]

The fact that the special conference gave him such a cool reception did not deter MacDonald. On 3 March 1914, in response to an invitation from Lloyd George, who was convinced that the run of events in the two parties would lead 'to the worst disaster which has befallen us',[33] MacDonald and Henderson met him and Illingworth, the Liberal chief whip. Lloyd George claimed he was speaking with the full approval of Asquith and the 'Inner Cabinet'. The Ulster crisis was such, he said, that three things had to be agreed upon. It is not clear from MacDonald's account whether they were agreed upon or merely noted, but, either way, they were plainly grounds for negotiation. The three were: a mutual withdrawal of candidates to eliminate three-cornered contests and a 'substantial' increase in Labour's parliamentary representation; an agreed programme to be carried out by the Liberals if they were returned; Labour membership of the cabinet if they sought it. All these were necessary, the Chancellor assured them, because the Ulster crisis was to be brought to a head by inducing the Lords to reject the army bill.

Without admitting that it was Lloyd George's plan MacDonald immediately gave public support to it. He said that if there were a Home Rule crisis he was ready to advise such 'electoral action on our part as will not unnecessarily jeopardise seats that ought to be kept or won by candidates in favour of Home Rule'.[34] It is at this moment, 'the spring of 1914', according to Fenner Brockway's famous piece of gossip, that MacDonald is said to have proposed 'an alliance with the Liberal Party at the next election'.[35] Brockway gives an affecting picture of himself and Hardie conspiring to kill the scheme; he describes how he raised the matter at the I.L.P. conference, how MacDonald denied it and challenged Brockway to produce the minutes, and how Snowden intervened to say that (at the appropriate meeting of the national executive) MacDonald demanded that the

[32] Labour Party, *Special and Annual Conference Report*, 1914, pp. 73–89.
[33] Marquand, ch. VIII, p. 59.
[34] Quoted in Marquand, ch. VIII, p. 60.
[35] Brockway, *Inside the Left*, pp. 36–8.

4

suggestion not be minuted 'so that the movement should be kept in ignorance'.

There are two things that ought to be said about this story. On the one hand, Snowden was not a member of the national executive and thus his evidence was at best second-hand. On the other, this is not altogether what happened at the I.L.P. conference. Brockway certainly raised the matter and MacDonald certainly denied it. Hardie, who was in the chair, took no part in the debate. Then Snowden spoke:

Referring to Mr. MacDonald's denial of a Labour–Liberal alliance, Mr. Snowden asked if it was denied that negotiations had taken place. It was something more than a rumour. At the recent Executive meeting of the Labour Party a definite proposal had been made and discussed.

But Hardie interjected that 'no such proposal had been made. The matter had been mentioned only.'[36]

It is unlikely that MacDonald was so obtuse as to present an 'alliance' to an executive which obviously would not have it. On the other hand, it really would be surprising if the matter of an electoral agreement was not raised. The executive was, after all, considering Labour's electoral position.[37] It is probable that MacDonald reported Lloyd George's offer and declared his support for an agreement with the Liberals of the kind he was already notoriously known to favour. Hardie was presumably against any agreement and told Brockway so. Apart from this not much more can be said, but it does appear as if the executive gave even MacDonald's more limited proposals a dusty reception. Lloyd George's offer came to nothing—because the Lords did not reject the army estimates, or because a nerveless government was not prepared to force a crisis over Ulster, or else because it was a genuinely private venture of Lloyd George's.

MacDonald, then, almost certainly wanted an arrangement with the Liberal Party. In the long term he might have looked to a political realignment, the creation of a new radical party, and Mr. Marquand's forthcoming biography of MacDonald suggests that this was so. But what he wanted for the immediate future was a Labour Party separate from the Liberal Party in its membership and its general aims, but modest in its short-run ambitions and restricted in its political activities. He was impressed, above all, with the weakness of the Labour Party in the country. He hoped it would contest only those seats where it was strong and where chances of success were good. In 1914 he was also pessimistic about Labour's political fortunes. As he was unquestionably determined that the Party should maintain its

[36] I.L.P., *Conference Report*, 1914, pp. 82–6.   [37] See above, p. 73.

parliamentary strength,[38] then there was no alternative, as he believed, to an agreement with the Liberal Party.

What arguments could support an electoral pact? Broadly speaking there were three. First, there was the apparent position of the Labour Party itself. Between 1910 and 1914 four seats, Hanley, Chesterfield, N. E. Derbyshire, and Bow and Bromley, had been lost in by-elections. Two others, Nuneaton and Mid-Derby, had effectively been lost as a result of the actions of their members, Johnson and Hancock.[39] Whether the by-elections were as bad as they looked is open to doubt,[40] but they seemed to show prima facie that the Liberals were holding on to the greater part of their traditional electorate and that Labour members held their seats on sufferance.[41]

As disquieting from MacDonald's view were the results of ballots conducted under the Trade Union Act. Though on the first ballot all but a few unions voted in favour of establishing a political fund, in many cases the minorities against were formidable, and the Engineers actually reversed themselves on a second. The votes of the principal unions are listed in Table 2.[42]

TABLE 2

Union	For	Against
Carpenters and Joiners	13,336	11,738
Ironfounders	6,854	2,576
Engineers	20,586	12,740
Boot and Shoe Operatives	6,085	1,939
National Union of Railwaymen	102,270	34,953
Miners' Federation	261,643	194,800
Railway Clerks	15,496	1,340
Amalgamated Weavers	98,158	75,893
Gasworkers	27,802	4,339

The ballots, *The Times* commented, 'show that a large section of members nominally supporting [the Labour Party] is indifferent and another large section positively hostile'.[43] These results were perhaps the most effective argument for a pact that would at least maintain the Party's strength until better times came.

Secondly, the political situation in 1914 was working to make an

[38] For a more detailed discussion see McKibbin, 'James Ramsay MacDonald', pp. 220–35.
[39] See above, p. 26–8.
[40] See below, p. 83–4.
[41] Snowden thought that Labour could win only 'half-a-dozen' seats on its own account. (Philip Snowden, *An Autobiography* (London, 1932), i, pp. 217–18.)
[42] Labour Party, *Conference Report*, 1914, App. V, p. 137.
[43] *The Times*, 28 Jan. 1914.

agreement appear not only desirable but necessary. Since it was always possible that an election could come before the passing of the Home Rule Bill—if Ulster did not actually precipitate an election—and since Conservative opposition to it seemed to threaten social disorder, and even the stability of the state itself, it would have required a thick-skinned leadership indeed to risk the defeat of the Liberal government in order to promote as many Labour candidates as possible. The crowing in the Unionist press after a by-election gain was bad enough; to forward Unionist aims by fighting against Liberal members might have appeared unthinkable.

Finally, an electoral understanding had tradition behind it. Many Labour M.P.s had been elected under the MacDonald–Gladstone agreement originally and had been re-elected without Liberal opposition since then. Nearly all of them had received some sort of help from the Liberals, including those, like Hardie, Snowden, and Lansbury, who were most opposed to any new agreement.

If he wished MacDonald could have marshalled an imposing argument. But was he right in thinking that Labour was in such low water in 1914? On any close analysis of events this interpretation is hard to sustain. The results in both the by-elections and the Trade Union Act ballots need some examination. It has been argued, for example, that in three-cornered by-elections in the period 1911–14 Labour fared 'abysmally'.[44] But the four seats Labour lost were by no means representative ones and in the remaining by-elections Labour made some significant gains. Three of the seats lost were in that Midlands mining belt where Lib–Labism remained uniquely strong.[45] In none was there any Labour organization; in none had Labour before fought an independent campaign; in Chesterfield it still did not do so. Though the Hanley result was certainly disappointing, it is not to be compared with by-election results in other mining constituencies; nor, indeed, is it to be compared with the N.-E. Derbyshire election which was remarkable less for its loss than for the size of the Labour vote. The fourth seat lost was equally unrepresentative: Bow and Bromley went to the Conservatives after George Lansbury resigned it and the Labour whip to fight a by-election as a women's suffrage candidate.[46] He had no official Labour support and women's suffrage was no more electorally popular in the East End than anywhere else.

Between December 1910 and the outbreak of the war, excluding

[44] T. Wilson, *The Downfall of the Liberal Party, 1914–1935* (London, 1966), p. 17.
[45] See above, p. 54.
[46] For Bow, see Labour Party, *Conference Report*, 1913, pp. 18–20; R. Postgate, *George Lansbury* (London, 1951), pp. 126–8.

the four seats lost, Labour fought twelve by-elections. Seven were first contests and they are listed in Table 3:

TABLE 3

Kilmarnock Boroughs (Sept. 1911)		*Keighley* (Oct. 1911)	
Liberal	6,923	Liberal	4,667
Conservative	4,637	Conservative	3,842
Labour	2,761	Labour	3,452
Oldham (Nov. 1911)		*Midlothian* (Sept. 1912)	
Conservative	12,255	Conservative	6,021
Liberal	10,623	Liberal	5,989
Labour	7,448	Labour	2,413
CONSERVATIVE GAIN		CONSERVATIVE GAIN	
Houghton-le-Spring (Mar. 1913)		*South Lanark* (Dec. 1913)	
Liberal	6,930	Conservative	4,257
Conservative	4,807	Liberal	4,006
Labour	4,165	Labour	1,676
		CONSERVATIVE GAIN	
N.-W. Durham (Jan. 1914)			
Liberal	7,241		
Conservative	5,564		
Labour	5,026		

Of these results, Keighley, Houghton-le-Spring, and N.-W. Durham are, on any judgement, good ones. There was little separating the Conservative and Labour candidates, and not very much more separating Labour from Liberal. Similarly, given the circumstances in which it was fought, Labour did surprisingly well in Oldham.[47] The three Scottish results were more disappointing for Labour. Yet South Lanark was as much an agricultural constituency as a mining one and Kilmarnock was not then, nor was it for a long time afterwards, by any means a safe seat for Labour. In Midlothian, Brown did much less well in a first contest than Adamson did in West Fife, but Midlothian was heavily influenced by Edinburgh's professional and mercantile families, many of whom lived in the division.[48]

Nor were the results in the five constituencies which had been contested before at all disastrous. They are listed in Table 4.

[47] It was widely alleged that the Textile Workers had done nothing to assist the Labour candidate, W. C. Robinson. (Labour Party, *Conference Report*, 1912, pp. 70–1.) The Oldham Trades Council had refused to endorse Robinson's candidature in 1910. For the political position of the Cotton Operatives, see Clegg, Fox, and Thompson, pp. 410–11.
[48] H. Pelling, *Social Geography of British Elections, 1885–1910* (London, 1967), p. 396.

TABLE 4

N.-E. Lanarkshire (Mar. 1911)		Last Contest (Jan. 1910)	
Liberal	7,976	Liberal	9,105
Conservative	6,776	Conservative	7,012
Labour	2,896	Labour	2,160
Holmfirth (June 1912)		Last Contest (Jan. 1910)	
Liberal	4,749	Liberal	7,761
Conservative	3,379	Conservative	5,419
Labour	3,195	Labour	1,380
Crewe (July 1912)		Last Contest (Jan. 1910)	
Conservative	6,260	Liberal	7,761
Liberal	5,294	Conservative	5,419
Labour	2,485	Labour	1,380
CONSERVATIVE GAIN			
Keighley (Nov. 1913)		Last Contest (Oct. 1911)	
Liberal	4,730	Liberal	4,667
Conservative	3,852	Conservative	3,842
Labour	3,646	Labour	3,452
Leith Burghs (Feb. 1914)		Last Contest (Jan. 1910)	
Conservative	5,159	Liberal	7,146
Liberal	5,143	Conservative	4,540
Labour	3,346	Labour	2,742
CONSERVATIVE GAIN			

In all these constituencies the Labour vote had increased compared with the last contest. In Holmfirth it was much more than doubled; in Crewe it was nearly doubled. In N.-E. Lanarkshire and Leith the Labour vote rose absolutely in reduced total polls. In Keighley it was static. Plainly Labour was not doing worse than in 1910, let alone faring abysmally. Professionals at the time were sure that Labour was gaining at the expense of the older parties: *The Times* correspondent wrote of the N.-W. Durham result that it

is chiefly interesting for the strength of the Labour poll. The Liberals sought to bring waverers to their side during the contest by pointing to the consistent lack of success of Labour candidates in three cornered fights since the last General Election. But this lack of success . . . is purely relative. The Labour Party has broken a good deal of new ground, and has proved to both Liberals and Unionists in the constituencies that it is a growing force, with which both the older parties will have to reckon seriously.[49]

In addition, it is useful to look at municipal elections for the period. They were often the only occasions when local parties put up candidates and were, for that reason, taken more seriously in many

[49] *The Times*, 2 Feb. 1914, 'Labour at the By-Elections'.

constituencies than parliamentary contests. Since the hand of Head Office fell less heavily and less frequently on local candidates divisional parties were readier to nominate them. From 1908 onwards Labour made an unbroken series of gains:

TABLE 5

Year	No. of Labour Candidates	Elected	Gains	Losses	Net Gains
1909	555	122	55	32	23
1910	330	113	52	19	33
1911	367	157	95	17	78
1912	596	164	63	21	42
1913	494	196	106	21	85

Compared with the number of candidates nominated by both major parties today these figures are undoubtedly small, and it would be wrong, of course, to read too much into them. Municipal politics are not national politics and too little is known of them to make firm judgements. But on any reading these results are not symptoms of electoral decrepitude. They were good enough, indeed, to force the non-Labour parties into fusion in some places. At the 1913 elections in Bradford, for example, all seventeen Labour candidates each faced only one opponent, the opposition parties having suitably distributed their candidates after an electoral pact.[50] In the same year similar pacts were arranged in Leeds and Sheffield.

That other election, the ballots under the Trade Union Act, also needs a little comment, though it is true that nothing too hard and fast can be said about it. Contemporary opponents of the Labour Party were gratified by the size of the minorities voting against the political funds. Pelling is impressed rather by the near unanimity with which unions voted for them. That only a minority participated in the balloting is, he points out, a characteristic of British trade-union politics.[51] P. F. Clarke has ingeniously suggested that voting for the Labour Party in the ballots and against it in parliamentary elections is perfectly compatible if 'both actions are seen within the framework of progressivism'.[52] But the ballots were not seen at the time as being within a progressive 'framework'. They were conducted after plebiscitary campaigns whose aim was to force union members to declare themselves for or against the Labour Party. It was the Lib-Labs who mounted the opposition, just as it was they who initiated

---

[50] *Conference Report*, 1914, pp. 31–2. See also P. J. Waller's review of P. F. Clarke, *Lancashire and the New Liberalism* (London, 1971) in *The English Historical Review* (Oct. 1972), pp. 843–6.
[51] Pelling, *Popular Politics*, p. 162.
[52] Clarke, *Lancashire and the New Liberalism*, p. 401.

the suits that led to the Osborne Judgement and who enthusiastically had their unions enjoined once the Judgement had been delivered.

As to the results, Pelling is surely right. There were, certainly, large minorities against the political funds in the Miners' Federation and the Textile Workers, but these were unions with long traditions of political activity in the two older parties. Nevertheless, a majority of their members voted in favour of a process by which political action in future would mean the Labour Party. Those unions, even old-established ones like the Railway Servants and the Railway Clerks, which felt themselves under employers' attack, voted emphatically for political payment.

Though the great industrial disturbances of 1911–14 do not appear to have done the parliamentary Labour Party any obvious good at the time, it can be presumed that they did the older parties even less good. But it is impossible to say with certainty what the political consequences of the strikes were; it is likely that they made the local parties more militant and increased tensions between Head Office and the rank and file. A probable consequence of this militancy was the attraction of many union members to the Labour Party who might not have been converted by the political activities of the Party alone. At the same time there was an unprecedented rise in trade-union membership.

TABLE 6

Trade Union Membership, 1910–14[53]

Year	Membership in millions	% Rate of Increase
1910	2·565	–
1911	3·139	22·5
1912	3·416	8·8
1913	4·135	21·0
1914	4·145	–

The extraordinary growth of the trade unions during the war is well known. Their growth before 1914 has been less often noticed; yet, for example, there was no year during or after the First World War in which the relative rise in union membership equalled that between 1910 and 1911.[54] For the Labour Party the industrial disturbances of the immediate pre-war years were probably less significant than the enrolment of nearly 2,000,000 more workers, many of whom were not on the electoral rolls until 1918, into the trade-unions, for the trade-unions had their own political party.

[53] B. R. Mitchell and P. Deane, *Abstract of British Historical Statistics* (Cambridge, 1962), p. 68.
[54] See below, p. 240.

Finally, it must be emphasized that Labour was operating on the basis of a highly restrictive franchise, and one which was probably peculiarly unfavourable to it. It is difficult for a mass working-class party to be politically successful when about half the working-class is voteless.[55] Thus the constant extension of organization—particularly the attempts to make trades councils do serious political work—was designed to, and did, yield electoral dividends in the future. Furthermore, the Liberals were aware that any substantial increase in the electorate could work to their disadvantage and to the advantage of Labour.[56] This, not surprisingly, helped to delay the long-promised franchise bill and to prolong the delicate and impermanent equilibrium upon which 'progressive' politics was founded.

The case that the Labour Party was a declining force is, therefore, difficult to argue successfully. Likewise it is hard to see how an electoral agreement with the Liberals could have been concluded. The Labour movement in the country could now scarcely have swallowed it, and there was no sign that, apart from MacDonald, any Labour leader seriously favoured one. In any case, there was no real evidence that the Liberals were willing partners. Their leaders, no doubt, would not have rejected Labour overtures out of hand, but many local Liberal associations would have done so. It was these things that made MacDonald's position so difficult, for the public espousal of a policy that was becoming increasingly repugnant to many in the Labour movement contributed to the increasing unpopularity of his leadership which was so obvious in 1914. Hardie or Henderson would probably have found leading the Labour Party as awkward as he did, but it is true that for MacDonald more than for them the war came just in time.

[55] See N. Blewett, 'The Franchise in the United Kingdom, 1885–1914,' *Past and Present*, 32 (1965).
[56] Pelling, Popular Politics, p. 119.

WAR AND THE NEW SOCIAL ORDER
1914–1918

1. *1914–1917*

MACDONALD and his critics had no further opportunity to engage before he retired from the field: the German invasion of Belgium converted the Labour movement to a vigorous, though not uncritical, prosecution of the war. The hastily organized 'peace protest committee' overnight became the War Emergency Workers' National Committee,[1] and MacDonald, unwilling to lead a party so committed to the war, resigned the parliamentary chairmanship on the night of 5–6 August. His successor, Henderson, like MacDonald, believed that it was necessary for Germany to be defeated, but was (also like MacDonald), in fact, ambiguous in his attitude to the war, and this ambiguity became more obvious as time passed. Though MacDonald was by no means ejected from the Party's affairs—that was a romantic invention—it is true that those decisions that ultimately gave the Labour Party its independence were, for the most part, made by others.

On the whole, the people who dominated the Labour Party at the outbreak of the war still did so at its end. There was no concerted move to the left and none of that confusion and reshuffling of the sort that Annie Kriegel has noticed in French socialism.[2] Everyone was more or less affected by wartime collectivism; even those unions suspicious of the state were impressed by its power. The trade unions, taken in the mass, were readier to throw their full weight behind the Party than they had been in 1914. But this was a paradoxical business. The Miners, for example, though notoriously patriotic, refused to sign the Treasury agreement of 1915,[3] while other unions, less enthusiastic for the war, signed the agreement and were more reluctant to strike. Similarly, throughout the war the left was divided and defensive, while the patriotic right was self-confident and more or

---

[1] This Committee was established partly to relieve unemployment and distress, which it was supposed would follow the outbreak of war, and partly to ensure that Labour would have some say in wartime social policy. See Royden Harrison, 'The War Emergency Workers' National Committee, 1914–1920', in A. Briggs and J. Saville (eds.), *Essays in Labour History, 1886–1923* (London, 1971), pp. 211–16.

[2] A. Kriegel, *Aux origines du Communisme français* (Paris, 1964).

[3] See H. M. Pelling, *A History of British Trade Unionism* (London, 1963), pp. 151–2.

less united. There was a consistent attack by the right against the left
within the unions and by the unions against the socialists within the
Party. Despite a couple of notable defeats this attack was largely
successful.

Within a few days of the outbreak of war the Labour Party went on
quarter-time. The national agent, Peters, joined the recruiting
campaign and took much of the Party's organization with him.
Henderson entered the government in May 1915 and from then until
the middle of 1917 Party affairs were of secondary interest to him.
Between August 1914 and August 1917 Labour was involved in only
three by-elections. Two were held unopposed under the Party truce,[4]
and one, Merthyr, Keir Hardie's old seat, was lost to an independent
patriotic miner after a divisive campaign.[5] Political work in the
constituencies slowed down steadily, and financial grants to constituency parties, a good index of local activity, fell continuously from
1915 to 1917.[6]

Head Office did its best under difficult circumstances. In February
1915 the two Party organizers were instructed to resume normal
duties and in the following year they moved to London where, it was
held, they would be more effective.[7] Henderson's pre-1914 reforms
worked themselves out haphazardly. The formation of new parties
continued, while the selection of new candidates, particularly from
the Miners' Federation, slowly increased the total. The number of
professional agents appointed under the 1912 scheme increased from
seventeen in that year to eighty in 1918, and for the first time a
substantial number of constituencies were organized in a more or less
full-time way.

No one at the time took much notice of organizational matters.
Leaving aside the great industrial disputes on Clydeside and in other
centres of heavy engineering (simply because we cannot say what
they meant in the evolution of the Labour movement's policies),[8]

---

[4] Bolton and Sheffield Attercliffe.

[5] The Merthyr by-election (Nov. 1915) was won by C. B. Stanton. The Labour candidate
was James Winstone of the South Wales Miners, who had narrowly defeated Stanton for the
nomination after three ballots. Stanton thereupon resigned as miners' agent in the constituency, stood himself, and defeated Winstone by 10,286 to 6,080. Stanton had much
support from patriotic trade-unionists and the newly formed British Workers' League.
For the by-election, see J. O. Stubbs, 'Lord Milner and Patriotic Labour', *English Historical
Review*, 87 (Oct. 1972), p. 723.

[6] 1915—£810; 1916—£725; 1917—£590.

[7] 'NEC', 2 Dec. 1916.

[8] For the best account, see Iain McLean, 'The Labour Movement in Clydeside Politics,
1914–1922', Oxford D.Phil., 1971; also James Hinton, 'The Clyde Workers' Committee and
the Dilution Struggle', in Briggs and Saville, pp. 152–84. Even Dr. Hinton, a historian
normally sympathetic to the class struggle, is forced to conclude that 'the revolutionaries
could not escape entanglement in the protective reflexes of the craftsmen . . .' (p. 184).

the war was an obsessive interest. Most, other than those whom Royden Harrison has called the 'super patriots', were usually confused in their attitudes, and it is too easy to say that the unions supported the war and the socialists did not. The British Socialist Party, for example, was rabidly jingoistic, while the Amalgamated Society of Engineers, a great and militant union, was genuinely divided.

Yet it is true that the unions tended to support Labour's representation in a coalition government and the I.L.P. tended to oppose it. This put the I.L.P. in difficulties, since its place in the Labour Party always depended on the goodwill or the indifference of the unions. Indeed, ever since the formation of the old Labour Representation Committee the numbers and wealth of the unions might have overwhelmed the I.L.P. Furthermore, opposition within the unions to socialists, if not necessarily to socialism, never far below the surface before 1914, was inflamed by the war. The disintegration of the Liberal Party further complicated the I.L.P.'s position. The appearance in the Labour movement, via the I.L.P., of a number of former Liberal radicals, often of middle- and upper-class origin, merely exaggerated the class-consciousness of some of the union leaders and damned the I.L.P. even more in their eyes.

The right mounted its offensive, first in the T.U.C., and then in the Party. The 1916 T.U.C. was wrecked by a first attempt—led by Williams of the Musicians, Davis of the Brassworkers, and Havelock Wilson of the Seamen—to form a specifically trade-union Labour Party. The attempt failed, yet it was more than a straw in the wind.[9] It came at a time when opponents of the war or of wartime policies were creating organizations which crossed party boundaries and which to more suspicious Labour leaders seemed to threaten familiar political demarcations. Yet if a root-and-branch onslaught of the type wanted by the jingoes could be resisted, a movement to strengthen the unions at the expense of the socialists clearly had much more support.

At the Party conference of January 1917 the unions combined to force a change in the method of electing the national executive. This had always been a weapon in their armoury, even if an unused one. Until 1917 each section of the Party elected its own members to the executive: thus the I.L.P. elected the I.L.P. members, the unions union members, etc. Now the Railway Clerks, supported by the Miners, proposed that all members of the executive should be elected by the whole conference voting as a single constituency, a change which would allow the unions to determine the membership of the executive. There is no doubt what the amendment was to do: to exclude those

[9] In the following argument I have been much helped by an unpublished paper on the 1918 constitution of the Labour Party by A. F. Thompson of Wadham College, Oxford.

I.L.P.ers whose policies both to the war and to socialism the unions found unacceptable. Henderson, who was at this moment ideologically disposed to the Railway Clerks, still begged the conference not to accept an amendment of such 'a drastic character'. It was, however, narrowly passed, by 1,123,000 to 1,107,000, and the majority might have been larger if Henderson had not been so unenthusiastic.[10]

On the eve of the revolution in Russia, therefore, and after two and a half years of a catastrophic war that showed no sign of ending, the political balance within the Labour movement seemed actually to be shifting to the right; the predominance of the patriots was unchallenged, and it was they rather than their opponents, who were making the running.[11]

2. The 1918 Constitution and the Socialist Objective

And yet, within a year, Henderson was out of the government, the Labour movement had agreed to meet German socialists in Stockholm, and the Labour Party had committed itself to the nationalization of the means of production, distribution, and exchange. How is this remarkable development to be explained? More particularly, how is clause IV, the socialist objective, to be explained?[12] Part of the answer is to be found, not in clause IV itself, but in the circumstances in which the constitution was written and passed. It is easy to be over-impressed with the socialist objective and to be unconcerned with the corpus of the 1918 constitution, whose uncharacteristic adornment clause IV was. That constitution embodied not an ideology but a system by which power in the Labour Party was distributed.

The real problem is not what is in the constitution, but why it came when it did. To a degree it was forced on the Labour Party. The war and the disruption of international socialism had landed the British Labour Party in a position it had not held before. Largely owing to the numerical strength—and to the wealth—of the British

---

[10] *Conference Report*, 1917, pp. 137–8.

[11] Mr. David Marquand discusses wartime policies extensively in his forthcoming biography of Ramsay MacDonald; I hope to do the same, from a different view, in my own biography of Arthur Henderson.

[12] There is a substantial literature on the socialist objective. Eldon Barry (*Nationalisation in British Politics* (London, 1965) puts clause IV in a unique British tradition of nationalization; Professor Beer (S. H. Beer, *Modern British Politics* (London, 1969), pp. 137–52) argues that clause IV was functional to the Labour Party's independence, though he suggests that it is also an affirmation of the Party's moral purpose. Royden Harrison, (loc. cit., pp. 211–59), and J. M. Winter ('The Development of British Socialist Thought', Ph.D. dissertation, Cambridge, 1970, pp. 189–245) have pointed to agencies such as the War Emergency Workers' National Committee which, they suggest, were responsible for developing a more or less specific socialist programme acceptable to the Labour leadership. Finally, Professor Miliband, *marxisant* if not Marxist (*Parliamentary Socialism* (London, 1964), pp. 60–2), argues that clause IV was the figleaf of Labourism, the first of a number of reformist treacheries.

N.B. not idealistic but practical

trade-unions, the Labour Party found itself willy-nilly the leading 'Allied' socialist party and the rock upon which European social democracy was already building its fortress against Bolshevism. Consequently, it appeared necessary to construct a political party appropriate to this industrial support.

As Dr. Winter has pointed out, Henderson's visit to Russia in 1917 convinced him that a powerful parliamentary and socialist alternative to Bolshevism was immediately required, and one that would meet the needs of the new 'democratic consciousness' of the masses.[13] Yet at the same time it is possible to exaggerate the extent to which Henderson was (so to say) converted to socialism while in Russia. There, after all, people had been 'permeated by pacifist theories', and the articles 'that appear in some of the papers read by the working classes are of a most destructive character'. As for socialism,

The men are not content with asking for reasonable advances ... but their demands are so extravagant that it is obvious that they are prompted not so much with [sic] a desire for economic improvement as to secure a complete change in the control of industry. They want to introduce a form of syndicalism, to place Directors and Managers in a subordinate position and the supreme control in the hands of the workpeople themselves. So far as I have been able to see if the experiment is tried, it can only have results that will be disaster to the whole concern.[14]

Fear of Bolshevism and the extreme left throughout Europe was almost certainly a preliminary to the new constitution, and international developments were the occasion for its drafting; it was, that is to say, written immediately upon Henderson's resignation from the government.[15] But fear of Bolshevism and the needs of international socialism were arguments that could go only so far with the unions. Henderson rather appealed to their self-esteem : he noted the immense advance made by the unions in size and importance. They had felt the powers of the state, now they must be able to control the state. He argued that there could be no going back to 1914, that only the Labour movement could consolidate wartime gains and supervise postwar reconstruction. Above all, he reminded his audience that the Representation of the People Act, in whatever final form it took, made reorganization necessary as the existing structure of the Party would be unable to cope with the new voters.[16]

[13] J. M. Winter, 'Arthur Henderson, the Russian Revolution and the Reconstruction of the Labour Party', *Historical Journal*, 15, 4 (1972), pp. 753–73.
[14] Henderson to T. W. Dowson, 19 June 1917, 'LPLF: HP/HEN/1/30'.
[15] For this, see C. F. Brand, *British Labour's Rise to Power* (London, 1941), passim.
[16] For the Act and its consequences, see D. E. Butler, *The Electoral System in Britain, 1918–1951* (Oxford, 1953), pp. 12–13. The electorate increased from 8,357,648 in 1915 to 21,932,322 in 1918.

None of these had much to do with socialism as a coherent programme, except in so far as collectivism is a sort of socialism. In the same way, socialism was remarkable for its absence in the presentation and drafting of the constitution. Henderson did nothing until he had the consent of the unions. On 6 September 1917 he addressed a joint meeting of the T.U.C.'s parliamentary committee (its executive body) and the national executive of the Party. It was a long and apparently difficult interview.[17] Some of the unions were as reluctant as ever to change the Party's structure. They were still suspicious of individual membership and feared that the establishment of local parties (both of which Henderson proposed) would strike at their own authority in the Party. A programme was not discussed but Henderson harped on the Representation of the People Act and Labour's electoral weaknesses. In the end it was agreed that he should be allowed to draft 'Reorganisation proposals *consequent upon the passing of the Representation of the People Bill*'.[18] Only a couple of weeks later was Middleton able to inform the Scottish secretary, Ben Shaw, 'that Mr. Henderson is now coming back to work steadily at the Office and is this week engaged in preparing a memorandum on Party re-organisation for discussion at our Executive next week'.[19]

Between then and 16 October, the date on which the first draft was circulated, Henderson saw much of Fabians, guild socialists, and sympathetic civil servants he had met while in office. Tom Jones records that on the evening of 10 October 'Henderson, Mallon,[20] Mary Macarthur, Middleton, Cole and, I think, W. C. Anderson met and talked over the re-organisation of the Labour Party on a constituency basis'. According to Jones (second-hand from Mallon) Henderson thought it 'should be possible to run about 200 candidates and steal the Government's thunder'.[21] It is unlikely that Henderson was thinking in such modest terms: 200 is not much more than Labour would have contested in any case. More probable, surely, is what Henderson told C. P. Scott. They 'might run as many as 500 candidates now that members were paid and election costs so greatly reduced as they were under the [Representation of the People Act]'.[22]

While these meetings certainly talked about a new programme, most of the discussion seems to have been about organizational questions. After the gathering of 10 October, Mallon told Jones that

[17] 'NEC', 6 Sept. 1917.
[18] My italics.
[19] Middleton to Shaw, 17 Sept. 1917, 'LPLF: Uncat. Scotland'.
[20] J. J. Mallon (1880–1968), at the board of trade and ministry of reconstruction, later warden of Toynbee Hall. Prominent Fabian and Labour candidate for Saffron Walden, 1918.
[21] R. K. Middlemas (ed.), *Thomas Jones' Whitehall Diary* (London, 1969), i, pp. 36–7.
[22] T. Wilson (ed.), *The Political Diaries of C. P. Scott, 1911–1928* (London, 1970), p. 317.

'there is some chance now of the trade unionists and the co-operators really joining up into a new political formation. The name suggested . . . was the People's Party.' The influence of this *équipe* is not hard to detect in Henderson's remark to Scott that his policy 'was to enlarge the bounds of the Labour Party and bring in the intellectuals as candidates. The Labour Party had been too short on brains.'[23]

Henderson presented a memorandum to a meeting of the national executive on 26 September. It proposed

> the re-organisation of the Party with a view to a wider extension of membership, the strengthening and development of local parties in the constituencies, together with the promotion of a larger number of candidates, and the suggestion that a Party programme be adopted.[24]

A sub-committee was appointed 'to consider details'. Its membership is worth noting. It consisted of Purdy of the Shipwrights and chairman of the Party, MacDonald, Henderson, W. C. Robinson of the Textile Workers, W. H. Hutchinson of the Engineers, Egerton Wake, a Party organizer, Sidney Webb, and G. J. Wardle (Railway Servants), who was a member of the government. There was an entrenched majority of unionists, and once again, as with the discussions of the preceding month or so, the I.L.P. was effectively excluded. Wake, though a pacifist and I.L.P.er, was now a Party organizer, very much Henderson's man, and in no way represented the interests of the I.L.P. Wardle's position was obscure : he was a 'super patriot' and drifting away from the Labour Party, but in so far as he had influence at all, it was not on the side of socialism.

On 16 October the first draft of the constitution was circulated to the full national executive, together with the 'model rules' for the new divisional Labour parties. Now there was not much in the draft that was very novel, or very surprising. Middleton told Ben Shaw that it incorporated those ideas that had been commonplace in the Party for the last couple of years[25]—but their ancestry was older even than that. The draft had four main provisions : individual membership of the Party, the establishment of new divisional parties and the amalgamation of trades councils with existing parties (these two complemented each other), the election of the national executive by the whole conference voting as a single constituency (with unions voting as an undivided unit—the 'block vote'), and, finally, the socialist objective.

As a notion, individual membership was not new. The national

---

[23] *Political Diaries of C. P. Scott*, 11–12 Dec. 1917, p. 316.
[24] 'NEC', 26 Sept. 1917.
[25] Middleton to Shaw, 17 Sept. 1917, 'LPLF: Uncat. Scotland'.

executive had attempted unsuccessfully to introduce it in 1912.[26] But whereas in that year there was only a rather confused recommendation for 'central office associates', now individual members were to be a basic constituent of a system of branch parties and were to join the local party through a ward association. But, of course, the evolution of ward associations before 1914 almost predetermined their reorganization in this way.[27]

The model rules were a formalized version of what had been the practice in most constituencies before 1914. There is no evidence to suggest that Henderson turned to his own party at Barnard Castle for inspiration. The new parties, like the old, were to be founded on the ward associations, and the latter were to be comprised, as they had been hitherto, of all members of affiliated societies and all individuals living in the ward. What had in the past been connived at, it was now proposed to make legal. Management of the divisional party was to be in the hands of a general committee of four sections: representatives of affiliated unions, of other societies eligible for affiliation, individual members, and a women's section. The general management committee was an innovation.

The decision to exclude industrial trades councils from affiliation and to encourage the amalgamation of trades councils with local parties also only confirmed years of development. It had always been the hope of Head Office that amalgamations could be arranged, if only for bureaucratic reasons of efficiency and convenience. In practice, amalgamation was exceptionally difficult: either the affiliation was simply transferred to the local party, or else the councils were so tenacious in defence of their political rights that Head Office caved in completely.

After the outbreak of war, and perhaps with an eye to later reorganization, the national executive again began to insist on amalgamation—with no more success than before.[28] But 'unity of the movement' was one of the voguish enthusiasms of the hour. Webb justified amalgamation by claiming that until now the Labour Party had been 'too centralised' (he meant too dependent on London). To be a majority in the country, he said, it was necessary to have strong

[26] In May 1911 the national executive asked Clynes, Tom Fox, and W. C. Robinson to examine whether 'individual membership is practicable'. People eligible for such membership might be 'managers, foremen, persons engaged in commercial pursuits on their own account'. Branch parties clearly were contemplated, but dismissed on the grounds that they would not harmonize 'with the other constituent parts of the Party'. Instead, the executive was asked to permit individuals to join as 'central office associates'. ('NEC', 26 July 1911.) At the 1912 conference the unions and the I.L.P. united to defeat the scheme. (*Conference Report*, 1912, pp. 92-4.)
[27] See above, p. 7.
[28] See McKibbin, 'Evolution of a National Party', p. 196.

constituency organizations; therefore, the 'local Labour party and the trades council everywhere should become one body, with separate sides for political and industrial work'.[29] But it was going to be difficult, if not impossible, to impose the model rules on amalgamated parties, and the attempt to shift the foundations of local organization from the trade unions to the amalgamated parties could never succeed so long as the unions remained as preponderant in the constituencies as they were.[30]

Finally, there was the socialist objective.[31] In Henderson's original draft[32] clause IV (or Party Objects 'd') was as follows:

To secure for the producers by hand or brain the full fruits of their industry by the Common Ownership of all monopolies and essential Raw Materials;
alternatively
To secure for the producers by hand or brain the full fruits of their industry, and the most equitable distribution thereof that may be possible, upon the basis of the Common Ownership of the Means of Production and the best obtainable system of popular administration and control of each industry or service.

The first alternative is almost certainly Henderson's: it bears the stamp of conventional trade-union attitudes.[33] The second would appear to be Webb's, especially if it is coupled with the almost redundant clause V (Party Objects 'e').[34] It certainly sounds like Webb, but does not sound like Henderson, and in the end it was adopted, though why, the minutes of the national executive do not say.

Then how did clause IV get there? Inevitably, for a number of reasons. The Party was committed to a 'programme', and clauses IV and V, though by no means prescriptions for political action, indicated the direction of the programme and offered the electorate a doctrine differentiated from that of the other parties. Further, the socialist objective served the useful purpose, as Beer has suggested, of sharpening the break between the Labour and Liberal Parties. Finally, clause IV, precisely because of its vagueness and lack of rigour

[29] 'Minutes of Conference on the Organization of Trades Councils and Local Labour Parties, 16 March, 1918', 'L.S.E. Passfield Papers: Miscellaneous Unnumbered'.

[30] See below, pp. 131–6.

[31] Strictly, the method of electing the national executive was also new. But that had been forced on Henderson by the 1917 conference.

[32] Filed as 'NEC', 16 Oct. 1917.

[33] Dr. Winter, however, thinks that the monopolies alternative was devised by Webb since it closely follows the 'Conscription of Riches' programme. The second, he argues, is Hyndman's. (Winter, 'Development of British Socialist Thought', p. 270.) This seems to me unlikely on two grounds. First, as A. F. Thompson points out (MS., p. 14), 'monopoly' was an 'old enemy' of Henderson's. He had long regarded the nationalization of 'monopoly' as more than a half-way solution to the social problem. Second, there is no evidence that Hyndman took any part at all in the preliminaries to the drafting of the constitution, still less the drafting itself.

[34] Generally 'to promote the Political, Social and Economic emancipation of the People, and more particularly of those who depend [on] hand or . . . brain for the means of life'.

(1) ∴ conscious
     ∴ expanded appeal to electorate - Henderson wanted
                              to do this edict

THE 1918 CONSTITUTION   97

paradoxically had an umbrella function: it was an acceptable formula
in a Party where there was otherwise little doctrinal agreement.

On the other hand, there were narrowly electoral reasons for
choosing Webb's alternative. Henderson had already told Middleton
that he did not care one way or the other.[35] Nevertheless, he was under
heavy pressure from Webb, Cole, Mallon, and others, and they would
certainly have argued for the 'common ownership of the means of
production'. This, they suggested, would be electorally popular, not
because the working classes had become socialist (that was undetermined, and they would probably support Labour in any case) but
because an important section of the middle classes had. It was always
fundamental to Fabian thought that the professional and salaried
managerial classes (the *nouvelle couche sociale*—a phrase borrowed from
Léon Gambetta, of all people) were socialist by class interest as much
as the proletariat; indeed, the Fabians were probably more interested
in them than they were in the proletariat.[36] The Fabians, and many
of the guild socialists as well, were convinced that the war had finally
revealed to these classes where their real allegiances ought to lie. For
their part, the Webbs did their best to bring the Labour Party and the
professional associations together,[37] and not the least remarkable
feature of Labour's electoral programme in 1918 was the lavish baits
to the middle classes which it contained. The socialist objective was
thus implanted into the constitution partly as a sop to the professional
bourgeoisie: that this was so helps to explain why the trade unions
swallowed it as easily as they did.

Likewise, the apparently surprising absence of discussion of doctrine
and policy throughout the debates on the constitution suggest what
secondary importance its programmatic clauses had. The minutes of
the national executive, derelict in recording clause IV, record, on the
other hand, every amendment to the draft's structural provisions and
endless discussion about the Party's electoral procedures. What was of

[35] Middleton to Shaw, 2 Nov. 1917, 'LPLF: Uncat. Scotland'.
[36] See A. Oldfield, 'The Labour Party and Planning—1934, or 1918?', *Society for the
Study of Labour History Bulletin*, 25 (1972), p. 53.
[37] Of which, surely, the most amusing and characteristic is Beatrice's intervention on
behalf of the B.M.A. On 9 Feb. 1918 she wrote to Middleton: 'I think Sidney reported to
Mr. Henderson that I had seen Dr. Cox, the Secretary of the British Medical Association . . .
I found him somewhat hurt that the B.M.A.—which considers itself the democratic organization of the Medical Profession had not in any way been recognized by the Labour Party
with regard to the organization of their own service. He said that on seeing the report of
the interview with the State Medical Association ("representing a very small and unin-
fluential and somewhat aristocratic section of the profession") he had written to Mr.
Henderson asking that a deputation from the B.M.A. might be heard. I am certain that,
in view of the next election and also from the standpoint of the Labour Party's principles
of Trade Unionism the B.M.A. ought to be heard.' (Beatrice Webb to Middleton, 9 Feb. 1918,
'LPLF: Uncat., JSM Misc.'.)

first importance was who elected whom to the national executive. That was also the I.L.P.'s order of priority. For twenty years its pedagogic aim had been to teach the Labour movement socialism, yet it was inflexibly opposed to a constitution that, formally at least, committed the Labour Party to just that. But the I.L.P. had long seen that a nominal adherence to socialism in no way diminished the power of the predominantly anti-socialist unions within the Party. After their successful amendment to the constitution in 1917, MacDonald told Webb that the unions were a 'terrible incubus' on the Party, and that the present organization 'failed totally to represent the rank and file'.[38] When he was appointed to the reorganization subcommittee in September, MacDonald actually presented an alternative draft. His, he noted in his diary, would make the Party 'more responsive to genuine political impulses'; the 'tyranny' of the block vote had 'become intolerable'.[39] On 9 October, he dismissed Henderson's draft, that is to say the one that included clause IV, as 'in spirit and in grasp just an election agent's document'.[40] Like the unions, the I.L.P. seems to have concluded that the composition of the national executive was the heart of the constitution. Jowett and Anderson attempted to restore sectional voting for the executive, but their amendment was defeated by five to four.[41] After that failure, and a number of successful organizational amendments, the new constitution was ready for publication.

As early as 16 October the national executive had, unusually, given Henderson 'plenary powers' in the presentation of the constitution,[42] and in November he went to the country. In practice, as the schedules show,[43] Henderson devoted himself almost entirely to those areas and unions where opposition might have been expected. Even before delegates assembled for the January 1918 conference it was clear that, though the majority of trade unionists were probably in favour of a new constitution, they were not united in favour of this one. Disapproval came most strongly from the great Lib–Lab unions: all those unions, plus a few others, where opposition to socialists was most strong. Henderson's propagandist tours concentrated on the mining districts—not merely because the miners were undecided about the constitution but because a large number of Labour candidatures was

---

[38] Sidney to Beatrice Webb, 23 Jan. 1917, 'Passfield Papers: Correspondence, II. 3. (i)'.
[39] Marquand, ch. X, p. 55.
[40] Ibid.
[41] 'NEC', 16–17 Oct. 1917. Apart from mover and seconder, the other two supporters of the amendment were MacDonald certainly, and probably Webb. (See Webb, *The New Constitution of the Labour Party*, p. 4.)
[42] 'NEC', 16 Oct. 1917.
[43] They are filed as 'NEC', 15 Nov. 1917.

involved—and on textile Lancashire. Places that might be awkward in principle, like London and Glasgow, also received more than their fair share of attention.[44] The tours were, therefore, highly and carefully selective.

To his audiences Henderson spoke about socialism not at all. He talked about how Labour might become a government, not about what a Labour government might do. His emphasis consistently was on the electoral needs of the Party. Individual membership and branch parties, he said, were both made necessary by the Representation of the People Act. At a lower though no doubt more heartfelt level, he warned them of Lloyd George's guile, and of the threat from the extreme left. He conceded the block vote and assured the unions that the socialists could not dominate the reorganized Party.

According to Henderson, the constitution's reception was almost universally favourable. In Manchester the draft was 'very favourably received'; at Bristol it was 'very cordially received'; at Cardiff it was 'well received'. Everywhere the results seem to have been 'very satisfactory' or 'successful'. Requests to the Miners and Textile Workers for more parliamentary candidates were also 'favourably received'. Yet there was evidence everywhere that enough of the important unions had not been persuaded. The Miners were wavering, and with their traditions that is not surprising. The *Cotton Factory Times*, the organ of the Textile Workers, dismissed the safeguards of the unions' position as 'totally inadequate'.[45] As conference amendments and resolutions came in it was obvious that the class-conscious unions were preparing themselves against a putative army of middle-class socialists. They attacked a draft constitution which had apparently committed the Labour Party to socialism on the ground that its executive might, at some time in the future, be controlled by socialists.

Even before the conference opened at Nottingham on 23 January 1918, Henderson knew that the draft would be lucky to get through. A couple of days earlier Beatrice Webb found him 'nervous about the rejection of his new constitution by the block vote [*sic*] of the big unions'.[46] On the eve of the conference Smillie told him privately that the Miners would move the reference back of the constitution.[47]

Henderson opened the debate with a long and predictable speech, which more or less repeated everything he had said on tour.[48] Smillie immediately moved the reference back. His position as both an

[44] For London, see *London Labour Chronicle*, Dec. 1917; for Glasgow, Glasgow Labour Party, 'Minutes', 10 Nov. 1917.
[45] *Cotton Factory Times*, 26 Oct. 1917.
[46] B. Webb, *Diaries, 1912–1924*, p. 106.
[47] 'NEC', 23 Jan. 1918.
[48] For the debate, see *Conference Report*, January 1918, pp. 98–104.

I.L.P.er and as president of the greatest of the Lib–Lab unions was an embarrassing one. He had no criticism of substance ('he would admit the truth of every word that Mr. Henderson said') but pleaded for more time to consider the draft. He was seconded by J. W. Ogden of the Textile Workers, who thought it was a matter of 'procedure'. A. G. Walkden also supported Smillie: he was worried about the membership of the national executive and was anxious that the industrial worker should not be overlooked.

But there was real hostility to the constitution as well. Sexton of the Liverpool Dockers claimed that the only thing left was the name of the Labour Party. He said that there were already enough avenues of entry for the middle classes (and if that was not enough 'there was still the brains of the movement in the Fabian Society'). There were too many cranks within the Party as it was: 'the cranks of the U.D.C. and the Council of Civil Liberties avowedly opposing the policy of the Labour Party'. Tom Shaw of the Textile Workers, a powerful union official indeed, joined Sexton in baiting the middle classes: he wanted to see the Party grow in 'a safe way, not by attracting every disgruntled Liberal and Tory they could find'. He was, he said, 'doing local political work when Mr. Henderson was gaining his valuable experience in the Liberal Party'.[49]

As was half expected the constitution was referred back, though only narrowly—1,337,000 to 1,318,000. The conference then adjourned for a month. In the interim the executive made three changes to the draft. Of most importance was the increase in the number of representatives from 'the affiliated organizations' (i.e. the unions) on the national executive from eleven to thirteen. It was hoped (successfully) to convince the unions they could then always outvote bourgeois socialists, who might, one supposes, just conceivably hold the remaining ten seats. The two other changes were comparatively minor ones, but had the same purpose. The parliamentary party (a union-dominated one so it was expected) was to be associated with the formulation of electoral policy, while individual Labour candidates could depart only slightly from the general electoral programme of the Party.

These concessions satisfied the Miners, and their executive approved the constitution on 25 February; the Engineers declared their support on the same day.[50] When the resumed conference met, approval was, therefore, assured more or less from the beginning. The opposition

---

[49] He was unkindly, though significantly, referring to the time when Henderson was agent for Sir Joseph Pease, Liberal Member for Barnard Castle.

[50] *Daily News*, 26 Feb. 1918. Because of wartime paper restrictions there is no official report of the resumed conference. The following account is based on reports in *The Times*, *Daily News*, and *Daily Telegraph*.

was the same as before, with the addition of the I.L.P. But the I.L.P.s tactics had been misconceived in every way. It had denounced the draft while Henderson had been parading it before the movement at the end of 1917; it had supported the draft at the first conference to spite the Miners and the Textile Workers; it then published a wordy resolution for the adjourned conference rejecting the constitution in terms designed to catch the votes of the Lib–Lab unions, and withdrew the resolution when the Miners announced that they had changed their minds.[51]

They first attempted to undo the block vote.[52] Henderson ('as restrained as the chairman of a railway company') protested that to carry such an amendment would be 'to drive a wedge into every union'.[53] The motion was defeated by 1,600,000 to 757,000, showing that there was some union support for it. The second amendment, to restore the right of the socialist societies to elect their own representatives to the national executive, was more heavily defeated (for obvious reasons)—1,839,000 to 345,000.

Like the I.L.P., the Railway Clerks had rather held their fire in January. Now they went closer to joining the patriotic right. They had already circulated a letter to other unions reminding them that individuals would be represented on the executive quite out of proportion to their financial contributions, while the unions would, by the same terms, be grossly under-represented. The Railway Clerks were prepared to accept individual members, but not branch parties under any circumstances. They proposed, therefore, *ex post facto* sanction for what in practice already happened. They called on each local party 'to broaden its rules (where necessary) so as to provide for the admission of individual men and women', but asked conference 'to adhere to the existing constitution of the national party'.[54] This amendment, supported by Sexton of the Dockers, was defeated on a show of hands.

The national executive's amendments were rapidly approved. The change in the size of the new executive was carried without opposition, and the following day the executive formally instructed Head Office to arrange for the immediate formation of local parties in all constituencies and for the nomination of parliamentary candidates wherever they were wanted.[55]

It was widely agreed at the time that the acceptance of the new constitution had been a personal triumph for Henderson. So it was to an extent: since his resignation from the government he had led the

[51] *Daily Telegraph*, 26 Feb. 1918.
[52] Thus allowing minorities within unions to vote differently from majorities at conference.
[53] *Daily News*, 27 Feb. 1918.
[54] *Daily Telegraph*, 26 Feb. 1918.
[55] 'NEC', 27 Feb. 1918.

movement with skill and tact. But a close examination of the events of 1917–18 makes it clear that in all essentials the trade unions had their way. They accepted the socialist objective partly because they had always been collectivist, partly because they had advocated nationalization of specific industries even before the war, partly to indulge the Fabians, and partly because they did not think it mattered very much. They swallowed individual membership for electoral reasons and on the fair assumption that things at a local level would not in fact really change. But in the apparently crucial matter of election to the national executive they insisted on having their way.

Even then a number of unions were unappeased. Within the T.U.C. itself the patriotic right was as active as in 1916, and rather more successful. Williams, Davis, and Havelock Wilson resumed their offensive as soon as the constitution had been passed. In March–April 1918 Williams circulated proposals for a Trade Union Labour Party to be governed by the T.U.C. itself. Both the T.U.C. and the Labour Party took the proposal sufficiently seriously to issue a joint resolution in April 1918, which concluded that the 'formation of a Trade Union Labour Party . . . in our opinion is calculated to disrupt a Movement built up by years of sacrifice'. They asked 'those responsible' to 'discontinue such action' and they hoped that nothing more would be necessary 'to enforce that loyalty our Movement has a right to expect from those holding such responsible positions'.[56]

When the T.U.C. met at Derby in September 1918, W. J. Davis, not at all abashed, moved that the parliamentary committee 'be instructed to take steps necessary to establish a Trade Union Labour Party'. In spite of (or because of) a piece of rodomontade from Wilson, the proposal was defeated by 3,815,000 to 567,000.[57] This was certainly a decisive vote, but a proposal from George Isaacs of the Printers that would have grouped the unions affiliated to the Labour Party into a self-contained political federation mustered over one million votes. Cole is probably right in thinking that both Isaacs and Wilson would have had considerably more support had not sectional voting for the national executive not been abolished.[58]

Like Henderson, the unions had decided 'to stick by the Federation'.[59] But they did so in such a way as to increase their predominance within the reorganized Party. There was no chance that they would accept any other arrangement, for they had, unlike the labour move-

[56] See *Conference Report*, June 1918, p. 17.
[57] T.U.C., *Congress Report*, 1918, pp. 251–9.
[58] Cole, *History of the Labour Party*, p. 48.
[59] This was the phrase used by Henderson when he presented the constitution to the Jan. 1918 conference. They had 'stuck by the Federation' rather than founding the party anew purely on branches and individual membership.

ments in other parts of Europe, been scarcely affected at all by any clear urge to the left, and this showed itself both in the attitude of the parliamentary committee to the Labour Party and in the personnel of the committee itself. The one elected in 1918 was at least as patriotic as any elected before it, and perhaps slightly more so: Havelock Wilson, unsuccessful in 1916, completed a year of international triumphs by being elected to the committee. Its full membership was as follows:

J. H. Thomas (N.U.R.)	E. L. Poulton (Boot and Shoe)
H. Gosling (Watermen)	R. Walker (Agricultural Labourers' Union)
J. Ogden (Weavers)	W. J. Davis (Brassworkers)
W. Thorne (General Workers)	M. Bondfield (Shop Assistants)
A. Onions (Miners)	T. Greenall (Miners)
J. Hill (Boilermakers)	H. Wilson (Seamen)
J. Sexton (Dockers)	J. B. Williams (Musicians)
H. Skinner (Typographers)	G. Stuart-Bunning (Postmen)
	R. Shirkie (Colliery Enginemen)

Though Thomas, who headed the poll, had been judiciously neutral in his attitude to the war, this was as solid and as patriotic a committee as could have been elected before 1914. In addition to Wilson, the two other promoters of the Trade Union Labour Party, Williams and Davis, were elected, as was their most famous supporter, James Sexton. And the membership of this committee was a more important determinant of the Labour Party's development than the break-up of the Liberal Party, the Russian Revolution, the work of the Webbs, or, even, what Henderson thought he was doing in 1917.

Yet if the unions were not much interested in socialism, what were they interested in? The riveting nature of clause IV tends to take our eyes off the really important discussions of policy embodied in the twenty-six resolutions of June 1918.[60] These formed the basis of Labour policy at the 1918 election and at succeeding general elections. Three of them dealt with what might be called substantive matters of socialism, and they were contradictory. The first was merely an expression of collectivist goodwill. It demanded

the gradual building up of a new social order, based not on internecine conflict, inequality of riches and dominion over subject classes ... but on the deliberately planned co-operation in production and distribution and exchange, the sympathetic approach to a healthy equality, the widest possible participation in power, both economic and political, and the general consciousness of consent which characterise a true democracy.

The second theoretical resolution emerged, after amendment, as a

[60] For the resolutions and debate on them, see *Conference Report*, June 1918, pp. 43-79.

'socialist' one. As proposed by the executive it talked of the need for increased production by elimination of inefficiency and waste. On the motion of F. O. Roberts and Will Thorne it was amended to read by 'socialisation of industry'. But neither Roberts nor Thorne was an obvious candidate for socialist fire-eating: Thorne, though an old Social Democrat, was a notorious jingo during the war and a militant opponent of the socialist societies. In opposing the amendment, MacDonald protested that the twenty-six resolutions were only 'elaborate footnotes to the constitution', a dubious assertion, since the constitution, in effect, said nothing about what a Labour government would do. As amended, therefore, the resolution was clause IV rewritten.

It was the twenty-fourth resolution, passed unanimously, and significantly called 'Control of Capitalist Industry', that said something precise about the relationship between state and industry.

That the Conference insists . . . on the necessity of retaining after the war and of developing the present system of organising, controlling and auditing the processes, profits and prices of capitalist industry; that the economies of centralised purchasing of raw materials, foodstuffs and other imports must be continued, and, therefore, the 'rationing' of all establishments under collective control . . . that the 'costing' of manufacturers' processes and auditing of their accounts, so as to discover the necessary cost of production, together with the authoritative limitation of prices at the factory, the wholesale warehouse, is the only security against the extortion of profiteering; and that it is as much the duty of the Government to protect the consumer by limiting prices, as it is to protect the factory operative from unhealthy conditions, the householder from the burglar.

This was the authentic voice of wartime collectivism, with perhaps a note of pre-1914 'efficiency' as well. It influenced an untheoretical man like Henderson as much as anybody. In his letters from Russia, those which had so firmly dismissed revolution and extreme socialism, he concluded 'that the only salvation for industry, at all events for the period of the war is that the state should act as a buffer between two warring sections'. What was wanted was that 'industry should be controlled in the same way as we have controlled railways, mines, shipping, agriculture etc.'.[61] If collectivism amounted to not much more than preserving those controls established under emergency regulations, it was still a very considerable advance.

The other twenty-three resolutions were, practically, legislative items that would fill out a large number of King's speeches. These 'legislative' resolutions included the nationalization of coal, electricity, railways, canals, and land. (Sidney Webb also called the fifteenth

[61] For the letters, see above, p. 92; also Henderson in the *Observer*, 25 Nov. 1917.

resolution 'nationalization of education', but that tended to obscure rather than to clarify, since it fell far short of that.) The rest dealt with housing, social services, temperance, 'complete emancipation of women', conscription of wealth, etc. To a considerable degree, successive Labour governments have executed these resolutions. They have not brought about socialism, but then in 1918 few imagined that they would.

The unions had always in a general way been collectivist: the Webbs noticed this as early as 1894.[62] The importance of the war is not so much that it made the unions collectivist as that it made them more anxious that collectivism should find its way into legislation. This meant encouraging and using the Labour Party in a way they had not thought really necessary in 1914. In his presidential address to the 1917 T.U.C., John Hill of the Boilermakers put it thus: 'the prejudice of Trade Unionists against politics has hitherto held us back . . . but the events of the last three years have taken the scales from our eyes'. The man, he said, 'in our ranks to-day who is neither a Government official nor a member of some Government Committee is unknown to the movement'. In these circumstances, the 'best scheme of reconstruction' was a 'strong and intelligent Trade Unionism linked with our political arm, the Labour Party'.[63]

But as soon as the unions came to this conclusion, the old socialist societies, and particularly the I.L.P., were at a disadvantage. Not only had they lost political power, as it were, within the Party, but the Party itself now wished to discharge many of those functions they had come to consider their own. The I.L.P. quickly understood this and there was a good deal of talk about disaffiliation at its 1918 conference.[64] MacDonald expressed himself 'surprised by the strength of feeling in the I.L.P. that it can serve better outside'.[65] The I.L.P. did not disaffiliate and it could only make the best of the situation. MacDonald, with his sensitive nose for changes in the wind, gracefully adjusted himself to the new situation; he was put up to defend the muted socialism of the twenty-six resolutions and few other men were more implicated in the 1918 constitution and its consequences than he.[66]

Thus in Britain alone the left wing of the working-class movement did not emerge from the war in some way stronger than it entered it. It is true, certainly, that the unions disliked socialists more than they

[62] S. and B. Webb, *History of Trade Unionism* (London, 1894), p. 477.
[63] *Congress Report*, 1917, pp. 54–6.
[64] R. E. Dowse, 'The Independent Labour Party, 1918–1932' (Univ. of London Ph.D. thesis), pp. 20–6. Since published as *Left in the Centre* (London, 1966).
[65] R. T. McKenzie, *British Political Parties* (London, 1964), p. 481.
[66] For MacDonald's position, see McKibbin, 'Evolution of a National Party,' p. 221.

disliked socialism and it is true also that dislike of socialists was generated by a highly developed class-consciousness. Were socialists suspect because they were socialist or because they were supposedly not working class?—it is often hard to tell. But in a way the result was the same, and if the war did not necessarily mean the defeat of socialism in Britain, it did mean the defeat of the socialists.

3. *To the General Election of 1918*

The events of 1918 can for simplicity be divided into two. There were several months of electoral and political consolidation which followed the passing of the constitution and this period more or less concluded with the Party conference in June 1918. The second period began with the abandonment of the electoral truce and ended with the general election in December.

Although Henderson had flooded the national executive with memoranda on the complete reorganization of the Party's institutions from the end of 1917 on[67]—it is important to remember on what a wide front he was operating—it was the immediate electoral problems that were pressing. The national executive had, of course, decided on the night that the resumed conference had completed its work to take the plunge and to sanction candidates wherever local parties wanted them. Henderson, and most other members of the executive, thereupon went to the country explaining the constitution, arranging for the establishment of new local parties and the nomination of candidates.[68]

So far as candidates went, there was no difficulty in finding them and neither unions nor local parties needed much encouragement. Candidates for most of the northern industrial and mining seats had been sanctioned by May. It was not until August that the county constituencies (and boroughs like Birmingham where Labour was untypically weak) began to be sanctioned in large numbers. There were a few troublesome constituencies, but, outside the ministers' seats, they were surprisingly few.[69] In June Henderson told the Party conference that they had a total of 301 candidates, inquiries 'for something like another 100', and made it plain 'that they intended to impose no limit'.[70]

On paper the growth in the number of local bodies between 1916 and 1918 was very rapid. In 1916 there were 199 affiliated local bodies; by the middle of 1919 the number had reached 400. But it

[67] See below, pp. 206–21.
[68] For S.-W. Lancashire, for example, see Liverpool L.R.C., 'Minutes', 1 June 1918; *Liverpool Courier*, 3 June 1918.
[69] See McKibbin, 'Evolution of a National Party', pp. 217–18.
[70] *Conference Report*, June 1918, p. 27.

is likely that many of the new parties were formed for the immediate
purpose of running candidates at the forthcoming elections and were
not much more than old *ad hoc* ward associations.[71] Not that it made
much difference, this remained true for many years after 1918 as well.

Delegates at the June conference, however, were less interested in
these matters than in political developments. Henderson's resignation
from the government in August 1917 and the launching of the new
constitution six months later had put the Labour Party in a false
position. Henderson was succeeded in the war cabinet by Barnes, who
then, Lloyd George thought, 'had automatically been made Labour
leader'.[72] The seven other ministers remained in the government and
the coalition was preserved intact.

Yet their continued presence there became something of an
anomaly. Many of Henderson's most persuasive arguments during the
drafting and acceptance of the constitution had, after all, been aimed
at the coalition government, and he had made no secret of his own
views about coalitions or, at least, this particular coalition. Furthermore, the passing of the new constitution removed most of the last
restraints on local parties, who began to attack the ministers in their
own constituencies. Barnes had long been under fire in Glasgow
Gorbals, and although the executive managed to shield him for a time,
it was clear by June that he would not be renominated. As early as
May 1918 the Gorton Trades Council had nominated J. Binns of the
Engineers to replace John Hodge. He was saved only by the refusal of
the executive to sanction Binns and by his timely agreement to
resign from the coalition.[73] In Norwich, G. N. Roberts had been
repudiated by his Trades Council even by August 1917.[74] Of the
senior ministers, only Clynes escaped serious opposition.

The position of the ministers was worsened when the June conference decided to abandon the Party truce. It is not altogether clear
who was responsible for this decision. As the executive pointed out, the
truce had existed only informally since 31 December 1916 and its
observance was due merely to 'the circumstances of the times'.[75]
Thereafter, Head Office had been under some pressure to approve
by-election contests. There had been a few independent candidates,
usually styled 'Peace by Negotiation', and mostly run by local
branches of the I.L.P.[76]

---

[71] For details, see McKibbin, 'Evolution of a National Party', pp. 217–18.
[72] Or so A. J. P. Taylor tells us. (*English History, 1914–1945* (Oxford, 1965), p. 90.)
[73] 'NEC', 23 July 1918; 31 Oct. 1918.
[74] *Conference Report*, Jan. 1918, p. 35.
[75] *Conference Report*, June 1918, p. 35.
[76] In April 1918 the executive had been seriously divided over a contest in Keighley. The
local party had asked it to endorse William Bland: in the end, the executive refused and
Bland stood as a 'Peace by Negotiation' candidate. (*The Times*, 29 Apr. 1918).

At the beginning of May, Charles Fenwick, the sitting Lib–Lab M.P. for Wansbeck, died, and the Miners' Federation announced that they would endorse any candidate 'who might be selected by the Northumberland Miners to contest the by-election'. A rather laconic message to that effect was sent to Henderson a day or so after it had appeared in the press. The Miners took everyone by surprise. They had kept well clear of the 'Peace' candidates and they had just been involved in a wrangle with MacDonald over Dunfermline Burghs, as a result of which he was actually censured by the executive.[77] Their break with the truce was not, therefore, forced on them by the I.L.P.

The national executive was evenly divided about a contest.[78] When the executive met on 8 May it decided to take no action. However, the following day, after only a brief discussion, it decided to recommend to conference that the truce be abandoned, at any rate for by-elections.[79] Presumably the Miners' action impressed the Party. It was an excellent example of the unions 'taking politics seriously' in a way that was recommended to them at the 1917 T.U.C. And where the Miners, with their Lib–Lab traditions, led, the Labour Party could only follow. But the Party's action was consistent and intelligible. It had publicly assumed the role of alternative to the government and its leading non-ministerial members were increasingly critical of that government. The result of the Wansbeck by-election, which the Labour candidate, Ebenezer Edwards, lost by only 548,[80] seemed further to justify the executive's action.

This action was approved by the June conference, though the Labour ministers came out strongly against it.[81] In July they wrote a joint letter to the executive setting out their objections and protesting against attacks on them in their own constituencies.

The mandate given in 1916 [they said] and continually re-affirmed, places us

---

[77] MacDonald had publicly supported the candidature of Arthur Ponsonby, the sitting member, who had resigned from the Liberal Party and was seeking re-election as an independent. Unfortunately the Miners had decided to contest the seat and had already nominated a candidate. The Miners' Federation formally reported MacDonald to the executive (Ashton to Henderson, 15 Apr. 1918, 'LPLF: MacD. Uncat. Misc.') as did the Fyfe and Kinross Miners. MacDonald put the best gloss on his behaviour that he could, but he was censured by the executive nevertheless. ('NEC', 30 May 1918: MacDonald's statement is filed as 'LPLF: NEC/MacD. Uncat. Misc.'.) Henderson and MacDonald obviously had words. There is a typically feline entry in MacDonald's diary: 'Labour Party Exec. censured me for going to Dunfermline. Henderson gave vent to spleen and his display of vanity . . . and jealousy was crushingly painful.' (Marquand ch. X, p. 61.) MacDonald wrote to Ponsonby that the affair was a 'terrible revelation of the mind and spirit of sections of the Labour Party . . . I am ashamed of my friends'. (MacDonald to Ponsonby, (?)30 May 1918, 'Bodleian MS. Ponsonby.')

[78] 'NEC', 8 May 1918.

[79] 'NEC', 9 May 1918.

[80] The result was Coalition Liberal 5,815, Labour 5,267.

[81] See Cole, *History of the Labour Party*, p. 41.

under an obligation as members of a Coalition Ministry to assist the Government in every honourable way ... But the effective discharge of such an obligation must be seriously hampered if the resolution to end the Party Truce is translated into actual fact. It is impossible to give whole-hearted assistance to any Government while claiming the right to fight it at the same time.

They also claimed that they were being 'undermined' in their own seats and that they were victims of constant 'sniping'.[82] G. H. Roberts, whose position had certainly been undermined, accused the executive of being 'unable to discipline revolters against authority'. The result 'of this supineness is that in some constituencies the sections most loyal to the Party now claim ascendancy. In a vain attempt to conciliate them the Executive invite loyal members to commit political suicide.'[83]

On behalf of the executive Henderson replied with surprising sharpness: the executive had done 'everything possible to promote better relationships between the Labour Ministers and the local Labour Parties', and he claimed that 'the "sniping" which had been referred to so often had not been confined to one side'.[84] To Roberts, he said baldly that the situation in Norwich was his own fault.[85]

Yet for all this, the ministers' position was logical enough. The Labour Party could not reasonably fight the coalition at by-elections while many of its leading members held posts in it. In the general euphoria of the moment the ministers had been overlooked. Therefore, though the Party had done little else since January than prepare for the next election whenever it might come, in July there was a bout of hesitation. On 24 July, Henderson suddenly 'warned' the executive that an election would take place in the winter and spoke against it. He concluded that such an election would 'tend to divert public opinion in a most undesirable way'—in short, would be a khaki one.[86] But that it would be a khaki election was not unexpected; it was one that Labour had long ago resigned itself to fighting. It is likely that Henderson was less worried about fighting a khaki election than about fighting one without the Labour ministers. It was in the Party's interest to postpone an election until the ministers could legitimately be asked to resign. In the end, the executive decided that though an election was not actually desirable, there was no point in objecting if one were actually held.[87]

[82] 'NEC', 31 July 1918.
[83] Roberts to Henderson, (?)1 Aug. 1918, 'LPLF: Uncat. Misc.'
[84] Henderson to Labour Ministers, 1 Aug. 1918, 'LPLF: Uncat. Misc.'
[85] Henderson to Roberts, undated, filed as 'NEC', 7 Aug. 1918.
[86] 'NEC', 24 July 1918.
[87] 'NEC', 27 July 1918.

If the position of the ministers was thus logical, then logically they ought to leave the government. This was the view of the national executive. It was not the view of the parliamentary party. On 15 October the executive decided to recommend to an emergency conference of the Party (14 November) that Labour should withdraw from the coalition.[88] But when the executive met the parliamentary party there was almost irremediable disagreement. The latter was convinced that withdrawal would end whatever chance Labour had of influencing reconstruction. Webb devised a way out of this impasse: conference would be asked simply 'whether or not' the Party should leave the coalition 'either on the actual cessation of hostilities, or on the Dissolution, or on the signing of the definite Treaty of Peace'.[89]

At the emergency conference, after a celebrated intervention by Bernard Shaw, delegates voted by 2,117,000 to 810,000 to leave the coalition when parliament was dissolved. An amendment by Clynes that would have enabled the Party to support the coalition until the signing of peace was defeated by 1,844,000 to 891,000.[90] After much hesitation, and many blandishments from the other side, Clynes, Hodge, and Walsh resigned, so enabling the Party, as *The Times* noted, to close its ranks 'much more effectively than seemed possible a fortnight ago'.[91]

Labour, therefore, went into the election more or less united, more united, *The Times* might have added, than seemed possible two years before. As an independent electoral effort Labour did well at its first time. Though most candidates were without official agents, and though all its leading members were confined to their constituencies by the abusive and enthusiastic campaigns of their opponents,[92] Labour made itself strongly felt throughout the country. *The Times* correspondent, a moderately sympathetic observer, repeatedly noted the effectiveness of the Labour Campaign: '. . . it really seems as if the Labour Party were better prepared for the election than any other' (6 December); '. . . Labour in the early days of the contest threw much more vigour into the campaign than the candidates and workers of any other party' (9 December). Henderson, for all the trumpetings about individual membership and new model parties in January and February, knew where the Party's electoral strength would come from. He told C. P. Scott that Labour would fight the election better than the other

[88] This motion was moved by MacDonald after some preliminary skirmishing. ('NEC', 15 Oct. 1918.)

[89] 'NEC', 15 Oct. 1918.

[90] *The Times*, 15 Nov. 1918.

[91] *The Times*, 27 Nov. 1918. Barnes, Roberts, Wardle, and Parker remained in the government.

[92] Many of them from the National Democratic Party, as the British Workers' League had now become. Both MacDonald and Henderson were defeated by candidates from this Party.

parties 'because they had existing trades union organisation in every town'.[93] In this election, as in the three succeeding it, successful Labour candidates rode the unions to parliament.

Nevertheless, the local parties (whatever they were) nominated 140 of Labour's 361 candidates, and this was clearly a result of the new constitution. Of the unions, by far the largest sponsor was the Miners' Federation, which put up fifty-one candidates, followed by the Engineers with seventeen and the Textile Workers with ten. But the election results did not correspond with the geographic distribution of candidates: the new parliamentary party was largely confined to the mining divisions and the north. Labour hoped for 100 seats and claimed fifty-seven. Accretions on the opening of parliament increased that number to sixty-one.[94] The Party polled 22·7 per cent of all votes cast, but the parliamentary party was overwhelmingly a union one: twenty-five M.P.s came from the Miners' Federation alone, and all but eight of the remainder (five from the local parties and three from the I.L.P.) were union nominees.[95] Of perhaps more importance were the seventy-nine seats where the Labour candidate finished ahead of the opposition (non-couponed) Liberal.

Most of the Party leaders were defeated. Henderson (who had thrown up Barnard Castle for East Ham South), MacDonald, Snowden, Anderson, and Jowett lost their seats, and all but Jowett lost them badly. Although Henderson got back in 1919 the performance of the parliamentary party in the 1918 parliament was always disappointing. It is unlikely that this mattered much, if at all, for the real work in the next four years was extra-parliamentary. Yet by the end of 1918 the Labour Party was 'independent' at last, and could look to the future free from old traditions and allegiances, and free also from those demoralizing disputes about how 'independence' might best be won.

---

[93] *Political Diaries of C. P. Scott*, p. 317.
[94] The four others were Sir Owen Thomas (Anglesey), Jack Jones (Silvertown), F. H. Rose (Aberdeen North), who stood as independent Labour candidates, and A. E. Waterson (Kettering), the successful Co-operative candidate.
[95] Details in *Conference Report*, 1919, p. 287 (Appendix VI).

VI

THE END OF THE PARTY
OF PROGRESS

To all those involved in the new constitution and Labour's 1918 electoral programme, it did seem as if the Party had finally broken with political Liberalism. Yet outside the Labour movement the idea or fear of 'progressive unity' had a tenacious grip on life. To those radicals who had always believed in the essential unity of progressive purpose, there was no less reason for continuing the partnership than there had been before. That the partnership had undergone an awkward *bouleversement* was not seen as a necessary obstacle. To the 'pure' Asquithians it probably was an obstacle, but one worth overcoming if the gratifying prospect of a return to parliament and office was to have any substance. For his part, Lloyd George was as productive of ingenious schemes, all of which looked for a transposition of parties, as were Asquithians and radicals. Furthermore, the existence of the coalition, though it in no way changed the basic structure of British political life, did give a large number of politicians time to indulge in a sort of elevated gossip which rarely intersected with reality,[1] but often involved the Labour Party in unlikely combinations.

Whatever may have been conceivable even as late as 1917, it was plain that with the drafting of the new constitution the Liberals could hope for little. Speaking with deep feeling to the first 1918 conference, Henderson said that now 'he had had experience of two Governments, as long as he ever lived he should never be a member of any other Government, whatever its colour, unless Labour was in control'.[2] When C. P. Scott asked him whether Labour would leave free those constituencies held by 'good democrats and Radicals', he replied that 'discrimination would be difficult and that broadly he thought the policy would be to run a Labour candidate wherever there was a tolerable chance of carrying him'. He thought that there might be a few radical seats left uncontested, but he put more hope in the proposed alternative vote and 'on a friendly understanding between Liberalism and Labour

---

[1] The volume of this gossip was such that Mr. Cowling has recently been able to write a rather large book based almost exclusively upon it. See M. Cowling, *The Impact of Labour* (London, 1971).

[2] *Conference Report*, Jan. 1918, pp. 116–17.

to give each other their second choice'. He went on to suggest that Labour might run as many as 500 candidates, and he implied, not very delicately, that if good radicals wished to avoid Labour competition, they ought to join the Labour Party.[3]

The failure of parliament to adopt the alternative vote did not change Labour's electoral policy. Immediately after the 1918 elections it was decided by the national executive that, so far as organizational considerations allowed, all seats should be contested in the future.[4] When the organization and elections sub-committee discussed by-electoral policy in February 1919, it cautiously recommended that 'it was not possible to lay down any general policy with regard to by-elections', but hoped that seats would be contested where there was a possibility of winning or 'even of making a substantial improvement on the result of the election [of 1918]', where the local party wished to fight 'and for which adequate support in money and organization is assured locally'.[5] But the full executive ignored this recommendation and resolved simply that 'in the event of a parliamentary vacancy occurring it be an instruction to Head Office to take immediate steps with a view to contesting same'.[6] As a direction, this was never rescinded or revised : it remained, therefore, a duty of Head Office, generally speaking, to contest every seat as it fell vacant.

In practice, however, nowhere near every by-election was contested. (See Table 7.)

TABLE 7

By-Elections, July 1919–October 1924

	1919–20	1920–1	1921–2	1922–3	1923–4
Total	26	34	21	18	16
Fought by Labour	22	15*	10	13	12

* Evan Davies (Lab.) was returned unopposed in Ebbw Vale.

But the distance here between policy and its performance is only an apparent one. Henderson had made it clear to the national executive at the beginning of 1919 that Head Office would sanction a by-election contest only if local organization were such as to justify one. Since Henderson had much autonomy in the day-to-day administration of the Party, and since he had a traditionally prudent attitude to by-elections, he refused to approve obviously hopeless contests. Yet 'steps' were always taken when a seat became vacant; if contests did not follow, it meant that the constituency did not have a party, or 'the

[3] *Political Diaries of C. P. Scott*, pp. 316–17 (11–12 Dec. 1917).
[4] 'NEC', 2 Jan. 1919.
[5] 'NEC', 4 Feb. 1919.
[6] 'NEC', 9 Apr. 1919.

organization had not been maintained', or a newly established local party was simply incapable of mounting a campaign. On the other hand, if it were considered politically desirable, reluctant local parties were pushed into candidatures: in March 1923 Chuter Ede was thus nominated for Mitcham, and defeated the minister of agriculture (Sir Arthur Griffith Boscawen) seeking re-election.[7]

Labour was also rather unlucky in the disposition of by-elections during the 1918 parliament. Many of the contests were in rural seats, where Labour organization was rudimentary or non-existent, or in suburban constituencies and county towns, or in places like Birmingham where Labour was at a disadvantage to start with. In 1920-1, for example, the seats not contested by Labour were Louth, Hemel Hempstead, Middleton and Prestwich, Hereford, Dover, Cardiganshire, Penrith and Cockermouth, Abingdon, Orkney and Shetland, Westminster St. George's, and a clutch of constituencies that fell vacant after a cabinet reshuffle: Birmingham West, Birmingham Moseley, Glasgow Pollok, Dorset East, Bristol West, Bewdley, Eddisbury, and Chichester.

With the exception of Middleton and Prestwich (which was uncontested because of a smallpox outbreak) none of these was a remotely likely Labour victory. Louth (which was contested disastrously the following year), Hemel Hempstead, Cardiganshire, Penrith, Abingdon —not to speak of Orkney and Shetland and St. George's—were quite impossible. Hereford and Dover could have been fought, but both were still very much county towns with strong Tory histories. The ministers' seats were no more hopeful. East Dorset, Bewdley (Baldwin's seat: he had just become president of the board of trade), Eddisbury, and Chichester were as difficult for Labour as any in the country. Pollok has been held by Labour only since 1966, and then socially much changed. Finally, though the Labour offensive was perceptibly making way in Birmingham, the Party had not yet even established bridgeheads in either the West or Moseley divisions. While there is no evidence, as the executive claimed, that 'extreme care was taken to fill the offices with Members who held safe seats in the country', it was true that they provided 'the Coalition with cheap victories'.[8]

However, disputes about the 'independence of the Party' had become a tradition, and one that was strong enough to survive the war. At the 1920 conference Wake was interrogated about by-elections unfought.[9] Similar questions in 1923 elicited from Henderson

---

[7] See Henderson's testimony to the 1923 conference, *Conference Report*, 1923, p. 198.
[8] *Conference Report*, 1921, p. 36.
[9] *Conference Report*, 1920, pp. 125–6.

a lengthy reply.[10] In 1921 and 1922 it was raised in a more general way. In the former year, a resolution from the Social Democratic Federation repudiating 'all suggestions for any alliance between the Labour Party and any section of the Liberal and Conservative Parties' was carried unanimously. In 1922 Robert Williams of the Transport Workers moved a resolution almost identical with that of the previous year, but embellished by an attack on the Party's 'intelligentsia'. It was a well-known fact, he said,

that kites had been flown assiduously in the *Daily News* and the *Nation* urging that the Party should make a pact or arrangement with the Asquithian Liberals. If such a pact were made he was confident that some members of the Labour Party considered themselves influential enough to get inside the Government. They all knew that well known members of the Executive of the Labour Party were flying kites of this character.[11]

Webb, appropriately enough, replied for the executive. He denied that any kites had been flown and blamed the Liberal press for circulating tendentious stories; he begged the movement to ignore 'insinuations against this, that or the other individual'.

The movement was not so easily put off. Shinwell was, he said, grateful for Webb's assurances but suggested that these 'intentions should be translated into the journalistic activities of Mr. Webb and his friends'. Presumably Shinwell was referring to the *New Statesman*, whose editor, Clifford Sharp, was notoriously favourable to an agreement with the opposition Liberals. Since the Webbs had founded the paper they could, perhaps, be held guilty by association. It was also true that Webb mixed socially with Massingham of the *Nation* and Scott of the *Manchester Guardian*—as, of course, did Henderson.

While it is likely that such social intercourse was as objectionable to many in the movement as purely political entanglements, the real problem was that a number of the newly prominent in the Party, and a few of the old, had not confined their political activities to Labour before 1914. Debates of this sort were the tribute that the Labour movement paid to the divisiveness of the old relationship with the Liberal Party. After the war, however, it appears as if only one member of the national executive ever actually raised the matter of an agreement. According to Hugh Dalton, Egerton Wake told him

that [C. G. Ammon of the Post Office Workers and an I.L.P.er] had been trying for a straight fight in North Camberwell and has been conducting, probably, clandestine negotiations with the neighbouring Liberals. Ammon put up Isaacs' [secretary of the London Liberal Federation] list to the

---

[10] *Conference Report*, 1923, pp. 197–8.
[11] *Conference Report*, 1922, pp. 210–12.

National Executive ... There was a look of disgust all around the table. It was unanimously decided to take no action.

Dalton added that 'he was authorised to state this'.[12] There is no other evidence that it was again considered by the national executive.

Webb did not, however, unfairly blame the Liberal press for circulating tendentious stories. It was perfectly legitimate for those Liberals, like C. P. Scott, who were seeking a new radical alignment to use their papers in order to encourage one. Unfortunately, it led to much highly imaginative and wishful reporting. Thus Professor Wilson, who has read the Liberal press, tells us that the Liberals regarded the Widnes and Rusholme by-elections of 1919 as a 'turning point' in relations between the two parties.[13] But in what sense were they a turning-point? Only in so far as they began to disabuse the Liberals.

Henderson's nomination for Widnes in September 1919 obviously had importance beyond the Labour Party: to many rudderless radicals he at that moment represented a more acceptable alternative to the coalition than any Liberal leader. Thus the Widnes by-election was not only a Labour show of strength, it became on the Liberal side a demonstration of 'progressive' unity, and Henderson went to the polls accompanied by a heavy barrage of 'progressive' propaganda. 'We could hope', the *Manchester Guardian* wrote, apropos of the straight fight he was allowed,[14] 'that the Widnes fight may be the beginning of a new co-operation between Liberalism and Labour which will allow to each party its place in the forces of democratic progress.'[15] Of the result (Henderson won), the same paper explained that 'Labour may be excused if, as the younger party entering a field already largely occupied, it asserts itself at times somewhat urgently. What is clear is that there must be give and take.'[16]

There is no doubt that the Liberals gave Henderson assistance and that he made a public show of accepting it. At the declaration of the poll he said that 'the Liberals ... without asking any pledges from him, threw themselves wholeheartedly into the fight, and had accomplished with Labour that which they had never accomplished themselves'.[17] He was even talked into writing an article for the *Manchester Guardian* congratulating all concerned on the 'spirit of determined hostility to the Coalition Government'.[18]

[12] 'L.S.E. MS. Dalton Diaries', 9 Feb. 1922.
[13] Wilson, *The Downfall of the Liberal Party*, pp. 205–6.
[14] Though Widnes had no Liberal tradition anyway. See Pelling, *Social Geography*, p. 269.
[15] *Manchester Guardian*, 26 Aug. 1919.
[16] *Manchester Guardian*, 13 Sept. 1919.
[17] *Widnes Guardian*, 2 Sept. 1919.
[18] *Manchester Guardian*, 13 Sept. 1919.

Henderson was not a man to offend his friends whoever they were, especially if he thought they might be coaxed into the Labour Party. But the opposition Liberals certainly expected more from him than his thanks. Shortly before the declaration of the Widnes poll the Rusholme division of Manchester became vacant. It was a predominantly middle-class constituency of the type the Liberals were increasingly coming to consider their own. The Liberal press made the point that Widnes implied a bargain.

It is therefore a time for all who take the state of the country to heart to combine in their attack. The attack has been ably conducted in several places by Labour, and Labour candidates would acknowledge that they have had valuable help ungrudgingly given by Liberals . . . We trust that in Rusholme the Liberals may count on the cordial co-operation of Labour.[19]

Liberal hopes for such an agreement were raised by stories appearing in some of the London press that Henderson favoured one.[20] Within a few days of the seat becoming vacant, the local Labour party had tentatively adopted Dr. R. Dunstan, a former Liberal candidate for Totnes. Even so, this was going to be a difficult contest for a party still noticeably weak outside its old industrial strongholds. The Rusholme Labour Party had just been formed, largely by I.L.P.ers, and was not expected to make much of a showing. Therefore it was decided initially to withhold endorsement of Dunstan's candidature on organizational grounds and on the advice of the national organizer, William Holmes.[21] As a precautionary measure, though, it was agreed to send Fred Jowett and A. G. Cameron to Manchester to examine the 'political' implications of a contest.

When they arrived it was made clear to them that the local people were set for a contest regardless. The president of the Manchester and Salford Trades Council, E. J. Hookway, had already publicly expressed the Council's view that a contest was essential.[22] Jowett and Cameron reported that a failure to fight the seat would be 'misunderstood' in the north-west, would, that is to say, be construed as an agreement with the Liberals, and recommended on those grounds that the candidature should go ahead.[23] This recommendation was accepted by the executive. Specifically to avoid rumours of 'progressive' collaboration, the executive was prepared to override their national organizer and sanction a campaign which he thought would be ill organized.

The decision having been made, Henderson typically abandoned any doubts that he might have had; to the chagrin of the Liberal

[19] *Manchester Guardian*, 6 Sept. 1919.
[20] See, for example, *The Times*, 6 Sept. 1919.
[21] 'NEC', 11 Sept. 1919.
[22] *Manchester Guardian*, 8 Sept. 1919.
[23] 'NEC', 17 Sept. 1919.

press he led the campaign in Rusholme. 'We prefer to say nothing', the *Manchester Guardian* nevertheless said, 'of what may be due on the score of gratitude for recent ungrudging support.'[24] The *Nation* reminded Henderson that in Widnes 'there was, of course, a large Liberal contribution. Mr. Henderson now chooses to forget this and intervenes at Rusholme (not an industrial constituency) to help a weak Labour candidate and destroy a strong Liberal one.'[25] Labour's decision was more than justified by the result: Dunstan gained 6,412 votes, and Pringle, the opposition Liberal, 3,923. Compared with 1918 the Labour vote had more than doubled.

Labour's behaviour, as much as Pringle's failure, shocked the Liberals, and for them it may well have seemed a turning-point. But for Labour there was no point to turn. The Liberals talked themselves into believing that an agreement was desirable and therefore possible, whereas it was impossible all along. In the case of the *Manchester Guardian*, whose editor, C. P. Scott, was as well acquainted with Labour's policy as anybody, the wish was almost certainly father to the thought.

Henderson's behaviour at Widnes, even allowing for the euphoria of the moment, was rather rash. Public acceptance of Liberal support, together with articles in the *Manchester Guardian*, was the very type of indiscretion that caused so many misunderstandings before 1914 and perpetuated misunderstandings after then. Henderson was, after all, like Webb, on friendly terms with many opposition Liberals: it was better not to advertise it, and certainly better to avoid providing grist for a Liberal press ready to mill endless stories about 'progressive' alliances. Yet Henderson was only doing what he had been trying to do ever since 1917—to entice Liberals into the Labour Party, and at the expense of the Liberals and not of Labour.

Furthermore, the Rusholme contest showed that if it were necessary to make public Labour's divorce from Liberalism, the Party would overlook the usual organizational niceties and go ahead anyway. This was so particularly in Lancashire where the 'progressive' tradition was a strong one[26] and where Liberalism was still infused with a certain radicalism. Thus in 1923, when the election was fought on an issue (free trade) more likely to force a 'progressive' *ralliement* than any other, and nowhere more so than in Lancashire, it was demanded of Labour almost to go out of its way in opposing the reunited Liberal Party. What happened in Manchester, for example, was not at all what the Liberal press hoped was going to happen. The *Manchester*

[24] *Manchester Guardian*, 15 Sept. 1919.
[25] *Nation*, 20 Sept. 1919.
[26] See Clarke, *Lancashire and the New Liberalism*, *passim*.

Guardian claimed that 'Labour will do something like they did in 1910. They will go on the policy of not fighting a seat merely for the sake of fighting it . . . Tacitly, they will make room for the Liberal Party.'[27] But, despite threatened Liberal candidatures in Platting (Clynes's seat) and Ardwick, Labour contested all Manchester and Salford seats except Blackley and Moss Side, leaving only those, as the *Manchester Guardian* admitted, 'because of lack of funds and a high degree of confusion in local organization'.[28] Rather than allow C. F. G. Masterman a free run in Rusholme the divisional party adopted William Paul, a Communist, as an eleventh-hour candidate, and a similar one appeared in Hulme.

All that has been said about Manchester can equally be said about the rest of urban and industrial Britain, with two obvious exceptions: Central Hull, where J. M. Kenworthy, a forceful personality sympathetic to Labour, was unopposed throughout the period, and Preston, a double-member borough, where John Hodge was always the only Labour candidate.[29]

Such agreements as there were between local Labour and Liberal parties were limited usually to agricultural constituencies or county towns. In these seats, where Labour typically was weak, there was an obvious temptation for divisional parties or union officers to support a Liberal candidate in the absence of a Labour one. In 1922 and 1923 it appears as if Labour deliberately stood aside for Liberal candidates in Eastbourne and Newark. Public support and assistance was apparently given to the Liberals in Denbigh, Huntingdonshire, and Hemel Hempstead.[30] In May 1923 the district organizer of the south-western region reported that in Tiverton the local trades council

has almost collapsed, as at the [1922] general election, 50% of them deserted [the Labour candidate] and signed [Sir Francis Acland, the Independent Liberal's] nomination forms, the reason being given that the fear of victimisation was so strong. Trade Unionism is in a very low state, and even during my visit, several members of the Transport Workers left their Union because the Divisional Secretary introduced Labour politics.[31]

In these circumstances, there was not much that the executive could do if a local party gave support to a Liberal candidate other than

[27] *Manchester Guardian*, 14 Nov. 1923.
[28] *Manchester Guardian*, 21 Nov. 1923.
[29] M. Kinnear (*The British Voter* (London, 1968), pp. 108–10) suggests that there were seven urban constituencies where there were fairly long-standing agreements. But there is no evidence, at least from the general elections of the period, that this was so. For details, see McKibbin, 'Evolution of a National Party', pp. 418–19.
[30] I am grateful to Mr. C. Cook of the London School of Economics for this information. In 1924 Labour contested all these seats except Huntingdon and Denbigh.
[31] 'NEC', 5 May 1923.

to protest after the event. Thus the Bodmin Labour Party was censured for directing its members to vote for the Asquithian Isaac Foot at a by-election in February 1922,[32] though it may be supposed that Labour voters, such as there were in Bodmin, would have done so in any case.

What is surprising, however, is the number of rural and county seats that there were not left to the Liberals. Though it was not until 1924 that Labour actually contested more than 500 seats, only about ten or so seats were covered by agreements, and then usually for just one election. In 1924 Labour left uncontested a mere forty-five of these seats, and they included real Tory dug-outs like Blackpool and Southport.

Both sides of the Liberal Party failed to understand what had happened since 1917. All of its members thought that some kind of 'progressive' alliance was possible: radicals were untiring in trying to arrange one, Lloyd Georgeites always suspected that one was being arranged.[33] Before 1914, after all, there had been close liaison between the two parliamentary parties, and, as the radicals saw it, there was still a large measure of political agreement between them—as there had been before 1914. Common sense, therefore, dictated that men of goodwill and progressive thinking should work together for their common ends.

Yet this did not happen. Throughout 1924, for example, when it could have been expected that Labour would treat the Liberals with consideration and delicacy, Labour, on the contrary, made not the slightest effort to do so. Rather, it attacked those who kept it in power with a greater violence than it attacked its official opposition. Many Liberals were puzzled by this and found it difficult to explain.

In part, it was due to the fact that Labour was, or thought it was, competing for the same electorate as the Liberal Party. Thus the electoral and, as it were, rhetorical strategy of the Labour Party in the 1920s was aimed less at upsetting the Conservative predominance than at forestalling a Liberal revival. And if, as in 1923, it looked as

[32] 'NEC', 5 Apr. 1922; *Manchester Guardian*, 21 Feb. 1922.

[33] See a memorandum by Sir William Sutherland, Lloyd George's private secretary and political fixer, dated 8 Sept. 1920. 'There is no doubt', he wrote, 'that some sort of deal is being attempted by the Asquithians and Labour in regard to the seat being vacated by Peel in Suffolk (Woodbridge), as well as in South Suffolk (Sudbury), the idea being that Labour should not oppose in the one case, nor the "Wee Frees" in the other.' Lloyd George's 'immediate line', he said, was to oppose 'the intrigues of the Henderson and Ramsay MacDonald sort', since (he added correctly) 'there is no doubt that the great bulk of the Labour men in the country are strongly opposed to any alliance with the "Wee Frees",' (Beaverbrook Library, MS. Lloyd George 5/22/2/4). Sutherland actually was right in this case. In 1920 and 1922 Labour fought Woodbridge, but not Sudbury. However, this was only because H. D. Harben, the wealthy Fabian, financed his own candidature. In 1918 Labour contested neither seat.

i.e. Achieved status as 2nd party – V. Imp – By denying
an 'alliance' + by widening electoral appeal.

END OF THE PARTY OF PROGRESS   121

though the Liberals might indeed have revived, then it was necessary
not to co-operate with them, and to govern in disregard of them. The
first Labour government cannot be understood other than in these
terms; it was, thus, a propaganda exercise as much as anything else.
It was seen as such by its leaders, and they, rather than trying to
prolong its life, looked for the best moment to bring it to an end. It
was not an accident that the cabinet unanimously and with astonishing
speed decided to treat as a matter of confidence a Liberal motion on
the Campbell case.[34] In 1924 the elimination of the Liberal Party
as a competitor for the 'progressive' vote was completed with an
unexpected success, though MacDonald received little credit for it at
the time.

In part, also, it was due to wider political differences than there
had been before the war. Though Labour became only notionally a
socialist party in 1918, it was committed to the nationalization of
specific industries, and most Liberals stopped short of that. Radicals
tended to exaggerate the common ground between the Liberal and
Labour parties: the behaviour of the Liberals both in the 1924 and
the 1929 parliaments suggests that an agreed programme might, in
fact, have been difficult to negotiate. Furthermore, from the moment
the Labour Party decided that it could encompass more or less everyone there was no real point in conciliating the Liberals or in doing
anything else other than to hasten their fall. Officially, there was
nothing to choose between the Liberals and the Tories. It was only
some ex-Liberals who believed that their former colleagues were
actually worse than the Conservatives.[35]

But in practice, of course, there was something to choose. Unless
tactical considerations had supervened Labour would unquestionably
have advised its supporters to give their alternative votes to the
Liberals, had such an electoral system been enacted. The ease with
which individual Liberals moved into the Labour Party is evidence
that the political differences between Liberal radicals and the Labour
movement were by no means unbridgeable. Nor was any real ideological
conversion required: J. C. Wedgwood, for example, was a single-
taxer all his life and his adhesion to the Labour Party was a change in
label only.

In the end, differences in policy were subordinate to social and
psychological resentments which powerfully directed Labour's
actions towards the Liberal Party. MacDonald, when pushed by

[34] For which, see R. W. Lyman, *The First Labour Government* (London, 1957), pp. 237–44.
[35] 'Better a Tory government than a Liberal–Labour government, Ponsonby declared,
for if Liberals were present in a Labour administration they would destroy all prospect of a
social reconstruction and international reconstruction in which Labour believed.' (Wilson,
p. 205.)

C. P. Scott, gave a number of explanations for his own and his Party's hostility to the Liberals. None of them in the strict sense was political. In January 1924 he said that the 'difficulty' was Lloyd George, not because he was doctrinally antipathetic, but because 'they could not trust him'. Further, MacDonald was tired of the Liberals 'flaunting' Labour's dependence on them.[36] By July he was asserting that he 'could get on' with the Tories: they were 'gentlemen', but the Liberals were 'cads'. Asquith was 'patronising' and Liberal members showed indifference and contempt for Labour ministers. Whereas Labour had simple disagreements with the Tories and then 'shook hands', the Liberals apparently were superior and stuck up.[37]

A good deal of this talk was presumably a result of MacDonald's own snobbery and social unease—the clubland argot, 'cads', 'gentlemen', 'shaking hands' is all too characteristic—but it was more than just that. The distrust of Lloyd George was common to the whole Labour Party and some in it had more reason to distrust him than MacDonald. Despite the hopes variously articulated in the 1920s and 1930s that Lloyd George would die on the left, in so far as individuals mattered at all, he, more than any other, stood in the way of a 'progressive' alliance. But the disintegrating effects of Lloyd George were only a secondary problem. It was what the Liberal Party represented, and the social classes that seemed to make it distinctive, that was the real one. As a Party, it was not just manifestly bourgeois—so was the Conservative Party; rightly or wrongly it appeared to many in the Labour movement to be bourgeois in a particular way. It was the Party of the self-consciously superior, the rich and clever lawyers, the effortless Oxford men, of those parliamentarians who never bothered to hide their contempt for Labour ministers or backbenchers. On an individual level many Liberal chickens had now come home to roost: the scarcely concealed snobbery of some of its leaders (and their wives) and the schoolmasterly behaviour of even sympathetic Liberals were two of them. Henderson, treated as a general dogsbody in both coalitions, regarded that as his sacrifice for the war effort, but one so humiliating that he was determined never to make it again. This feeling was sharpened by pre-war experience. Though the relationship between the two parliamentary parties was always fairly amicable before 1914, from the Labour side it was always a client one. This was not a foundation on which any alliance could be built, and MacDonald was not alone in detecting and immediately resenting 'patronising' and 'condescending' tones when the roles of the two parties had been reversed.

But much of the active rank and file of the Labour movement had

[36] *Diaries of C. P. Scott*, p. 453.   [37] Ibid., pp. 460–1.

never been a partner even to this sort of relationship. The Liberal Party now paid dearly for the social origins of its leadership, for the middle-class character and exclusiveness of its local caucuses. And in the mining divisions the Liberal Party was now what it had only been incipiently in 1914—a bosses' party. To the rest of the Labour movement, it is true, it may not have seemed necessarily a bosses' party, but even less did it seem a party of the newly enfranchised working-classes.

VII

PARTY AND RANK-AND-FILE
1918–1924

1. *Head Office*

OF all Head Office institutions, only the national executive itself bore obvious marks of reorganization. Its size (it now had twenty-three members) and the volume of work it had to handle made it too unwieldy for the old casual methods to be any longer effective. After July 1918, therefore, the pre-war emergency subcommittees of the executive were replaced by four standing subcommittees—organization and elections, policy and programme, literature, research and publicity, and finance and general purposes—whose tasks were to relieve the full committee of most of its routine work.[1] From 1918 onwards, much of the full executive's administrative work was done by the sub-committees; for the most part, unless a problem was peculiarly contentious the full executive merely approved the actions of its sub-committees.

As before, the secretary of the Party was responsible to the national executive. In practice, Henderson had much freedom of manœuvre. Though he had a couple of scrapes with some members over the Party's finances and his own position when Labour was in office, he was overruled on only one important issue, the place of Wales in regional reorganization,[2] and even that was only part of a wider decision about which the secretary very much had his way. Indeed, the national executive's almost total compliance with Henderson's wishes, even when he was treating it with less courtesy than it could have expected,[3] is remarkable even in a party where the professional bureaucracy had a tradition of administrative authority.

Henderson was now at the height of his powers and the years 1917–22 were probably the most productive of his career. The international successes of 1929–31 were passing ones. His final assumption of the Party's leadership was soon overwhelmed by electoral disaster and his presidency of the disarmament conference was a sad anti-climax. Although nearing sixty (he was fifty-five in 1918) he still had immense resilience—he attended almost all organization conferences between 1919 and 1922, spoke at most major by-elections (including

[1] 'NEC', 10 July 1918.   [3] For one example, see below, p. 160.
[2] See below, pp. 167–70.

three of his own),[4] directed four general elections (1918, 1922, 1923, and 1924), supervised the regional reorganization in 1920 and the creation of the joint departments, worried himself sick over the *Daily Herald*, and all this apart from his industrial, political, and international socialist work.

Yet even his prodigious energy flagged occasionally. In 1919 the accumulated strains of the previous two years seem to have caused a bout of nervous exhaustion which showed itself in continuous, petulant, and quite uncharacteristic threats to resign: 'I have felt strongly inclined to get out altogether' he wrote to Webb.[5] In 1920 he had a complete physical collapse followed by a major operation, from which his recovery was slow. This illness emphasized his indispensability to the Party—'Henderson's dangerous illness and his doubtful recovery have made one realise his relative superiority to all other men. He is really the only Labour man who considers the welfare of the Party as a whole . . .' Beatrice Webb noted.[6]

Yet this indispensability had its disadvantages. Henderson had a tendency to accumulate responsibilities but a disinclination to shed them. It is hard to avoid the conclusion that the Party became too dependent on him and he too determined to maintain his hold on the Party. In 1924 he was most reluctant to give up the secretaryship, and did so only under heavy pressure from the national executive. Though his management of Head Office was thus unimpaired, the irascibility which inevitable overwork produced did not help personal relations there.

The national agent's office changed hands in 1918. Egerton Wake succeeded Peters in September when the latter became deputy housing commissioner at the ministry of health. This change had long been foreseen : Wake had taken on more and more of Peters's responsibilities during the war, while Peters was increasingly criticized for his obvious Liberal political inclinations. They had been known at Head Office for some time,[7] but became embarrassingly public when Peters was accused of signing the nomination papers of the Liberal candidate in Croydon : an accusation which neither Peters nor Head Office bothered to deny.[8] Wake was a much more vigorous agent than Peters, but the changeover was to have consequences other than just that. Wake was a Head Office man, a centralist, and Henderson had gained a formidable and loyal ally.

[4] Widnes, 1919; Newcastle East, 1923; Burnley, 1924.
[5] Henderson to Webb, 17 May 1919, L.S.E. MS. Passfield: Correspondence, II.4.9. His only other 'resignation' was in 1910. See above, p. 3.
[6] Beatrice Webb, 'Transcript Diaries', 35, 18–25 June 1920, L.S.E. MS. Passfield.
[7] Information provided by Lord Henderson.
[8] *Conference Report*, 1919, pp. 124–5.

Most of the routine work was now done by Middleton and Wake. Once the work ceased to be routine, that is to say, when it became a question of policy, then it went to Henderson. Whereas before the war Henderson was as much involved in day-to-day work as anybody else, after the war his tasks were more directive ones, the clerkly duties being left very much to his subordinates.

In matters of organizational policy the executive tended to be dominated by the 'trade union centre', the majority of the executive members who were unionists. Though this majority was itself divided on many issues, it tended to support Henderson in his direction of the Party. Some of the I.L.P. members, notably Jowett, had a tradition of opposition, and this was strengthened by the advent of men like Maxton, who was not only an I.L.P.er, but a Scot as well. Yet the most consistently lively members of the executive were its women members, and this was probably a development not foreseen by its more conventional male members: it was Susan Lawrence, Ethel Bentham, and Mrs. Harrison Bell, for example, who led executive opposition to Henderson's remaining secretary in 1924. They were all the model of the emancipated woman and other members of the executive probably felt as awkward in their presence as Henderson seems to have done.[9]

But in an average year, and the women aside, Henderson seems to have had the generally consistent support of men like A. G. Cameron, W. C. Robinson, Ben Turner, C. T. Cramp, Frank Hodges, J. R. Clynes, F. O. Roberts, and W. H. Hutchinson, but not, on the whole, Robert Smillie or Robert Williams, for example. Trade-union support was fairly solid because Henderson, for the most part, governed the Party's organization in their interest.[10]

All the evidence suggests that the chairman of the executive (the 'chairman of the Party') had little influence on events—certainly none of the chairmen of this period had much influence—and were content to leave the running of the Party to Henderson. Even a man like Purdy, who, as chairman in 1917 and 1918, might have been in a position to exercise some power, has left no visible mark on reorganization except to make an embarrassing speech on its virtues. For the rest, though the chairman may have had some importance in the conducting of negotiations or in the handling of intra-Party disputes,[11] it does appear as if the title was more or less honorific.

[9] But Henderson was on very easy terms with Marion Phillips, the chief women's officer, whom Egon Wertheimer called 'a typical Continental phenomenon' and who was very much an independent professional woman. (E. Wertheimer, *Portrait of the Labour Party* (1929), p. 190). Margaret Bondfield, as a union leader herself, did not count.

[10] See below, pp. 131–7.

[11] For one example, see below, p. 186.

Similarly, though for different reasons, it is likely that MacDonald's position as treasurer was largely a grace-and-favour one. Party finances were securely in Henderson's hands[12] and MacDonald looked after the exchequer only formally. But the treasury was a useful way of keeping him on the executive when it was not certain that he would be elected to it in the ordinary way, while leaving him free for other political work and for his long awaited (and delayed) return to parliamentary life. Relations between Henderson and MacDonald were polite, distant, strained, and confined to general Party business. There were no repetitions of Henderson's resignation in 1910 and MacDonald was presumably more tactful, at least before he became prime minister. Until 1922 Henderson was clearly the dominant partner, and since he was working hard to bring MacDonald back to the House it was in MacDonald's interest to be tactful.[13] Both, in a sense, used each other.

2. National Organization

It cannot be said that the methods of pre-war organizing techniques changed very much after 1918. But they were greatly intensified and the number of people involved in them substantially increased. While there was always local initiative in the establishment of constituency parties or in the assumption of political functions by existing trades councils, that initiative usually followed one of the great regional conferences which were held in large numbers between 1918 and 1922. These meetings had a fairly standard form. There were two sessions: a private one addressed either by Henderson or the national agent, and a public one, almost certainly addressed by Henderson together with a leading parliamentary figure. The first was occupied solely with organizational matters, the second with policy and was usually inspirational in aim. The first session was small, only party secretaries, prospective candidates, and sitting members, numbers appropriate to a meeting technical in its nature. The second session was usually very big, carefully filled out with delegates and sympathizers.

Sidney Webb has left a good description of the thirtieth regional conference at Newcastle. One hundred delegates attended the morning session, addressed by himself and Wake—though not by Henderson and Clynes ('I dare say they are right not to make themselves "too cheap" ').[14] The afternoon meeting, which Webb thought

[12] See below, pp. 156–62.
[13] H. Dalton, *Call Back Yesterday* (London, 1953), p. 75.
[14] Sidney Webb to Beatrice Webb, 24 Sept. 1921, 'L.S.E. MS. Passfield: Correspondence,' II.3.(i).

'magnificent', was attended by 2,000 people, and enthused by Clynes ('in fine form') and Henderson ('ponderously impressive'). The *Newcastle Daily Chronicle* put it more picturesquely : 'Flood of Labour Oratory on Tyneside'.[15] Henderson, as usual on occasions of this kind, spoke lengthily (he opened the Clayton by-election of February 1922 with a near two-hour speech), thus showing that verbosity was by no means characteristic only of the Marxist tradition in European socialism.

By 1922 each of the Party's nine regions had assembled about three times for such conferences, and on nearly all these occasions they were addressed by the national agent, the secretary, or the parliamentary leader, or even both, together with some other 'star' speaker—in Newcastle's case, Webb. It meant, therefore, that there was more contact between the leadership and constituencies than might have seemed possible. With the appointment of the regional organizers in 1920 and the regional propagandists in 1922, the links between the constituencies and Head Office were strengthened, particularly as several of the propagandists were ex-M.P.s from marginal constituencies, like Tom Myers from Spen Valley, which he had lost to Sir John Simon in 1922.

Speaking was a pre-war tradition that Head Office continued and encouraged, not merely because it was often regarded as a substitute for more expensive organization, but because it was a popular method of electioneering. Every election campaign, quite apart from regional conferences and other flag-showing occasions, groaned under the weight of public meetings. Webb, for one, found them both tiring and conceivably redundant. Writing to Beatrice from East Newcastle, where Henderson was the Labour candidate (he had been defeated in 1922), Webb recorded speaking at four meetings '... in crowded school-rooms being taken on in taxis from one to the other, whilst Trevelyan and Maclean and other speakers, along with Henderson were also being taken around. The meetings are crowded and enthusiastic, far too numerous for my liking, but apparently the people insist on them ...' Webb was not proficient at this kind of speaking, which had its origins in the old days of I.L.P. and trade-union evangelizing.

Tonight I shall be taken on the same sort of round. It is difficult for me to do any good at such a business as the speeches have to be short and scrappy and they are pitchforked in between others, which may be entirely different in subject and must be very different in kind. But they seem to think it necessary to have us all ... [16]

[15] *Newcastle Daily Chronicle*, 26 Sept. 1921.
[16] Sidney to Beatrice Webb, 12 Jan. 1923, 'L.S.E. MS. Passfield: Correspondence,' II.3.(i).

It is unlikely that any other political party relied so much upon its leadership for these purposes. For example, Labour's public meetings were a remarkable feature of an already remarkable by-election in Woolwich (March 1921), when MacDonald was the Party's candidate. He had the support of Henderson, Thomas, Clynes, Smillie, Adamson, Snowden, and innumerable other union leaders and M.P.s.[17] The enormous popularity of such meetings—the Plumstead Baths were filled with people at least an hour before the meeting—did not, however, prevent MacDonald's defeat. The *Labour Organiser*, the journal of the agent's association, criticized the Party's excessive reliance on 'showy enthusiasm' and its lack of 'hard doorstep work'. A little more of the doorstep, it thought, and MacDonald would have been elected.[18] Clynes was always much in demand as chairman of the P.L.P. and as one of the best speakers in the movement. Thomas was popular and could be relied on to give a good performance, as could Snowden. MacDonald spoke less often; he did not really like these packed nightly meetings, nor was he very good at them. On an off-night he could be truly awful.[19]

Yet, if he chose his moment, he was excellent, particularly after 1922 when his performance was sustained by an *ex officio* glamour. The best example of this was his 1924 election campaign. Whatever else may be said about his leadership in 1924—and some other things have been said[20]—the election itself was a professional triumph. He began with a valedictory speech at the Party conference which created scenes of unprecedented enthusiasm. On re-reading, it appears quite as embarrassing and incoherent as many of his later ones, and, clearly, MacDonald always teetered between disaster and success. A good deal depended on the mood of both his audience and himself: so long as people listened not to the meaning of his words but to their sentimental suggestions the effect was nothing less than spectacular. When he arrived at the 1924 conference on its last day, dissolution already being

---

[17] *Woolwich Gazette and Plumstead News*, 8 Mar. 1921. For the by-election, see *Woolwich Herald* and *Woolwich Gazette and Plumstead News*, Feb.–Mar. 1921. For MacDonald's candidature, see below, pp. 133–4.

[18] *Labour Organiser*, Apr. 1921. See also Herbert Morrison in the *London Labour Chronicle*, Apr. 1921: '. . . it is possible for star turns to be overdone and . . . canvassing on the doorstep is of *much* greater consequence than holding forth at the street corner.'

[19] For Clynes, see Wertheimer, *Portrait of the Labour Party*, p. 183; for MacDonald, A. H. Booth, *British Hustings, 1924–1950* (London, 1956), pp. 19–20.

[20] Notably by Snowden. See his letters to Jowett in Brockway, *Socialism over Sixty Years*, pp. 222–3. Snowden spoke of opportunities 'recklessly thrown away by the most incompetent leadership which ever brought a government to ruin'. MacDonald showed 'an incapacity I never thought him capable of'. The worth of Snowden's judgement must be a matter of opinion, though I am inclined to think that the government was bound to fall sooner rather than later. Nevertheless, it cannot be doubted that the election came at psychologically the right moment for Labour, and that MacDonald's campaigning was not at all incompetent, but confident and vigorous. (See below, p. 130.)

known, he received a 'tumultuous ovation'. He spoke to the delegates thus :[21]

Business-like to the end! Business-like at our birth, business-like during our term of life, business-like at the moment of our death, business-like in our resurrection! No Charles II with us, having to apologize because we are taking a long time to die. No! Clean!! When we are done why cumber the ground? ...

... Back you go now from here, back to your constituencies, back to your parishes, back to your towns, back to your villages and start the fight, the greatest fight, the most memorable fight, involving the largest issues of any of the many fights that you and I have engaged in during the last thirty years.

Be of good heart my friends. Some of us are getting old; and yet who gets old in the Labour Movement? Our surroundings are so perennially young that we drink them in and by some magic of assimilation the youth of our circumstances defies the length of our years ...

Spoken by anyone else than MacDonald, these words would probably have provoked the reaction they certainly deserved. In fact, they had the conference constantly on its feet and were the prelude to his astonishing automobile tour of the country, which began in Glasgow and ended in Aberavon (his constituency), and which for dramatic interest seemed to some observers to exceed anything since Chamberlain's protection campaign in 1903.[22] The climax of the tour was appropriate.

Scenes of tremendous enthusiasm greeted the return of Mr. Ramsay MacDonald to his constituency on Friday, crowds lining the roadside from the Station-square to Margam. So eager were the Socialists to accord their leader a welcome back to Wales that charabancs came from Llanelly, Aberdare, Growerton, Bridgend, Mountain Ash, and Ogmore Vale, while a long arrival of conveyances proceeded from Briton Ferry, their occupants flying streamers of red, white and green, and waving multi-coloured paper caps ... It was 8.30 when Mr. MacDonald arrived, his passage being held up all along the route by throngs of people. A halt was made near the station where he addressed a few words to the crowd, his opening greetings ... being wildly cheered ... He was escorted to his hotel by a procession displaying flags and banners ... Long after he had retired his following thronged the streets, singing election songs and cheering loudly outside the windows![23]

Similar scenes were repeated in other parts of south Wales—in Swansea they even surpassed those in Aberavon.[24] In 1924 MacDonald was Labour's most valuable electoral weapon.

[21] *Conference Report*, 1924, pp. 182–4.
[22] *The Times*, 18 Oct. 1924; for the tour generally, see *The Times*, 14–24 Oct. 1924.
[23] *South Wales Daily Post*, 18 Oct. 1924.
[24] *South Wales Daily Post*, 25 Oct. 1924.

3. *Selection of Candidates*

On the whole there is little to be said about the selection of candidates which has not in a general way already been noted, but something more specific needs to be written about Head Office's influence in the nomination of candidates and the extent to which constituencies could resist or ignore such influence.

For the most part, the nomination and selection of candidates was perfectly regular. Trade-union candidates, those for whom responsibility had been accepted by a union, were usually approved by the executive without question. The same can be said about candidates from the socialist societies or about candidates whom local parties might select on their own account so long as they were prepared to make the necessary financial guarantees. Refusal to endorse a candidate was uncommon and occurred, if it occurred at all, usually when the candidate was a Communist.[25] And then the national executive could not prevent a local party from running him anyway. Occasionally, if the executive did not think local organization was up to supporting a candidate, endorsement would be refused even if the candidature went ahead on an independent basis.

Head Office rarely tried to force candidates upon constituencies. On the contrary, the executive was criticized for not using its powers to ensure the return to parliament of 'national' figures. At the 1920 conference, W. A. Robinson of the Warehouse and General Workers expressed his surprise that the names of MacDonald and Snowden 'had not been before the country'. He wanted to know whether they had been asked.[26] In a vague reply Wake said (in effect) that they had not, and there was nothing that the executive could do about it. He added that most parties had already selected candidates, but if a party wished to choose either of these two (MacDonald or Snowden) 'the full resources of the Party would be used to return them'. Shinwell (then an I.L.P. delegate) thought that in future '. . . whenever a bye-election appeared imminent the National Executive should immediately consult the local Labour Party with a view to the selection of any person who in the opinion of the National Executive was a fit candidate . . . Bye-elections were the property of the National Movement.'

In practice Head Office made little attempt to turn by-elections into the property of the national movement, and on the three occasions when it tried to insert its own candidate into a by-election there was a good deal of surprise and some resentment in the local party. Of these

[25] For the position of the Communists, see below, pp. 191–204.
[26] *Conference Report*, 1920, p. 125.

three, one, Stockport, is discussed in the next chapter.[27] The other
two, Widnes (August 1919) and East Woolwich (March 1921), were
attempts to return Henderson and MacDonald to the House. In both
contests the local party was induced to abandon its own nominee and
somewhat reluctantly to accept the executive's candidate.

Henderson's nomination for Widnes was the least troublesome of
the two. When the seat became vacant the local party appears to have
approached Tom Williamson of the National Amalgamated Union of
Labour.[28] Since he had fought the seat in 1918 he could reasonably
have expected to do so again. But with the exception of Bothwell
(Lanark), where it would have been impossible to ease out John
Robertson of the Miners, Widnes was the best prospect that had fallen
vacant since the election. The executive decided, therefore, that the
opportunity should be seized for restoring Henderson to the parliamentary party. On 16 August three members of the executive were
sent to St. Helens to meet delegates from the Widnes party.[29] Heavy
pressure must have been put upon the delegation since they not only
agreed to accept Henderson's nomination, but then made selection
certain by inducing Williamson to withdraw. Henderson later claimed
that he became candidate only when Williamson said he was 'out of
it'.[30] He even put up a public show of reluctance to accept:[31] but when
he met the Widnes party he told them, in an obviously well-prepared
address, that 'it would be a serious thing for the Labour Party in the
constituency and for himself if he were defeated in the election'.[32]

The *Manchester Guardian* claimed that Williamson's friends were
'a little mortified at the rapid turn of events at the weekend, but his
splendid example of loyalty is bound to have an excellent effect on
the constituency'.[33] Unlike MacDonald's candidature in Woolwich,
however, Henderson's nomination did not become an issue itself in the
local party. Henderson was widely trusted in a way MacDonald was
not, and this was important in a local party dominated by union
delegates. He had recently shown his willingness to 'think of the
movement' by abandoning his claims on Chester-le-Street, a real
sacrifice since that quite literally would have been a seat for life.[34]
Finally, Widnes was not by any means a sure victory. Henderson was

[27] See below, pp. 183–5.
[28] *Widnes Guardian*, 19 Aug. 1919.
[29] *Widnes Guardian*, 19 Aug. 1919.
[30] *Widnes Guardian*, 22 Aug. 1919.
[31] *Manchester Guardian*, 20 Aug. 1919.
[32] *Manchester Guardian*, 20 Aug. 1919.
[33] *Manchester Guardian*, 20 Aug. 1919.
[34] *Glasgow Herald*, 19 July 1919. Chester-le-Street was one of the two seats in Durham—
the other was Spennymoor—held by Labour in 1931. He gave it up on the grounds that the
publication of the Sankey Report made it necessary to have a miners' candidate.

willing to make a fight of it and the local party stood to gain as much as he did.

If it were an advantage not to be planted in a safe seat, then MacDonald was at a disadvantage. The resignation of Will Crooks early in 1921 made available East Woolwich, a presumably certain victory for the prospective Labour candidate. The details of MacDonald's emergence as candidate are a little obscure but can be more or less reconstructed. The *Conference Report* of 1921 merely noted that the 'Woolwich Labour Party in consultation with the National Executive decided to put forward Mr. J. Ramsay MacDonald as the Labour candidate'.[35] The executive minutes, though more complete, are only a little less reticent. According to them the initiative was taken by the 'officials of the Woolwich Labour Party'[36] which placed the candidature in the hands of the national executive. The minute then reads:

A suggestion that, owing to the strength of the Movement in Woolwich, the contest should be made a national one with a national figure was considered. Ultimately, as a result of a joint meeting of a deputation from the Woolwich Labour Party and the Sub-Committee, it was decided to recommend to the Executive that Mr. J. Ramsay MacDonald be the candidate, and that the Executive assume responsibility for the contest. This proposal was put before the Woolwich Party . . . and full enquiry was made as to prospects and the condition of the organisation. The Conference of the Woolwich Labour Party, after a full explanation and survey of the whole position unanimously selected J. Ramsay MacDonald as their candidate.

But this clotted prose tells us only that the executive had dealings with the Woolwich party. To start with, the fact that financial responsibility was accepted by the executive shows that it very strongly wanted MacDonald as candidate. In the 1920 debate on candidates and constituencies,[37] Wake had said '. . . it was quite true that the National Executive had been told by some of the local Parties that they were quite prepared to accept a National candidate if the Party would provide the funds. As they had no funds at their disposal it was quite impossible to undertake that policy'.[38] With these words only a few months behind them it was unlikely that the Woolwich people asked Head Office for a 'National Candidate'. Had they done so they would probably have offered to accept financial responsibility themselves. Yet the executive offer to accept financial responsibility was an unsolicited one. So, one suspects, was MacDonald's candidature.

Furthermore, it does seem unlikely that the officers of the Woolwich party, who must have been as aware as anybody of the self-interested

[35] *Conference Report*, 1921, p. 39.
[36] 'NEC', 15 Feb. 1921.
[37] *Conference Report*, 1920, p. 125.
[38] *Conference Report*, 1920, p. 125.

patriotism of the Woolwich electors, would want MacDonald as their man: it might have been thought that they would want anyone but MacDonald. The (unsympathetic) *Woolwich Herald* wrote that MacDonald's nomination 'is not altogether welcomed by a section of the Labour voters. Many of them, particularly ex-Service men, would have preferred to give their support to a local man . . .'.[39] But the (sympathetic) *Woolwich Gazette* also regretted the introduction of MacDonald to East Woolwich, carrying in train his war record ('with which Woolwich people have special reason to be conversant'), and thought that the Woolwich agent, Will Barefoot, should have been selected.[40] The following week it announced that 'local people now recognize the folly of allowing themselves to be dictated to by head-quarters'.[41] Finally, *The Times* quoted MacDonald as saying that it was 'largely owing to pressure from the Central Labour Party that he was running'[42]—a curious, though familiar, indiscretion from a man not normally given to direct statements.

It is, therefore, probably fair to assume that MacDonald was chosen by Head Office and only reluctantly accepted by the Woolwich party. His defeat justified their reluctance.[43]

Head Office was not, in principle, disposed to select candidates for constituencies, and constituencies, for their part, were not in principle prepared to accept them. They would, of course, look to Head Office for candidates if they were unable to find any of their own, but having found a candidate for a constituency they were not likely to have him replaced. The executive was able to secure contests for MacDonald and Henderson precisely because it was done so rarely.

But why was it done so rarely? While so many of the local parties were dominated by the unions it was simply impossible to direct them to select a particular candidate, and while the majority of the executive's members were trade-unionists it was unlikely that they would want to. Above all, the trade-unions, generally speaking, still controlled the sources of the Party's finances, and while this was so Head Office was in no position to tell them whom they were to spend it on.

The South Norfolk by-election (July 1920) provides a good example of the way a union could destroy a candidature which did not satisfy its members. At the general election of 1918 the seat had been

---

[39] *Woolwich Herald*, 11 Feb. 1921. (The 'local man' was Leslie Haden Guest, L.C.C. member for Woolwich.)

[40] *Woolwich Gazette*, 1 Mar. 1921.

[41] *Woolwich Gazette*, 8 Mar. 1921.

[42] *The Times*, 10 Feb. 1921.

[43] MacDonald was opposed by Captain Gee, V.C., a Bottomley candidate, and the election was fought largely on MacDonald's supposed wartime record. After an extraordinarily scurrilous campaign, and a huge turnout, MacDonald was defeated by 683 votes. Ironically, of course, all the defeat did was to confirm him as a man martyred for his principles.

contested by George Edwards of the Agricultural Labourers. In May 1920 he had given up the nomination due to ill health and thereafter the emergence of a candidate followed a somewhat confused, if not exactly irregular course. According to Edwards, who remained president of the divisional party, it then asked the Agricultural Labourers to find a new candidate and they nominated William Holmes, one of the organizers of the national Party. At the same time (again according to Edwards) the local officers asked for nominations outside the union. As a result, the former candidate for East Norfolk, W. B. Taylor, a farmer, was selected.[44]

When the seat fell vacant, therefore, a candidate had been regularly selected and should have been ready to fight the by-election. But the local party, meeting on 29 May 1920, decided not to contest the seat. Because Taylor was not officially sponsored by the Agricultural Labourers he was not, the unions said, entitled to any financial assistance. The divisional party was 'in the cart financially',[45] and unable to fight any sort of campaign. It feebly announced that 'it was prompted to this decision by the generally accepted assurance that the Government is not likely to survive the autumn session, and that a general election is certain at an early date'.[46] However, on 17 June 1920, delegates from all fifty-five branches of the Agricultural Labourers' Union in the division met and decided to contest the seat after all. George Edwards was coaxed into renewing his candidacy; Taylor gracefully withdrew and Edwards was then formally nominated.[47] These rather odd proceedings need some untangling.

The secretary of the divisional party told an Agricultural Labourers' demonstration on the same day that

... the last four days had not been of the pleasantest possible description from the standpoint of Labour ... in South Norfolk ... That announcement [not to contest] had caused considerable comment ... and it was made plain that there was a widespread determination among the organised workers of the Division that even the opportunity of contesting a by-election should not be allowed to pass unchallenged by the Labour Party ... [48]

Edwards, himself, when asked why Taylor withdrew, said that the 'necessary financial help could not be found locally for Mr. Taylor'.[49] Walter Smith, the president of the Agricultural Labourers' Union, claimed that '... the same funds were not available for the other

[44] George Edwards, *From Crow-Scaring to Westminster* (London, 1922), pp. 211–12.
[45] *Norwich Mercury*, 3 July, 1920.
[46] *Norwich Mercury*, 17 July 1920.
[47] *Norwich Mercury*, 17 July 1920. Edwards went on to win the by-election.
[48] *Norwich Mercury*, 17 July 1920.
[49] *Eastern Daily Press*, 16 July 1920.

candidate as were available for Mr. Edwards. We have had to make certain rules and regulations for the government of our union . . . and the rules do not make the political fund available to the candidate to whom you refer.'[50]

This was too pat and not altogether true. The rules of the union did not forbid individual branches from making contributions to the campaign funds of a Labour candidate, particularly as that candidate (Taylor) was himself a member of the union. Indeed, there was no reason why Taylor should not have been placed on the union's panel of candidates and formal responsibility taken for him. The real reason for Taylor's resignation appears to have been his unpopularity with important sections of the union in Norfolk.

In the same month that Taylor resigned his candidacy an inaugural meeting of the East Norfolk Divisional Labour Party was held, at which delegates from the Agricultural Labourers' Union were in the majority. The convener, E. G. Loades (Agricultural Labourers), said that in selecting a candidate '. . . he hoped they would have a Labour candidate. They did not want any more farmers' candidates. The railwaymen put forward a farmers' candidate last time [Taylor]. Let them have a workers' candidate next time.'[51]

That was putting the point fairly bluntly. A few days later a letter-writer to the *Eastern Daily Press* asserted that the real reason why Taylor was dropped was that he was an 'opportunist' and not a true Labour man. Taylor had filled 'nearly every political role except Tory'. He was an adept at 'riding three horses at the same time, Farmers' Union and Liberal–Labour'. He was too conservative even for many Liberals—'to wit his support of the Farmers' Union, who, we believe, footed his last election bill'.[52]

In these circumstances it is probably fair to assume that Taylor, though he had been regularly selected by the divisional party and endorsed by the national executive, was forced to withdraw because the most important union—the vital union—in the constituency was not prepared to accept him.

TABLE 8*

General Election	1922	1923	1924
Union M.P.s	85	98	86
All other M.P.s	57	93	65
Union percentage of total	60	52	57

* These figures are extracted from Cole, *History of the Labour Party*, pp. 130, 155, 171.

[50] *Norwich Mercury*, 17 July 1920.
[51] *Norwich Mercury*, 19 June 1920.
[52] *Eastern Daily Press*, 22 June 1920.

The hold the unions had on 'safe' Labour seats can be seen from Table 8. These figures, of course, do not include candidates returned for constituencies where the unions were the chief props, like Seaham (Webb), or Aberavon (MacDonald). It is likely that the great majority of the constituencies won by Labour in the period were, in one way or the other, dependent upon the unions. This being so, they had a not surprising autonomy in the selection of candidates; by extension, as the divisional parties began to return an increasing number of members the same autonomy was given to them.

To this, however, one important qualification needs to be added. Though Head Office did not, and with some notable exceptions could not, choose a constituency's candidate, this was a diminution of its authority of only a limited kind. For financial considerations did not prevent the executive from gaining an almost absolute control over the sort of candidate which all constituencies were required to adopt.[53] Although local parties could inconvenience Head Office, this privilege was in a wider sense, a circumscribed one.

4. Growth and Character of Local Parties

The copious use of 'star' speakers was one way that Head Office encouraged local organization; the regional conferences, themselves heavily dependent upon these same 'stars', were another. The rapid growth of divisional Labour parties (to use the term loosely) was partly a consequence of these efforts and the expansion of the Head Office's organizational facilities. The actual increase can most simply be put in numerical form (Table 9).

TABLE 9

No. of Affiliated Divisional Labour Parties and Trades Councils, 1918–1924

Jan. 1918	June 1918	1919	1920	1921	1922	1923	1924
215	397	400	433	498	527	573	626

Since, however, many constituencies were affiliated twice, these figures can be misleading. Thus, for example, the Aston division of Birmingham was affiliated to the national Party through the Aston divisional party and through the Birmingham Central Labour Party. A rather more accurate way of assessing constituency organization is to look at the number of constituencies without a divisional Labour party. After 1921 (when the national Party's statistics became more reliable) they were as shown in Table 10.

[53] See below, pp. 191–2.

TABLE 10

No. of Constituencies without a Divisional Labour Party, 1921–1924

1921	1922	1923	1924
140	109	54	19

Unfortunately, these figures are also to some extent misleading. Many of these constituencies were in divided boroughs which were, nevertheless, organized by a united party. Neither East nor West Woolwich had a divisional party in 1924 but both were organized by the Woolwich Trades and Labour Council.

In 1921 not much short of half of the constituencies without formal divisional parties were in the cities, and this remained so until 1923 when the real growth of local parties there occurred; but that preceded only by a year a similar growth in the number of county town and rural parties (Table 11).

TABLE 11

No. of Divisions without Local Parties in 14 Cities of England and Scotland

	Total no. of divisions	1921	1922	1923	1924
London (L.C.C. area)	61	15	16	11	11
Glasgow	15	12	4	0	0
Birmingham	12	9	6	4	0
Liverpool	11	2	3	1	1
Manchester	10	2	1	0	0
Sheffield	7	1	1	1	1
Leeds	6	1	0	0	0
Edinburgh	5	4	3	0	0
Bristol	5	1	1	0	0
Bradford	4	4	1	1	1
Newcastle	4	4	2	0	0
Nottingham	4	2	2	2	0
Leicester	3	3	0	0	0
Plymouth	3	3	2	0	0

Yet these figures do not tell us what kind of local party had been affiliated to the national Party, nor how effective such parties were. There is not much point in trying to get anything from the official name of a local party: by 1921 a majority of them were called either 'Divisional Labour Party' or 'Trades Council and Divisional Labour Party' (it was still Head Office policy to amalgamate the two). In fact, it was much more likely that the great majority of them were glorified trades councils, and that the majority of them also had no significant individual membership.[54]

At the outset, it ought to be said that it is impossible to quantify such conclusions as are reached about local organization, and they must be impressionistic, but all the evidence points to these conclusions nevertheless. It is clear from Sidney Webb's correspondence to Beatrice that he was utterly dependent on trade-union officials and the devoted efforts of an honorary agent.[55] When the affairs of the Motherwell Trades Council were being so publicly exposed in 1922–4, two things became apparent: it was not a divisional Labour party, though it was called one, and if it had an individual members' section it was of the most dubious kind.[56] Similarly, rows with the Co-operative Party in Stockport and Paisley showed that the new divisional Labour parties there were quite indistinguishable from the old trades councils. James Griffiths, appointed agent-secretary in Llanelly in 1922, was sure that the reorganization of the Party made not the slightest difference to the local parties in South Wales. In April 1921 the *Labour Organiser* was lamenting the small number of the Party's individual members;[57] yet three years later it was still able to find only two parties with significant individual memberships: Ardwick (Manchester) and Woolwich.[58]

Despite its declining membership after 1919, it is likely that the I.L.P. was still absorbing some of the people who might otherwise have joined the Labour Party directly. The I.L.P. can claim, therefore, to have organized a number of new constituency parties— Marwick points to Leicester, Bradford, and Norwich in England, to much of Scotland, and to some of the constituencies in south Wales, like MacDonald's seat of Aberavon,[59] though the last was as much the responsibility of the iron and steel unions as of the I.L.P.

However, if a new party were to be formed in England or Wales it was most common for the industrial side of the movement, with the co-operation of the I.L.P., to call a foundation meeting, often following a regional conference, and it did not matter what sort of constituency it was. The primary bases of most new constituencies, as of the old, were the trade-union branches, on to which an individual members' section may or may not have been tacked.

Sidney Webb's 'party' in Seaham consisted of his agent together

[54] There are no published figures of the Party's individual membership until 1928.
[55] See Sidney Webb to Beatrice Webb, 28 Nov. 1920; 2 Dec. 1920, 'L.S.E. MS. Passfield: Correspondence,' II.3.(i); also *Seaham Weekly News*, Oct.–Nov. 1922.
[56] See below, pp. 196–203.
[57] *Labour Organiser*, Apr. 1921.
[58] *Labour Organiser*, Aug. 1924.
[59] Marwick, *Independent Labour Party*, pp. 54–60.

with sympathetic union officials, usually from the miners.[60] When Henderson went to Widnes in 1919 he found the Widnes divisional party merely a renamed trades council.[61] John Robertson of the Scottish Miners, the first man to gain a seat for Labour in the 1918 parliament, was nominated by the 'Bothwell Trades Council and Divisional Labour Party'—in reality the old trades council constitutionally unaltered.[62] Chuter Ede, candidate at the Mitcham by-election (February 1923), discovered that the local Labour party, founded in 1918, was a secretary and what few trade-union branches there were in the division.[63] When it came to organizing Merthyr Tydfil, the old trades council was split in two, one half for Merthyr, the other for Aberdare, and both were called divisional Labour parties.[64] The Abertillery Labour Party was a collection of miners' lodges to which was appended a women's section.[65] The newly formed East Norfolk and South Norfolk parties were, both of them, merely colonies of the Agricultural Labourers' Union.[66] In the depths of rural Lincolnshire, the Gainsborough divisional party was formed by a retired congregational minister and the local district organizer of the Engineers and remained very much an Engineers' party.[67]

However much Labour's professional organizers might have disliked the old trades councils, they recognized that it was only upon trade-union branches that the new parties could be founded. Of the organization of new constituencies the *Labour Organiser* wrote:[68]

... the first endeavour would be to try and get possession of all possible information concerning the latent Trades Unionism in the Division. If, as anticipated, it turned out that there was a number of branches scattered about, it would rather depend on the facilities for getting to a centre, whether or no a central conference was decided upon at once.

Assuming for a moment the most difficult case i.e. where a central conference cannot be thought of for a time, there remains the steady slogging work of finding out when these branches meet and of securing invitations to meet them in order that their co-operation might be obtained in future movements.

It can probably be assumed, therefore, that most of the divisional

[60] Sidney Webb to Beatrice Webb, 3 Dec. 1920, 'L.S.E. MS. Passfield: Correspondence,' II.3.(i).
[61] *Widnes Examiner*, 30 Aug. 1919.
[62] *Lanarkshire News*, 5 July, 1919.
[63] *Manchester Guardian*, 28 Feb. 1923.
[64] 'NEC', 15 Feb. 1921.
[65] *Labour Organiser*, Jan. 1921.
[66] For East Norfolk, *Norwich Mercury*, 19 June 1920; for South Norfolk, Edwards, pp. 202–6.
[67] *Retford, Worksop, Isle of Axholme and Gainsborough News*, 10 Nov. 1922.
[68] *Labour Organiser*, Jan. 1922.

Labour parties were, in reality, not strikingly different, if they were different at all, from the pre-war delegate parties—that is, parties whose only members were delegates from affiliated societies, the delegates being elected proportionately to the size of the society, and that these parties gained their strength essentially from trade-union branches. In the few constituencies where there was absolutely no union organization, then, the national Party had to rely on sympathizers and on open public meetings. It was in this sort of constituency, of course, that the I.L.P. came into its own, but it was also one that had to rely on Head Office for most of such organizational success as it had.

At the local level, the other side of the strength of the unions was the weakness of the individual members' sections: in the early 'twenties individual membership of the Party was neither large nor formally important. To this general comment, however, four qualifications ought to be noted. First: although the individual members' sections did not grow at all impressively after 1918, the women's sections did. Some constituencies had very large women's memberships indeed. The 1923 *Conference Report* listed twelve constituencies as having women's memberships of over 200 (Table 12).[69]

TABLE 12

Woolwich	1,008	Newport	300
Barrow	900	North Norfolk	280
Blackburn	500	Heywood and Radcliffe	280
Watford	500	Wood Green	270
York	500	Colchester	220
Gloucester	400	Rugby	210

In the same year the national executive estimated total women's membership at 'over 120,000'.[70] In 1924 it was 'over 150,000' with Barrow joining Woolwich in having a membership of above 1,000.[71] The development of the women's sections was not a new phenomenon; before 1914 they were relatively well filled and much of the work had been done by women then as was done after 1918.

Second, it was possible for any individual to join his local party if he wished. While the section he entered may have been very small, he could be fitted in. This was particularly the case with prominent former Liberals who joined the Party after 1918 or who were only vaguely associated with it before then: J. C. Wedgwood (an M.P.), H. D. Harben (a Fabian), R. L. Outhwaite, E. G. Hemmerde (M.P. for Crewe, 1923–4), E. T. John, Brig.-Gen. C. B. Thomson, and

[69] *Conference Report*, 1923, p. 61.   [71] *Conference Report*, 1924, p. 19.
[70] *Conference Report*, 1923, p. 60.

C. R. Buxton were all, at one time or another, delegates from their local parties to conference, and in their capacity as individual members. If, therefore, the local party were still a delegate one, without permanent ward associations on the lines of the model rules, then delegation from a tiny individual members' section did open up local parties to individuals. This did not give the Labour Party a mass membership, but it allowed in anyone who was determined to join.

Third, just as the name 'Divisional Labour Party' was often misleading, so was the name 'Trades Council'; and it was just as misleading to assume that constituencies without 'model' constituency parties were necessarily deficient in organization. That London had eleven of the nineteen unorganized constituencies looks at first sight surprising. But it was not so. Indeed, under Herbert Morrison's vigorous direction London was one of the most effectively organized parts of the country. Of these eleven, three—St. George's, Abbey, and the City—were as close to impossible for Labour as any in Britain (though even St. George's was capable of unearthing over 6,000 votes for Fenner Brockway in 1924). Two more, Battersea North and South, were certainly not the sort of local organization recommended by Head Office; but North Battersea was Saklatvala's constituency and Communist influence was strong. Similarly, Paddington was the property of the eccentric Hugh Roberts[72] and his trades council successfully avoided any kind of reorganization. But Hammersmith (North and South), though a borough party, had a full-time agent (one of a comparatively small number of parties that did) and it worked effectively;[73] while the organization of Woolwich (East and West) was almost notoriously good, with what was supposed to be the highest number of individual and women members in the country (though if Morrison is to be believed that honour goes to South Poplar with 'a very large individual membership—something over 2,000').[74] Thus, in effect, of the London Labour Party's sixty constituencies, only three (excluding Battersea and including Abbey) could be considered ill organized.

Finally, it ought to be noted that any kind of local organization was able to raise volunteer or informal 'membership'. Before the war,

---

[72] For Roberts, see *Conference Report*, 1919, p. 124.

[73] R. T. Windle, the district organizer for London was by no means convinced that divisional parties in small divided boroughs were more effective than a united borough party: 'The borough parties are in the position of being able to get into contact with all organisations in the borough; irrespective of the constituency in which its members reside ... borough parties are also in the position to make big appeals for finance throughout the borough and to develop schemes for making money ...' (*London Labour Chronicle*, May 1921.) Christopher Addison made his debut as a Labour candidate in North Hammersmith and was entirely satisfied with organization. (See *The Times*, 14 Oct. 1924.)

[74] *Conference Report*, 1923, p. 228.

most ward associations and local parties recruited members for electoral purposes even when there was no statutory form of individual membership. Much the same happened after 1918; it was always easy to bolster local organizations with sympathizers—from the under-nourished unemployed who could be relied on to cause embarrassment at Tory meetings,[75] to the Countess of Warwick's forelock-tugging retainers.[76]

The figures for the number of the Party's full-time agents are also a little deceptive. Certainly, the final product of the much-trumpeted agents' scheme[77] was disappointing; at no time did the number of agents appointed under the scheme exceed 133. The figures were:

1920	112
1921	127
1922	133
1923	111
1924	113

But at election time these numbers were significantly increased. In addition to the official Party agents, there were a number of so-called 'supplementary agents' employed by affiliated bodies, most of them by the Miners. Their numbers were:

1920	24
1921	22
1922	23
1923	26
1924	36

In County Durham, for example, the constituencies of Barnard Castle, Spennymoor, Blaydon, Chester-le-Street, Durham, Sedgefield, Houghton-le-Spring, and South Shields were organized by Miners' agents; Party agents organized Darlington, Gateshead, Stockton-on-Tees, Consett, and Jarrow. Thirteen of the nineteen Durham seats in this way were permanently organized.[78]

Even this excludes from consideration the efforts of volunteer agents who could be either more or less permanent or recruited for the period of the election. Ernest Hunter went to Aberavon to act as agent for MacDonald in 1922,[79] and Sidney Webb had his retired

[75] *Manchester Guardian*, 10 Feb. 1922.
[76] For an amusing account of the Countess's campaign in Warwick and Leamington, see *Birmingham Post*, 6 Nov. 1923.
[77] For the scheme, see above, pp. 32–3.
[78] *Conference Report*, 1923, Appendix VI.
[79] *Western Mail*, 30 Oct. 1922.
6

Congregational minister.[80] When Hugh Dalton won Peckham from the Conservatives in 1924 he was told by Egerton Wake,

You are quite right to attach so much importance to having a good agent. In this constituency I think that will just make the difference between defeat and victory. I have waiting in the next room a most capable and experienced agent, who has already conducted several Parliamentary elections. He happens to be free and I want to use him to the best advantage of the Party. I am prepared to put him at your disposal . . . [81]

The official list, of course, must also exclude the work of district organizers as agents. In by-elections, particularly, it was common for organizers to act as agents: often it meant that constituencies were getting better services than they might have done with a permanent agent of their own. Following T. E. Naylor's by-electoral gain in Walworth (December 1921), the *London Labour Chronicle* noted that victory would not have been possible but for the recent appointment of R. T. Windle, the district organizer who acted as agent, and who ran the campaign.[82]

These preceding explanations and qualifications need obvious recapitulation. In summary, therefore, we can say that the official list of affiliated local parties tells us, prima facie, only a little about the growth of constituency organization, which was always variable, frequently makeshift, and not usually founded upon a stable individual membership. It is clear, furthermore, that the new model parties were slow to develop, that their real strength lay, as it had always done, in trade-union branches and that the absence of a permanent agent by no means meant that a constituency was not working effectively.

5. *Effectiveness of Local Parties*

Although there were constant complaints in Labour circles that the enemy had superior forces at his disposal, these complaints came from men who overrated the importance of organization and who found anything less than perfection displeasing. All the evidence, on the contrary, suggests that outside the rural, semi-rural, and overwhelmingly bourgeois constituencies, the enemy was taken aback by the intensity and vigour of Labour's attack. What Labour lost in cars and money was more than made up by volunteer support and energetic canvassing.

---

[80] Sidney wrote: 'I am writing every day to Herron [his agent] reporting progress . . . I am much impressed by his devotion and philanthropy, mixed with a curious, practical Macchiavellianism. The place would be hapless and hopeless without him . . .' (Sidney Webb to Beatrice Webb, 3 Dec. 1920, 'L.S.E. MS. Passfield: Correspondence,' II.3.(i).)

[81] H. Dalton, *Call Back Yesterday* (London, 1953), pp. 152–3).

[82] *London Labour Chronicle*, Jan. 1922.

After 1918, though the Tory constituency parties continued to function, or were supposed to continue to function, with their usual effortless competence, it was Labour, more than any of the other parties, that tried to construct a 'scientific' method of constituency organization. To some extent this meant making the best of known deficiencies. In place of automobiles and elaborately financed propaganda campaigns, Labour was forced back, as we have seen, on the very extensive use of speakers and public meetings together with a very thorough canvass of the constituency. Outside London, speakers tended to be preferred; London, where the 'scientific' bent was very pronounced,[83] favoured the canvass. Commenting on T. E. Naylor's victory in Walworth, the women's organizer for London, Annie Somers, wrote[84]

Public meetings, though they were held, were a minor matter in our campaign. It was not too much to say that this election *was won on the doorstep.* The fact that such success was scored by this method should lead us to think that the most important duty of the election worker is that of canvassing.

The *Manchester Guardian* was impressed by the success of these methods when C. G. Ammon gained Camberwell North (February 1922).[85] Its correspondent believed that Camberwell was one of those south-side constituencies which were 'the despair of political organisers aiming at efficiency'. Political meetings did not attract constituents (though they went 'to the kinemas whether trade and employment is good or bad') and the only means of touching this electorate was by 'laborious house-to-house canvassing'. This, the *Guardian* conceded, Labour had more than done. The Party had recruited canvassers for every street, who, in the nature of things, were also propagandists. It was a most 'valuable instrument' and Ammon would be 'the first to acknowledge that this is a workers' rather than a candidate victory'.

The same paper was even more struck by Labour's canvassing in the Mitcham by-election. The *Guardian* noted that the Labour Party had 'invented' what is called 'mass canvassing for women'.[86] 'They send several canvassers into a street. These knock at the doors. The women, attracted by curiosity come out, and they are immediately addressed by a speaker in waiting for the purpose, and while the meeting goes on the canvassers are at work.' Chuter Ede's campaign, 'exceptionally well organised on the latest methods by experts from

[83] See Morrison's lapidary comment of 1923: 'The new school of Labour politicians is a scientific school. It knows that noisy tub-thumping does not make up for careful organization.' (*London Labour Chronicle*, Nov. 1921.)
[84] *London Labour Chronicle*, Nov. 1921.
[85] *Manchester Guardian*, 21 Feb. 1922.
[86] *Manchester Guardian*, 28 Feb. 1923.

headquarters'[87] so riveted the Tories that they asked their candidate to imitate it. Sir Arthur Griffith Boscawen (the candidate), with true *hauteur*, refused. It might have served him better had he not, since he was defeated; Ede won the seat, and at Labour's first attempt.

Outside London, observers were equally impressed by Labour's organization, by both its novelty and its energy. It was to be expected that when Henderson was seeking re-election at Widnes no efforts would be spared. The *Widnes Guardian* said that Henderson had the assistance of 'expert organisers', of hundreds of volunteers from Widnes and neighbouring constituencies: 'it is scarcely possible to conceive an election being fought more keenly or more "scientifically"'.[88] Once again the Tories were reluctant admirers of Labour organization. Their candidate was not disappointed: 'Mr Henderson brought with him a powerful and enthusiastic organisation which deserved to win.'[89]

Widnes, after all, was only on the outskirts of Liverpool; the Conservatives might be forgiven for thinking that in the city itself such things could not happen. When J. H. Hayes, of the Policemen's union, was conducting his successful campaign to become the first Labour member for a Liverpool constituency (Edge Hill) in March 1923—an obviously less important by-election than Widnes—this was at first the attitude of the press. The *Daily Courier* announced that Labour had 'no confidence in its own local organisation' and had been forced to import the district organizer, J. H. Standring. It noted that 'Edgehill Conservatives will show these heroic visitants what organisation really means'.[90] By the end of the month it was less sure: it noted the army of Labour women canvassers and the ever-present propaganda which was thoughtful and attractive.[91] The *Liverpool Echo* believed that only in the matter of cars was the Conservative organization superior and agreed with Standring when he said that Labour's poll 'would have been much heavier if they had had more vehicles, the only point in which Labour was beaten'.[92] Once again, it was the seemingly infinite number of canvassers and election-day workers that astonished the reporters.

The rule seemed to be, the more trade unionists the more enthusiastic the organization. The last time a Labour candidate was opposed in Abertillery (in December 1920), the South Wales Miners, who

[87] Ibid.
[88] *Widnes Guardian*, 29 Aug. 1919.
[89] *Widnes Examiner*, 13 Sept. 1919.
[90] *Liverpool Daily Courier*, 21 Feb. 1923.
[91] *Liverpool Daily Courier*, 3 Mar. 1923. That Labour's pictorial propaganda was good is not surprising: its advisers and frequently its draughtsmen were Low and Will Dyson.
[92] *Liverpool Echo*, 7 Mar. 1923.

conducted the by-election, rallied 750 canvassers for the campaign and no less than 1,000 scouts for polling day.[93] A tenth of this number, or even none at all, one imagines, could have held Abertillery. Hugh Dalton recalled that in Cambridge, although he had considerable support from the university, the real strength of the borough Labour party was its railwaymen and building workers.[94]

In general elections all local parties, of course, were to some extent thrown upon their own resources. A constituency without a trained agent, for example, could no longer count on the full-time assistance of the district organizer, nor was it as easy as in a by-election to borrow workers from neighbouring constituencies. Yet the difficulties of organization during a general election can easily be exaggerated. Because constituencies depended for the most part on volunteers and the trade-union branches, electoral organization had a degree of resilience which was pretty constant. It can be argued, indeed, that a general election was more effective in mobilizing support than the less significant demands of a by-election. In any case, because the district organizers were essentially roving agents they did remain in contact with all constituencies in their districts and could rescue any party which got into trouble. Similarly M.P.s for very safe constituencies lent their organizations to neighbouring candidates in more difficult seats: in 1922 most of James Sexton's St. Helens divisional party was sent to Widnes in an unsuccessful attempt to save Henderson.[95]

But dependence upon the trade unions did emphasize certain inequalities in the resources available to different candidates. Those nominated by the larger unions or the Co-operative Party were much more lavishly funded than those who were not. Excluding certain individuals of private means[96], much the best financed of all Labour candidates were those of the Miners' Federation. In 1918 it contested fifty-one constituencies: the average expenditure of candidates for these same seats in 1922 (excluding three unopposed), 1923 (excluding three unopposed), and 1924 (excluding eight unopposed) was respectively £804, £662, and £624.[97] In 1923 and 1924 the average expenses of a miners' candidate were higher than the average expenditure of Labour candidates in any of the county constituencies in

[93] Labour Organiser, Jan. 1921.
[94] H. Dalton, Call Back Yesterday, p. 130.
[95] Widnes Guardian, 14 Nov. 1922.
[96] There were a few of these, like Noel Buxton in North Norfolk, J. C. Wedgwood in Newcastle-under-Lyme, Susan Lawrence in East Ham South, and, to the good fortune of Tyneside Labour, C.P. Trevelyan in Newcastle Central and David Adams (the shipowner) in Newcastle West. Their 1922 election expenses are in Parliamentary Accounts and Papers, 1924 (2) XVIII, pp. 681 ff., as are all other figures for 1922 expenditure.
[97] The figures for 1923 are in Parliamentary Accounts and Papers, 1924 (51), XVIII, pp. 775 ff.; 1924 are in Parliamentary Accounts and Papers, 1926 (1) XXII, pp. 523 ff.

England, Scotland, and Wales, and at least 50 per cent higher than the average for all candidates.

The only county seats in the United Kingdom where Labour candidates spent anywhere near the legal maximum were in Wales. The expenditure of candidates in industrial Welsh county seats (1922) is shown in Table 13.

TABLE 13

Constituency	Expenditure £	Legal Maximum £
Llanelly	715	1,423
Wrexham	500	1,151
Caerphilly	377	1,044
Gower	960	965
Neath	1,410	1,273
Ogmore	792	1,157
Pontypridd	1,373	1,198
Ebbw Vale	1,003	966

To this list should be added Aberavon, where MacDonald was largely financed by the iron and steel workers' unions, and Pontypool where Tom Griffiths was candidate of the Steel Smelters.

Aberavon	1,013	1,104
Pontypool	787	946

Of these constituencies, only Llanelly, Wrexham, and Caerphilly were well below the legal limits. Caerphilly was anyway outstanding: its funds had been drained by a by-election in August 1921 and although the constituency was organized by the South Wales Miners, its member, Morgan Jones, was a nominee of the I.L.P. Like Caerphilly, Llanelly was organized by the Miners, but its member, Dr. Williams, was nominated by the local party. Similarly, Wrexham, though it fielded an official of the South Wales Miners in 1918, was the responsibility of the local party in 1922.

The position in Scotland, where so many of the candidates were

TABLE 14

Constituency	Expenditure £	Legal Maximum £
South Ayrshire	925	889
Bothwell	742	909
Hamilton	647	799
North Lanark	794	885
Midlothian and Peebles N.	735	727
Midlothian and Peebles S.	684	777

nominated by the I.L.P. or the local parties, was even more striking. In 1922 the expenditure of Miners' candidates in Scottish county seats was as shown in Table 14 on previous page.

But expenditure in many of the other county constituencies was almost ludicrously low (see Table 15). Only William Westwood in Perth and Shinwell in Linlithgow were reasonably well provided for.

TABLE 15

Constituency	Expenditure £	Legal Maximum £
Bute and North Ayrshire	190	1,160
Kilmarnock	208	968
Berwick and Haddington	145	966
Dumbarton County	364	1,125
Coatbridge	250	895
Lanark	317	848
Rutherglen	326	948
Renfrew East	316	828
Renfrew West	232	842
Stirling and Clackmannan East	361	921
Stirling and Clackmannan West	387	670

In the Scottish boroughs, similarly, only those candidates, like Morel in Dundee,[98] who had support from a strong local union

TABLE 16

Constituency	Expenditure £	Legal Maximum £
Bridgeton	113	761
Camlachie	217	730
Cathcart	215	688
Central	451	902
Gorbals	386	840
Govan	129	641
Hillhead	171	545
Kelvingrove	179	785
Maryhill	198	704
Partick	400	588
Pollok	137	659
St. Rollox	214	776
Shettleston	133	619
Springburn	147	714
Tradeston	554	702

[98] See W. W. Walker, 'Dundee's Disenchantment with Churchill', *Scottish Historical Review* 49, 1 (April 1970), p. 103.

(Juteworkers), or who were nominated by the Co-operative Party, could hope for much. This was certainly so in Glasgow, where the only two candidates who drew on substantial funds were the two Co-operative candidates, Andrew Young (Partick) and Tom Henderson (Tradeston). The others showed an appropriately contemptuous disregard for the cash nexus. In 1923 the figures for the fifteen Glasgow divisions were as shown in Table 16 (on previous page).

Obviously too much should not be made of this rather austere attitude to constituency finances: it was matched by the scarcity of national finances and its effect on organization may have been slighter than Labour organizers cared to admit. In spite of the figures Labour did win Coatbridge, Rutherglen, East Renfrew, and West Renfrew. The majority of the Glasgow constituencies were consistently won by Labour in this period while Maxton, Wheatley, Campbell Stephen, Buchanan, and McLean could presumably have been elected without money ever changing hands.[99] The volunteer work for local parties could not be measured in money terms, and this was, after all, the backbone of almost all local organizations. But if a candidate wished to fight an elaborate or expensive campaign then it was in his interest to be a drummer boy for the big battalions.

6. *The Rural Constituencies*

The Labour Party never defined precisely what it meant by the 'rural' constituencies it thought necessary to win. In the almost infinite discussion of how they might best be conquered, there was a good deal of confusion as to what they were. In practice, Labour's professionals tended to regard any constituency which had little or no industry, and few, if any, union members, as a 'rural' constituency, and that is a useful enough definition.

The rural divisions presented Labour with unique problems. Outside parts of Norfolk none of the usual props of the Labour Party was in evidence—yet Labour was as anxious to win the rural seats as it was to win any other kind. It was not, of course, unusual for European socialist parties to write their programmes with an eye to the peasantry, but this was usually grudging and accompanied by protracted theoretical disputes. Labour's position, characteristically, was not affected by such complications; the Party assumed, with its customary disregard for a rigorous ideology, that it was as fully

---

[99] This was true elsewhere: one need look no further than John Beckett's victory at Gateshead in 1924. In one of the most extraordinary results of the whole election. Beckett turned a Liberal majority of 655 into a Labour one of 9,366. His expenditure was £323 and the legally allowed maximum £1,180.

entitled to represent both the agricultural labourers and farmers as it was to represent workers by hand and brain in the cities.

Attending closely such beliefs was the sentimental feeling that the rural seats ought to be won—that it was the Party's mission to liberate them from the feudal burdens under which they were supposed to languish. Squire and parson were as much a part of Labour's demonology as they were in that of any Liberal land reformer.

Finally, Labour organizers, from Head Office downwards, all shared the mistaken view—and one would have thought an obviously mistaken view—that the rural county constituencies must be won before Labour could expect a parliamentary majority. At the 1923 Conference MacDonald stated this as unquestioned fact.[100] The next year Wake said that the seats Labour had not previously contested (by which he meant, for the most part, unorganized rural seats) were 'the whole problem in regard to the future of the Labour Party'.[101] The Labour candidate for Lewes, Captain Basil Hall, wrote to Francis Galton, the corresponding secretary of the Fabian Society, that the 'Agricultural Constituencies south of the Thames are the only door left open before Labour can enter into real power'.[102]

Organizing the rural seats was generally recognized to be a job without quick returns. The Labour propagandist, one agent wrote, 'must be content with a faith like some of the religious pioneers, satisfied that they were doing the right thing, leaving time to tell in their or in another's day'.[103] The problem was : how did the organizer make the rural constituencies even aware that a Labour Party existed? If there were trade-union branches, they were used by organizers with the greatest relief; if not, then the Party had to rely on public meetings run by sympathetic locals—'a socialist vicar, a Labour schoolmaster, an enlightened small farmer'.[104]

H. N. White, the agent for Warwick and Leamington, thought that short, sharp campaigns were all that could be expected. For a by-election at Warwick he was given the services of a national organizer, J. W. Kneeshaw, for a six-day campaign, while Kneeshaw brought with him a couple of 'famous tub thumping orators'.[105] Seventeen meetings were held—two each evening—and five afternoon meetings.

Arrangements were made for the first meeting to commence at 7.30, both speakers being present—the first speaker being allowed 30 minutes, after

[100] *Conference Report*, 1923, pp. 204–5.
[101] *Conference Report*, 1924, pp. 180–1.
[102] Basil Hall to Galton, 14 Apr. 1924, 'FHD', Box 16, 'Elections'.
[103] *Labour Organiser*, Apr.–May 1923.
[104] *Labour Organiser*, Oct. 1923.
[105] *Labour Organiser*, July–Aug. 1922.

which he was conveyed to the second meeting place—which was anything from three to six miles away, the conveyance returning for the second speaker, who was timed to leave 40 minutes later . . . When within five miles of a local party, one of the members was sent out to act as chairman. Advantage was taken to sell the *Labour Searchlight* [the local Labour paper] which, if the villagers showed diffidence, was preceded with a copy gratis, of 'The Labour Party's Fight for the Agricultural Wages Board.' Where that bait did not succeed, the agent challenged the sporting instinct, which resulted in a copy being pocketed, if not paid for.

Other agents merely relied upon fairly frequent meetings without any of the trimmings White thought necessary.[106] George Edwards, however, was one of the few candidates who could collect thousands at his meetings, but then South Norfolk was one of the handful of rural seats that Labour could win.

Practically all of Mr. Edwards' meetings were held outside, and even his eve-of-the-poll rallies, chiefly Attleborough and Wymondham were attended by some thousands. Coming on from Attleborough Mr. Edwards was played into Wymondham by the Soldiers' Federation Brass Band, and was given the reception of his life on the Fairland where he was supported by the Earl of Kimberley and three Labour Members of Parliament.[107]

In most areas, fighting rural constituencies was much more difficult than this. Some campaigns were disasters: the executive was always torn between a desire to establish Labour in a constituency and a not surprising fear of the débâcles which often followed. The physical size of many constituencies made it very difficult for Labour's essentially amateur organization to work, presuming there were any volunteers to start with. Even in a county seat like Seaham, which Labour could win very easily, Sidney Webb found the distances and bad roads almost intolerable—while the back seat of his agent's motor cycle was physically exhausting, not to speak of its effect on his piles.[108] Lack of mobility was thus the most obvious and insurmountable problem. All remaining obstacles, from the British Legion to the women's institutes, had to be taken in a candidate's stride.

On several occasions Head Office was pushed into candidatures by local enthusiasm and much against its better judgement. In August–September 1921 the executive sanctioned a candidature for a by-election in Louth. At a first contest the Labour candidate finished bottom of the poll. Apparently the contest was approved over the objections of Henderson since Webb found him a few days later

---

[106] See Minnie Pallister, *The Orange Box* (1925), pp. 47 ff.
[107] *Norwich Mercury*, 21 July 1920.
[108] Sidney Webb to Beatrice Webb, 2 Dec. 1920, 'L.S.E. MS. Passfield: Correspondence,' II.3.(i).

'self-congratulatory at the Labour collapse at Louth which he had predicted'.[109]

In March 1923 the Ludlow division of Shropshire fell vacant and the local party decided to seek Head Office approval for a contest. Labour had not previously fought the seat and great difficulty was had in finding a candidate.[110] One of the national organizers, Harry Drinkwater, was sent to the constituency and returned strongly opposed to fighting; his '. . . own reasonings were those that are natural to an officer of the organisation department in whose opinions considerations of strategy, prestige and a certain ordered disposition of the forces always weigh'.[111] It seems as if Head Office agreed to a candidate only because the few trade unionists in Ludlow itself would have been put out had it not.

The contention of the Labour headquarters is that now the Labour Party are H.M. official opposition every vacant seat must be contested by the Labour Party. Locally they were informed that there would have been serious trouble among the miners and railwaymen in the Division if the seat was not fought on this occasion.[112]

This, presumably, was one of the problems of having a few unionists in an essentially non-union constituency; without them a candidate could have been decently refused. At any rate one was found, an I.L.P.er who candidly confessed that agricultural problems were new to him,[113] and he finished very badly bottom of the poll.[114]

Among the Party organizers there was a good deal of recrimination after the event: the 1924 conference report noted tartly that the time was 'too short, and the area too wide, for an effective campaign, but the contest has probably opened up the constituency for future development'.[115] Harry Drinkwater, whose advice had not been followed, wrote a long article criticizing contests of this kind.[116] He dismissed the old argument that they were good for propaganda as no longer acceptable. More consideration should have been given to the state of organization in the constituency. With a nod in the direction where Labour's strength really lay, he commented '. . . upon the utter lack of any Labour or Trade Union movement. It is, indeed, rare to

[109] Sidney Webb to Beatrice Webb, 24 Sept. 1921, 'L.S.E. MS. Passfield: Correspondence, II.3.(i).
[110] Labour Organiser, Apr.–May 1923.
[111] Ibid.
[112] Ludlow Advertiser, 7 Apr. 1923.
[113] Ludlow Advertiser, 7 Apr. 1923.
[114] The figures were: Cons. 9,956; Lib. 6,740; Lab. 1,420.
[115] Conference Report, 1924, p. 56.
[116] Labour Organiser, Apr.–May 1923.

discover a constituency of seven or eight hundred square miles without a single Trades Council or properly organised party. There are whole villages, even towns, without a Trade Union branch . . .'. He concluded with the observation that the result ought to lead to the 'undeceiving of the blindness which could lead so many of us to believe that a Labour Government was yet possible with rural England in its present temper'.

One might have expected, therefore, that since rural England had to be vanquished before Labour entered into the fullness of power and since organization was so frail, Head Office would take fairly drastic measures to assist rural parties. Fortunately this did not happen. Certainly, a few days after Ludlow, Henderson took up suggestions for propaganda tours made by Drinkwater and some of the rural agents.[117]

What Henderson was unable to do, however, was to redistribute electoral finances so that agricultural constituencies got more, and the industrial seats less. Though money was granted to rural constituencies from the so-called 'Fighting Fund', the funds were themselves so small that the Party in practice could do very little to help them. Everything suggests that in seats other than those where unions had accepted responsibility expenditure was minimal and the position of candidates pretty desperate.

Basil Hall, candidate for Lewes in 1923, wrote that the

Election cost £350 of which I have supplied £250 and £100 was collected by other means. I personally have absolutely no funds left, and though the Divisional Party is setting about the collection of money it is not likely that a constituency which is mainly agricultural will be able to collect enough to meet the expenses of an election especially one in the near future, and it looks at present doubtful whether the seat can be contested by a Labour candidate.[118]

The agent for Cromer, S. G. Gee, thought in 1923 that the Party had only enough money to contest half the rural constituencies in the kingdom, and those unsatisfactorily. In giving his estimate of the financial needs of the rural constituencies, Gee wrote that he could not see how '. . . an average rural constituency can be run on less than £600 per year for the first two or three years of a prospective candidature . . . Then for the Parliamentary Election the sum of £1,000 should be available for the contest.'[119] Clearly, this was an ideal to which all rural parties would have liked to aim : but it was a literally

---

[117] 'NEC', 24 Apr. 1923.
[118] Hall to Francis Galton, 14 Feb. 1924, 'FHD', Box 16, 'Elections'.
[119] *Labour Organiser*, Oct. 1923.

fantastic sum and one which, as Gee himself recognized, had no relation to what was financially possible.

The continued financial weakness of the agricultural constituencies can best be seen by looking at the expenditure of some of those rural constituencies which took responsibility for their own candidates as against those where a union had taken responsibility.

In the county divisions of Warwick, for example, which Labour contested in 1923, T. Barrow of the Warwickshire Miners spent £1,035 in Nuneaton against a maximum of £1,443, while in neighbouring Warwick and Leamington the Countess of Warwick could find only £475 against £1,259. In Gainsborough (Lincolnshire), a hopeless constituency, James Read of the Engineers, and secretary of the Coventry shop stewards' movement,[120] could spend £863 (maximum £974), while not far away, A. E. Stubbs, who lost Cambridge County by only 679, collected just £171 (maximum £1,069).[121]

More or less the same thing happened in those Norfolk constituencies contested by the Agricultural Labourers and those (excluding Noel Buxton, who had private funds) which were not (see Table 17).

TABLE 17

Norfolk County Divisions in the 1922 General Election

Constituency	Candidate	Expenditure £	Legal Maximum £
Norfolk East	G. E. Hewitt	327	939
King's Lynn	R. B. Walker	838	1,025
Norfolk S.-W.	W. B. Taylor	205	942
Norfolk South	G. Edwards	495	943

Of the four candidates, two, Walker and Edwards, were nominated by the Agricultural Labourers. Edwards's expenditure is low only because a by-election had been fought there two years before. But at the following general election, when Edwards was the only union nominee, his expenditure rose while those of the others fell or remained the same (Table 18).

[120] For Read's nomination, see *Retford, Worksop, Isle of Axholme and Gainsborough News*, 27 Oct. 1922.

[121] See the testimony of a delegate from the Cambridge Labour Party at the 1923 conference: 'This particular constituency [Cambridge County] was fought without a penny piece from the Central Office, and it showed what could be done in rural constituencies.' (*Conference Report*, 1923, p. 203). Stubbs was one of those Labour stalwarts whose career was almost heroic. He stood for Cambridgeshire on eight successive occasions (1922, 1923, 1924, 1929, 1931, 1935, 1945, and 1950), winning it sensationally in 1945 and losing it narrowly in 1950.

TABLE 18

Constituency	Candidate	Expenditure £	Legal Maximum £
Norfolk East	G. E. Hewitt	314	958
King's Lynn	J. Stephenson	452	1,043
Norfolk S.-W.	W. B. Taylor	212	949
Norfolk South	G. Edwards	561	961

It must be concluded that, for the most part, the rural constituencies were either badly organized or not organized at all. Aside from the social and political obstacles that stood in the way of Labour successes in the rural areas, it was clear that without substantial assistance from Head Office the rural parties could not hope for effective organization. But since Head Office did not control the sources of Labour's electoral finances, this could not be done. It is appropriate, therefore, to look at these finances in a little detail.

7. Party Finances

One of the principal governors of the way Party organization developed was the origin and relative scarcity of its funds. While there was always sufficient available for the needs of Head Office itself, its failure to centralize Labour's political finances meant that the unions remained masters of their own political expenditure. Organizational strength, at least as measured by money, found, so to speak, its own level without the executive being able to do much else than marginally adjust it.

The 1918 constitution levied the unions' affiliation fee at 2d. per member per annum but optimistically provided for the establishment of a central fund to supplement the electoral expenses of each candidate. In 1918 about £15,000 was distributed to the constituencies from this fund and the Party thereupon had a minor financial crisis. In January 1919 Henderson presented a slightly panicky memorandum to the executive reporting that the estimated deficit for the year would be £7,000 and that planned expenditure was running well ahead of presumed income.[122] The executive, therefore, decided to ask the 1919 conference to abolish the central fund and at the same time to raise the union levy to 3d. per member per annum.

The debate on these two proposals almost exactly paralleled that in 1912 when the executive tried to raise the union levy to 2d. per member. Henderson began with a long statement explaining that 'it

[122] 'NEC', 2 Jan. 1919. The income from affiliation fees in 1918–19 was £20,882 and the deficit that year was made good by the sale of treasury bills and war-bearer bonds.

was absolutely impossible for them to go on at the present rate of contribution' and certainly impossible to increase the number of parliamentary candidatures at the next general election. Indeed, he suggested that without the increase there was no chance of the Party expanding at all in any direction.

The attack on both these amendments—the abolition of the central fund and the increase in the levy—was led, as it had been in 1912, by Will Thorne of the Gasworkers. Thorne was simply opposed to any increases (or 'monetary penalties' as he called them) in the trade-union contributions and this he did by bombarding conference with details of the minute contributions paid by the socialist societies—as he had done in 1912.

He said unhesitatingly that the method of payment was absolutely rotten. If they examined their balance sheet and the fee paid by some organisations and examined the membership they would have to come to the conclusion that they were not playing the square game, and not paying to the Parliamentary Funds [the central fund].

After a good deal of wrangling between unions and unions, and unions and Snowden, a compromise suggested by MacDonald (as Party treasurer) was accepted. MacDonald proposed that the conference agree to the abandonment of the central fund, while Head Office would drop plans for raising the levy. But if, by next year, the financial position had not improved then the conference could be approached again to raise the levy. Should an election occur in the meantime MacDonald assured the conference that the ending of parliamentary grants would make 'no difference to the number of members they returned to the House of Commons'. MacDonald did not explain how this might be done, but he rather undid the force of Henderson's argument.

By the following year, however, the drafting of the General Scheme of Organisation[123] and the appointment of the district organizers had made the 3d. levy essential, and this was accepted by everyone. At the 1920 conference the increase was approved without opposition and without debate.[124] This greatly expanded Head Office's income and gave Henderson more room for manœuvre in developing national organization. Annual payments from affiliation fees were thereafter as in Table 19 on following page.

But the increases did little, if anything, for the local parties: 1920 was the first of three successive conferences at which delegates attempted to direct funds from the unions and union-sponsored candidates to less well-endowed constituencies. D. B. Foster of the

[123] For which, see below, pp. 174-6.   [124] *Conference Report*, 1920, pp. 121-2.

TABLE 19

	£
1919–20	30,244
1920–1	48,776
1921–2	54,869
1922–3	42,671
1923–4	49,341

Leeds Labour Party moved that trade unions be asked to give a greater proportion of their political funds to the local parties.[125] Seconding the motion, G. R. Shepherd, the future national agent, significantly added that if the trade unions 'were going to control the local Labour parties they ought to pay more to the upkeep of the parties than they did now'. The resolution was carried on a show of hands, but as the chairman, W. H. Hutchinson, said, it 'was merely a declaration of opinion and did not commit the conference to anything'.

The same conference, however, also instructed the executive to examine the whole basis of local party finance and to report the following year.[126] This report, presented to the 1921 conference,[127] contained not a crumb for the hard-pressed local parties.

In the present stage of the Party's development [it said] . . . it is not practicable to equalise the financial support available for candidates in all constituencies. This could only be accomplished by the centralisation of political funds of all our affiliated organisations, and at present the Party, even if such method [sic] were deemed advisable, is not ready to take such a step.

It could only urge all union branches to affiliate to their local parties and hope that the parties 'would make an earnest attempt to develop the individual membership . . . this development has not received the attention it deserves'. At the same conference a resolution from the Blackburn Labour Party asking the executive to 'devise suitable minimum affiliation fees payable to local Labour parties' was also defeated.[128]

The local parties returned to the attack for the third time at the 1922 conference when the Broxtowe divisional party moved that '. . . this Conference thinks the time has arrived when all political Labour funds should be pooled, and requests the National Executive Committee to arrange a Conference of all affiliated Societies to discuss this and report to the next Conference'.[129] MacDonald, as

[125] See *Conference Report*, 1920, pp. 130–1.
[126] Ibid., pp. 122–3.
[127] *Conference Report*, 1921, pp. 46–8.
[128] *Conference Report*, 1921, pp. 203–4.
[129] Debate in *Conference Report*, 1922, pp. 216–17.

treasurer, opposed this and was obliged to indulge in much necessary nonsense about electing 'free men' who would accept 'a discipline which was not servitude'; that, it turned out, could best be achieved by local parties finding their own finances.

But the general election of 1922, both by drawing so heavily upon the Party's resources and showing how comparatively meagre they were, made it apparent that some kind of central fund would have to be restored. So far as the election went, the Party did not do too badly (see Table 20), but the strain on finances was severe.

TABLE 20

Expenditure of Labour Candidates at the General Election of 1922*

London Boroughs		English Boroughs	
No. of Candidates:	45	No. of Candidates:	140
Average Expenses:	£304	Average Expenses:	£534
Scottish Burghs		*Welsh Boroughs*	
No. of Candidates:	23	No. of Candidates:	10
Average Expenses:	£408	Average Expenses:	£608
English Counties		*Scottish Counties*	
No. of Candidates:	153	No. of Candidates:	19
Average Expenses:	£614	Average Expenses:	£479
Welsh Counties		Total All Candidates:†	407
No. of Candidates:	17	Total All Expenses:	£221,300
Average Expenses:	£823	Total Average:†	£541

* These figures are extracted from lists of expenses of parliamentary candidates in *Parliamentary Accounts and Papers etc.*
† Excluding three unopposed.

When the 1923 conference met Henderson called for the establishment of what he called a Fighting Fund, so that Head Office could assist struggling local parties in a way that had not been possible before, an assistance which was even more necessary now that accumulated reserves had disappeared.[130] Henderson's speech was caustically received by a delegate from the West Ham party, who said '. . . he was very glad to hear that the Executive had come to the conclusion that the Local Labour Parties might be of some use to them. They had been taking the wrong line when they depended entirely on Trade Unions for support.'

Between this conference and the general election, £23,565 was collected, of which £10,000 came from the National Union of Railwaymen and about £8,505 from Party appeals and conference contributions. In addition, Henderson raised £4,045 from his 'friends'. Of this total about £18,000 was distributed: £5,175 to

[130] *Conference Report*, 1923, pp. 201–7.

fifty-seven rural constituencies and £11,600 to 158 urban constituencies. Each candidate received from £25 to (in three cases only)
£200. Total expenditure for the election of 1923 was as shown in
Table 21:

TABLE 21

Expenditure of Labour Candidates at General Election of 1923

London Boroughs		English Boroughs	
No. of Candidates:	48	No. of Candidates:	56
Average:	£351	Average:	£460
Scottish Burghs		Welsh Boroughs	
No. of Candidates:	28	No. of Candidates:	10
Average:	£325	Average:	£569
English Counties		Scottish Counties	
No. of Candidates:	144	No. of Candidates:	21
Average:	£510	Average:	£425
Welsh Counties		Total All Candidates:*	422
No. of Candidates:	15	Total All Expenses:	£194,627
Average:	£638	Total Average:*	£463

* Excluding three unopposed.

It is clear from these figures, apart from the obvious decline in
expenditure in all types of constituency, that the urban divisions were
still relative to their needs better financed than the county divisions and
that, if anything, the disparity had increased, despite the establishment
of the Fighting Fund. This situation caused embarrassment at Head
Office. When A. G. Cameron asked why no details of the Fund had
been given to the executive, Henderson replied that the election sub-
committee (MacDonald, Henderson, and Webb) 'had always been
prepared to answer any questions regarding the Fund, but that it had
been deemed unwise to indicate the comparatively small amount
upon which the Party had fought the General Election'.[131]

In fact, the Fighting Fund always remained something of a mystery.
Though total receipts and total expenditure were given to the executive, there was no information about its actual distribution or the
names and contributions of Henderson's 'friends'.[132] Despite the
vaunted publicity of Labour's accounts they remained a secret
between Henderson and the contributors. It is obvious, furthermore,
that (unlike today) it was the Party secretary and not the treasurer

---

[131] 'NEC', 26 Mar. 1924. Susan Lawrence protested at the way (she said) Henderson was
concealing information from the executive.

[132] One name was revealed in 1924 when Henderson, *pour encourager les autres*, read a
letter from his close friend, Bernhard Barron, the founder of Carreras Cigarettes, donating
£5,000 to the Party's campaign funds. (*Conference Report*, 1924, p. 185.)

(MacDonald) who collected the Party's private funds; indeed, all the finances appear to have been in Henderson's hands. Had MacDonald not treated his post as a sinecure to ensure *ex officio* membership of the executive, details of finances might have been less obscure.

In the general election of 1924, though a total of £20,150 was distributed to the constituencies, Head Office was unable to reverse the unfavourable position of the county divisions. The differential between them and the urban divisions became considerably larger and many constituencies appear to have been on their last legs.[133] The London boroughs were actually able to increase their average expenditure while the decline in county expenditure had accelerated more than elsewhere (Table 22).

TABLE 22

Expenditure of Labour Candidates at the General Election of 1924

London Boroughs		English Boroughs	
No. of Candidates:	53	No. of Candidates:	175
Average Expenses:	£412	Average Expenses:	£412
Scottish Burghs		Welsh Boroughs	
No. of Candidates:	31	No. of Candidates:	9
Average Expenses:	£325	Average Expenses:	£517
English Counties		Scottish Counties	
No. of Candidates:	185	No. of Candidates:	32
Average Expenses:	£456	Average Expenses:	£367
Welsh Counties		Total All Candidates:*	501
No. of Candidates:	16	Total All Expenses:	£222,166
Average Expenses:	£623	Total Average:*	£433

* Excluding eight unopposed.

8. Summary

The refusal to centralize funds or equalize expenditure was not, despite what MacDonald said, due to a desire to encourage healthy independence in the Party's M.P.s, but because the trade unions were not prepared to surrender the autonomy of their political expenditure. The whole debate about constituency organization and finance assumed that trade-union domination of the local parties was not only a fact but an inevitable fact. It may not have been inevitable, but it was true, at the very least until 1924, that local party organization

---

[133] Webb's party at Seaham was pretty close to exhaustion even by 1923. He wrote to Beatrice that 'he had warned them of the probable election, and of the Party's poverty, and it would have to be done entirely on a voluntary basis'. (Sidney Webb to Beatrice Webb, 28 Oct. 1923, 'L.S.E. MS. Passfield: Correspondence,' II.3.(i). James Griffiths recalls that his party in Llanelly was saved only by a meeting addressed by MacDonald at which £150 was collected.

was utterly dependent upon the unions as institutions and upon their officers and members as individuals. And this was as true in the rural constituencies as it was anywhere else: because unions were weaker in the rural areas so was organization. To say that the constituencies were dependent upon the unions is not to deny the importance of the I.L.P. or of individual sympathizers. But the importance of the I.L.P. had been steadily diminishing since the war and it was to be years before individual members began to take its place.

The inability of Head Office to centralize funds had one important consequence. It meant that organization was strongest and best financed in those constituencies Labour could win; it was most shaky in those constituencies Labour could not. Equalization might have diverted resources to the rural parties, but that could have meant the loss of potential Labour seats without any compensating gains. It is probably fair to say that, with the exception of a few in Wales and a couple elsewhere, Labour had won as many rural seats by 1924 as it ever would win.

VIII

REGIONS, CO-OPERATORS AND COMMUNISTS

1. The Regions

THE problem of the regions was a left-over from the pre-war years[1] and had been the subject of long and not always successful negotiations. It was obvious that these negotiations would have to be taken up again anyway, but made more so by the turn of events in Scotland's politics during the First World War. It was plain at the first conference of the Scottish Advisory Council of the Labour Party in 1915 that the lurch to the left in the west of Scotland was going to cause difficulties only secondarily concerned with organization itself, but whose effect on organization would be considerable.[2] Almost everything that happened in Scotland between 1915 and 1924 was a product of the strength of the Scottish left—of the power of the I.L.P., of the relative weakness of the trade unions outside Glasgow, of the smallness of many of the local parties, and of the ease with which they were dominated by I.L.P.ers, Socialists, and later Communists.

The original Henderson scheme for Scotland, and the one under which the Scottish Advisory Council had first met in 1915, had not really satisfied anyone there. From the beginning the Council freely considered matters—such as the war and Labour's representation in the government—that were, strictly speaking, outside its competence. Delegates from the national executive were, they felt, not given the respect due to them; after the September 1916 conference the executive felt obliged to insist on the right of their delegates to participate in any conference business.[3] By 1917 Scotland's dissatisfaction with the *status quo* was evident both at the Scottish conference of that year[4] and in the attempts of the Scottish executive to gain that autonomy it had failed to obtain in 1913–14.

From the position, therefore, of a Scottish executive which tended to be at odds with the executive over important matters of policy, there

---

[1] See above, p. 43.
[2] See above, p. 42.
[3] 'NEC', 19 Oct. 1916. Egerton Wake was the delegate, a fact of some later importance. See below, p. 164.
[4] S.A.C., *Conference Report*, 1917, pp. 43–6.

was a good case to be made for constitutional alterations that would give it a certain political autonomy, as well as autonomy in organization. Furthermore, the end of 1917, despite what Henderson later said, did seem an appropriate moment to think about Scottish organization. With the national Party being reorganized there was no good reason why regional organization should not be considered at the same time. Thus, when the Scottish executive met on 1 December 1917 to draft revisions to the Scottish constitution, its members hoped to exploit the favourable situation in Scotland as well as the new conditions created by Henderson's draft constitution.

The new constitution for Scotland, drafted in December 1917,[5] opened boldly by transforming the Advisory Council into the 'Scottish Labour Party' (and the reminders of Hardie's Scottish Labour Party of 1888[6] may not have been unconscious). It renewed Scotland's demands for a special position in the national Party. The Scottish executive was to have two delegates at the national conference, quite apart from the number of delegates the Scottish unions and local parties would have had in any case. Even more importantly, the Scottish executive was to be automatically represented on the executive, again apart from any other Scots who were elected in an ordinary capacity. The executive reaffirmed its right (which it already possessed in limited measure) to endorse Scottish parliamentary candidates and to draw up a specifically Scottish parliamentary programme. At the last minute, Ben Shaw, the Scottish secretary, accurately anticipating Henderson's likely reaction, talked the executive into reintroducing the word 'Council' into its name.[7] When the constitution was sent to London on 8 December it was headed 'The Scottish Council of the Labour Party'.

Henderson was profoundly irritated by the amendments, as much by their timing as their content. He thought that it was absolutely the worst time to raise questions of Scottish revision. This irritation was almost certainly reinforced by Wake, who accompanied Henderson and Peters when they met the Scottish executive on 22 December 1917. Henderson opened his long statement with the pointed observation that 'notwithstanding very great pressure at the office, they had come specially to discuss with the Scottish executive' the proposed draft.[8] While Head Office hoped to be as fair as possible to Scotland, the Scottish executive must realize that 'such proposals could wait in view of the enormous importance of creating the new Divisional organisations'. Henderson again emphasized (as he was to do at both Party conferences the following year) that it was the next election

[5] 'SEC', 7 Dec. 1917; also 'NEC', 9 May 1918. [7] 'SEC', 7 Dec. 1917.
[6] Pelling, *Origins of the Labour Party*, pp. 69–71. [8] 'SEC', 22 Dec. 1917.

which should most concern the Party and that all other considerations must be subordinate to it.

It was true that they at Headquarters were making revolutionary proposals of organisation, but it was absolutely essential at this moment to make a strong National Party ... Mr. Henderson further emphasised the supreme necessity of the fixing of as many parliamentary candidates as possible at the earliest moment.

These arguments did not mollify the Scots and the meeting became increasingly acrimonious. Maxton claimed that the real issue was Scotland's right to be heard.

Mr. Maxton [Scottish Council of the I.L.P.] urged that the two serious matters were Scottish representation on the National Executive and at the National Conference arguing that such representation would remove the need for interviews like the present.

Mr. Henderson said that much more was claimed in the draft; changes of a revolutionary character as regards Executive powers being suggested by the removal of the word 'Advisory' from the title of the Scottish organisation.

Mr. Maxton pointed out that there was no proposal for any change in the financial arrangements or the status of the Secretary.

Mr. Smillie [Chairman of the Executive] asserted that Headquarters were reading into the draft what it was not intended to contain.

Wake intervened to

express his decided concurrence with Mr. Henderson and urged strongly that, if put forward, all those proposals for adoption by the National Conference showed that it was intended to change the character of the Scottish organisation, and that definite independent Executive powers were being claimed. Were this granted Wales would make a similar claim. (Mr. Maxton interrupted to say that in that case such a claim would be backed). Mr. Wake, continuing, asserted that the presentation of such a claim at the National Conference would imperil the whole revision of the National Constitution without success so far as the Scottish claim was concerned. There was some disposition to sympathise with the development of local aspirations, but the present proposals would destroy the unity of organisation in front of the next general election.

At this point the Scottish executive raised certain individual matters that interested them, and interested the left of the I.L.P. and the British Socialist Party particularly.

Mr. Mulholland [Hugh Mulholland, Scottish Council of the British Socialist Party] claimed that the Scottish people knew best what was good for Scotland, and if the unity of the Party were to be maintained, Scottish discontent would have to be settled first.

Mr. Wilson [Thomas Wilson, Scottish Shop Assistants] asked, assuming that the word 'Advisory' were retained in the title, would the claim for Scottish representation on the Executive be admitted?

Mr. Mulholland said he was not much concerned about the name; he wanted more Executive power in Scotland, and made reference to the right of the Gorbals L.R.C. to run a candidate against the sitting Labour member.[9]

Henderson remarked

... that such a policy would be suicidal, and asked if the Gorbals L.R.C. would be willing to submit the decision to a ballot of all the elements of the S.A.C.

Mr. Mulholland claimed that a ballot of the Gorbals elements should be considered sufficient ...

Mr. Wilson asserted that whilst there was responsibility in the minds of the Scottish Executive towards Headquarters, there was the feeling that it was necessary to go cap in hand on occasion.

Mr. Maxton claimed that the Scottish programme had been turned down.

Mr. Henderson explained that the National Conference, contrary to his own views, had turned down the proposal to have any programme, but there never had been any interference by the National Executive with the terms of Scottish propaganda or candidatures.

When Smillie asked, with some justification, whether the introduction of a Scottish draft at the conference really would jeopardize the new constitution, Henderson replied that it would: he reverted to Wake's argument and embellished it.

Mr. Henderson affirmed that the subject was so large that the Conference might tire of it [the new national constitution] before it had been completed if further disputable matter were introduced, and shelve the whole question. The presentation of the Scottish draft to the Conference would raise wide territorial issues and it would be impossible to reconcile the territorial and other elements at this Conference, *as the main structure was, and must remain, largely one of Trades Union and Socialist Organisations, most of which were national bodies stretched throughout Great Britain.* [Emphasis mine.] Were Scotland granted separate representation, London, Lancashire, Yorkshire, Wales and perhaps other sections of the country differing in type, would each present a similar claim, with a great show of reason. He suggested the withdrawal of the proposals presently, and that, after the great work of the Conference had been got through, the two Executives should confer upon proposals which might be agreed upon to be submitted to the Annual Meeting of the Scottish organisation first ...

After some further desultory discussion the Scottish executive

---

[9] Gorbals had already repudiated its sitting member, G. N. Barnes (since Henderson's resignation, the Labour member of the war cabinet) and had selected the socialist and pacifist, John MacLean, as its candidate. As Barnes was still an official Labour member of the government, Head Office repeatedly refused to endorse MacLean—though he went to the polls as the official Labour candidate in December 1918. (See above, p. 107.)

decided to withdraw its draft scheme 'when the assurances given by Mr. Henderson have been endorsed by the National Executive'. These 'assurances' (which were scarcely that) concerned a specifically Scottish programme, the right of deputation to the national executive, and increased financial assistance to the Scottish office.

On 9 May 1918, Maxton presented the Scottish executive's constitutional amendments to the national executive, where they appear to have been given a pretty rough reception.[10] This was so, not because the executive was (in Scottish eyes) being even more unreasonable than usual, but because the Scottish amendments were the same ones that Henderson had so strongly objected to the previous December and that the Scottish executive had agreed to withdraw. The annoyance of Head Office is, therefore, not as surprising as the Scottish executive later pretended to find it. The organization committee of the national executive considered the Scottish amendments on 27 August 1918—in this case the delay was not due to the usual reluctance to discuss Scotland but to genuine overwork—and found them as displeasing as Henderson had done. It rejected entirely the proposed clause 4, which provided for separate union and local party affiliation to the Scottish Advisory Council (as distinct from affiliation to the national Party), struck out the clause which would have permitted separate Scottish representation at the national conference and similarly rejected separate Scottish representation on the national executive.[11]

In September, on the eve of the Scottish conference, Wake, as organizing secretary for Scotland and Wales, took these objections to Scotland. The Scottish executive could do little else than withdraw the offending amendments—indeed the whole draft was withdrawn—and it agreed to meet again in January 1919 to reconstruct its draft.[12] The new amendments gave Scotland an autonomy more nominal than real: a change of name to the 'Scottish Council of Labour', an increased budget, and certain rights in regard to the Scottish programme of the Party.[13] In the long run it proved to be not much of a solution, though for the immediate future such changes as there were, together with the regional reorganization of the Party in 1920 and the electoral successes of Labour in the west of Scotland, helped to still dissatisfaction.

Welsh Claims for Autonomy. It was the claims of Wales and London that finally forced Head Office into drafting a scheme of reorganization that would satisfy demands for regional devolution and yet maintain the national executive's central direction of the Party.

[10] 'NEC', 9 May 1918.
[11] 'NEC', 27 Aug. 1918.
[12] 'SEC', 20 Sept. 1918.
[13] 'SEC', 13 Jan. 1919.

Having conceded the Scots a nominal autonomy, in principle before the war and, in fact, during it, Head Office had been under pressure to do the same thing for Wales. Yet there were differences. Even if the Party only followed the administrative system of the United Kingdom (which it tended to do) then there was no real case for Welsh autonomy, or anything approaching it. England and Wales were one governmental unit, and on this view of things, there seemed as little reason (in 1918) for conceding the Welsh autonomous powers as in conceding them (say) to Lancashire. Furthermore, the heads of some of the big trade unions had made known their objections to 'federalizing' the Party before 1914,[14] fearing perhaps the same thing in their own unions, and the Scottish Advisory Council had been established over the protests of some of them. It was duly circumscribed to satisfy their, as well as Henderson's, fears.

In 1911 one attempt was made to give Wales a 'federal' relationship to the Party and that was immediately rejected by Head Office. Nothing more was done by the Welsh until 1916—the year following the inaugural conference of the Scottish Advisory Council—when, largely under the prodding of the South Wales Miners' Federation,[15] a conference of South Wales Labour parties was held on 2 December 1916, at which the national executive was officially represented.[16] This group met again in 1917. In May 1918, with the Party in a state of reorganization, the South Wales Labour Federation (the title assumed by the conference) formally requested the establishment of a Welsh Advisory Council: the request was laid before the executive,[17] but not taken up again before August 1918, when Henderson and Wake met the Federation and considered their claim for a separate Welsh council. The executive offered a couple of palliatives: a grant for propaganda and the appointment of Wake as organizing secretary for Wales. The problem of a Welsh Council was referred to a subcommittee which, as far as one can see, never met.[18]

The appointment of Wake as secretary was significant and rather ominous. He was no friend of devolution; he merely bolstered Henderson's dislike of regional organizations with all the 'difficulties' and inefficiency which went with them. Though it might have been

---

[14] See above, p. 41. Dr. Pelling makes the point that the unions were also opposed to the federal administration of the National Health Insurance Act which was embodied in the Act. Their opposition was unsuccessful and the Act was administered independently in England, Wales and Scotland. (*Popular Politics*, p. 108).

[15] Significantly, it was the Miners alone of the large unions who organized themselves in a genuinely federal way: the Miners' Federation was still a confederation of reasonably autonomous bodies.

[16] 'NEC', 2 Nov. 1916.

[17] 'NEC', 25 May 1918.

[18] 'NEC', 21 Aug. 1918.

expected that Wake's personality would have adjusted easily to what he called the 'celtic temperament', on the contrary, it seems to have infuriated him. In April 1918, after conducting a 'difficult' by-election[19] in Aberdeenshire, he wrote to Middleton, with customary hyperbole, that 'the poll takes place here on Wednesday and I shall heave a sigh of relief deep enough to shake the snowcaps of these frowning mountains. "Oh, bonnie Scotland, what I'm sufferin' for ye noo." '[20] The effect of Wales was likewise; in 1919, he insisted, the East Swansea by-election would have been won '. . . if our people had worked to instructions . . . This Celtic temperament persists in wasting itself with fever and raving. If they had expressed their energy in work they would easily have wiped the remaining 1,000 of the majority out'.[21] Wake was not the man to argue the case for devolution with persuasion, if at all.

Since the 1918 subcommittee appears not to have met, or at least not to have reported, the question carried over into 1919. In October of that year, after another meeting of the South Wales Federation, Henderson and Wake were asked to report on the situation in Wales.[22]

They reported back on 11 November 1919 and appended to the report[23] a scheme for the administrative decentralization of the Party, and one that was to give it a fairly elaborate system of regional organization. This system was created not because Henderson was struck by the beauties of regional organizations but because he wished to avoid giving Wales autonomy and hoped to put an end to Herbert Morrison's ambitions for London.

After reviewing the state of the Party in Wales, they made some legitimate objections to treating Wales as a unit.

The real problem of organising Wales as a whole consists in the distances, the railway system and the geographical difficulties. North and South Wales are effectively divided from each other. Economically and industrially North Wales is much more associated with Liverpool and Manchester than with Cardiff. From an organising point of view, North Wales is much more accessible from Liverpool, Chester etc. than from South Wales, while Newport, Cardiff and Swansea are much more accessible to London than many parts of England . . .

The report went on to admit that 'on the basis of nationality, Wales certainly appears to have a claim, and, if Devolution is decided upon, some organisation to give the Party in Wales a corporate means of

---

[19] In his correspondence 'difficult' is much the most common of his own adjectives.
[20] Wake to Middleton, 14 Apr. 1918, 'LPLF: Uncat.'.
[21] Wake to Middleton, 25 July 1919, 'LPLF: Uncat.'.
[22] 'NEC', 7 Oct. 1919.
[23] Which is filed as 'NEC', 11 Nov. 1919.

expressing itself will be necessary'. The problem, however, remained—
and the arguments against an extension of Scottish autonomy were
more or less repeated.

Whether the grant of an Advisory Council to Wales will act as an incentive
to similar claims for London and other Federation areas . . . are matters that
require serious consideration. In London, there are 61 constituencies with
special difficulties and problems and their case is under consideration . . .
Federations exist in Lancashire and Cheshire on the North Coast and other
areas, and a Midland Federation is being formed. Appeals for assistance in
various ways by these Federations have been declined in the past, and the
probable effect of the creation of a Welsh Advisory Council upon these bodies
needs to be faced in coming to a decision on the matter.

The Problem of London. Now, as Henderson noted, by the time he had
come to write the report the situation had been further complicated.
During the war London had emerged as a region in its own right, and
something, therefore, needs to be said about this and how it affected
Henderson's thinking on the wider question of regional devolution.

As a political unit London probably had claims at least the equal of
Scotland. The L.C.C. area alone had only ten fewer parliamentary
seats (61 as against 71), as large a population and a government whose
budget and complexity equalled that of the Scottish Office. Moreover,
the formation of the London Labour Party, a huge federal party
whose affiliated membership surpassed that of the Scottish council in
1920,[24] increased expectations, certainly within London, that it
should gain some form of autonomy, as seemed only fitting to its
size and prestige. It is fair to say that these expectations increased
after Herbert Morrison's appointment to the Party secretaryship in
1915.

Morrison was ambitious, hard-working, and devoted to the interests of his city and his Party. Though he always had designs on
national politics, it was the London County Council that first
fascinated him, and, as his otherwise reticent autobiography shows,
always did.[25] Morrison's attachment to what he took to be sound
principles of organization was famous. Like so many other Labour
men, he was engrossed in the earlier successes of the S.P.D. and
over-impressed with its feats of organization.

Before the war [he wrote] the Social Democratic Party in Berlin could have
an executive meeting on Saturday afternoon, pass copy to its printers paragraph by paragraph, have the manifesto printed on its own press during the

---

[24] It reached 364,000 in 1920 (London Labour Party, *Report of the Executive*, 1919-20,
p. 8) and 385,000 in 1921 (*Report of the Executive*, 1920-1, p. 9).
[25] Morrison, *Autobiography*, pp. 74-80.

night, and through its Party organisation have copy delivered to every residence in Berlin by the Sunday dinner-time.

London is larger than Berlin, but let us set about the task of organisation with the vision of making practicable for London Labour what the Social Democrat organisation was able to do in Berlin.[26]

Labour would be successful only if it gave to politics the 'scientific intensity' which he supposed that the German Social Democrats gave to it.[27] The 'card index frame of mind', he said in one of those characteristic utterances that gave him a reputation for philistinism, 'makes organisation a thing of beauty whilst the Labour and Socialist ideal makes patience and determination worthwhile'.[28]

It was in this spirit of organizational symmetry that the London Labour Party created its sporting clubs, its choral unions, its dramatic associations, its picnic societies, its women's clubs and debating groups. There is no doubting that Morrison did infect others with his own enthusiasms. The flood of hectorings and exhortations from London Party headquarters through its newspaper[29] and the innumerable *Organisation Points from the London Labour Party* had their effect: London did develop a genuine kind of Labour community and the three decades' rule following the victory of 1934 owe as much to Morrison's 'patience and determination' as to his love of London.

Yet it is clear that in the first years Morrison failed to achieve what he wanted for London, that his plans were consistently opposed by Head Office and, even more than that, his hopes both for himself and London raised real apprehension at Head Office. Nor did Morrison's personality smooth his path: he was never tactful about matters that seemed important to him—while his perkiness and self-confidence irritated people who might otherwise have admired his political abilities.[30]

Between September 1917 and October 1920 the London Labour Party was persistently at odds with the national executive about the nature and desirability of London's autonomy. As early as September 1917 Morrison had suggested to Henderson that London be given special consideration in the drafting of the new constitution, due 'to

[26] Morrison, *Labour Party Organisation in London* (London, 1921), p. 5.
[27] Morrison, *Organisation Points*, No. 1, 4 Nov. 1920.
[28] Morrison, *Labour Party Organisation in London*, p. 5.
[29] It had various names. It was the *London Labour Party Circular*, May 1917 to Oct. 1918; the *London Labour Party Chronicle* from Oct. 1918 to Oct. 1924; thereafter the *London News*.
[30] Henderson's personal relations with Morrison were always difficult. This was due partly to Morrison's closeness to MacDonald and partly due to Morrison's public displays of rudeness to the trade-unions. For his part, Morrison always believed that Henderson deprived him of the Labour Party secretaryship in 1934.

the exceptional position of the London Labour Party'.[31] Although the national agent, Peters, assured Morrison that 'the claims of London will not be overlooked', nothing, in fact, was done.[32] In May 1919, the London Party, through its chairman, Fred Bramley, presented Head Office with 'a suggested scheme of organisation and financial estimates'.[33] Peters later told Bramley that, although the executive felt obliged to postpone any decisions until after the annual conference and the election of a new executive, 'some measure of assistance to the London Labour Party' had been considered sympathetically.[34]

It is most unlikely that assistance to London was considered 'sympathetically'—there was no reason why a question of rooms and rents (as it was) should be considered of sufficient importance to be left to another executive; nor was there much chance that a new executive would differ from the old in a matter of this kind.

The new executive dealt with it expeditiously by rejecting London's claims out of hand: Middleton delicately informed Morrison that 'there appeared to be no prospect of affording [London] accommodation'.[35] Three days later Morrison and Bramley saw Henderson, MacDonald, Middleton, and Wake (the new national agent) and were told that a subsidy was impossible. Henderson's argument was the old one: if London were granted special privileges then 'others would claim them'.[36]

London returned to the attack the following month with a letter to Wake complaining that 'London organisation was almost completely neglected by Head Office' and asking for 'a definite reply to the question whether the National Executive were willing to make a grant annually equivalent to the value of one full time official'.[37] The following February (1920) the executive finally rejected Morrison's request for assistance, though Wake suggested that the executive might give London £40 for their agents. The final humiliation came in March when the executive refused to grant even the £40.[38] With some justification Morrison replied that despite 'its real record of organising work accomplished, the London Labour Party has not been assisted even to the extent of one constituency Labour Party'.[39]

[31] Morrison to Henderson, 29 Sept. 1917, in 'Summary of Correspondence Respecting Relations with the London Labour Party', filed as 'NEC', 14 Oct. 1920.

[32] Peters to Morrison, 4 Oct. 1917 in 'Summary of Correspondence'.

[33] Bramley to Peters, 6 May 1919, in 'Summary of Correspondence'.

[34] 'NEC', 12 Oct. 1919.

[35] 'NEC', 12 Oct. 1919 and Middleton to Morrison, 13 Oct. 1919, in 'Summary of Correspondence'.

[36] Text of Discussion, 16 Oct. 1919, in 'Summary of Correspondence'.

[37] Morrison to Wake, 24 Nov. 1919, in 'Summary of Correspondence'.

[38] Wake to Morrison, 15 Mar. 1920, in 'Summary of Correspondence'.

[39] Morrison to Wake, 22 Mar. 1920, in 'Summary of Correspondence'.

After the national conference of 1920 had approved Henderson's regional reorganization Morrison again approached Head Office—this time with the aim of increasing London's autonomy as well as its budget. Considering the number of times he had been kicked downstairs one can only marvel at his persistence. He, and the treasurer of the London Party, Alfred Salter,[40] met the organization sub-committee on 12 October 1920. According to the national executive minute,[41]

> The deputation regretted that the National Executive would not make a grant to the London Labour Party but, in lieu, they were prepared to accept in principle the idea that London should be a separate area with its own District and Women's organiser attached to the London Labour Party working at the general discretion of the London Executive and instructions given through the London secretary [Morrison].

This, of course, was the last thing envisaged by the national executive; it should be remembered, furthermore, that the Scottish executive had not long ago fought, and lost, a battle over precisely this. Anyway, presumably on the principle that he had nothing to lose, Morrison was emboldened to ask for more. He asked 'that the National Executive should make either a fixed or a percentage contribution towards the general office and administrative expenses of the London Labour Party'.

Henderson's reaction was exactly as one might have expected, though couched in language made more decorous if less lucid by the executive minute.

> The Secretary pointed out in the first place, with regard to a subsidy, this was a principle to which the National Executive were opposed and with regard to which a precedent could not be established in London, as it would mean preferential treatment for that area. Further, that he could hold out no hope of the National Executive agreeing to appoint two officers and being responsible for their salaries but placing them entirely at the disposal of and under the control of the London Labour Party.

The deputation and the executive failed to agree on any of these matters. Indeed, the only concession London gained had already been made. By a decision of the executive in August[42] London was made a separate region—in Henderson's original scheme London was counted with the so-called southern counties, Middlesex, Kent, Surrey, Sussex, and Hampshire.[43]

[40] Dr. Alfred Salter (1873–1945), bacteriologist and pathologist, leading London I.L.P.er and M.P. for West Bermondsey, 1922–3, 1924–45. His wife, Ada Salter, was also prominent in the Labour Party. See A. F. Brockway, *Bermondsey Story: The Life of Alfred Salter* (London, 1949).
[41] 'NEC', 12 Oct. 1920.
[42] 'NEC', 31 Aug. 1920.
[43] See below, pp. 174–5.

In many ways it appeared that London was treated somewhat churlishly. It was not just that no substantive request made by London was conceded: all requests made by London, even the absurd £40, were rejected. It is clear that the national executive regarded almost any concession as a precedent and thus undesirable. There was as well, perhaps, a feeling that Morrison's ambitions were far too extensive, if not actually insatiable. Writing to Ethel Bentham, a prominent member of the London Party and a friend of Morrison's, Middleton said that Henderson 'was afraid that a situation might develop in London as had developed in Scotland during the War and that this would be unsatisfactory to the National Party in every way'.[44] Though Morrison might legitimately be able to complain of Head Office's attitude to him, in principle he was treated no differently to Scotland, Wales, or any of the other regions.

The 'General Scheme'. It was in these circumstances of Scottish, Welsh, and London demands for some kind of autonomy that Henderson produced his 'General Scheme of Organisation'. In his report to the executive he justified the regional reforms on strictly organizational grounds.[45] 'The present method', he wrote, 'of having two organisers travelling the whole country has served its purpose and with the growth of the Party and the increase of the constituencies, some more direct and more comprehensive method is required.'

It is unlikely, however, that organizational requirements alone produced the reforms. The fact remains that the scheme was appended to a memorandum on Welsh affairs which rejected any autonomy for Wales and was written at a time when Head Office was having difficulties with London. It is hard to avoid the conclusion that Henderson was trying to smother the claims of Wales and London in a scheme of regional organization which would at the same time forestall similar claims from elsewhere. While Henderson assured the executive that his suggestions were only put forward as a 'basis of discussion', he was anxious that they should be given 'full consideration' before what he euphemistically called 'any other developments' were decided upon.[46]

This draft scheme divided England, Scotland and Wales into seven regions: Scotland (centre Glasgow); North Eastern (centre Leeds); North Western (centre Manchester or Liverpool); Midlands (centre Birmingham); South Western (centre Bristol); Eastern (centre London) and London and Southern (centre London). This was a rather remarkable decision. By adhering so closely to what he took to

[44] Middleton to Ethel Bentham, 18 Oct. 1920, 'LPLF, Uncat.'.
[45] 'General Scheme of Organisation', 'NEC', 11 Nov. 1919.
[46] 'NEC', 11 Nov. 1919.

be the general lines of development of the British economy and its linking communications, he tended to ignore traditional and still powerful national and regional loyalties which were represented in the Labour movement as elsewhere. It was most unlikely that the Scots, the Welsh, or even the Londoners on the national executive or in the country would consent to the break-up of Wales as an independent and historic unit within the Party. What the draft does show is the extent to which Henderson was prepared to go in the creation of a unified national organization and how far he thought Labour was to be the Party of what he understood to be modern Britain.

Not unexpectedly the draft was too much for the executive, which added to it an eighth region, Wales and Monmouth, extracted from Henderson's South Western and North Western regions.[47] In doing so the executive was clearly right. It was one thing to direct Welsh demands into safe channels; quite another to repudiate them openly. The 1920 conference, therefore, approved Henderson's draft together with Wales as a separate region.[48]

In August 1920 the scheme was further refined. London was detached from the southern counties to create a ninth region, London, having the boundaries of the L.C.C.[49] The reasons for this second retreat from the draft were pretty much as they were for the first. Once again it could scarcely be held that the best way to meet London's 'special difficulties and problems' was to maintain in public that they did not exist. As with Wales, the executive was probably right to have second thoughts; Henderson's draft would almost certainly have increased London's dissatisfaction. Furthermore, while the original arrangement for London had all the logic of Henderson's original premises, in practice it would have been an administrative monster. London was itself big enough to consume the energies of one organizer, without his having to oversee half the home counties as well. The L.C.C. area (London district) was a much more manageable unit.

The amendments to the original draft had, therefore, somewhat altered its territorial divisions. The nine districts of the final scheme are shown in Table 23 on following page.

Once it had been admitted that London and Wales were to have separate representation, this certainly was a tidier scheme than Henderson's. But so far as devolution was concerned Henderson had won the battle, not that it required much winning. In no sense did the scheme mean a change in administrative authority within the Party.

[47] *Conference Report*, 1920, p. 17.
[48] What was approved was not the scheme as such, but a rise in the affiliation fee necessary to finance it. The increase was 1*d*. per member: from 2*d*. to 3*d*. It was approved unanimously and without discussion. (*Conference Report*, 1920, p. 122.)
[49] 'NEC', 31 Aug. 1920.

TABLE 23

DISTRICT A. North Eastern: Northumberland, Durham, Yorkshire.
DISTRICT B. North Western: Cumberland, Westmorland, Lancashire, Cheshire, Derbyshire High Peak.
DISTRICT C. Midlands: Worcester, Derbyshire (except High Peak), Nottinghamshire, Warwick, Leicester, Northampton, Hereford, Gloucester (except Bristol), Staffordshire, Shropshire.
DISTRICT D. Southern and Home Counties: Middlesex, Kent, Surrey, Sussex, Hampshire, Bedford, Hertford, Berkshire, Buckinghamshire, Oxford.
DISTRICT E. The L.C.C. area.
DISTRICT F. South Western: Dorset, Wiltshire, Somerset, Devon, Cornwall and Bristol.
DISTRICT G. Eastern: Lincoln and Rutland, Norfolk, Suffolk, Huntingdon, Cambridge, Essex.
DISTRICT H. Wales and Monmouth.
DISTRICT J. Scotland.

Even the bureaucratic changes were not striking: there were to be no regional 'head offices', while it was proposed that most of the clerical work was to be done through the national agent's department in any case. Furthermore, two of the districts—London and Southern Counties—were to have their centres at Head Office, while the other seven organizers were to work from their homes.

What the regional organizers did was to relieve Head Office of much of the mechanical, but heavy, work of electoral management. They did the kind of work that had been left to the secretary, the national agent and the two roving organizers before 1914, the necessary but drudging work of organizing the constituencies. And their work could be very heavy. Since there were no more than 133 official agents at any one time[50] most of the constituencies relied upon the district organizers for a good deal of what formal organization they had. In most by-elections, organizers acted as agents or campaign supervisors. In either case, they usually ran the contest. For the most part, however, the old task of propaganda, an important one for the organizers before 1914, was not, strictly speaking, one for the organizers after 1920. Only in the South Western area (Dorset, Wiltshire, Somerset, etc.), where 'the movement is in the pioneer state',[51] was the organizer expected also to be a propagandist. Normally, as we have seen, propaganda was treated as a national business and left to Head Office.[52]

A fairly good idea of what the organizers actually did can be gained from the reports circulated to the members of the national executive.

[50] See above, p. 143.
[51] 'NEC', 26 Feb. 1924.
[52] See above, pp. 127-31.

Those that immediately followed the 1922 general election are good examples and can be quoted fruitfully.[53]

District A. North Eastern. As reported by Mr. F. Gibbin [the organizer] the organisation in Newcastle East, Central and West division appears to be satisfactory and well maintained. Mr. Gibbin has assisted in the formation of the Divisional Labour Party for the North division, which has not yet been fought by Labour . . . Special visits have been paid to Gateshead where the agent has resigned and a new appointment will have to be made and to Cleveland where some difficulty over the candidature has developed. Attention has been given to the Barkston Ash Division, where a selection has been made, and the Berwick-on-Tweed Division has also received visits as there is the possibility of a by-election there.

District B. North Western. In addition to the ordinary work of visitation, Mr. Standring was engaged upon clearing up the Edge Hill accounts, and before these were complete he was transferred to Anglesey to assist in the by-election there . . . He is endeavouring to arrange for the formation of a Party in Northern Cumberland . . .

District D. Home and Southern Counties. Mr. Shepherd has cleared up the Mitcham election [Mitcham by-election] accounts and has given attention to the Division in order to lay the foundations for an effective Divisional organisation in future. He has paid special attention to Watford, Kingston and Eastbourne, and in each case has advised upon the rules and disputes arising therefrom. He has paid organising visits to Hendon, Chichester, Chislehurst, Wood Green and the Isle of Wight . . . A special visit was paid to the Isle of Thanet where the conditions are changing owing to the development of the mining industry and a candidature may result. He has also visited Canterbury Division where local differences have created difficulties for some time past, and also visited Tottenham where reorganisation of the two divisions is being considered.[54]

District E. London. Mr. R. T. Windle attended the Annual Meeting of the Young Labour League in order to express sympathy with the education of youth in Labour principles . . . Special visits have been paid to North Lambeth to reorganise the Divisional Party on the lines of the constitution . . . Special attention has been given to Rotherhithe and the DLP has been persuaded to put its house in order. Conferences with the Executive Committee and the candidate for Central Hackney have taken place in view of the possible by-election . . .

District G. Eastern. Mr. Holmes has visited the Saffron Walden Division and has also paid organising visits to S.E. Essex, Maldon and Colchester Divisions . . . Special visits have been paid to the Eye Division where a new Divisional Labour Party has been developed and where they are anxious to secure a candidate . . . He has also spent some time visiting the Norfolk strike area [the

[53] 'NEC', 24 Apr. 1924.
[54] Both divisions of Tottenham were then controlled by the single borough Labour party.

strike of agricultural labourers in Norfolk, March 1923] devoting attention to pushing the Party's interests as opportunity occurred.

District H. Wales & Monmouth. Mr. Morris has been engaged during the month in the Anglesey Division where he acted as agent for Mr. E. T. John in the by-election. The constituency was a difficult one, and it was Mr. Morris' first experience of having charge of a by-election, but he was assisted by Mr. Standring [the organizer for the North West].

District J. Scotland. Following the Annual Conference of the Scottish Council, the new Scottish Executive has got to work and Mr. Ben Shaw has been busily engaged at the Scottish Office in getting their various committees into operation. He has visited Dumfriesshire, Roxburgh and Selkirk, Perth, Dumbartonshire and has spoken at a variety of meetings at Tollcross, the Glasgow Fabian Society ... He has visited the Scottish T.U.C. at Dundee as the representative of the Labour Party, and is now visiting several constituencies in Aberdeen and the North.

It was obvious from these reports that most of the work was routine: the organizing of by-elections, the replacement of agents, the strengthening of local parties, assistance in the formation of local parties—generally speaking, keeping local organization up to the mark. The appointment of district organizers made it possible to organize the constituencies more rapidly and more efficiently. The presence of an organizer nearby, moreover, made the solution of difficult constituency problems more expeditious than had they been left to the rather cumbrous procedures of the secretary's department and the national executive. For example, it took only one visit from the Scottish organizer, Shaw, to the Motherwell constituency to end a difficult situation that gave every sign of going on indefinitely.[55] But the rights of Head Office remained intact. The organizers worked strictly within boundaries set by the executive and to that extent Henderson had his way.

2. *The Labour Party and the Co-operative Union, 1915–1924*

Until 1915 the Labour Party's relations with the Co-operative movement had not been as satisfactory as the leadership of either had wished. The Co-operative Congress, following the seemingly permanent political divisions within its affiliated societies, repeatedly rejected any arrangements with the Labour Party. It remained, in addition, confused about its wider political role.[56] By 1917, however, it appeared as if the war might have dissipated this confusion: many in the Co-operative Union now assumed that to participate in politics was a legitimate function and that the Union might effectively mobilize the

[55] See below, pp. 196–204.   [56] See above, pp. 43–7.

working classes as consumers as the trade unions had mobilized them as workers.

The Co-operative Union had rejected an alliance with the Labour Party in 1915. But as the war went into its second half, the co-operators found, somewhat to their surprise, that neither coalition government was seized with an anxiety to include them in the war effort. Whereas the Labour movement was, at the least, consulted, the Union was ignored, or actively discriminated against, in military contracting and in wholesaling and retailing. While the offices of trade unions and the three political parties were, if necessary, exempted from military service *pro forma*, co-operative employees were often required to face frequently hostile tribunals—composed, the Webbs tell us, 'in the main of retail shopkeepers, the smaller manufacturers, auctioneers, and agents of various kinds, and others directly interested in profit-making enterprise'.[57] The result was that an awkwardly large number of officials were called up, seriously interfering with co-operative business. The last straw was the imposition on the societies of an excess profits tax—the first tax ever to be levied on them—which aroused the deepest resentment. Tom Jones, after a talk with Middleton and Harry May, the secretary of the Co-operative Joint Parliamentary Committee (the Union's old political liaison body), noted that they were

very bitter at the Government's treatment of the Co-operative movement in the Ministry of Food and denounced the farce of offering Smillie the Food Controllership early in the weeks of the Leeds Conference.[58] I said why had not the C.W.S. [Co-operative Wholesale Society] taken on the Food Controllership? . . . May replied that it would be the cemetery of the C.W.S., as Devonport [Lord Devonport, H. E. Kearley, the tea merchant, previous Food Controller] filled all the billets with private traders, all of whom would have to be dismissed if a co-operator took the helm.[59]

The situation was considered serious enough for the central board of the Union to place before the 1917 congress in Swansea a motion urging 'direct representation in Parliament'. This was carried, over the objections of the veteran E. O. Greening, by 1,883 to 199, and a motion to extend this activity to municipal politics was carried by 1,979 to 201.[60] But it was the refusal of Lloyd George even to see a deputation from the Union that had the most galvanizing effect on

---

[57] S. and B. Webb, *Consumers' Co-operative Movement*, p. 247.

[58] He was referring to the Leeds Conference of June 1917, summoned by sections of the Labour movement to celebrate the Russian revolution. Smillie was one of the signatories of its manifesto, as was MacDonald.

[59] Jones, *Whitehall Diary*, 29 Aug. 1917, p. 36.

[60] *Co-operative Congress Report*, 1917, pp. 549–69.

co-operators: some of the more 'advanced' societies even set up local defence associations.[61] The Union summoned an emergency congress in October 1917 which empowered a committee to organize co-operative political representation and, as an earnest of the Union's new political enthusiasm, it nominated Harry May as its candidate for a by-election at Prestwich (May 1918).

May's campaign and its outcome were hardly inspiring. The Manchester and Salford Labour Party, which had been prevented from contesting the seat by the political truce, regarded the co-operative conversion to politics as spurious and took, therefore, a less than positive part in the battle. But the behaviour of the C.W.S. itself was even more disturbing. Of its thirty-two directors only four supported May, while the society refused to place any of its (many) automobiles at his disposal. The local co-operative society (in its official capacity) refused to contribute to his campaign fund, which was provided by a voluntary defence association. Even as a propaganda demonstration, the result was pretty bad. May polled 2,832 votes to the 8,520 for his Coalition Liberal opponent.[62]

Labour leaders must have watched these developments with some dismay, partly because they feared co-operative political competition (though the extent of that remained undetermined, and, on the strength of Prestwich, possibly negligible), but more because it meant that the irritating business of dealing with the Union would clearly have to begin again. Following the disappointments of the pre-war years the Party was understandably less disposed to negotiate with the Union than it had been. In fact, it was inclined actively to oppose attempts to link the co-operative societies with Labour. In November 1915 the executive rejected a proposal from the Scots that local co-operative associations should be allowed in one way or another to affiliate to the Party.[63] Middleton wrote to Shaw that the executive was convinced that the co-operative organizations generally were 'as yet either hostile or immature in Political Opinion'.[64]

The following year Henderson told the Scottish executive that it would be a mistake in policy

> to alter the Constitution in order to provide a cheap and easy way for the inclusion of Co-operative elements in the National Party ... whilst practically every Co-operative Society had a great majority of members opposed to affiliation with the National Labour Party. They at Head Quarters had done

[61] Cynthia I. Arditti, 'The History of the Co-operative Party in the Manchester District' (University of Manchester M.A. thesis, 1953), p. 10.
[62] For the by-election, see Arditti, 'Co-operative Party in Manchester,' pp. 12–14.
[63] 'NEC', 8 Nov. 1915.
[64] Middleton to Shaw, 8 Nov. 1915, 'LPLF: Uncat.'.

everything possible for a long time past to encourage closer relations politically with the Co-operative Movement and . . . with practically no success.[65]

In October 1917, nevertheless, a co-ordinating committee, the Scottish Co-operative and Labour Council, was established in Scotland. In February 1918, this Council, which represented the Labour Party, the Scottish T.U.C., the Scottish section of the Union, and the Scottish C.W.S., met Wake, then organizing secretary for Scotland and Wales. While Wake welcomed the formation of the committee, and while he was sure that 'a conflict could and must be avoided', he emphasized the 'lack even of Co-operative consciousness by the Co-operators as shown at the Prestwich election . . .'.[66]

At the 1918 elections, as a result of the efforts of a hastily organized and informal joint committee, the co-operators were given a free run in ten constituencies of which they were successful in one, Kettering.[67] Yet in the one constituency where the co-operators wished to field a candidate, but where the local Labour party absolutely refused to support him, West Salford, the executive strongly took the side of the local party and the co-operators were forced to withdraw.[68] Had other constituencies been less responsive to Head Office persuasion than they were, it is likely that the Co-operative Representation Committee—in 1919 to become the Co-operative Party—would not have been able to contest as many seats as it did. A. E. Waterson, the member for Kettering, recognizing the real source of his electoral support, immediately joined the parliamentary party when parliament assembled.

Labour was clearly disappointed by the performance of the Co-operative candidates. When the executive met in January 1919 it was decided that the joint committee should examine in detail relations between the Party and the Union.[69] The *ad hoc* joint committee decided to make itself permanent and after nudges from the Labour representatives the Co-operative delegates agreed to seek from their annual congress powers either to affiliate to the Labour Party or to federate with it for electoral purposes.[70] When the Co-operative congress met in June 1919 the central board did its best to promote the Labour Party. It told delegates that in all constituencies contested by

[65] 'SEC', 17 Mar. 1916.
[66] 'SEC', 9 Feb. 1918.
[67] See *Co-operative Congress Report*, 1919, pp. 184–7. The ten seats were Kettering, Paisley, Kilmarnock, Clackmannan and East Stirling, Bradford South, Birmingham King's Norton, Birmingham Sparkbrook, Sheffield Hillsborough, Leeds Central, Mossley (Lancashire).
[68] 'NEC', 29 May 1918.
[69] 'NEC', 2 Jan. 1919.
[70] 'NEC', 26 Mar. 1919.

the Representation Committee they had 'not only the moral, but the very active support of the local Labour and Trade Union forces'. It thought that 'the gathering together of vested interests' in the coalition may have proved to be 'one of the most effective driving forces towards the formation of a federation of democratic parties, whether in the shape of a Democratic or People's Party, or a working agreement between sympathetic organisations'.[71]

It is not clear who inserted the notion of a 'Democratic or People's Party' into the report, but it was one that had commended itself to many co-operators for years,[72] and had, of course, done the rounds in the second half of 1917.[73] It was in these rather dubious terms that a resolution was presented to the congress which voted to instruct 'the National Co-operative Representation Committee to negotiate with the Labour Party and the . . . Trades Union Congress with a view to a federation for electoral purposes, and with the ultimate object of forming a United Democratic or People's Party'.[74]

Another motion to affiliate the Representation Committee directly to the Labour Party was defeated.[75] Armed with this somewhat ambiguous authority the co-operators met the Labour Party and the T.U.C. on 9 July 1919.[76] The Labour delegates hurriedly dismissed the concept of a 'People's Party' or anything like it. The co-operative delegates, though vaguely disappointed, do not appear to have been surprised. In the event, the meeting drafted a scheme for a nine-man board, three members each from the Labour Party, the T.U.C., and the Co-operative Party. The functions of this body (the Labour and Co-operative Political Alliance) were straightforward and harmless enough—they certainly did not commit the Co-operative Party to Labour in any binding way. Yet when the scheme was placed before the 1920 congress, the chairman, G. A. Ramsay, ruled it out of order, to the stupefaction of the central board and amidst 'much disorder in the Congress Hall', on the ground that the affiliated societies had had insufficient time to examine it.[77]

The plan was submitted to the 1921 congress and the behaviour of the co-operative societies was even more bewildering than usual. An amendment rejecting the proposed alliance was defeated by 1,999 to 1,953. But when the resolution was placed as a substantive notion it was defeated by 1,686 to 1,682.[78] This was the last time before the

[71] *Co-operative Congress Report*, 1919, p. 187.
[72] See above, p. 30.
[73] See above, p. 94.
[74] *Co-operative Congress Report*, 1919, p. 527.
[75] Ibid., pp. 532–3.
[76] Minutes of the meeting filed as 'NEC', 9 July 1919.
[77] *Co-operative Congress Report*, 1920, p. 515.
[78] *Co-operative Congress Report*, 1921, pp. 482–96.

late twenties that anyone tried to institutionalize relations between the Labour Party and the Union. Electoral questions were sorted out, often unsatisfactorily, as they always had been, in the old informal way. The truth was that the co-operative movement was as politically divided as it had been before the war. Furthermore, as Cole points out, much of the co-operative enthusiasm for political action had vanished since the war. After 1918 the number of distributive and productive societies affiliated to the Co-operative Party fell sharply. By 1924 the majority of co-operators were not affiliated to the Co-operative Party, though they were entitled to vote on Party matters at Congress.[79]

The most important consequence of this failure to establish any formal co-ordinating body was an electoral one. Because problems could only be sorted out as they arose, there was no way of preventing problems occurring in the first place. Nor was there any accepted procedure for arbitrating demarcation disputes between the two parties. This meant that the difficulties themselves were compounded and often prolonged: they were solved either by *force majeure* or muddle. It is worth looking at a couple of these disputes to see how complicated they could and did become.

The Stockport By-election (March 1920). The first parliamentary vacancy for Stockport was created late in February 1920 when the sitting Coalition Liberal member died. On 22 February the local Labour executive met and unanimously decided to contest the seat.[80] Though they had not chosen a candidate two names were on hand, one from the I.L.P. and one from the Postal Workers.[81] But Stockport was a good co-operators' town with a large purchasing membership and an active political movement. The local Co-operative Party had already decided to contest the seat[82] and it, too, had a couple of nominees on hand. They asked for a joint meeting with the Stockport Labour Party, a meeting which that body refused to attend.[83] Even before the vacancy the local Labour offices had made it clear to Henderson that they would not support a co-operative candidate; he, therefore, had written to S. F. Perry, the secretary of the Co-operative Party, asking him to 'see' his Stockport affiliate and making it fairly plain that Labour would claim the seat.[84] On 22 February Perry arrived in Stockport to meet the co-operators. There was a protracted

[79] G. D. H. Cole, *A Century of Co-operation* (Manchester, 1944), p. 320.
[80] 'NEC', 9 Mar. 1920.
[81] *Cheshire Daily Echo*, 25 Feb. 1920.
[82] 'NEC', 3 Feb. 1920.
[83] 'NEC', 9 Mar. 1920.
[84] Henderson to Perry, 5 Feb. 1920, 'LPLF: Uncat.'.

discussion on relations with the Labour Party and it was tactfully concluded that they 'were prepared to contest the parliamentary by-election' if a candidate 'acceptable to both parties' were selected.[85]

The national agent, Wake, met the local Labour party on 27 February. Much to their astonishment he told them that the executive was not only ready to support their claim to the seat but even had a candidate for them—Sir Leo Chiozza Money. This was very much a Head Office choice (the local party was about to choose George Middleton of the Post Office Workers) and was accepted only reluctantly by the Stockport people: 'after all, the Labour Party wants brains', the Stockport secretary told a reporter.[86] At a joint meeting with Wake the next day the local co-operators agreed to support Money, though with little enthusiasm.

However, some of these problems were unexpectedly eased. Since the Tories and Liberals were in the same predicament as their opponents—how to divide one place between two claimants—a way out was found by inducing the second member, G. J. Wardle (Coalition Labour), to resign. The coalition partners each then took one vacancy and, it seemed, so could Labour and Co-operative.

This did happen—but only just. The local Co-operative party met on 11 March and insisted on the second nomination, while the local Labour party refused to give up its claims.[87] Even the national executive was divided: the secretary's motion that the second vacancy should be left to the Co-operative Party was carried by only six votes to four.[88] The only candidate it would accept was Perry himself, who was duly nominated. Wake had difficulty in persuading the local Labour party to support even Perry.[89]

Everything went wrong with the campaign, which was confused by the entry of two Bottomley candidates and a Sinn Feiner. It was generally noticed that Labour workers neglected Perry, while co-operators themselves were prominent by their absence.[90] The result was a blow, even more to the co-operators than to Labour.[91] Wake noted that

... this result may be regarded frankly as a disappointment... The chief cause ... of the lack of our success, was the chaotic condition of the local

[85] *Cheshire Daily Echo*, 25 Feb. 1920.
[86] *Cheshire Daily Echo*, 28 Feb. 1920; 'NEC', 9 Mar. 1920.
[87] *Cheshire Daily Echo*, 12 Mar. 1920.
[88] 'NEC', 10 Mar. 1920.
[89] 'NEC', 20 Apr. 1920.
[90] *Cheshire Daily Echo*, 15 Mar. 1920.
[91] It was: V. Greenwood (Co. Unionist) 22,847; H. Fildes (Co. Liberal) 22,386; L. Chiozza Money (Labour) 16,042; S. F. Perry (Co-operative) 14,434; A. G. Kindell (Bottomley) 5,644; J. J. Terrett (Bottomley) 5,543; W. O'Brien (Sinn Fein) 2,336.

movement, due partly to the effect of internal quarrels long drawn out ...
The Co-operative Movement while bringing resources and funds to our aid,
brought little else in the way of support or effective work.[92]

In private, he was more caustic. To G. R. Shepherd (his successor as
national agent), Wake wrote that 'we might have been landed with a
white elephant [in the Co-operative movement]'.[93] The lesson appeared
to be a twofold one : that local Labour parties were perhaps unwilling
to associate themselves with Co-operative candidates, and that the
electorate was probably unlikely to vote for Co-operative Party
candidates even if the electors were co-operators themselves.

Paisley (1923–1924). In 1924 Asquith suffered his second and last
parliamentary defeat when he lost Paisley to Rosslyn Mitchell. Yet,
had it not been for a bitter dispute within the 'democratic' forces of the
constituency he would have lost to a Co-operative candidate the
previous year. Before 1923 J. M. Biggar, the Co-operator, had three
times contested Paisley as the joint candidate of the Labour and
Co-operative Parties: in 1918, in 1920 at the by-election which
returned Asquith, and in 1922. Twice he had been within several
hundred votes of victory and it was a reasonable expectation that in
time the seat would be his.

But in 1923 an unendorsed Labour candidate was put up and
Asquith's return for a third time was made certain. The result was :

Asquith (Lib.)	9,723
Biggar (Co-op.)	7,977
Shaw (Cons.)	7,758
Cormack (Lab.)	3,685

The origins of Cormack's candidature were to be found in Glasgow's
housing problems. Biggar was a house factor whose attitude to rent
restriction and eviction angered many members of the Paisley Labour
Party.[94] It was alleged by the co-operators that this 'anger' was just
Communist mischief-making,[95] and in a sense this was true. Opposition
to Biggar was strongest in the Housing Association and the Unemployed
Committees, both of which had large Communist memberships. But
the fact that the dissidents allowed themselves to be addressed by
Harry Pollitt (still calling himself a Labour candidate) and met in the
Communist Hall tells us little.[96] The position of the Communist

[92] 'NEC', 20 Apr. 1920.
[93] Wake to Shepherd, 30 Mar. 1920, 'LPLF: Uncat.'.
[94] *Glasgow Herald*, 14 Nov. 1923.
[95] See Scottish Committee of the Co-operative Party, *History of the Paisley Constituency* (1924), p. 2.
[96] For these details, see *Glasgow Herald*, 17 Nov. 1923.

Party within the Labour movement was confused: individual members of the Communist Party could still be individual or affiliated members of the Labour Party.[97] In any case, there were many who felt strongly about Scottish housing but who were not Communists. Thus on 17 November 1923, after the Co-operative D fence Association decided to renominate Biggar, D. D. Cormack, a Dumbarton journalist prominent in the Housing Association, was nominated by the local Labour party. He was endorsed neither by the national executive nor by the S.A.C.[98]

At the end of April 1924, Biggar withdrew and was succeeded in the Co-operative candidature by Hugh Guthrie. Both the Co-operative Party and the Scottish executive seem to have assumed that the seat was still to be a Co-operative one: as a former I.L.P. candidate (for Camlachie in 1918) Guthrie was chosen specifically to satisfy the local Labour party. However, the Paisley Labour Party, with the full support of the Scottish I.L.P., decided to nominate a candidate of its own, Rosslyn Mitchell, who had made himself famous during a highly publicized campaign against Bonar Law in 1922.[99] They did so on the grounds that with Biggar's withdrawal the Co-operative claim to the seat automatically lapsed. W. Stewart, secretary of the Scottish I.L.P., wrote indignantly to the Scottish executive of the Labour Party complaining that Guthrie had been selected 'without consideration of the rights of the Labour Party' and demanding that the Paisley Party 'should have its proper share' in the choosing of a candidate—should be allowed, that is to say, to nominate Rosslyn Mitchell.[100] The Scottish executive, always anxious to keep the Co-operators on its side, deprecated the 'attempt to introduce Mr. Mitchell or another Labour candidate in the fashion proposed' and hoped that both parties would accept Guthrie.[101] A local attempt at conciliation failed and the whole affair was left to the national executive.

On 21–22 June, C. T. Cramp, the chairman of the national executive, and Wake went to Glasgow and there met the rival candidates, and deputations from the Co-operative Party, the I.L.P., and the Paisley Labour Party.[102] The I.L.P. deputation

---

[97] See below, p. 191

[98] 'SEC', 24 Nov. 1923.

[99] In Central Glasgow. See Margot Asquith's typically malicious description of him: 'Mitchell is better dressed than Peter Flower, is highly educated and no more Labour than you [Lord Islington], an orator wind-bag and dangerously courteous with a face like the actor John Hare, only handsomer.' (R. Jenkins, *Asquith* (1964), p. 504.)

[100] 'SEC', 10 May 1924.

[101] 'SEC', 10 May 1924.

[102] 'Report of a Deputation . . . into the Paisley Labour Party, 21–22 June 1924', filed as 'NEC', 2 Sept. 1924.

claimed that to allow the Co-operative Party to keep Paisley as their preserve was to place an unaffiliated organisation in a superior position to any of the constituent parts of the Labour Party. They were not prepared to agree that when the Co-operative Party had once fought a seat the constituency was regarded as preserved to them in the future . . .

The Paisley Labour Party asserted, probably accurately, that 'the Co-operative Party as an efficient fighting organisation does not exist in Paisley. The political work, so far as organisation and propaganda were concerned had been carried out by the Labour Party even for Co-operative candidates in the past.'

When Wake met the Scottish executive of the Labour Party he emphasized the 'national position': that Paisley could not be considered by itself but only as part of the national relationship between Labour and the Co-operative Party. 'We had to consider whether the Co-operative Party was to be exploited by other elements or was to work in harmony with us.' This was an argument that did not much impress the local Labour party, nor, in the end, did it much impress Wake. A general meeting of the Paisley Party was (with one dissentient) 'entirely in favour of persisting in claiming their rights under the Constitution and going forward with a Labour candidate'. An addendum to the report noted that a joint meeting had been held of the local Co-operative and Labour Parties but that 'neither Party was prepared to modify its position'.

The report's recommendations were distinctly unfavourable to the Co-operative Party: it should understand that 'the agreement can only operate in cases where mutual arrangement is obtained locally'. It was also considered that the basis of membership of the Co-operative Party[103] and its method of selecting candidates needed the closest examination. In the circumstances, Cramp and Wake concluded, it would be impossible to resist the claim of the Paisley Labour Party to select and run a Labour candidate for this constituency. The final justification for this was a constitutional one: 'there is no doubt that the National Executive has no power to withhold the endorsement if the candidate is otherwise satisfactory'. Now this was not strictly true. Head Office could not stop a local party selecting a candidate but it could defer endorsement—as it did to several Communists nominated as Labour candidates. Cramp and Wake, anyway Wake, would have known this as well as anybody; what, in fact, they were doing was recommending endorsement without actually saying so.

The executive had qualms about doing this and the endorsement was deferred.[104] Neither side was ready to compromise and a three-cornered contest was avoided only by the withdrawal of Guthrie for

[103] See below, p. 195.   [104] 'NEC', 2 Sept. 1924.

health reasons. Rosslyn Mitchell was left as the only Labour candidate.

The most striking thing about the Paisley dispute was the hostility of the local Labour party to the Co-operative candidates—even Guthrie to whom they had no personal objections. The Labour people were simply opposed to any candidate of the Co-operative Party. Cynthia Arditti has commented on the same hostility even in the Manchester area, that fortress of the Co-operative movement, where the local Labour parties doggedly refused to concede any of the city's seats to the Co-operative Party.[105] While it is certainly true that in most constituencies where the Co-operative Party was able to make a good case for a candidature the national executive was ready to give the Co-operators a free run, it seems equally true that in many constituencies local parties were not ready to give way and (with the possible exception of Stockport) the national executive made no attempt to impose a candidate on them.

Local Labour parties usually justified themselves by saying that the Co-operators left all the work to them, that they were erratic and suspect political partners. Of that everyone had plenty of evidence. But there were other disconcerting tendencies in the Co-operative Party. No one, for example, was ever really sure who belonged to it. In their report on Paisley, Cramp and Wake noted this: they referred specifically to the Kelvingrove division of Glasgow where an inquiry into the candidature of Aitken Ferguson (a Communist) revealed that anyone could, and did, join the Co-operative Party. Since the local Co-operative parties were affiliated to the local Labour parties[106] it was the done thing to 'rush' the Co-operative Party in order to increase support for a particular nominee. Aitken Ferguson owed his nomination to the doubling in membership of the affiliated Co-operative Party a week before the selection conference. Unease over this practice was only increased, rather than lessened, by the I.L.P.'s free admission that it had done the same thing.[107]

In the end, it was the political mutability of the Co-operators that made working with them so difficult. There was always a possibility that a change in the political complexion of a board of directors would make Co-operative political activity impossible in a constituency with a tradition of Co-operative candidatures. Thus, for example, the election in 1923 of a new board of directors for the Ten Acres and Stirchley society abruptly halted the Co-operative candidacy in Birmingham King's Norton. This development was unpredictable

---

[105] Arditti, 'Co-operative Movement in Manchester', pp. 68–70.

[106] This was peculiar to Glasgow and had been specifically forbidden by the executive. (See above, p. 180.) This, like so many other Head Office instructions, had been ignored in Scotland.

[107] 'NEC', 21 July 1924. See below, p. 195.

enough; even more unpredictable was that the board should have come under Liberal control; in the environment of Birmingham that was an act of defiance not so much of the Labour Party as of politics in principle.[108]

It seems probable that by the end of 1924 Head Office was much more sceptical about the possible value of an alliance with the Co-operative movement than it had been before the war. It is doubtful whether London was ever as enthusiastic as Glasgow, yet even Glasgow gave the air (at least) of being sadder and wiser for its experience. In August 1923, after Wake had told the Scottish executive that Labour should keep friendly relations with the Co-operators (or rather 'hoped' that Labour would do so), the Scots replied that the Co-operative Party was 'of doubtful value to the democratic movement' and asked, furthermore, the Scottish secretary to prepare a memorandum on the 'non-committal attitude' of the two great wholesale societies.[109]

It is unlikely that Labour gained many votes from its alliance with the Co-operative Party that it would not have got anyway. Of the six seats won by the Co-operative Party in the period—Kettering, East Ham South, Tottenham North, Sheffield Hillsborough, Glasgow Tradeston, and Glasgow Partick—Labour was perfectly capable of winning them all on its own account. It is just possible, indeed, given the confusion that sometimes accompanied Co-operative campaigns that Labour might have won some of the seats unsuccessfully contested by the Co-operative Party. In any case, it was assumed—and the experience of King's Norton is some confirmation[110]—that politically active Co-operators were also usually politically active members of the Labour Party.

The Co-operative Party had become neither of the things it was feared and hoped it might. Since it was impossible to mobilize a 'consumer-vote', or to nurture a 'consumer-consciousness' which would have a political function, the Co-operative Party did not emerge as a competitor of the Labour Party. But for the same reasons neither did it emerge as a bulwark of it: entanglements with the Co-operators disrupted national organization and were of questionable electoral worth. Then why did Labour persist?

[108] The seat had been contested by the Co-operative Party in 1922 and the national Co-operative Party wished to keep it on their panel of constituencies. The King's Norton Labour Party protested and the executive not unexpectedly decided in the latter's favour. There is a full account in 'NEC', 26 July 1924. The whole thing caused 'great dissatisfaction' in the central board of the Co-operative Union. *Co-operative Congress Report*, 1925, p. 98.

[109] 'SEC', 13 Aug. 1923.

[110] The King's Norton Co-operative Political Council, it was noted, was dominated by Labour supporters, while its secretary was one of the founder members of the divisional Labour Party and one of those who insisted on a Labour candidature.

In effect, the Labour Party was trying to buy ancillary benefits from the Co-operative Party. In theory these benefits were considerable. The co-operatives conducted a whole range of financial and merchandizing activities, already an important part of working-class life, and to that extent also of emotional significance to the Labour movement. But it was also hoped that these institutions could be more formally tied to the Labour Party and to the T.U.C. Basically what the Labour Party wanted was finance: finance for the Labour Party and, above all, funding for trade-union activities and for strikes. Thus, nearly all the schemes floated by the Labour Party, particularly in Scotland, involved an extension of the C.W.S.'s banking facilities, to be dependent heavily on trade-union investment. In return the C.W.S. banks were to extend credit at low interest rates to trade unions, trade councils, and local Labour parties. The schemes envisaged elaborate funding and provisioning of unions and union members during times of prolonged strikes.[111]

There is no evidence that these schemes ever got off the ground in the 1920s. The Scottish ones petered out and harmonious relations between the leadership of the trade unions and the Co-operative headquarters during the general strike were remarkable only by their absence. Many local co-operative societies, indeed, did extend credit to striking unionists, and clearly at the local level relations between the unions and the co-operatives could be close, but the most obvious impression at the time was the lack of co-ordination at the top between the T.U.C. and the co-operatives, not to speak of actual hostility between the two.[112] This, of course, was by no means the fault alone of the co-operatives. In 1926 the T.U.C. made little attempt to work with them; in 1920 the Scottish Council of the Labour Party had to report that trade-union indifference to the draft scheme of that year was almost as great as that of many of the local co-operative societies.[113]

At the time, before 1924, the Labour Party thought that the potential value of the Co-operative movement was presumably worth the electoral and organizational sacrifices that might have to be made. But the fact that these hopes were not realized was partly the result of what was essentially a political misjudgement by the Labour Party itself. The somewhat triumphalist mood of 1918 arose from certain

[111] See *Scottish Conference Report*, 1920, p. 11.

[112] Emile Burns (*The General Strike: May 1926. Trade Councils in Action* (London, 1926), pp. 55–61) concludes that local co-operative societies were almost equally divided on the question of extending credit but that the refusal of the T.U.C. to give transport permits to co-operative stores caused great annoyance. Julian Symons (*The General Strike*, (1957), pp. 129–72) agrees on credit extension and points out that, except in Manchester, the co-operators refused to print the *British Worker* on co-operative presses. But the T.U.C. had called out the co-operative printers with the rest.

[113] See *Scottish Conference Report*, 1920, p. 11.

assumptions about the unity of purpose of the British working classes. These assumptions did not concern the Co-operative movement alone and the disappointments, consequently, were not confined to it. But the Labour leadership did not assume that groups within the working class might see themselves as having different interests—that the largely commercial and financial activities of the co-operative societies might make them unsympathetic to some of the aims of the Labour Party.

3. The Labour Party and the Communist Party

The Communist Party might have been a much more formidable competitor of Labour than the Co-operators. The Communists, for the most part, had their strength within the Labour movement and such expansion as they had would be at the expense of the official Labour Party. However, though the ideological divisions between the Communist Party and the Labour Party were debated with much passion, it turned out that the existence of the Communist Party had only a relatively slight effect on Labour's organization.

It is not the point of this book to recount the Communist Party's repeated attempts and ultimate failure to affiliate itself or its members to the Labour Party. That has been told elsewhere and exhaustively.[114] But the chronology of the affiliation question is as follows. At the 1920 Labour Party conference the first Communist attempt to affiliate was rejected and the executive ruled that local Labour parties could not accept the affiliation of Communist Party branches. In December 1921 the Labour Party met a delegation from the Communist Party and the latter agreed to give written answers to a series of questions. These were found unsatisfactory and the executive again recommended to the annual conference (1922) that affiliation be refused. A motion to refer this back was defeated by 3,086,000 to 261,000. Affiliation was again rejected in 1923 by 2,880,000 to 366,000. It was not until 1924 that individual members of the Communist Party were excluded from membership of the Labour Party by conference decision. The position was clarified by three votes. Affiliation was again (and finally) rejected by 3,185,000 to 193,000. Members of the Communist Party were disbarred from Labour candidatures, at either parliamentary or municipal levels, by 2,456,000 to 654,000, and (most

[114] See L. J. Macfarlane, 'The Origins of the Communist Party of Great Britain and its Early History, 1920–1927', Ph.D. thesis, London, pp. 112–43; since published as *The British Communist Party* (London, 1966), pp. 94–109. All references in this text are to the doctoral manuscript. The problem is dealt with succinctly in H. Pelling, *The British Communist Party* (1958), and more lengthily than one would have thought possible in J. Klugman, *The Communist Party of Great Britain* (1969), i. pp. 75 ff.

important) all Communists were made ineligible for membership of the Labour Party—by 1,804,000 to 1,540,000.[115]

This uninterrupted series of defeats gives a pretty fair picture of the national importance of the Communist Party, but the growth of Communism did have some effects on the structure of the Labour Party and they need examination. Communist strength within the Labour Party was patchy. In the period 1920–4 Communist candidates were returned in two constituencies. In 1922 J. T. Walton Newbold won Motherwell as a Communist, though nominated by the local Labour party, while S. Saklatvala, standing as an endorsed Labour candidate, won Battersea North in 1922 and 1924. But there were several other Communists who stood unsuccessfully as endorsed Labour candidates.

There were two reasons why a fairly large number of Communists should still have been in the Labour Party. In the first place, leaving aside those who joined after 1920, most members of the Communist Party were formerly members of the British Socialist Party which was affiliated to the Labour Party. It was, therefore, natural enough to assume that since Communists had once been members of the Labour Party there was no reason why they should not continue to be so. Secondly, there was nothing in the Labour Party rules (until 1924) which prevented individual Communists from belonging to the Labour Party, from acting as union delegates to Party conferences, or, so long as their nominations were otherwise in order, from standing as Labour parliamentary candidates.

In 1922, the national executive was able to insist that Communist candidates nominated by local Labour parties should satisfy certain requirements. At the 1922 conference Henderson repeated the conditions that Saklatvala had accepted:[116]

... the candidate should appear before the constituency with the designation of 'Labour Candidate' only, independent of all other political parties, and if elected should join the Parliamentary Labour Party; that at the General Election he should, in his election address and in his campaign give prominence to the issues as defined by the National Executive from the General Party programme; that if elected he should act in harmony with the Constitution and Standing Orders of the Party.

Saklatvala and the Battersea Trades Council adhered to these requirements without question, as did most of the other Communist candidates until after 1924, when either the change in the Party constitution or the behaviour of the Communists themselves made acceptance or endorsement difficult.

[115] Macfarlane, 'The Communist Party', pp. 113–41.
[116] *Conference Report*, 1922, p. 175.

Consequently in 1922 only one Communist, Newbold in Mother-well, and in 1923, only two Communists, Newbold again, and Aitken Ferguson in Kelvingrove, stood as 'Labour' candidates (were, that is to say, nominated by the local Labour party) without the endorsement of the national executive.[117] Newbold stood as an avowed Communist, Ferguson as Independent Labour. Both these constituencies are good examples of what happened to local organiza-tions which were either controlled by Communists or in which Communists seemed to have a predominant influence. The two constituencies will, therefore, be examined in a little detail: Kelvin-grove, as it were, from the point of view of the executive in London, and Motherwell from that of the local constituency itself.

Glasgow Kelvingrove. In 1923 the Kelvingrove Party nominated as their candidate Aitken Ferguson, a member of the Boilermakers' Union, a former member of the Clyde Workers' Committee, a pro-minent Communist, and a future leading light in the National Minority Movement.[118] Ferguson seems to have been a popular candidate and an effective one. But on the advice of the Scottish executive the national executive refused to endorse him.[119] He had, nevertheless, support from the parliamentary party and he reduced the Conservative majority to 1,004. He did so well, indeed, that Labour optimists became convinced that any person other than Ferguson would have won.[120]

At the beginning of May 1924 the sitting Conservative died and the Boilermakers again nominated Ferguson for the candidature. The I.L.P. strongly opposed this nomination, as it did all Communist nominations in Scotland—and put up Patrick Dollan, the leader of the Labour group on the Glasgow Council. Yet support for Ferguson in the local party was so strong that Dollan withdrew and Ferguson was chosen unanimously as candidate on 9 May.[121] The Scottish secretary, Ben Shaw, always a good weathercock, immediately wrote to Wake urging Ferguson's endorsement.

If you want my personal feeling, I believe it would go against the General Labour opinion here to refuse endorsement; it being difficult if not impossible

---

[117] In 1922 Willie Gallacher was the only Communist candidate to oppose an endorsed Labour candidate. He finished bottom of the poll at Dundee.

[118] See R. R. Martin, 'The National Minority Movement' (Univ. of Oxford D.Phil. thesis, 1964), p. 230. (Since published as *Communism and the British Trade Unions, 1924–1933* (Oxford, 1969.) Ferguson edited the Minority Movement's newspaper, the *Worker*, from 1924 to 1926.

[119] 'NEC', 28 May 1924.

[120] See *Scottish Conference Report*, 1924, p. 8.

[121] *Glasgow Herald*, 10 May 1924. Dollan withdrew in order to prevent a 'split'—he said. The *Glasgow Herald* was inclined to think that he withdrew to avoid an inevitable defeat.

in the conditions of emergency to resist the unanimous findings of representatives and unanimous D.L.P. meetings backed by Scottish Executive recommendation[122]. . . and backed as it is now certain to be by unanimous Trades Council. In these circumstances it would also be judicious that our staff co-operate, personal feelings being put aside! As far as practicable.[123]

On 13 May, Wake wrote to all members of the national executive giving them a brief history of Ferguson's candidature and asking them to vote (by telegram) for or against endorsement.[124] They voted by fourteen to five in favour.[125] Three days after Wake's letter an advertisement sponsored by the Communist Party appeared in the *Worker's Weekly* asking for contributions to Ferguson's campaign and carrying a statement of his policy.[126] The latter was even more unlike the Labour Party's (and the Labour government's) policies than his earlier pronouncements had been. Two days later (18 May), on the urgent direction of Henderson, Wake again wrote to all members of the executive. He told them that the elections sub-committee had 'been consulted' and they were 'of opinion that several of these points are not only at variance but in conflict with the policy of the government and they feel that they cannot authorise further support in the way of speakers etc.'.[127] He asked members whether they were still in favour of endorsement. In fact, endorsement was not withheld but no official support was given.[128] Ferguson, for his part, made no attempt to camouflage himself: *The Times* was astonished at 'the astounding boldness of his Communistic, revolutionary, and confiscatory avowals'.[129]

The Conservatives managed to lift their majority to 4,321 and this Head Office thought the fault of Ferguson.[130] The Kelvingrove situation seemed so deplorable that the executive sent C. T. Cramp, Will Lawther, and Wake to Scotland. Their findings and their

---

[122] The Scottish executive had recommended endorsement by six votes to four. But eight members were not present. ('SEC', 10 May 1924.)

[123] Shaw to Wake, 11 May 1924, 'LPLF: Uncat. Scotland'.

[124] Wake to Members of the national executive, 13 May 1924, 'LPLF: Uncat.'.

[125] 'NEC', 16 May 1924.

[126] *Worker's Weekly*, 16 May 1924. The real point at issue was his criticism of the government's Russian policy. Ferguson advocated scrapping the so-called Expert's Report on Reparations, the cancellation of all British claims against Russia, an immediate £100,000,000 credit and the appointment of a trade unionist, nominated by the general council of the T.U.C., as ambassador.

[127] 'NEC', 17 May 1924.

[128] *Glasgow Herald*, 19 May 1924.

[129] *The Times*, :7 May 1924.

[130] 'NEC', 21 July 1924. The figures were: Cons. 15,488; Lab. 11,167; Lib. 1,372. It is unlikely that another candidate would have done better. The main cause of the Conservative success was the collapse of the Liberal vote and this was a nation-wide phenomenon in 1924. In the general election of 1924, when there was an endorsed Labour candidate in a straight fight with the Conservative, the figures were Cons. 18,034; Lab. 12,844.

conclusions, as was expected, had a national significance and guided much of Labour's behaviour towards the Communist Party for the rest of the year.[131]

The three met representatives of the S.A.C., the Glasgow Trades Council, the Kelvingrove Party, and the Scottish Council of the I.L.P. They interviewed no Communist official except Ferguson, who confessed that he was the paid Glasgow organizer of the Communist Party and candidly admitted that his agent was a Communist, as indeed he was, and destined to be remembered long after Ferguson. He was that same Campbell whose 'case' was immediately responsible for the fall of the first MacDonald government. Ferguson claimed that neither of these facts in any way made his candidature irregular.

The I.L.P. submission, however, was replete with accusations against Ferguson and the way he was selected.

They declared that in 1923, when Ferguson was selected for the General Election, there were irregularities in his nomination. They expressed the view that a different type of candidate would have won the seat for Labour, declared that the election address was unconstitutional, the campaign a burlesque of electioneering, and that the Tory candidate declared with truth that not a single speaker had defended the Labour Party throughout the election.

The I.L.P. claimed that 75 per cent of the 'so-called Co-operative Party' were not 'purchasing members'; were in other words, Communists.[132]

The Glasgow Trades Council merely noted that Ferguson was an accredited delegate of the Boilermakers' Society to the Council and, therefore, perfectly entitled to nomination. The Scottish executive agreed: '. . . the Communists should be in or out altogether . . . the unsatisfactory position at Kelvingrove with regard to Mr. Ferguson . . . has arisen out of the present vague and unsatisfactory state of our rules.' By and large, the national executive delegation agreed with

[131] The report is filed as 'NEC', 21 July 1924. The three visited Glasgow on 20–21 June 1924.
[132] 'NEC', 21 July 1924. See above, p. 188. The way the co-operative associations were affiliated to labour parties in Glasgow provided interested persons with heaven-sent opportunities. Co-operative representation to the Glasgow Labour parties was regulated by the number of purchasing members resident in the constituency. In Kelvingrove there were 4,000 and this entitled the co-operators to twenty delegates. These delegates, in turn, were appointed by the Co-operative Party which consisted of members of co-operative societies or their families who had 'signified' a desire to join the Co-operative Party. This party consisted of 100 members a few weeks before the by-election, but in the week before the selection meeting from 75 to 100 new members joined. The secretary of the Co-operative Party cheerfully admitted that this 'was due to a desire to influence the Co-operative vote at the selection conference'. Both Communists and I.L.P.ers admitted that they had attempted to 'rush' members into the Co-operative Party. The Communists plainly won the rush.

this. The constitution and rules of the Kelvingrove Party were in order; selection procedures were also regular, if somewhat delayed. The only thing which demanded correction, they said, was the affiliation of the Co-operative Party. They concluded that they were 'strongly of opinion that in order to prevent the recurrence of a candidature of this kind the rules require revision and strengthening to safeguard the Party against increased exploitation by the Communists'. And this clearly anticipated the resolutions presented to the 1924 conference and accepted by it.[133]

As for Kelvingrove, Ferguson did not offer himself for nomination again, presumably because endorsement would be refused unless he perjured himself before the electorate as (say) Saklatvala did. This apparently he was not prepared to do, or else the Kelvingrove Party regarded his performance as so unsatisfactory that a 'proper' Labour candidate was required. Yet it was probably his candidature at the 1924 by-election that was the occasion for, if by no means the only cause of the changes in the Party's constitution whereby the process of eliminating Communists from its membership began.

Motherwell. At the 1922 general election Motherwell became the first British constituency to return to parliament a candidate standing as a Communist, J. T. Walton Newbold.[134] Newbold was selected by the Motherwell Trades Council, a body affiliated to the national Labour Party, though exactly who nominated him was to be a matter of much dispute. He had been the endorsed Labour candidate in 1918, but as a nominee of the I.L.P. Since then he had left the I.L.P. and joined the Communist Party.

The exact membership of the Motherwell Trades Council is difficult to determine. Among the unions, the Miners, the Iron and Steel Trades Confederation, and the A.E.U. predominated, though there were a couple of fairly strong N.U.R. branches.[135] There was a strong and active I.L.P. in Motherwell. In Wishaw, the other important town in the constituency, as to whether there was an I.L.P., and if so, whether it was constitutional, there was much contention. Similarly, it was a matter of opinion whether there was an individual members' section before 1924 or not. There was a women's section which was once grotesquely inflated before a selection conference. The

[133] See above, pp. 191–2.

[134] (1888–1943), a man of most erratic career. Joined Fabian Society, 1908; I.L.P., 1910; Plebs League, 1917. Member, executive of Labour Research department, 1922–6; executive committee, Communist Party and Comintern, 1922–3. Resigned Communist Party, 1924. Rejoined Labour Party and contested Epping (Churchill's seat), 1929. Member Macmillan Committee, 1929. Followed MacDonald in 1931, thereafter supported Conservatives.

[135] *Motherwell Times*, 4 Aug. 1922.

Housing and Unemployed Committees were certainly and un-constitutionally affiliated and these were Newbold's real source of strength.

The Trades Council had been more or less acting in defiance of the national Party since May 1922 when it decided narrowly that Newbold's candidature should be continued. The Scottish secretary, Shaw, criticized the decision and regretted that he was not invited to attend the meeting.[136] In September the Trades Council decided to ignore the decision of the 1922 annual conference regarding eligibility of delegates to local parties, thus ensuring that the basis of Newbold's support would remain intact.[137]

At a meeting on 1 November, the secretary of the Trades Council, W. G. Ballinger, notified the delegates that he had advised the Scottish executive against selecting a 'Labour' candidate, as 'Labour was very much divided in its opinion regarding supporting Mr. Newbold'. Labour opinion could not have been all that divided: Newbold was unanimously endorsed by the Trades Council.[138] Furthermore, after the declaration of the poll, Ballinger admitted that no less than three circulars inviting nominations were sent to affiliated societies. Only one name had been received and that was out of order.[139]

Newbold's victory in a four-cornered contest was something of a sensation, as much in Motherwell as in the country.[140] It cannot be said there was much elation. At a meeting of the Trades Council immediately after the poll, the chairman was criticized for not publishing a telegram from the national executive refusing endorse-ment. He proffered the ingenious explanation 'that they had no instructions to send the telegram to London and therefore did not feel obliged to publish the reply'.[141] The following year, the two Trades Council delegates to the Scottish conference of the Labour Party, one of whom was certainly a Communist, were refused admission to the Conference hall.[142]

[136] 'SEC', 19 June 1922.

[137] *Motherwell Times*, 15 Sept. 1922. The two rules accepted by conference were as follows:
(a) Every person nominated to serve as a delegate shall individually accept the Constitution and principles of the Labour Party.
(b) No person shall be eligible as a delegate who is a member of any organisation having for one of its objects the return to Parliament or any Local Government Authority of a candidate or candidates other than such as have been endorsed by the Labour Party, or have been approved as running in association with the Labour Party. (*Conference Report*, 1922, p. 177.)

[138] *Motherwell Times*, 3 Nov. 1922.

[139] *Motherwell Times*, 24 Nov. 1924.

[140] The result was: Newbold (Comm.) 8,262; Ferguson (Ind.) 7,214; Maxwell (Lib.) 5,359; Colville (Nat. Lib.) 3,966.

[141] *Motherwell Times*, 1 Dec. 1922.

[142] *Scottish Conference Report*, 1923, pp. 31-2.

Newbold continued to have much personal support in the constituency. Despite the fact that in April (1923) the Trades Council had actually voted in favour of implementing the new rules for the eligibility of delegates,[143] Newbold's candidature was endorsed in November for the general election the following month—and, as the vote makes apparent, as much by the unions as the Housing and Unemployed Committees.[144] Newbold was, of course, a celebrated M.P. and he eased himself into this role with his customary panache.[145]

Yet his victory in 1922 had been somewhat adventitious; much depended on the divisions within the non-Communist vote. In 1923 he had only two opponents and was defeated by Ferguson who stood, on this occasion, as an unabashed Orange-Protestant.[146]

The recriminations which followed Newbold's victory in 1922 were nothing as to those which followed his defeat. At the meeting of the Trades Council after the election it was unanimously resolved to call nominations for a 'Labour candidate' and to hold a selection conference.[147] The circular calling for nominations, signed by Ben Shaw and the local secretary, W. G. Ballinger, pointed out emphatically that neither the Housing Association nor the Unemployed Committees were entitled to nominate a candidate, while Ballinger gratuitously added that Newbold was not a member of a union or of the individual members' section, thus disqualifying him on both counts.[148] The terms of this circular were clearly framed with an eye to the I.L.P. The Motherwell branch of the I.L.P. had met a couple of days before and had denounced the present system *tout court*. It put itself on record as believing that a Labour candidate would have won the seat, and that Newbold was necessarily bound to lose it.[149]

The addendum to the circular and the I.L.P. meeting led to a revealing exchange between Newbold and Ballinger. In a letter to the *Motherwell Times* Newbold justified his non-membership of the Labour Party:

---

[143] *Motherwell Times*, 20 Apr. 1923.

[144] *Motherwell Times*, 30 Nov. 1923.

[145] MacDonald made heavy play of Newbold's manner at the 1923 conference. Speaking on a resolution that instructed the parliamentary party to give the whip to Newbold, he assured the conference 'that it was not because Mr. Newbold was away on the left that they would not have him, because . . . he was not on the left. His mild conduct in the House of Commons had been a model to many other members on both sides. Nor was it because he was not respectable. The greatest contribution which Mr. Newbold had made to parliamentary procedure had been a new method of bowing to the Speaker'. (*Conference Report*, 1923, p. 191.)

[146] The figures were: Ferguson (Orange) 9,793; Newbold (Comm.) 8,712; Maxwell (Lib.) 4,799.

[147] *Motherwell Times*, 14 Dec. 1923.

[148] Ibid., 28 Dec. 1923.

[149] Ibid.

I am not . . . a member of the Individual Members section of the Motherwell D.L.P., but that is only because it does not exist. For some reason not explained there never has been formed such an Individual Section. There is a bitter antipathy on the part of the branches of the I.L.P. to the formation and development of such sections. Where the I.L.P. can cramp their growth it invariably does so.[150]

The following week Ballinger replied by saying that 'there has always been a small individual section attached to the Motherwell and Wishaw Trades and Labour Council, and I.L.P.ers have never at any time attempted to retard its growth'.[151]

To this, Newbold said that 'every Communist candidate in England was nominated'—he meant every Communist candidate was endorsed —but that in Scotland this was made impossible by the influence of the I.L.P. He attacked Fenner Brockway for supporting D. D. Cormack in Paisley and claimed that 'like Mr. Biggar in this respect, the front that I break is the I.L.P. front'. As to individual membership of the local Labour party, 'it must be very small, and it is certainly very inconspicuous. I was the official Labour candidate until September 1921, and I never met it. I should be very interested to see a chart of its growth'.[152]

There are two things that ought to be noted about this correspondence, for while both of them are incidental to the story of Newbold they do tell us a good deal about local organization. The first is the obvious irregularity of the Party's structure. Newbold called it a Divisional Labour Party, Ballinger a Trades and Labour council, and it was affiliated to the National Party as a D.L.P.,[153] that is, a party under the model rules, which it clearly was not. Ballinger, as secretary, was responsible for providing Head Office with this inaccurate information and we have only his word for it that an individual members' section existed, at least until 1924 when one nominated Newbold for the candidature. But clearly the organization of the Motherwell Party was quite as loose as most parties had been before the war, confusion surrounding the constituent parts of the Trades Council (or D.L.P.) was of long standing, and both were certainly not the responsibility of the Communists alone.

The second is Newbold's position. His thrust at the I.L.P. was expected and rather shrewd. The I.L.P. had vigorously opposed Communist candidatures wherever they had emerged in Scotland— that was true and well known. As to the I.L.P. impeding the development of D.L.P.s, even if that were not true, it was certainly widely

[150] *Motherwell Times*, 4 Jan. 1923.
[151] *Motherwell Times*, 11 Jan. 1923.
[152] *Motherwell Times*, 18 Jan. 1923.
[153] *Conference Report*, 1924, p. 42.

believed,[154] and was the sort of accusation that might evoke sympathy for Newbold in quarters not otherwise well disposed to him. But his remarks on Biggar's candidature in Paisley are a reminder that ideological differences in Scotland could be more apparent than real. Though Newbold's fellow-feeling for Biggar was genuine enough, much of the opposition to Biggar's candidature was Communist as well as I.L.P., and from the Communist position perfectly justifiable.[155]

The Trades Council held its selection conference shortly after this outburst of polemic and had before it three nominees: Bailie Taylor (I.L.P.), Bailie Walker (Iron and Steel Trades) and Newbold (Housing Association and two Unemployed Committees). Newbold's nomination was plainly unconstitutional and Ballinger immediately said so.[156] There was immediate discussion about the Unemployed Committees and this led to some further interesting revelations about local organization.

Councillor Donnelly (Unemployed) stated that in the Trades Council they had set up a procedure whereby the local Unemployed Committees were allowed to nominate candidates at the local elections. It was the Unemployed Committee who nominated him as a Parish Council candidate at the last election, and they also nominated Mr. Ballinger.
Councillor Ballinger: The body who nominated me was the No. 3 branch of the A.E.U.
Councillor Donnelly: That is not correct.
Councillor Ballinger: It is correct. I was nominated by A.E.U. Motherwell No. 3 which fulfilled all obligations . . . except providing an organising committee. This was mainly supplied by the Unemployed Committee who distributed addresses, [and] canvassed on behalf . . . of myself.[157]

Whether Ballinger was nominated by the A.E.U. or the Unemployed Committee is not the point. What is clear is that the Unemployed Committees provided much of the enthusiasm and probably most of the hard work at election time. Any attempt, therefore, to disaffiliate these bodies was bound to be difficult, not only because there were many sympathetic to them on the Trades Council, but because organization was to some extent dependent upon them. Despite Ballinger's objections to Newbold's nomination, the Council not unexpectedly decided to go ahead with selection (on 15 March) without bothering to inform the national executive until after a decision had been made.

The executive's reaction was prompt. A few days later Ballinger was told that Motherwell's delegates to the Scottish conference of the

[154] Marwick, 'Independent Labour Party', p. 54.   [156] Motherwell Times, 8 Feb. 1924.
[155] See above, pp. 185–6.   [157] Motherwell Times, 8 Feb. 1924.

Party (due to meet on 1 March) would not be accredited, an announcement that caused consternation in the Trades Council since it meant exclusion for the second year running. The chairman of the Council, T. C. Moore, generally assumed to be a Communist, or at least sympathetic, said that

they would never get out of the bit unless they considered this question from the point of view of what was going to be best for the workers of this particular district . . . It has been said that the present position in the Trades Council had been brought about by the Communist element entering the Council. That might or might not be true, but even supposing it was there was nothing to prevent Hughie Ferguson [the Orange M.P.] from entering the Trades Council and seeking to control it in the interests of his Party . . .

Ballinger, characteristically, tried to play both sides against the middle.

Motherwell would really be a test case for the whole country. He thought that they should say to the Scottish Executive – 'We will give you every information about the nomination and you may attend the selection conference when we are making the final choice but we will not allow you to question the eligibility of our nominee'. The real question was whether the workers here wanted Newbold or not. That was the issue of the Conference and he thought that the Scottish Executive would do well to leave the issue in the hands of the workers of Motherwell themselves.[158]

No final decision could be reached and the meeting was adjourned until 27 February. When delegates reassembled on that date, to their surprise, they found Ben Shaw present. Shaw, as he made clear, was primarily interested in the disaffiliation of the Unemployed Committees and the Housing Association.[159] As to the rejection of the Motherwell delegates, he said that the Council 'should disaffiliate the

---

[158] *Motherwell Times*, 15 Feb. 1924.

[159] *Motherwell Times*, 29 Feb. 1924. The disaffiliation of these bodies was always demanded by the Scottish executive before it considered reconstruction as satisfactory, but it was often the only thing demanded. Greenock is a good example. In the middle of 1923 the Trades Council was 'captured by an extreme Labour–Communist section', as the *Glasgow Herald* put it, (14 Nov. 1923) and decided to renominate as candidate the Communist, Alex Geddes. As a result, the I.L.P. and some union branches withdrew from the Council. On 3 Nov. 1923 the Scottish executive formally disaffiliated the Trades Council ('SEC', 3 Nov. 1923) and circularized trade unions 'with a view to reconstructing a loyal D.L.P.'. Despite pressure from Wake and the I.L.P., who wanted the immediate formation of a new party, the Scottish executive had second thoughts, and decided to postpone a decision until the position of Communists within the Labour Party became clearer. ('SEC', 7 Jan. 1924.) On 4 February a deputation from the Greenock Trades Council met the Scottish executive in order to reaffiliate. They assured the executive of their loyalty to the constitution, but admitted that the Housing Association and the Unemployed Committees were affiliated locally. ('SEC', 4 Feb. 1924.) Shortly afterwards Shaw visited Greenock and was satisfied that the Housing Association and the Unemployed Committees were disaffiliated. The Greenock Trades Council was reaffiliated to the national Party on 28 April. ('SEC', 28 Apr. 1924.)

Unemployed Committees and the Housing Association, and if they did so, he had no doubt their delegates would be received'. He told the meeting that somebody else might nominate Newbold and he added (misleadingly) that 'the fact that a man is a member of the Communist Party is no longer a bar, as long as he is a member of the Labour Party'. Though Shaw had been steadily heckled throughout his speech his advice was accepted: a motion cancelling the selection conference and calling for new nominations was carried by a large majority. A second motion, to disaffiliate the Unemployed Committees and the Housing Association, was also carried, but only by 31 votes to 29 and amidst constant uproar.[160]

At the beginning of May the Trades Council received three nominations for the postponed selection conference. They were as before—Newbold, Taylor (I.L.P.), and Walker (Iron and Steel Trades), the difference being on this occasion that not only had Newbold at last discovered the individual members' section—he was its nominee as well.[161] This was obviously suspicious. Two weeks later there were allegations that the women's section of the Council had been 'rushed': until the beginning of May there had been forty to sixty members, but within a week there were about 100 applications. The Trades Council decided that to 'keep harmony' it would be necessary for women to apply individually to the Council for membership.[162] This, of course, had caused so much trouble in Kelvingrove, and it is reasonable to assume that there was some 'rushing' of the individual members' section by Newbold's supporters. Such an assumption is given more weight by the balance of voting at the selection conference—the women's sections, whose membership was under the general supervision of the Council, supported Walker; the individual members supported Newbold.

At the frequently postponed conference Newbold was selected by 44 votes to 34.[163] Ben Shaw was there and made no objection to the choice or the manner of the election. Once again it seems as if Newbold had a good deal of personal support: the majority of the Iron and Steel

---

[160] The meeting was not without its entertaining moments. During a noisy row over the terms of the nominating circular the following exchange took place between a delegate from an Unemployed Committee and the chairman:
'Mr. Robertson protested that the Chairman had taken up one attitude on the last occasion the circulars were mentioned and he was taking up another now.
The Chairman: I order you to sit down, Mr. Robertson.
Mr. Robertson: I am not going to sit down.
The Chairman: Am I the chairman of this meeting or are you?
Mr. Robertson: I suppose I'll be chairman.
The Chairman: I wish you'd shut up.'
[161] *Motherwell Times*, 2 May 1924.
[162] *Motherwell Times*, 16 May 1924.
[163] *Motherwell Times*, 30 May 1924.

Trades' delegates, for example, voted for Newbold against their own nominee, Walker. He also had a considerable following among the Miners and the Railwaymen. He may even have had some discreet sympathy from the I.L.P. itself. At one meeting of the Motherwell I.L.P., the proceedings of which were leaked to the *Motherwell Times*, Ballinger is supposed to have come to the same conclusion 'as most people—that from the point of view of ability there was only one candidate that filled the bill, namely: Newbold . . .'.[164]

Yet Newbold had given no written undertaking to adhere to the Labour Party constitution; though his nomination was accepted by the Scottish executive it was not endorsed by the national executive.[165] His position, like that of all Communist candidates, became more difficult after the decisions of the 1924 conference, which gave the national executive the right to exclude Communists from membership of the Labour Party.[166] It was partly this that led to Newbold's totally unexpected abandonment of his candidature and the Communist Party in September 1924. He blamed ill-health, a desire to return to 'intellectual pursuits', and the unsuitability of his temperament to parliamentary life.[167]

With Newbold gone, the Housing Association and the Unemployed Committees disaffiliated, and Head Office armed with new powers, all the problems surrounding Newbold's career disappeared. Another selection conference was held, under Shaw's supervision, and the I.L.P. nominee, the Rev. James Barr from Glasgow, was quickly and triumphantly nominated.[168] The Communist nominee, Willie Gallacher, a formidable personality in his own right, received only six votes. At the beginning of the conference Shaw merely told the delegates that if Gallacher were nominated he would not be endorsed, and it was not necessary to say anything else. Barr went on to win the seat at the following general election, thus perhaps vindicating those who said the seat would always have been won had there been an endorsed Labour candidate.[169]

In many ways Motherwell's politics were distorted by the size of Newbold's personal following and the reluctance of anyone in Glasgow or London to intervene, but in a general way they only exaggerated tendencies that were apparent in other constituencies. Three characteristics of Motherwell were typical. The first was an organizational one. Because the Communists seemed often to have provided a good

[164] *Motherwell Times*, 7 Mar. 1924.
[165] 'NEC', 23 Apr. 1924.
[166] See above, pp. 191–2.
[167] *Motherwell Times*, 19 Sept. 1924.
[168] *Motherwell Times*, 17 Oct. 1924.
[169] The result was: Barr (Lab.) 12,816; Ferguson (Orange) 11,776.

deal of such electoral organization as existed there was an under-
standable reluctance by local officers to exclude them.[170] That the
Housing Association and the Unemployed Committees were frequently
the channels through which Communists filtered into local parties
explains the eagerness of both the Scottish and the national executives
to disaffiliate them. But the success of these two heterodox bodies (as
with so many others of a voluntary kind in the Labour Party) shows
how far local Labour organization differed from the model parties of
1918.

Second, the course of events in Motherwell showed that Head
Office, either in London or Glasgow, did possess decisive authority so
long as it cared to exercise it. While the strength of Communists in a
constituency usually signified a general irregularity in organization,
what was remarkable was not so much the irregularity but the power
of London or Glasgow to end it. Shaw, for example, achieved more by
his presence at only one meeting in Motherwell than had been achieved
by three years of mixed threats, cajolery and indifference.

Finally, the events in Motherwell showed that the Communist
Party was electorally strong only when it worked within traditional
Labour organization. Although Communists could gain influence by
their own ingenuity, perseverance, plain hard work, a skilful and
decisive exploitation of local grievances, and by the inertness or
complaisance of others, once they were excluded from that organization
they were ineffective.

4. Summary

The policies taken up by the Labour Party towards its regions, to the
Co-operative movement, and to the Communist Party were all closely
related. There was, to be sure, one obvious difference between the
Communist Party and the other two : some kind of regional autonomy,
and some form of Co-operative parliamentary representation could be
contained within the centralized structure of the Labour Party. The
Communists could not and had, therefore, to be expelled. Head
Office's policy towards the Co-operative and Communist Parties
needs no elaboration : the first was tolerated for its putative associated
benefits; the second was ideologically incompatible.

The executive's attitude to regional autonomy, and Henderson's
more particularly, needs a little further explanation. At first sight
it appears as if the regions were treated with excessive severity, and
perhaps they were, but to the national executive, and even more to

---

[170] It was this reason, as much as anything else, that led the 1924 Scottish conference
to vote in favour of affiliating the Communists. See, particularly, Ballinger's speech
(*Scottish Conference Report*, 1924, pp. 36–8).

Henderson, there were good reasons for this. They were very conscious of creating a party to suit what they took to be contemporary conditions: a party that would be able to exploit modern social and economic forces. This meant to the Labour Party, as it did to the great unions, central control over a national organization. It meant, furthermore, casting aside traditional and declining props of political power. Henderson was only too aware of the Liberal Party's fatal dependence on Scotland and Wales and the slow disintegration of its electorate in the crucial industrial and urban areas of England. His 'General Scheme of Organisation' was written quite consciously to follow what he understood to be the main lines of British economic development. Thus he drafted Wales out of existence—implanted it in England on the reasonably plausible grounds that north Wales was now part of Lancashire and Cheshire, or was, at least, becoming part of it—while south Wales was so closely linked with southern England as to make it impossible to disentangle the two. This was an analysis that did not recognize sentiments of nationality and was on that ground redrafted by the national executive.

In addition there were reasons of a more directly political kind. Autonomy, it was thought, would give opportunities for individuals and groups to cause 'difficulties' for the national Party. The General Scheme ensured that, on the whole, this would not happen.

The decision not to devolve authority followed the notions and prejudices of nearly all on the national executive: of men like MacDonald, who were suspicious of the socialist societies, of the leaders of the great unions who disliked devolution in principle, of Party professionals like Middleton and Wake, who had an interest in keeping the Party intact and, above all, of Henderson, whose trade-union and political career encompassed the attitudes of all of them.

IX

SHAPING THE PARTY'S INSTITUTIONS

1. *The Research Departments*

TENTATIVE discussions about a research department were held long before Party reorganization in 1917. Webb wrote of a joint meeting of the national executive and the parliamentary committee of the T.U.C. in October 1916 at which C. W. Bowerman, Secretary of the T.U.C., mentioned that they 'hoped for accommodation for each [committee] to have its own Statistical Department, and also a common Statistical Department! All that [Webb added] is, however, very far off.'[1]

Yet in the Fabian Research Department (F.R.D.)[2] the unions and the Party had a well-established institution with an active membership and an enormous amount of collected material at its disposal. While the Labour Party, therefore, was looking for research facilities the Webbs were eager to associate the F.R.D. with the Labour movement. During 1916 they were probably thinking of the unions rather than the Labour Party, partly because the F.R.D. was already doing some work for them.[3]

As early as 1 June 1916, Beatrice noted that she 'wanted an organisation on a more catholic basis [than the F.R.D.]' and that she 'proposed gradually to alter both the name and the constitution of the Department into a Labour Research Society, to include members of all recognised Socialist and Labour organisations...'. If the parliamentary committee failed to co-operate, then the 'larger unions' would be approached individually.[4]

The difficulty she faced in linking the F.R.D. with the Labour movement lay in the F.R.D.'s constitutional position. It was not just a part of the Fabian Society, but an autonomous body with its own executive. At the elections for that executive in 1916, G. D. H. Cole

---

[1] Sidney Webb to Beatrice Webb, 12 Oct. 1916, L.S.E. MS. Passfield: Correspondence, II.3.(i).

[2] For the early history of the Fabian Research Department see Cole, *History of the Labour Party*, p. 60.

[3] The *Labour Year Book*, though financed by the national executive and the parliamentary committee, was written by the F.R.D. and published in December 1915. Of 700 pages it was the most comprehensive handbook on the Labour Movement yet produced. See R. Page Arnot, *History of the Labour Research Department* (London, 1926), p. 13.

[4] Beatrice Webb, 'L.S.E. MS. Passfield: Transcript Diaries', p. 33, 1 June 1916.

was at the head of the poll and, aside from the Webbs and Bernard Shaw, the F.R.D.'s most conspicuous members were the guild socialists, Cole, Mellor, and Arnot. Beatrice claimed that there was an element of design in this ('we let [the guild socialists] make every possible use of the F.R.D. and then they cease to attack us')[5] and there may well have been, but this point was not always taken by the trade-union leaders or the older members of the Party.

Thus when she began seriously to think about 'converting' the F.R.D. Beatrice had to undertake some delicate negotiations with Cole. She candidly admitted that the national guildsmen, who 'abhored' [sic] the Fabians, were the core of the F.R.D., and naturally disliked the idea of their work 'redounding to the credit of the Labour Party'. The problem was to reconcile the guild socialists to the Labour movement without actually asking the guildsmen to identify themselves with the Labour Party. She was very anxious 'to see a separate and distinct organisation for research and publication purposes for the benefit of the Trade Unions and the Labour Movement, in which all sects of socialists can combine . . .'.[6] Cole replied, with the more-than-usual tactlessness he reserved for Beatrice, that

I do not like being regarded as a Fabian or having anything I do mixed up with the Fabian Society . . . which, to be candid, I detest.

I am no less averse than I am to the Fabian connection to the proposal to hand over the Research Department to the Labour Movement. I should simply resign if that happened, because it would mean the tying of our hands to serve the immediate ends of people who cannot see an inch beyond their noses.[7]

Some of this was probably tongue in cheek, but even so there seemed little likelihood that the F.R.D. could be assimilated with the Labour Movement. The required *deus ex machina* was Henderson.

Until September 1917 it had been the unions and the F.R.D. that had made the running, but in that month Henderson set his mind to research and information as he did to so many other things. Adequate research facilities were always an important item in the full equipment of what Henderson understood to be a proper political party. They were not even considered necessarily subordinate to the reorganization of the Party at the constituency level, and the possibility of establishing a 'statistical and information bureau' was raised by Henderson at a joint meeting of the parliamentary committee and the national executive in October 1917.[8]

[5] Ibid.
[6] Beatrice Webb to Cole, 14 Mar. 1917, 'L.S.E. MS. Passfield: Correspondence', II.4.8.
[7] Cole to Beatrice Webb, 15 Mar. 1917, Ibid.
[8] 'NEC', 16 Oct. 1917.
8

Henderson clearly wished to unite the research work of all three bodies—the parliamentary committee, the national executive, and the F.R.D.—in a single research department. This conformed to the belief in the virtues of amalgamation then fashionable at Head Office. However, if the parliamentary committee was ready to join with the Labour Party, it was not ready to join with the Fabians. Henderson, on the other hand, was committed to the Fabians. Not only was his partnership with Webb proving extraordinarily productive, but another member of the executive of the F.R.D., J. J. Mallon, was close to him at the time of his resignation from the government and the writing of the draft constitution.[9] In addition, and to some people's surprise, Henderson liked and respected Cole. The Fabians had come into their own in the second half of 1917 and it was unlikely that even a rebellious child like the F.R.D. would be overlooked. In March 1918, consequently, it was decided to negotiate with the F.R.D., the parliamentary committee being asked to participate if it wished.[10] The parliamentary committee did not so wish,[11] and on 9 April 1918 the Labour Party regretfully decided to go ahead with the Fabians alone.[12] Under a contract drafted by Webb and Cole, it was agreed that the Labour Party should provide the F.R.D. with accommodation at the new Party headquarters and that it should pay the F.R.D. £150 per annum for the issuing of a daily Labour news service.[13] In return the F.R.D. was to place its accumulated stores of documents and information at the disposal of the Party, to assist the advisory committees in their work and to publish the annual Labour directories.[14]

At the same time the constitution of the F.R.D. was redrafted along the lines suggested to Cole by Beatrice Webb.[15] Membership was open to both individuals and institutions and the department—the Labour Research Department (L.R.D.)—was organized into four sections: the so-called trade union survey, which supervised research into union matters, the co-operative section, the trades councils and local Labour parties section, and finally, the general section, which handled research matters not specifically related to the other three. Trade unions affiliated individually to the trade union survey committee, co-operative societies to the committee of the co-operative section and so on.

Despite the growing opposition to the L.R.D. in certain union

[9] See above, p. 93.
[10] 'NEC', 13 Mar. 1918.
[11] 'PC', 14 Mar. 1918.
[12] 'NEC', 9 Apr. 1918.
[13] 'Agreements and Memoranda relating to the F.R.D.', 'NEC', 4 Sept. 1918.
[14] 'NEC', 4 Sept. 1918, for 'F.R.D.: Revision of Rules'.
[15] See L.R.D., *Annual Reports*, 1918–21, *passim*.

circles, affiliation of societies to all its sections increased steadily from 1918 to 1921. Even when the L.R.D. and the Labour Party parted company, the number of affiliates (with the exception of the co-operatives) had trebled. This was so, although it was often not admitted, because the L.R.D. was very successful at the tasks it had contracted to do. The *Monthly Circular*, a diary of Labour events as well as a magazine, had a very large circulation amongst trade unions, despite those spirited leading articles which landed it in so much trouble.[16] As a service department for the Advisory Committees and the unions it had an excellent record, while its own publications were of an astonishingly high standard.[17] And if some of them, like the Hammonds' *Village Labourer* lost money (£230), others made a great deal: £1,100 was made from a reprint of *Economic Consequences of the Peace* and £3,600 from a reprint of the Webbs' *History of Trade Unionism*.[18]

Despite this, and the large number of union affiliations, the L.R.D. was in continuous financial difficulties. The *Annual Report* was never slow to put the blame where it thought it lay.

If the Labour Movement were unable to pay, this would be satisfactory enough. But as Labour can quite well afford to pay, and to pay handsomely, and is holding back solely because it does not yet know the value of such work as well as capital does, such a state of things is quite unfair, and cannot be expected to last . . . [19]

This was the sort of imprudence that was so characteristic of the extra-departmental activities of the L.R.D. But the foundations of the department rested on an unlikely proposition: that the unions and the *beaux esprits* of the L.R.D. could live together.

Those in the department who, like Arnot, became Communists, were no more objectionable to the union leaders than guildsmen like Cole and Mellor, who were broadcasting their own schemes for trade union organization. Cole, particularly, became associated with attempts to use the trades councils as the basis of a new national industrial organization. As early as June 1920, after a visit to the Scarborough conference of the Party, Beatrice Webb was struck by the 'unpopularity of the L.R.D.'.[20] The proposal to establish a general council (of the T.U.C.) with its own research department was due 'purely to a revolt against Cole and Co. who, they say, use the Research

[16] See L.R.D., *Annual Report*, 1919–20, p. 11; Page Arnot, *Labour Research Department*, pp. 18–19.
[17] For a list of publications, see Page Arnot, *Labour Research Department*, pp. 55–62.
[18] L.R.D., *Annual Report*, 1919–20, pp. 16–17.
[19] L.R.D., *Annual Report*, 1918–1919, p. 2.
[20] Beatrice Webb, 'L.S.E. MS. Passfield: Transcript Diaries', p. 35, 18–25 June 1920.

Department and its affiliated membership for promoting their own views of trade union organisation'. Among its opponents she noted Bramley, Bevin, and Tom Shaw of the T.U.C., 'not to mention Bowerman', and Gillies and Tracey of the Labour Party. On the national executive 'Sidney is its only friend'. MacDonald was opposed to it for the (fanciful) reason that 'he scents in Cole a more dangerous rival than even the Webbs'. This was placing too much importance on personalities; Communists were now making themselves felt in the unions, and as a result of this union leaders were perhaps more alarmed at the activities of the L.R.D. than they would have been in other circumstances.

But these resentments were only a partial explanation for what was to happen to the L.R.D. It was true that individual members of the Department were out of favour, but the origins of the general council are by no means to be found in this alone. Nevertheless, one of the consequences of the reorganization of the T.U.C. was to be the official separation of the L.R.D. from the Labour movement.

In 1916 and 1917 both the unions and the Party had conceived of a joint research department, and Bowerman, it will be remembered, specifically mentioned this to Webb. At the same time Harry Gosling had spoken of equipping the T.U.C. as well as any 'Department of State'.[21] The unions had long been aware that a 'great process of centralisation'[22] was under way and that the T.U.C. as it was then organized failed to represent that process. In 1918, however, the T.U.C. had wavered in its reforming tendencies. While the Labour Party and the T.U.C. moved into joint offices (33–5 Eccleston Square), the joint research department, and all other joint departments as well, were put aside.

In 1919 the wartime movements for reform were revived by the recommendations of the *ad hoc* committee which mediated between the National Union of Railwaymen and the two other unions of the triple alliance. It suggested that the parliamentary committee should be given a number of permanent departments, as might have been appropriate to the civil service.[23] This was followed by a memorandum from Bevin proposing a general council with its own administrative departments and a group of joint departments (research, legal, and publicity) to be shared with the Labour Party and the Co-operators.[24]

[21] John Lovell and B. C. Roberts, *A Short History of the T.U.C.* (London, 1968), p. 57. For a more detailed account of the reorganization of the T.U.C., see B. C. Roberts, *The Trades Union Congress, 1868–1921* (London, 1958), pp. 331–5.

[22] Lovell and Roberts, p. 58.

[23] V. L. Allen, 'The Reorganisation of the Trades Union Congress, 1918–1927', *British Journal of Sociology*, 11 (1960), p. 26.

[24] Ibid., p. 29.

A special congress (December 1919) endorsed these recommendations and authorized the establishment of a Trade Union Co-ordination Committee, of which both Henderson and Cole were members.[25] The reorganized T.U.C. was a consequence of these developments, and not of a desire to put an end to the L.R.D., however gratifying its end might be.

All this was watched with the greatest interest by the Labour Party. It now seemed as if the long-hoped-for joint departments could get under way. With his usual speed and skill in matters of administrative reform, it was Henderson who seized the initiative, and in November 1920 presented the T.U.C. (rather to its annoyance) with a scheme for joint services.

On 20 October 1920 he distributed to the members of the N.E.C. an elaborate plan for the co-ordination of union and Party activities— the celebrated 'Memorandum A'.[26] Henderson began by repeating his emphatic belief in the necessity of unifying the industrial and political wings of the movement: 'the developments which are taking place and the general circumstances of the time demand [it]'. The possibility of trade-union objection was swept aside: 'there can be no doubt that there is a widespread desire amongst the rank and file . . . for such a measure . . . and any comprehensive proposal towards this end would meet with approval'. He claimed that 'immediate steps' were required.

The Parliamentary Committee is undergoing a transformation which must be followed by great developments, and its new organisation will embark (in the absence of any co-ordinated scheme) upon research, information and publicity work which will tend to overlap with what is done by the Party and the Labour Research Department.

Therefore, he went on, the 'first need' was for some plan 'which will ensure as far as possible that on all matters of common interest there is a common policy and a common action'. To meet this need he put before the executive two proposals. The first provided for daily consultation between the secretaries of the T.U.C. and the Party. The second was an institutional one. He wanted to establish what he called, and what was eventually called, the National Joint Council of Labour. This body was to consist of the chairman, secretary, and three members each from the parliamentary committee, the national executive, and the parliamentary party. He also provided for a National Joint Conference, to consist of the parliamentary committee, the national executive, and 'a number of Parliamentary members, which with the Labour Party Executive will be equal in number to the

[25] Lovell and Roberts, p. 56.
[26] Filed as 'NEC', 20 Oct. 1920, 'Memorandum "A": Co-ordination'.

members of the newly constituted Parliamentary Committee'. He hoped that the National Joint Council would assume control of the press and publicity department, the advisory committees, the information bureau, and the international department of the Labour Party together with similar T.U.C. institutions.

The biggest obstacle in the way of this reorganization, as Henderson recognized, was the L.R.D. He thought it possible that the new joint body might come to some arrangement with the L.R.D., but unlikely. He concluded that '. . . if the industrial and political wings of the Labour Movement can combine for common purposes, there is no justification for the L.R.D. retaining its separate identity, unless its activities can be shown to be such that they would suffer by being brought under the National Joint Committee'. He dismissed the notion that research 'cannot be successfully carried on under official restrictions'; the L.R.D.'s functions, he said, did not differ substantially from those of the Advisory Committees 'and their freedom of enquiry has never been questioned'—an assertion which was not strictly true.[27]

He had decided, in effect, to abolish the L.R.D.: '. . . it is proposed, therefore, that the National Joint Council and the joint department under its supervision should combine the research, information and publicity activities of the Labour Party, the Parliamentary Committee and the Labour Research Department.' The new joint research department was to be under a research sub-committee of the National Joint Council which was 'to suggest lines of enquiry, advise upon methods etc. and should report to the National Council its views as to the form in which it thinks complete researches should be published'.

'Memorandum A' was administrative in its origins. Henderson had always favoured a joint research department, as he had favoured all forms of amalgamation between both sides of the movement. Under almost any conceivable scheme of joint departments the L.R.D. would either become redundant or be taken over directly. How far Henderson ensured that his administrative reforms would make the L.R.D. redundant we cannot tell, but it is almost certain that the unions would have insisted on the separation of the L.R.D. from the Party before agreeing to 'Memorandum A' or anything like it. The weight of the evidence suggests that the supersession of the L.R.D. was an administrative fact primarily and only secondarily a result of (nevertheless) widespread hostility to it.

Bramley, the acting general secretary of the T.U.C., was rather irritated by Henderson's draft. He did not dislike its contents but felt that they were the business of the T.U.C. and not of the Labour Party.

[27] See below, pp. 219–20.

It did, however, at least force the T.U.C. to write their own. In most essentials theirs differed little from Henderson's. It suggested four joint departments—research, publicity, legal affairs, and international affairs, each department to be headed by a permanent official.[28] Henderson again seized on this draft and rushed everyone into accepting it. In July 1921 he named Labour's representatives on the National Joint Council and presented the T.U.C. with a draft series of agreements about the joint departments and their staffing. This, on top of 'Memorandum A' was, as Allen says, too much for Bramley. He scrawled at the head of his copy: 'No attempt to submit same to joint committee. They just make plans and ask us for endorsement.'[29] Yet the T.U.C. could have few objections to what was basically its own draft: the joint departments were accepted by it in September 1921, and the general council named its members to the national joint council in October. The proposed legal department remained putative, and only three departments—research and information, international affairs, and press and publicity—finally came into operation on new year's day, 1922.[30]

The talents of the new research and information bureau were as impressive as those of the L.R.D. Arthur Greenwood was its permanent secretary, C. de Lisle Burns was head of the information bureau and W. Milne Bailey and Barbara Wootton were the senior research workers.[31]

So far as the L.R.D. was concerned the general view was that its sad fate was largely the fault of its more exuberant elements. On 12 July 1921, the day that Henderson announced Labour's participation in the National Joint Council, Beatrice Webb lamented to her diary:

Meanwhile exit the L.R.D.! Cole, Arnot and Co. have destroyed it ... by exciting antagonisms in every direction ... by rousing the malicious jealousy of J. R. MacDonald ... by alienating many members of the Labour Party Executive and nearly all the Parliamentary Committee, and finally by Arnot and his group joining the Communist Party, writing abusive paragraphs in the *Communist*, and helping to found the British section of the Red Trade Union International, they have made themselves quite impossible.[32]

In any case Cole's indiscretions may have forced a break sooner rather than later. The L.R.D.'s decision in September 1921 to accept £6,000 a year from Russia to finance an inquiry into the nature of

[28] Allen, p. 34.
[29] Ibid., p. 34.
[30] Ibid., p. 36.
[31] 'NEC', 4 Jan. 1922.
[32] Beatrice Webb, 'L.S.E. MS. Passfield: Transcript Diaries,' p. 36, 12 July 1921.

capitalist industry appalled Labour and union leaders. 'Cole really is an idiot', Beatrice Webb commented, 'if he thinks he can take money from the Bolshevik government without upsetting the mind of his present supporters and ruining himself...'[33]

The L.R.D. continued its activities; indeed it flourished, and the annual meeting of 1921 decided to maintain all the L.R.D.'s functions.[34] It remained, therefore, in very obvious competition with the joint department for the custom of the movement. It still did union work and for some time a number of its writers, Hugh Dalton, Susan Lawrence, John Scurr, even Ben Tillett, were individuals not sympathetic to the general political tendency of the L.R.D.

The Labour Party lost much when it unburdened itself of the L.R.D. However irritating and tendentious the latter's publications could be, they were all lively contributions to social research. Its work had an interest and variety not achieved by the joint department. The work of Greenwood's officers was solid and they always gave the Party such information as it wanted. Yet its research was necessarily limited by the requirements of the movement. Despite Henderson's assurances, it was not free, as the L.R.D. had been, to commission its own inquiries or to use its own initiative in the collection of material. The reasons for this are to be found both in the conception and in the development of the Advisory Committees.

2. *The Advisory Committees*

The functions of the Labour Party's Advisory Committees were closely allied to those of the L.R.D. The idea of small committees of specialists advising the national executive on all aspects of policy came from Henderson's time in cabinet office, from the experience of the war emergency committee, and, to a lesser degree, from the working traditions of the Fabian Society. Tom Jones records a typically *de haut en bas* conversation with the Webbs; they were

satisfied that Labour was not yet intellectually and administratively equal to the responsibility [of government]. They might be in five or ten years time — the task was now to rope in all the intellectual assistance possible. The Labour Conference next week would probably set up a whole series of new Committees, for the consideration of foreign affairs, industrial and Commercial legislation etc. The experience in the Cabinet had done one great service to Henderson. He was no longer unwilling or ashamed to depend on the help of intellectuals, having seen how dependent Cabinet Ministers were on such assistance.[35]

[33] Ibid., 7 Oct. 1921.
[34] L.R.D., *Annual Report*, 1920–1, p. 14.
[35] Tom Jones, *Whitehall Diary*, pp. 45–6 (12 Jan. 1918).

The analogy with cabinet ministers was apt: the Advisory Committees were to feed information to potential cabinet ministers and were established at a time when Labour thought of itself as at least a competitor for government. They were promoted also, in part, by a belief characteristic in the British Labour movement that social change would follow almost automatically upon the requisition of the necessary facts. The Advisory Committees would put those who possessed such facts to work for the Labour Party—sympathetic intellectuals and civil servants. In return they were to work with the Labour leadership, so satisfying that lust for power that all intellectuals are supposed secretly to nourish.

Jones's 'new committees' were presented to the national executive by Henderson on 13 March 1918. The executive accepted without discussion his draft of nine provisional committees and a provisional membership list.[36] The extent to which Labour had mobilized support from the intellectuals, either in the civil service or outside it, can be seen from the list of luminaries who accepted with apparent enthusiasm the invitation to sit on the committees.[37] In their final form, there were two changes from the original draft. A separate standing committee on women's questions which the chief women's officer, Dr. Marian Phillips, had established was accepted in the place of the proposed advisory committee, while, after much energetic lobbying from Ben Tillett, and somewhat to everyone's embarrassment, it was agreed to appoint a committee on the 'Drink Traffic'.[38] The Committees and their members as they were presented to the 1918 conference are shown in Table 24[39] on the following page. The work of the Committees was co-ordinated by a secretary—G. D. H. Cole until his resignation in March 1920 and Arthur Greenwood thereafter.

Inevitably, there was much overlap between the Advisory Committees and the L.R.D. Even in the first year of working the Committees produced 142 memoranda and reports,[40] any one of which might have been written by the L.R.D. Indeed, if Cole is to be

[36] 'NEC', 13 Mar. 1918.
[37] Henderson to the national executive, 'NEC', 16 Apr. 1918.
[38] 'NEC', 16 Apr. 1918. Labour's attitude to temperance is a topic in itself, but why a party whose leadership was top-heavy with teetotallers should have been so lukewarm towards temperance needs explaining. One explanation, however, is possibly related to the requirements of Party organization. Unlike the Liberals, who could usually build their own committee rooms, the Labour Party then, as so often it does now, was forced to meet in a private room of a centrally located pub. In such circumstances temperance could not be taken up with vigour. The fact that delegates were prepared to meet in a pub, and the practice was almost universal, also suggests that they were not ready to take up temperance in any case.
[39] Conference Report, 1918, p. 2.
[40] Conference Report, 1919, p. 48.

TABLE 24

International Questions ...	Chairman	Sidney Webb
	Secretary	Leonard Woolf
Trade Policy and Finance	Chairman	J. A. Hobson
	Secretary	G. D. H. Cole
Industrial Policy	Chairman	W. F. Purdy
	Secretary	J. J. Mallan
Education	Chairman	F. W. Goldstone*
Machinery of Government	Chairman	J. R. MacDonald
	Secretary	Beatrice Webb
Local Government	Chairman	F. W. Jowett
Public Health and	Chairman	W. C. Anderson
Medical Services	Secretary	G. P. Blizard
Rural Problems	Chairman	F. E. Green
	Secretary	Margaret Cole
Drink Traffic	Chairman	J. H. Thomas
	Secretary	E. R. Pease

* F. W. Goldstone of the Teachers and M.P. for Sunderland, 1910–18.

believed, the secretariat of the advisory committees was almost overwhelmed with work. In giving the reasons for his resignation Cole said that

... it is quite impossible to combine it with other work. The volume of work increases steadily, and the amount of interviewing and straightening out of difficulties, in addition to actual organising work, is a very heavy burden. An examination of the overtime sheets will show that the clerical staff ... is ... most seriously overworked ...

He added that much of their work was done by the L.R.D., nevertheless.[41] It would appear almost as if research work proliferated to meet the number of Committees there to undertake it. It is also possible that the intellectuals were suffering from bouts of enthusiasm and doing more work than the executive or the parliamentary party were capable of absorbing. Were other reasons not present, there were clearly administrative ones for deciding in 1920 to reorganize the Committees.

It was the slack, not to say slovenly, performance of the parliamentary party after 1918 that was responsible for the first change in the structure of the Committees. As early as May 1919 Henderson was complaining bitterly to Webb about the parliamentary party[42] and in December, Scott Lindsay, secretary of the parliamentary party,

[41] Cole to Middleton, 5 Mar. 1920, 'LPLF: Uncat. Advisory Committees'.
[42] Henderson to Webb, 17 May 1919, 'L.S.E. MS. Passfield: Correspondence', II. 4.8.

told J. S. Middleton that M.P.s were so poorly equipped that when 'questions ... are put to them about some action of the Party in the House ... it is not always possible [for them] to remember the line the Party took'.[43] In January 1920 Henderson circulated to M.P.s a rather schoolmasterly letter, pointing out 'how difficult it is to answer the allegations made' in the press criticizing the parliamentary party.[44] As a corrective Henderson tried unsuccessfully to have MacDonald appointed paid adviser to the parliamentary party,[45] and later (successfully) forced him on a rather unwilling Woolwich Labour Party.[46]

At the same time as Henderson was making known his dissatisfaction with the parliamentary party, the M.P.s, for their part, appeared to feel that the national executive was making policy without regard to them. Adamson, the parliamentary chairman, told Beatrice Webb that the executive had taken the 'initiative in deciding policy' and M.P.s found themselves committed to programmes 'with which they might not agree'. A way out would be to associate the M.P.s with the experts.[47] The parliamentary party itself, furthermore, made this point after much prodding from J. C. Wedgwood, who was (presumably) used to something better. In July 1920, he suggested, with great vehemence, that the Committees ought to be remodelled on the lines of government departments and that members of the parliamentary party should sit on each committee. Although Middleton told Woolf that 'the weight of opinion was against applying his ideas rigidly' he thought that 'it would be possible to meet him in certain directions'.[48] The M.P.s not only supported Wedgwood but also suggested that the Committees should sit in the House of Commons and be chaired by M.P.s.[49] Middleton asked Cole for his views.

Cole agreed that the Committees should sit in the House, and that 'in some cases at least' they should be chaired by M.P.s.[50] He felt that the principle of matching Committees with government departments could not be carried too far; he thought that a couple of new Committees were required, one for the home office and one for transport. As for temperance—'it is difficult to say where it stands now'. The reconstructed Committees followed closely Cole's draft.

[43] H. S. Lindsay to Middleton, 17 Dec. 1919, 'LPLF: Uncat. Misc.'.
[44] Henderson to Members of the Parliamentary Party, 31 Jan. 1920, 'LPLF: Uncat. Misc.'.
[45] See 'Report of a Meeting between James Ramsay MacDonald and the P.L.P.', undated, 'LPLF: Uncat. JRM Misc.'.
[46] See above, pp. 133-4.
[47] Beatrice Webb, 'L.S.E. MS. Passfield: Unpublished Diaries', p. 34, 14 Jan. 1919.
[48] Middleton to Leonard Woolf, 24 July 1920, 'LPLF: Uncat. JSM Misc.'.
[49] H. S. Lindsay to Middleton, 9 July 1920, 'LPLF: Uncat. JSM Misc.'.
[50] Cole to Middleton, 18 July 1920, 'LPLF: Uncat. JSM Misc.'.

The second, and more important, cause of reconstruction was the decision of the T.U.C. to reorganize[51] and this had the same consequences for the Advisory Committees as it did for the L.R.D. Given Henderson's determination to unite the research, information, and publicity facilities of the T.U.C. and the Labour Party, the Committees could no more escape amalgamation than the L.R.D. Appended, therefore, to 'Memorandum A' (on the L.R.D.) was 'Memorandum B',[52] concerning specifically the future of the Advisory Committees.

Henderson saw their functions as fourfold: they were 'to work out a general policy for the consideration of the . . . Executive', to assist the parliamentary party, to advise the executive on 'current questions', and to help Labour representatives on local government bodies. He followed the parliamentary party by agreeing that the chairmanship of each Committee, except those of a purely technical nature, should be held by an M.P. The Committees were to become, as it were, the day-to-day service departments of the Party. Parliamentary candidates and 'those who regularly speak on Labour platforms'

. . . should be supplied with all the reports and memoranda issued. As a rule they should be accompanied by comments and a statement as to their probable political importance. Labour representatives on local bodies should be supplied with such reports and memoranda as are likely to be of assistance to them in their public work.

Most significant, all the Advisory Committees were to come within the general authority of the new joint department of research and information, which was also to supervise the reconstructed L.R.D. This had two results. In an administrative way it removed much of the overlapping and confusion of work between the L.R.D. and the Committees. But it also meant that control of the Committees was now shared by the unions. Henceforth they had two masters, and of these two the general council was to be much the most rigorous.

Henderson's scheme was adopted by the two executives, and the form in which the Committees were reorganized owes much to Cole. The Committee on temperance quietly disappeared, an act of symbolic importance in the history of British radicalism—though anything more likely to discredit a temperance body than putting Jimmy Thomas in the chair can scarcely be imagined. The proposed Committee on transport was not yet established. The eleven committees were as follows:[53]

[51] See above.
[52] 'Memorandum on the Future of the Advisory Committees', ('Memorandum B'), 'NEC', 20 Oct. 1920.
[53] *Conference Report*, 1922, p. 43.

1) Agriculture and Rural Problems
2) Army, Navy and Pensions Problems
3) Education
4) Finance and Commerce
5) Home Office and Mines
6) Industrial Affairs
7) International Questions
8) Legal System and Administration of Justice
9) Local Government
10) Machinery of Government
11) Public Health

Every Committee had an M.P. as chairman (though that seemed to help neither the Committees nor the M.P.s, who were usually absentee).[54] In 1923 the structure of the Committees was altered slightly: their number was increased to thirteen by the creation of two new committees—housing and science.[55]

But the work of the Committees was no less enormous than it had been before 'Memorandum B': Leonard Woolf was amazed at the amount of material his Committee (international questions) alone managed to produce.[56] By 1924 work had become so heavy that the great inquiry *Trade Union Organisation* had to be abandoned after the completion of only four sections.[57] Whatever the failings of the first two Labour governments, they were not due to lack of information. No party has entered office so elaborately equipped with the impedimenta of research and information. If, in many cases, little use was made of such equipment, this was not due to an absence of advice, but to a failure of political nerve in a generation of Labour leaders.

Yet even after reorganization, the Advisory Committees, like the L.R.D. and the *Herald*, occupied a rather peculiar position in the Party. Though they were responsible jointly to the national executive and the general council, they retained a certain independence, if only because so many of their 'expert' members were recruited from outside the Labour movement. No one, therefore, really knew how much initiative lay with the Committees in matters of policy. This question was not settled until 1924 and then somewhat unsatisfactorily. The 'test case' was the unemployment insurance bill and its provisions for the agricultural labourers.

When the first MacDonald ministry took office, Greenwood, the secretary of the joint research department (and himself now a junior

[54] See Arthur Greenwood to Middleton, 4 Mar. 1921, 'LPLF: Uncat. JSM Misc.'; attendance records of M.P.s enclosed.
[55] *Conference Report*, 1924, p. 69.
[56] Leonard Woolf, *Downhill all the Way, 1918–1939* (London, 1967), p. 221.
[57] *Conference Report*, 1924, p. 67.

minister) wrote to each minister suggesting ways he could keep in touch with the work of the Committees.[58] There were, Greenwood thought, three procedures that could be adopted. First, all memoranda prepared by the Committees could be sent to the ministers concerned; second, ministers could consult the Committees whenever they wished, and, finally, the P.P.S.s of ministers might be members of the Committees. Most ministers accepted these arrangements. According to Milne Bailey, who became acting secretary of the joint department, when Greenwood entered the government, '. . . it was not intended that Committees should send formal deputations [to ministers] or put forward matters of policy that had not previously been endorsed by the executives, but merely that informal discussions should take place on current matters . . .[59]

However, the Agricultural Affairs Committee decided to send a deputation directly to the minister of agriculture, N. E. Buxton, about the inclusion of agricultural labourers in the unemployment insurance legislation. The vice-chairman of the Committee, R. B. Walker, himself a member of the Agricultural Labourers' Union, strongly objected to this and said so to Milne Bailey. Milne Bailey agreed with the objection and circulated a letter to all the secretaries of Committees.[60] He told them that 'it was contemplated that useful informal discussion would take place' but not 'recommendations on policy, this being a matter for the National Executives'. In cases of emergency, he wrote, recommendations on policy should first be submitted to the two secretaries for endorsement.

The proposed action of the Committee caused much resentment in the T.U.C. It was not a question of disagreeing with the Committee's policy, since the agricultural labourers probably stood to gain by inclusion, but a question of the right of any body outside the executives to present policies to Labour ministers. The general council were sure that the Committee had no such right. On 23 April 1924 it resolved that the Committees were not competent to decide on matters of policy 'without the authority of the executive bodies'.[61]

When the matter was first considered by the National Joint Council, the Labour Party delegates managed to amend the general council's resolution to read:

That in view of the fact [that] the function of the Joint and Advisory Committees appointed by the National Committees is advisory, their duty is

[58] The letter is filed as 'NJC', 24 Apr. 1924.
[59] 'NJC', 24 Apr. 1924.
[60] This letter, as well as an account of what happened, is filed as 'NJC', 24 Apr. 1924.
[61] 'GC', 23 Apr. 1924.

to deal with matters referred to them by the National Committees . . . and to make recommendations to the two National Committees.[62]

The next meeting of the National Joint Council had before it a letter from the secretary of the Committees defending their right of direct access to ministers 'on questions relating to the application of principles which have already been laid down in the policy of the Party'.[63] But Bramley, now general secretary of the T.U.C., stood firm by the decision of 23 April that the Committees had no independent right to propose policy.

At the same meeting Middleton pointed out that the T.U.C.'s position would excessively limit 'the facilities and powers already possessed by the advisory committees'. The general council could not accept this and their delegates made the point emphatically. With the reluctant consent of the Party delegates it was agreed that the Committees did not have the power of independent access and their work was to be supervised more closely by the two executives in the future.[64]

Now it would be a mistake to make too much of this incident. It is plain that the Committees themselves were originally misconceived. Despite their name it was never made clear that their functions were purely advisory and that they were always to be subordinated to the two executives. The institutional arrangements drafted by Henderson gave the Committees an apparent autonomy it was not intended they should possess. Nevertheless, the unions had decided in their own favour a matter of some importance—they had ensured that the Committees would not make their apparent autonomy a real one; that it was not the task of the Committees to advise Labour ministers even on a matter of settled principle. Furthermore, it was significant that it was the T.U.C. rather than the Labour Party that brought the Committees to heel. The fate of the Advisory Committees was another example of the way in which the unions were giving form and character to the Labour Party and also an example of the simultaneous decline in the influence of the socialist societies, whose members, for the most part, staffed the Committees.

3. *The Subordination of the* Daily Herald

The third of the Party's semi-independent institutions whose independence had been circumscribed by 1924 was the *Daily Herald*, and the story of the *Herald* tells us a good deal about the men who were leading the Labour Party and about the kind of Party they wished to lead.

[62] 'NJC', 23 Apr. 1924.
[63] 'NJC', 26 June 1924.

[64] Ibid.

The collapse of the old *Daily Citizen* in 1915 left the Labour movement without a newspaper. It was left without one, furthermore, at a time of great expansion—for a party almost obsessed by the needs of propaganda and the precedent of the German socialist press, this was an obvious deficiency. There was on hand, of course, the *Daily Herald*, which could conceivably replace the *Citizen*. But the movement had lost heavily on the *Citizen* and as an official newspaper it had been an almost total failure. This not unnaturally made it reluctant to acquire a successor; particularly one already losing money.

Furthermore, even if the principle of an official paper were admitted there were many in the Labour movement who had objections to its being the *Herald*. It had been founded before the war, originally as a strike sheet, by men of suspected syndicalist sympathies[65] and in direct competition with the *Citizen*. It had conducted a sort of guerrilla campaign against official policy during the war and had followed a highly unpredictable path since then; its reputation for faddishness was increased rather than diminished by the bright young men who followed G. D. H. Cole on to its staff.[66]

Finally, the fate of the *Citizen* seemed to show that party political newspapers were successful in Britain only if they occupied the same territory as the 'capitalist' press—if they were ready to write about sport, horse-racing, and 'general interest' stories. The British Labour movement, the Fabian W. S. Sanders told the 1912 Party Conference, should not be misled by the German example. In Germany there was 'no desire for sporting news, there was no desire for news about horse-racing and football; in fact, the ordinary German newspaper was a very easy thing to produce . . . That was impossible in this country.'[67] But the Labour Party leadership did not really want a 'capitalist' newspaper: some of its members disliked horse-racing for religious reasons, and of those who did not, most found the reporting of it trivial.

The Labour movement for these very reasons only slithered into possession of the *Herald*, but it did so because the *Herald* had one indispensable quality—it was the only paper Labour had. Further to its credit, it had in Will Dyson a powerful cartoonist of national repute and it had mounted a number of effective and irreverent political campaigns. In 1919, therefore, an unofficial trade-union committee, Arthur Henderson, W. C. Robinson, Frank Hodges, Ben Turner, and Ernest Bevin, organized financial assistance for the paper. Despite some ludicrously optimistic propaganda by Bevin and Robert Williams[68]—

[65] For the early history of the *Herald*, see G. Lansbury, *Miracle of Fleet Street* (London, 1925), pp. 10–13.
[66] H. H. Fife, *My Seven Selves* (London, 1939), p. 249.
[67] Labour Party, *Conference Report*, 1912, p. 80.
[68] 'PC', 7 Jan. 1920.

both of the Transport Workers' Federation—a price rise, and hopeful resolutions from the Labour Party Conference,[69] it was apparent by 1921 that without lavish assistance from the movement the paper would be forced to cease publication. At the suggestion of Lansbury it was agreed that in exchange for a bloc of shares the movement should provide the paper with bridging finance and should also place a levy upon the unions.[70]

The Labour Party itself was still very cautious. It refrained from 'taking over' the *Herald*; Henderson agreed to hold his shares only as a 'trustee' and refused a seat on the board of directors. Even at this early stage some members of the national executive were becoming restive, not so much because they believed the Party was funding a paper which would be a financial disaster—though many felt that as well—but because they believed it was funding one whose editorial policy it did not control. And that mattered very much to the unions. Charles Duncan, the general secretary of the Workers' Union, for example, wrote that he was 'somewhat confused as to who the other shareholders will be, and *who will, therefore, control policy . . .*'.[71]

The paper, despite assistance, continued on an inexorably calamitous path. By the end of February 1922 liquidation seemed imminent; a crisis was reached at the beginning of March 1922. Lansbury, therefore, decided to act on his own account and to act spectacularly. It is not clear what he intended or whether he thought his *coup* would be successful. More probably he assumed that whatever followed, the movement would be forced to sustain the *Herald*. On the morning of 2 March all the directors resigned and elected Henderson and C. W. Bowerman in their places. They did so, Lansbury wrote, in the confident expectation that the movement 'will assume the responsibility of continuing and developing the *Daily Herald*, and place it in the front rank of Labour newspapers in the world'.[72]

Henderson replied to this disconcerting letter in great agitation: Lansbury's action was 'premature' and would only further annoy the unions. This apprehensiveness was indeed confirmed by the union members of the national executive, who immediately and inevitably raised the question of control. 'If the *Daily Herald* is to be taken over', Tom Shaw wrote,

there ought to be no doubt whatever as to two points:

1) The unqualified control of paper, works and policy by the Labour Movement

[69] Labour Party, *Conference Report*, 1920, p. 175.
[70] *Daily Herald* Sub-Committee of the Two National Committees, 'Minutes', 10 Jan. 1922, 'LPLF: DHF'.
[71] Duncan to Henderson, 13 Jan. 1922, 'LPLF: DHF' (emphasis his).
[72] Lansbury to Henderson, 2 Mar. 1922, 'LPLF: DHF'.

2) The right of either the National Committees or the National Congresses to directly appoint their own directors.

He was 'dead against any method of a hybrid character which will entail the danger of the Labour Movement finding the money and a few individuals directing the policy of the paper, possibly in a spirit contrary to that of the decisions of the Party itself'.[73] Should this attack be unavailing, the unions could, and did, retreat to the argument that the *Herald* was a financial bottomless pit. If such a veteran of the ins and outs of the City as Frank Hodges could not understand its finances then no one could.[74]

Yet Lansbury had been rather shrewd. He put the movement into the position of having to devise urgently new schemes for saving his paper, if only to avoid the kind of commitment he had gratuitously accepted on its behalf. Thus on the very day that Bowerman wrote to Lansbury refusing the transfer of ownership, the T.U.C. sent out a desperate reminder to the trade unions exhorting them to support the $\frac{1}{2}d.$ levy.[75]

At the same time Lansbury agreed to prepare a scheme for converting the paper into a weekly. In fact, no such preparations were made. He was determined that the *Herald* should be maintained as a daily, and again he succeeded. Six days later the *Daily Herald* joint sub-committee of the two national executives was presented with a scheme drawn up by the 'staff' (that is Lansbury) for continuing the paper as a daily. This scheme was accepted and the committee even agreed to subsidize the paper's losses until the conference of the Labour Party in June (1922) and the T.U.C. in September.[76]

What made acceptance possible was (as usual) the sheer momentum of events: each step taken to assist the *Herald* made it more difficult for the movement to extricate itself.[77] It was Henderson who came up with the idea that the unions should be levied to the extent of 2*d.* per member per annum and this was probably the only way out. But Henderson also seems to have thought that the paper's losses should be a permanent charge on the movement: that this was not the view of the unions accounts partly for the *Herald*'s failure.

The general council of the T.U.C. reluctantly agreed to continue the paper as a daily, but with two conditions: first, that it should be under the control of the movement and second, that Lansbury should not be managing director—presumably the success of the first condition

[73] Shaw to Henderson, 7 Mar. 1922, 'LPLF: DHF'.
[74] See Hodges to Henderson, 7 Mar. 1922, 'LPLF: DHF'.
[75] T.U.C. Appeal for the *Daily Herald*, 6 Mar. 1922, 'LPLF: DHF'.
[76] Joint Committee, *Minutes*, 9 May 1922, 'LPLF: DHF'.
[77] See Sidney Webb to Beatrice Webb, 29 May 1922, 'PP: Correspondence', II.3.(i).

depended largely upon the implementation of the second. Lansbury agreed, as indeed he had to.[78] This, together with the fact that the *Herald* was manifestly still there, induced the congress to vote in favour of the levy.[79] On the strength of this vote the price of the paper was reduced to 1*d.* and Lansbury was succeeded as editor by Hamilton Fyfe. Lansbury had told the national executive as early as July that ill health would force him to resign, but it is likely that the T.U.C. would have required this in any case. Nevertheless, as general manager Lansbury retained considerable authority and Fyfe, though an impressive choice, was a somewhat surprising one. He had had much experience on the Northcliffe press and he was a forceful and independent-minded journalist, but it is doubtful if he was the sort of editor the unions were seeking in their then state of mind. He was not the man to accept direction readily from them or to edit the paper as the solemn organ of conventional trade-union wisdom which many union leaders wished it to become. Under Fyfe's sprightly editing the *Herald* became even more obnoxious to many Party and union officers than it had been under Lansbury.

Anyway, it was hoped that Fyfe could 'save' the *Herald* as it was supposed he had 'saved' the *Mirror* for Northcliffe. It was not saved. By November, just two months after congress, the *Herald* was once more on the point of collapse. The stream of letters and circulars from the Party and the T.U.C. had not significantly raised the paper's circulation. On 23 November (1922) Henderson and Lansbury despatched a confidential circular to all societies making plain both their anxiety and annoyance.[80]

We are in serious and immediate danger of losing the *Daily Herald*. We have written to you many times on the subject, but so far most of our letters and speeches have bought us little else than enthusiasm and kind words. Now we must tell you that we are at the end of our resources and unless you personally come to our aid the paper will be down and out.

Since the paper had proved so irredeemably profitless it is curious that a sub-committee to examine its lack of popularity was not appointed until February 1923. It asked Norman Angell to write a critique of the *Herald*.[81] By implication Angell's memorandum was an attack on the obsession with the German analogy that many Labour leaders had. The reason for its low circulation, Angell wrote,

[78] 'NEC', 31 May 1922.
[79] T.U.C., *Congress Report*, 1922, pp. 90–7.
[80] Henderson and Lansbury to Branch Secretaries, 21 Nov. 1922, 'LPLF: DHF.'
[81] Memorandum on the Position of the *Daily Herald*, 3 Feb. 1923, 'LPLF: DHF.'

comes from the necessities of the *Herald*'s situation. Persistent, energetic and clever as the campaigns have been . . . they were mainly directed at getting money or help . . . *asking something from the reader instead of offering something to him* . . . and the nett psychological impression of a burden to be borne . . . The very insistence on the duty of the workers to support it . . . had been equivalent to repeated suggestions that the paper could not sufficiently appeal to them . . . Little space is devoted to creating the impression that the paper is itself attractive, amusing, interesting . . . This is a trap into which most political and nearly all Party organs fall, and perhaps explains their all but universal failure . . . The reason is plain; in normal times, when there is no general strike or election, the mass of the workers are indifferent and . . . are guided in their newspaper reading by the subtle pull of 'entertainment value' — news, sport, curiosity etc.

He then went on to the only conclusion: 'So far as the *mass* is concerned, the appeal should not be to "Labour", "Socialism" and "Anti-Capitalism" but the merits of the paper as a paper . . . Even the political features should be presented to the readers on their non-political side.'

It ought to be said that, on the whole, the members of the sub-committee took Angell's point. They therefore made one last attempt to break out of the financial restraints that bound the paper's development. The financial scheme of 26 February 1923 provided for a twelve-page 1*d.* paper, financed by new grants, and borrowing from the Labour Party, from 'Co-operative assistance', and from private investment.[82]

Even this scheme, however, failed. The only source of funds that proved moderately productive (somewhat maddeningly) was private investment. The circulation drive was not successful; the co-operative societies, as might have been expected, were not forthcoming, and the unions' contributions were not sufficient to cover the *Herald*'s now immense weekly losses.

On 22 August 1923 the general council of the T.U.C. decided that the unions could no longer sustain the paper which should cease publication on 30 September. This decision was accompanied by much political criticism of the paper, of its excessive left-wing

---

[82] Joint Meeting of the *Daily Herald* Joint Committee and the Board of Directors, 'Minutes', 26 Feb. 1923, 'LPLF: DHF'. Much of the private investment came from those who were delicately called 'friends of the movement'. In his *Miracle of Fleet Street* (p. 166) Lansbury singles out for mention the Countess De la Warr and H. D. Harben, but implies that Harben, an old Fabian, also acted as agent for other investors. Much came from Clifford Allen's Quaker acquaintances and he was, indeed, specifically asked to drum up investment in face of opposition from Smillie and other members of the national executive ('Minutes', 14 Feb. 1923). It is likely, also, that Henderson's friends invested, including Bernhard Barron, the founder of Carreras Cigarettes, and a large public benefactor of the Labour Party.

sympathies, and the extent to which it was supposed to be staffed by Communists.[83] A joint meeting of the general council and the national executive confirmed their decision the following day, though with a large number of abstentions and after two votes.[84] This was a reluctant decision and the reasons for this were as they had always been: the paper was still there; an enormous amount of money and effort would have been wasted should it disappear; and it was the only paper whose support was (more or less) assured. As MacDonald wrote: 'from what I hear Congress is likely to abandon the paper, and what we shall do then God only knows'.[85]

Thus the somewhat exciting proceedings at the T.U.C. in September, when the *Herald* was given a last-minute reprieve, are not as unexpected as they appeared at the time. The excuse for overturning the general council's decision was provided by a scheme of economies drawn up by the *Daily Herald* chapel of the National Union of Journalists (N.U.J.).[86] There was some dispute as to who actually saved the paper: Fyfe, no admirer of A. J. Cook (of the Miners), nevertheless thought the credit was his,[87] and Cook's intervention in the debate does appear to have been decisive. Congress voted to sustain the paper's losses while a Committee of Enquiry prepared plans for the *Herald*'s future.

The Committee of Enquiry, which had five representatives from the general council, five from the national executive and six from the *Herald*'s directors, held its first working session on 11 October 1923. They met delegates from the N.U.J. and the Printing Trades Federation (P.T.F.) to consider a scheme of economies drawn up by the unions. At least, it was intended that the session should be about this: in effect, it was about politics. There had already been much grumbling in the unions about the *Herald*'s political inclinations and these complaints came at a time when many union leaders felt themselves engaged in a struggle against Communist 'penetration'. The political problems of the paper in these years cannot, therefore, be understood outside the context of the 'Communist question' in the British Labour movement.

Even at the preliminary meeting of the Committee of Enquiry, J. R. Clynes, by no means one of its dogmatic opponents, expressed the view that the *Herald* 'had to be brought more under the control of the Movement. There was a feeling that the Movement had a right to

[83] 'GC', 23 Aug. 1923.
[84] 'NEC', 24 Aug. 1923.
[85] Fyfe, *My Seven Selves*, p. 257.
[86] See '*Daily Herald*: statement on behalf of staff to Congress', 1 Sept. 1923, 'LPLF: DHF'.
[87] Fyfe, *My Seven Selves*, p. 257.

expect more support from its own newspaper.'[88] The submissions from the Printers and Journalists showed how much this view was shared by the rank and file as well. Technically, they accused the paper of being over-manned; they meant that it was manned by the wrong people. Fyfe, the editor, began by taking up the Printers' charge of overstaffing.[89]

Mr. Fyfe: ... I do not see how you could produce a newspaper with a less staff than Mr. Lansbury and I propose. You could produce a different kind of paper, but you could not produce a newspaper.

You see here, they say, on p. 3 —'Reuters Agency could be depended on for foreign news'. . . That means we must rely entirely on capitalist agencies . . .

Mr. Holmes [P.T.F.]: It is very interesting to us to learn that foreign correspondents had six months agreement . . .

Mr. Henderson: Do let us ask Mr. Holmes to keep in mind the stages through which the paper has gone . . .

Mr. Hutchinson: What could Mr. Holmes suggest would be a reasonable period? . . .

Mr. Isaacs [George Isaacs, P.T.F.]: Perhaps Mr. Fyfe can answer that.

Mr. Fyfe: The Chairman is conducting the meeting.

Mr. Isaacs: I thought you were by the way you were behaving up there.

Mr. Richardson [Secretary of the N.U.J.]: One of the journalists dismissed is my brother. I do not wish to mention names as I do not wish anyone else to be victimised . . .

Mr. Morrison [Herbert Morrison]: The Federation is aware, I suppose, that complaints have been made as to the news which Reuter supplies.

Mr. Holmes: It is not as unreliable as that from special correspondents of the *Daily Herald* . . .

I want to say that information has come to us that since it has been decided to reduce the size of the paper of course the staff has been reduced.

That part of the editorial staff that is possibly more favourable to the Trade Union movement is being dispensed with. And men who have advanced political opinions in accordance with those running the show at the present time are retained. I think that can be proved by reference to the names . . .

We feel strongly we are not being treated properly by the Management. There are certain men in the Editorial Department . . . who had no experience whatever of journalistic work before they went to the *Daily Herald*. I could give instances if that were necessary.

Mr. Walkden: How long have they been there, Mr. Holmes?

Mr. Holmes: I could not say how long; but all the time the paper has been going from bad to worse.

Mr. Fyfe: What does Mr. Holmes mean by the paper going from bad to worse?

Mr. Holmes: I mean the whole tone has gone from bad to worse.

[88] Committee of Enquiry, 1 Oct. 1923, 'LPLF: DHF'.
[89] Committee of Enquiry, 11 Oct. 1923, 'LPLF: DHF'.

The Chairman [Arthur Pugh]: I really must say this line of argument does not seem to come within the purview of the committee.

These elevated exchanges show how suspect the paper now was in the eyes of at least a number of unionists. Furthermore, it would be unfair to the unions to maintain that there was not some substance in their charges. For if it were not true that unionists were discriminated against in employment, it was true that Communists were well represented in the paper's editorial direction. The foreign editor, Norman Ewer, was then a well-known Communist and the paper was noticeably favourable to the Third International. The assistant editor, William Mellor, was (temporarily) a Communist and had got himself into a scrape with both Fyfe and the Labour Party over a projected visit to Russia. Another member of the editorial department, Francis Meynell, had made himself notorious during the 'Russian gold' affair—the '*Daily Herald* catastrophe' Scott Lindsay called it[90]—as had Lansbury himself.[91] Other criticism, particularly MacDonald's belief that the paper's correspondence columns were 'stacked' against the Party, was more or less unfair. But while they could legitimately regard attacks upon the paper's industrial reporting as misguided (which is not to say they were misguided), Lansbury and Fyfe ought really to have understood how sensitive Labour leaders were to the reporting of relations between the Communists and other labour and socialist movements. It was their treatment of the Internationals that lost them the support of Henderson, hitherto a formidable friend of the *Herald*. Finally, Lansbury's attempts to defend the staff produced the opposite of his intended effect: when he wrote to Henderson that 'as to people being discharged my son-in-law [Raymond] Postgate is one and he is a full-blooded Communist',[92] all he did was to emphasize that there were Communists on the staff, and that there was conceivably nepotism as well.

Had the Printers been in a position to carry their criticisms further there might have been fairly immediate as well as drastic changes in the paper, but the unexpected general election of 1923, and the even more unexpected formation of a Labour government in January 1924, made it necessary to keep the *Herald* intact. At the same time, however, the formation of MacDonald's ministry made the paper's editorial direction, as it was then constituted, doubly difficult. Firstly, if the paper's circulation did not rise during a period of Labour government—as it did not—then people wished to know why. Secondly, since it was supposed to be an act of duty to give the government the support the

---

[90] H. S. Lindsay to Middleton, 14 Sept. 1920, 'LPLF, CA/ADM/34'.
[91] For the catastrophe, see Fyfe, *My Seven Selves*, pp. 254–5.
[92] Lansbury to Henderson, 13 Oct. 1923, 'LPLF: DHF'.

movement thought owing it, many Labour leaders considered the *Herald*'s position little short of treasonable, though in retrospect the paper appears remarkably loyal to the government—if to the left of it. Its real guilt, in effect, was consistency: it remained vaguely sympathetic to the Third International—though with the formation of the Labour and Socialist International the previous year the break between social democracy and Communism had been made more or less permanent; it was ardent for the Russian negotiations and had little time for the argument that the delicate parliamentary position made necessary all sorts of unpleasant shifts and arrangements. This position was resented by many, from the prime minister downwards.

By July MacDonald was already convinced that the paper was 'fast becoming a Communist organ'.[93] On 11 August, prompted by the *Herald*'s treatment of R.A.F. police action in Iraq, MacDonald, who had manfully restrained himself so far, wrote a formal complaint to Henderson:[94]

If Communists are to enjoy the luxury of a daily paper they ought to find the money and the patronage for themselves, and not play the cuckoo game. Because the article this morning surpasses in its mischief what has been done by the paper, I cannot refrain from drawing your attention to it, as a culpable piece of disloyalty to the Party . . .

Nor was Fyfe exactly tactful in his responses to criticism. Towards the end of his ministry, MacDonald wrote to Fyfe accusing the *Herald* of being 'a dumping-ground for rubbish which would be put in the waste-paper basket for anyone who knew his business or who was not out for mischief'.[95] This was an impertinent letter, but it is doubtful if it deserved the cheeky reply it got.

I have had to do with so many Prime Ministers [Fyfe wrote] . . . that I am not surprised by the petulant tone of your letter . . . The *Herald* is the organ, not of your government, not of a Party, but of the Labour Movement. In that Movement there are many currents of opinion. It would be foolish to aim at making the policy of the *Herald* fit in with all these currents of opinion, but it is very important that no section should feel resentment at not being allowed to express its own views in its own newspaper . . . It should be a help for a Prime Minister to keep in touch with the sentiments and convictions, the reactions and perplexities of those who have put him where he is. Many things you have said and done . . . prove that this advantage is not shared by you . . . You tell me I do not know my business as editor . . . but I have been

---

[93] Rose Rosenberg [MacDonald's secretary] to Middleton, 28 July 1924, 'LPLF: JSM Uncat. Misc.'.

[94] MacDonald to Henderson, 11 Aug. 1924, 'LPLF: JSM Uncat. Misc.'.

[95] Letters quoted in Fyfe, *My Seven Selves*, pp. 257–9.

in training for thirty years. You have been Prime Minister for eight months
... Isn't it just possible that you have something to learn too.

This was a shrewd reply, and a wounding one; but it was wounding
only if one accepted Fyfe's definition of what the *Herald* should be.
There were many in the movement who did not accept that definition,
and they were, furthermore, highly placed—quite apart, of course,
from the prime minister.

This criticism became explicit with the fall of the Labour government. After a long controversy over the paper's reporting of that
well-known sore spot, the affairs of the Internationals, Tom Shaw, the
secretary of the Labour and Socialist International and minister of
labour in MacDonald's government, wrote to Norman Ewer:

> I cannot say that I am astonished at the feeling which exists in Continental
> Socialist and Labour Movements respecting the *Daily Herald*. I agree with
> my Continental friends that the *Daily Herald* is the worst informed paper in
> Europe so far as the Socialist Movement is concerned.[96] It never attempts to
> state the point of view of the Socialist Parties, but wherever Communist or
> minority opposition exists it appears to be able to state that opposition.[97]

On the same day that this damning letter was composed, Middleton
received from Ben Shaw a resolution from the Scottish executive, not a
stronghold of the right, noting that the *Herald* 'publishes inadequate
and distorted reports of Labour Party affairs in Scotland'.[98]

The *Herald*'s deviation might have been tolerable had the paper won
commercial success. But between the general election of 1923 and the
dissolution of parliament in October 1924 circulation fell from a high
point of 419,000 to 354,000. It was disappointing, and not just to the
Herald (as Lansbury sadly admitted),[99] that the presence in office of a
Labour government made no difference to circulation one way or the
other—though Lansbury did feel that political criticism might have
been partly responsible for this.[100] Happily for the *Herald* another

---

[96] The minutes of the Labour and Socialist International are filled with views of the
Continental friends. In June 1924 Fritz Adler, joint secretary of the International, attacked
the *Herald* for suggesting that only in Russia was May Day observed as a holiday. The
Menshevik, Abramovitch, claimed that 'comrades of all countries were of opinion that the
Daily Herald was purely and simply a Communist organ. How little it tells except about
Communist Russia, and how many lies are told in it about France and Germany. Everyone
recognizes that it is not a Social Democratic paper ... '. (Exec. Comm. L.S.I. 'Minutes',
5–7 June 1924.) In November there were complaints to the Administrative Committee of
the International that the German Communist paper, *Rote Fahne*, was reprinting verbatim
articles on German socialism from the *Herald*. The national executive was instructed to
take action. (L.S.I. 'Administrative Committee Minutes', 21 Nov. 1924.)

[97] Shaw to Ewer, 11 Feb. 1925, 'LPLF: DHF'.

[98] Ben Shaw to Middleton, 11 Feb. 1925, 'LPLF: DHF'.

[99] General Manager's Report, 20 May 1924, 'LPLF: DHF'.

[100] General Manager's Report, 14 July 1924, 'LPLF: DHF'.

general election intervened to inflate its circulation at a time when it was on the point of liquidation. By the end of 1924, however, with election excitement behind it, the paper was once again in low water and the directors contemplated its supersession by a weekly.[101]

In December (1924) the *Herald*'s critics finally organized themselves: yet another sub-committee was appointed to examine the paper, but this committee was much more union-dominated than its predecessors—there were four members from the general council, four from the national executive, but only two from the *Herald*. Its leading lights were Ernest Bevin and Robert Williams, both early supporters turned public critics of the *Herald*. The line of development now seemed fairly clear.

The committee was due to meet on 12 January 1925; Lansbury relieved everyone of much embarrassment by resigning as general manager nine days before. His letter began perfunctorily and inaccurately by noting that the paper was in a healthy state and 'there was no question of leaving a sinking ship'. However, he continued

I continually find myself in conflict with the views and opinions of others as to how the office shall be managed. There is no doubt that the place could be much more efficiently run than it has been, but poverty and poverty alone is responsible for whatever defects exist in the organisation of this business.

Apart from all personal questions . . . there is the further fact that many of our leaders on the political and industrial side do not give the paper the support that it is entitled to receive. We have a great abundance of critics in high places . . . [102]

His resignation was accepted on 27 January 1925, and he was succeeded by Robert Williams.[103]

The departure of the old guard was completed by the resignation of Philip Millwood, the secretary of the *Herald*, at the end of March. Millwood was almost automatically suspect. He had been a conscientious objector in the war, was a Quaker friend of Clifford Allen's, and was one of those who had entered the Labour movement all too obviously via the I.L.P. His resignation was accepted speedily and without regret.[104] He wrote to Ben Turner, the chairman of the *Herald*, that the way his department was disposed of 'makes it evident that our work is not held in much esteem; and all the efforts during five years' service have thus not found much favour in the minds of the Directors'.[105]

---

[101] Philip Millwood [Sec. of the *Herald*] to Henderson, 6 Nov. 1924, 'LPLF: DHF'.
[102] Lansbury to Ben Turner, 3 Jan. 1925, 'LPLF: DHF'.
[103] *Daily Herald* Board of Directors, 'Minutes', 27 Jan. 1925, 'LPLF: DHF'.
[104] Ibid., 5 Apr. 1925.
[105] Millwood to Turner, 7 Apr. 1925, 'LPLF: DHF'.

The resignations of Lansbury and Millwood, and the arrival of Robert Williams as a trade-union nominee, ended this second phase in the *Herald*'s life. Between 1912 and 1919, the most vigorous period in the paper's history, it was entirely independent; between 1919 and 1925 it attempted to remain independent in editorial policy, while more or less totally dependent upon the movement for finances. This could only end as it did—in the subordination of the *Herald*'s editorial independence to its economic needs. All this aside, however, it needs to be said that the fate of the *Herald* was not different from the one that overtook the Labour Research Department and the advisory committees—organizations which all fitted rather awkwardly into the structure of the Labour Party. Thus the process of administrative 'streamlining' and more or less unremitting trade-union pressure in all likelihood would have absorbed the *Herald* anyway, and certainly would have after the unions had detected the Communist threat.

But though trade-union pressure is the most insistent theme in the story of the *Herald*, the source of its difficulties can also be found elsewhere. There was, to start with, great confusion as to what sort of paper it should be. It may have been true, as the unions claimed, that it was overstaffed; it may also be true, as Fyfe claimed, that, apart from Henderson, none of the union leaders had the faintest understanding of how a paper should be managed. What was important, however, was the disgreeement between Lansbury and Fyfe, on one hand, and the movement on the other, about the paper's content. The movement wanted an industrial-political paper, one that did the rounds of the local parties and the trades councils, earnestly reporting the movement and closely supervised by it. Lansbury wanted an independent left-wing paper, Labour in its sympathies but not tied to official policy. In the event, the *Herald* was not official enough to satisfy the people who paid its bills, but too heavily encumbered with political reporting to gain a mass circulation.

Both sides must accept their share of blame. It was Lansbury more than anyone else who forced the *Herald* on a reluctant Labour movement and did his best to make their fortunes inextricable. Yet he resented it when its editorial policy was criticized by those on whom he had imposed it. However, the Party and the unions wanted a paper, as Angell told them, that was bound to be uninteresting and difficult to sell. But they also wanted one that was profitable, instead of accepting the *Herald*'s losses as a general charge upon the movement as Henderson seems to have wanted and as the much admired S.P.D. did. Some found it offputting to see the Labour leadership railing against the capitalist press as a principle, while desperately trying to hawk the *Herald*'s advertising space to every large capitalist in Britain.

Finally, the experience of the *Herald* seemed to show that the Labour leaders, as they did with so many other things, seriously overestimated the part that politics normally played in the lives of the British working classes. Britain was not Germany: the British working class was enmeshed in its national culture in a way the German working class was not—partly, and the *Herald* felt this, because sport as a working-class pastime was so much more important in Britain than anywhere else in Europe. However unpalatable it probably was, the Labour leaders had to recognize, and eventually did recognize, that a newspaper which at the very least did not emphasize sport, entertainment, and general news as much as politics represented a formula for commercial failure of almost mathematical perfection. Thus the *Herald* staggered from crisis to crisis, rescued by fitful bouts of political enthusiasm at election time, while the *Daily Mail* and the *Daily Express* added hundreds of thousands to their already large circulations.

4. *Summary*

In summary, there are three things that need to be said about the L.R.D., the advisory committees, and the *Daily Herald*. In the first place, they were all conceived as necessary parts of a Party not only competing for government, but one that would be 'fit' for government. The *Daily Herald* was to be the paper of the movement, the propagator of the Party's activities and the necessary prophylaxis against infection from the capitalist press. The L.R.D. and, later, the advisory committees were consciously designed as Labour's civil service performing those functions that the civil service was supposed to do in Whitehall.

In the second place, the institutional position of these three bodies within the Labour Party was vague. It is clear that the semi-independence they could claim at the outset was unlikely to last. They could not hope to escape that process of absorption and centralization that was the characteristic feature of the Party's development. Henderson's passion for unifying the industrial and political side of the movement—a rather indiscriminate passion reinforced by Webb and a few others but not always held by union leaders—was bound to make an organization like the L.R.D. redundant. The eagerness with which Henderson drafted 'Memorandum A' was not a result of any real objection to the politics of the L.R.D., but of his conviction that the Labour Party must evolve in this direction.

Finally, the three institutions were subject to strong and successful trade-union pressure. Not only was this another example of the way the unions were moulding the Labour Party in a way probably not foreseen in 1918, but union intervention of this kind had political consequences as well, quite apart from the obvious one that all three (except the L.R.D. which saved itself by withdrawing from the Labour Party *in toto*) lost such autonomy as they had: it ensured that the kind of reformism enthroned by the 1918 constitution would have few well-placed and effective critics within the Party. To that extent, the proponents of socialism within the Party suffered another defeat.

CONCLUSION

BY the end of 1924 the Labour Party was recognizably the same Party that we know today. There have been, it is true, some intervening disasters: the events of 1931 effectively removed Henderson and MacDonald from its leadership and ended in a bizarre and poignant way the curious relationship which had begun twenty-eight years before. The same events also disposed of the remainder of that founding generation which made its début in the parliaments of 1906 and 1910. There are also some important differences. The triumphant Party of 1945 had many more votes than in 1924; it had, too, more seats, more individual members and relatively fewer trade-union sponsored M.P.s. Above all, the parliamentary party and the parliamentary leadership were much less obviously working-class.

This was a remarkable development which has its own interest. But it also involves wider questions, for the Labour Party became the second party of the state in only fourteen years and did so in a country with tenacious social and political habits. The rise of Labour and the fall of the Liberal Party are, therefore, intrinsically connected. Equally, the triumph of Labour is related to the influences that gave the Party its distinctive character.

The decline of the Liberal Party has understandably fascinated historians; apart from its general political significance it had a gifted and all-too-articulate *dramatis personae*. Furthermore, its decline has not lent itself to obvious historical explanations. On the whole, historians have pointed to the First World War as decisive. George Dangerfield, it is true, saw in the political and industrial crises of the pre-war years symptoms of the oncoming 'strange death of Liberal England'.[1] But his is rather a literary confection which does not attempt serious analysis.[2] The war itself, however, is useful in two ways. It can in the first place be manipulated to give historical form to the parliamentary disintegration of the Liberal Party after August 1914: the ideology and structure of the Liberal Party, the 'war' argument runs, was unsuited to 'total war' and both collapsed under its pressure. Then again, the argument is presented by those historians who see 'total war' as the cause of profound social and economic

---

[1] G. Dangerfield, *The Strange Death of Liberal England, 1910–1914* (New York, 1961).
[2] See, particularly, pp. 426–42. For a discussion of Dangerfield, see Pelling, *Popular Politics*, pp. 102–3.

changes in this country which made the Liberal Party either redundant or actually antipathetic.

Clearly, the two forms of this argument are different. One is, so to speak, superstructural, concerned with policy and leadership; the other looks to society and popular attitudes. The first is a contingent one: on the eve of the war, the Liberal Party, though showing some signs of senescence, was still more or less vigorous and healthy.[3] But quarrels over wartime policy enfeebled and divided its leadership,[4] thus leaving a vacuum into which the Labour Party slipped.[5]

This is an unsatisfactory explanation. To begin with, it assumes that the Liberal Party did split. It would be idle to pretend that there were not deep divisions in the Party; nevertheless Asquith's self-assumed pose after the formation of Lloyd George's government in December 1916 was not that of leader of the opposition, but of the leading Liberal outside the government. Some of his followers were less Roman in their forbearance than he, but they in no way constituted an opposition. What is surprising about the period is the degree to which the Asquithians worked to preserve the unity of the Party, rather than to divide it. Yet, in the long run, it might have served the Liberals better had Asquith really split them, had he gone into the 1918 election not just outside the government, but vigorously opposed to it. The Liberal Party had, after all, in the past survived fundamental divisions. Those who seek to explain the decline of the Liberals in terms of a divided leadership must also explain why the Party weathered the break between Gladstone and Chamberlain. Within seven years of their own disruption Asquith and Lloyd George were back in harness; Gladstone and Chamberlain never re-united but the post-1886 Liberal Party still regained office.

Even if it is true that divisions lost the Liberal Party popular support, it is hard to see why the Labour Party, which was even more divided, should have been the beneficiary. Labour had split first on the outbreak of the war, then again in August–September 1917, and finally in November 1918.[6] In proportion, Labour's divisions received as much publicity as those within official Liberalism; that the Liberals alone appear to have suffered from their divisions suggests that there were other reasons for their decline than the divisions themselves.

There is, then, a second variant of the argument from contingency. This is to suggest that what brought the Liberals to ruin was their

[3] Wilson, *Downfall of the Liberal Party*, p. 18; Clarke, *Lancashire and the New Liberalism*, pp. 402–7.

[4] Wilson, ibid., pp. 49–164.

[5] See R. Skidelsky, *Politicians and the Slump: the Labour Government of 1929–1931* (Penguin ed., London, 1970), p. 433.

[6] For these, see above, pp. 88–110.

doctrinaire adherence to *laissez-faire*.[7] The country, however, wanted to win the war and was ready to accept any control or direction necessary to do so. But (so the argument runs) the great bulk of the Liberal Party was not prepared to give up negligent peacetime habits. It was, therefore, and more or less by popular demand, brushed aside.

This argument is almost certainly fallacious. To suppose that, even in war, the Conservatives were instinctively more collectivist than the Liberals is to ignore everything that happened after 1906. As a general proposition it is unquestionably true that the Liberal Party was more committed to state intervention than the Conservatives, and this was so after 1914 as it was before it. Differences in wartime policy were not argued in categories of economic liberalism, but over the right of the state to conscript. Military conscription has never been, at least not in Britain, part of conventional collectivism, and there were thus more collectivists hesitant about the war than there were those eager to get on with it.

Furthermore, the Labour movement was even more reluctant than the Liberals to accept state control and direction. It may be so that Labour would support any government which would organize the war, but opposition to the kind of measures that Lloyd George was expected to introduce was stronger in the Labour movement than anywhere else. Liberal radicals left their own Party and entered the Labour movement, though not in such numbers as is usually maintained, because official Liberalism seemed all too ready to prosecute the war with vigour. Fighting the war was no index of collectivism, it was a register of patriotism, and the Conservatives were always better at that than their opponents.

The other way out is to suggest that the war itself was so voracious in its needs and so penetrating in its consequences that it completely, or almost completely, overturned accepted political traditions.[8] Marwick has written that whether

we talk of 'rising expectations' or changing 'reference groups' it is apparent that the taste of affluence, afforded to some workers during the war, greatly accelerated that quest for a higher standard of living which in itself was so potent an agent for continuing social change. While it would be absurd to deny that the actual tally of social legislation fell dismally below that promised by the politicians, it is also instructive to make two comparisons: the post-1918

[7] It is urged most strongly by A. J. P. Taylor. See *Politics in Wartime* (London, 1964), pp. 21–40; *English History*, pp. 34–77.
[8] See A. Marwick, 'The Impact of the First World War on British Society', *Journal of Contemporary History*, Jan. 1968; *The Deluge: British Society and the First World War*, (London, 1965), pp. 206–9.

Labour Party with the pre-1914 Labour Party, and the post-1918 franchise with the pre-1914 one—only in 1918, as Mr. Noel Blewett [*sic*] has clearly demonstrated, did Britain become a political democracy.[9]

It is a question how obvious or how true these apparently obvious truths are. There seems little doubt that by 1919, emotionally anyway, people tried to return to 1914 and to behave as if the war had only been an interruption. This applied to their political as much as to their social and economic lives and was perhaps more powerfully felt than those changes the war actually did bring about.[10]

In any case, had the structure of Britain changed so much as a result of the war? The towns were no larger than they had been; there were few new industries; there was no increase in the mobility of the population; despite fashionable forms of social dissent there was little of that political disorientation so noticeable on the Continent. Though the staple industries were soon to be in difficulties, they had also been in some before 1914, and the labour disturbances of 1917–19 were no worse than those of 1911–13. The war had clearly extended the role of the state, but so had the most important social legislation of the Campbell Bannerman and Asquith governments. As to those two 'instructive' comparisons made by Marwick: the post-war Labour Party was, of course, not nearly so different from its predecessor as he believes. Of the franchise reform it is worth noting that suffrage bills had been before parliament in 1912 and 1913, and, despite the dilly-dallying of the Liberal government, some kind of legislation would have been passed before long. The 1918 Act, for its part, was the most conservative that could have been devised in the circumstances. The vote for all men over twenty-one was irresistible, but for women the suffrage was limited by age and property qualifications, a franchise widely admitted to be illegitimate even before 1914.

Furthermore, it is easy to exaggerate the importance of the war in encouraging both trade-union membership and industrial militancy. These were even more marked features of the years before the war than of the war itself. Between 1910 and 1920 the sharpest annual rates of increase in trade-union membership were at the beginning and end of the decade (see table on following page).

Thus the rise in union membership during the war was more than equalled by the rates of increase before it; the wartime industrial disputes and the exceptionally low levels of unemployed had their precedent in the inflationary conditions of 1911–14, which, as

[9] Marwick, 'Impact of the First World War', p. 62. Cf. W. G. Runciman, *Relative Deprivation and Social Justice* (London, 1966; Penguin ed. with postscript, London, 1972)
[10] See C. L. Mowat, *Britain between the Wars* (London, 1955), pp. 8–9.

9

Table 25[11]

Total Trade Union Membership, 1910–1920

	Membership	% Rate of Increase
1910	2·565 million	–
1911	3·139	22·5
1912	3·416	8·8
1913	4·135	21·0
1914	4·145	–
1915	4·359	5·0
1916	4·644	6·5
1917	5·499	18·3
1918	6·533	18·5
1919	7·926	21·4
1920	8·347	5·3

Pelling convincingly argues, were the real cause of the great strikes of the last years of peace.[12]

It becomes, therefore, difficult to avoid the conclusion that the war itself was not of first importance in the Labour Party's post-war successes. Everything points to Labour's enduring *ante-bellum* character: continuity of leadership and personnel at all levels, effective continuity of policy, and, above all, continuity of organization. The Labour Party, the 'old' pre-1931 Party, remained as it had been before 1914—propagandist and evangelical. It saw its function as the political mobilization of an already existing industrial class-consciousness: in practice, it concentrated more upon the extension of organization than upon the perfection of policy. But this organization, particularly in the constituencies, was itself only the political side of an industrial organization that had grown rapidly in the late nineteenth and early twentieth centuries. Almost everywhere the proliferating trades councils became the local agencies of the Labour Party. The councils themselves were a response to the industrial pressures of late Victorian and Edwardian capitalism, and these pressures affected craft and general unions alike. But a more or less mature capitalism imposed upon the British working-class not only its own technological and vocational demands, but in addition, a sensitive and tenacious pattern of class loyalties whose political expression was the Labour Party.

'Objectively,' there seems little reason to suppose that the Labour Party should not have advanced as quickly as its counterparts in Western Europe and Australia did. It is true that the British Liberal Party—and also the Conservative Party—had a hold on sections of

---

[11] From Mitchell and Deane, *British Historical Statistics*, p. 68; see also above, p. 86.
[12] Pelling, *Popular Politics*, p. 149.

the working-class which had no parallel elsewhere, and that there was much in common between the political objectives of the Liberal and Labour Parties. But this was probably of less significance than the electoral impediments to Labour's activities. By 1914, of those countries with a functioning representative system of government, Britain alone did not have universal manhood suffrage; indeed at least half her working-class were excluded from voting. The war ended that, and, at the same time as it enfranchised all men and some women, it renewed the upward rush in trade-union membership and intensified two important tendencies of Edwardian capitalism: industrial agglomeration and the destruction of the social and economic bases of regional and parochial life. But why was it Labour, and not the Liberal Party which benefited from these changes?

The answer is to be found in the nature of the relationship between the Labour Party and the trade-unions on the one hand, and between the trade-unions and the industrial working-classes on the other. Since the Labour Party was inextricably linked to the unions, it, like them, followed the main lines of British economic development. Because it had no life apart from the unions it gained electorally from their growth. Like the unions, the Labour Party was national in its organization and centralized in its institutions. It deliberately overrode regional boundaries and local interests. Its leaders were positively suspicious of the regions and disliked attempts to make use of the 'nationalist' aspirations of the Scots and the Welsh.

This can be seen nowhere better than in the national executive's opposition to 'federalizing' the Party. Its members, and Henderson in particular, were actively conscious of creating a Party to suit what they took to be contemporary political needs. This meant to Labour, as it did to the unions, centralized authority in a national organization. Henderson's 'General Scheme'[13] was deliberately written to assert the supremacy of national organization over regional. Thus he wished to draft Wales out of existence on the reasonably plausible grounds that north Wales was now part of Lancashire and Cheshire—or was becoming part of it—while south Wales was so closely linked with southern England as to make it impossible to disentangle the two. Of course, this was too much for the national executive and Wales survived intact, but the principle was clear.

In its formal organization the Party had consistently imitated the great unions. With its national executive, secretariat, and pyramidal structure, it was (and is) quite unlike any other British party. Since the unions had always been the model, even during the heyday of the 'federation of federations' before the war, there was in practice an

13 See above, pp. 174–6.

almost unbroken line of continuity in the development of Party organization: the 1918 constitution, for the immediate future at least, made little difference. Throughout the period increasing centralization of the Party was accompanied by growing dependence on the unions. Head Office successfully defeated regional devolution and won more or less complete power to regulate the political complexion of candidates local parties might choose. This explains the comparative ease with which the Communists were excluded from the Party and their lack of success in local organization once Head Office had intervened.[14] The Labour Party's own departments were victims of the same process. Semi-independent bodies like the Labour Research Department, the Advisory Committees, and the *Daily Herald* soon lost whatever independence they had.[15]

But it was the unions as much as anyone else who were responsible for what happened to these departments; similarly Party centralization stopped whenever the unions felt their interests threatened. Thus Head Office was unable to redistribute constituency finances, as the unions would tolerate no interference with their political funds.[16] For the same reasons the executive was reluctant to force candidates upon constituencies: the unions controlled local finances. The fate of W. B. Taylor in South Norfolk, or even MacDonald himself in Woolwich, showed what the unions could do to a candidate who did not please them.[17]

These two tendencies—increasing centralization of Party organization and a growing union predominance—went *pari passu*. But union predominance was felt at all levels. While it is possible to distinguish the national Party from its union affiliates, in the constituencies it is much more difficult to do so. This had been the case before the war as well, but the links between the Party and the unions locally were tightened by the failure of the 1918 reorganization to work as it was expected to. Few 'model' parties were established and individual membership grew sluggishly almost everywhere and in some places not at all. In the rush to contest as many seats as possible Labour fell back on what was already there: fell back, that is, on trade-union organization. For the most part, the unions and their officials made up the deficiency of individual members. They provided the volunteer workers, the local party officers, and the money. Local parties with strong union branches were usually well organized; those with a union-sponsored candidate were well financed too. It must also be

[14] See above, pp. 191–204.
[15] See above, pp. 206–35.
[16] See above, pp. 156–62.
[17] For South Norfolk, see pp. 133–6; for Woolwich, pp. 132–3.

said that in these constituencies Labour organization worked as effectively as that of the Conservative Party. Even in the rural divisions Labour organizers turned instinctively to the local unions. The only county constituencies, therefore, that were competently organized were those where either the Miners or the Agricultural Labourers had an interest. Even in a rural constituency with scarcely any union membership, so long as a union had taken responsibility, then the local party would at least have enough money. What emerged was informal, often improvised, but remarkably tough. It was this resilient and complicated organization that held the Labour Party together in the First World War at a time when the parliamentary party more or less fell apart. If the Labour Party had been a vehicle of ideological belief, as to a considerable degree the S.P.D. still was, or existed even primarily for specific political objectives, it might have been rent as some of the European socialist parties were. Yet the Labour Party was not based upon broadly articulated principles, but rather upon a highly developed class-consciousness and intense class loyalties. The trade-unions cultivated this consciousness and these loyalties; they also contributed to the disintegration of regional and traditional allegiances and to their supersession by allegiances imposed by class and occupation.

To this development the war did not act so much as a generator as an accelerator: the years before 1914 are, therefore, as important as those after the outbreak of the war. The disputes between the two partners in the great Party of Progress which followed the 1910 general elections[18] were a result of heightening class-consciousness in the industrial working-class. Not a consciousness which is easily definable, that is to say, let alone a Marxist one, but an implicit consciousness that the Labour Party stood for them in a way no other party did. John Vincent has suggested that the emerging Liberal Party in fact offered its electorate little: but it was the Party 'of moral ideas' and of personal liberation—as such it excited passionate enthusiasms.[19] In an oddly analogous manner, the Labour Party also presented no great programme, but it meant much to its adherents and elicited the same enthusiasms. Indeed, in programmatic terms the idea of a 'progressive party' was convenient and sensible—hence its attraction to *parliamentarians* of both the Liberal and Labour Parties. To politicians who thought that legislation and policies created party loyalties disruption of progressive unity was absurd and self-defeating. Yet party loyalties were not conditioned by parliamentary require-

---

[18] For Labour–Liberal relations before the war, see above, pp. 48–71.

[19] J. R. Vincent, *The Formation of the Liberal Party* (London, 1966); there is a brilliant summary of his position in *Pollbooks: How Victorians Voted* (Cambridge, 1967), pp. 43–50.

ments, but increasingly by class. 'Labour representation' in consequence became an issue in itself. Those active in constituency affairs understood this better than the grandees of the parliamentary Liberal Party ever did. As early as 1902 Herbert Samuel noted that 'when the forces of progress [i.e. the Liberal Party] are divided in the House of Commons it is usually on some question of Empire policy'. When the progressive forces 'were divided in a constituency it is usually on the question of Labour representation'.[20]

The eclipse of the Liberal Party, therefore, was not due to 'the war', or a wrong-headed pursuit of *laissez-faire*, or the split between Asquith and Lloyd George, or the conversion of the workers to socialism, but to a slow change in the way popular political affiliations were decided. As political allegiance became more and more determined by class self-awareness, the Liberal Party found it could make no claim on the loyalties of any class. The widening of the suffrage hastened this change: it enrolled millions of people who had no reason to vote Liberal and the Liberal Party had no agency to recruit them. It is possible that the Liberals held on to a fair part of what they had, but more and more in areas outside the perimeters of industrial Britain.

Within the Labour Party itself the preponderance of the unions meant that class loyalty drove out socialist doctrine. The war, far from representing a general movement to the left, was responsible for a confident and aggressive attack from the right. This attack was partly successful: clause IV, the 'socialist objective', was inserted in a constitution that confirmed the triumph of the unions and the defeat of the socialists. The real class warriors were the jingo trade-unionists who were able to win a usually illegitimate support by pointing to the middle-class origins of many of the socialists. For the I.L.P. this had always been a difficulty, but when it became, after 1917, a haven for dissenting radicals from the superior classes, what was in 1914 only a difficulty became then a catastrophe.[21]

It is true that the exclusion of the I.L.P. was partly a technical matter and the expansion of Labour's organization after the war was a disaster for it.[22] Yet it received no help from either Henderson or MacDonald. Henderson, ineradicably a trade-unionist in his outlook, disliked it precisely because it was 'independent', because it could not easily be absorbed into the Labour Party, and because it was not prone to the kind of loyalty that was expected in the circles from which he came. But MacDonald, anything but a trade-unionist in his attitudes, also connived at the diminution of its influence. Before 1914 he tried

---

[20] *New Liberal Review*, 21 (Oct. 1902).
[21] For the socialist objective, see above, pp. 96–8.   [22] See above, p. 105.

to curb the socialists by extending the national Party's activities; after 1917 he hastily (and realistically) associated himself with a constitution which he had publicly opposed at the time of its presentation and which would, it was thought, make the socialist societies redundant. By 1919 the last strongholds of socialist thought in the Party were the L.R.D., and, to a lesser degree, the Advisory Committees. Five years later the L.R.D. had been totally reformed, largely at the command of the unions, and its more independent spirits left the Party entirely. Similarly, the Advisory Committees were brought to heel; again, mostly on the insistence of the unions. The fate of the *Daily Herald*, a socialist stronghold of a different sort, needs no repetition.[23] Those of Labour's post-war intellectuals who remained within the Party and with whom Henderson had such close rapport, were not usually I.L.P.ers; they were more often Fabians or guild socialists who presented no challenge to the Party's government: the Fabians, because, in the end, they respected power more than doctrine, the guild socialists because their doctrines were too quirky to be taken seriously by anyone.

A Party with a socialist objective but no socialist ideology needs something else: the movement, and service to the movement, became a substitute. But though a real sense of the movement did develop (as it was bound to do) its development consistently disappointed the hopes of those who, like Henderson and Morrison, were bewitched by the German example. The monolithic movement, embracing both political and industrial wings, and carrying with it all but the socially vicious and obscurantist, was a tantalizing phenomenon. Yet it was an impossible one, and much of the social and political history of the Labour Party in these years is a history of failure.

At the centre, in London, the combined T.U.C. and Labour Party lasted much less than a decade.[24] In the constituencies the formally amalgamated Labour parties and trades councils had a continuous lack of success; many of the complicated fusions that were forced upon them in the 1920s had to be disentangled ten years later. It was impossible to inculcate that feeling of unity which was (however exaggerated) apparent in Germany before 1914.[25] The British working-classes maddeningly refused to read a Labour newspaper, at least one that did not in more than equal parts report sport and sensations. They did not lead their social lives within the confines of their Party, nor did they regard Party allegiance as the judge of their cultural values.

[23] See above. pp. 221–34.
[24] See above, p. 234.
[25] For this, see J. P. Nettl, 'The German Social Democratic Party, 1890–1914, as a Political Model', *Past and Present*, 30 (1965), pp. 76–8.

There were three reasons for this comparative failure. First, the Labour leaders greatly overestimated the interest in politics that members of the working-classes would normally have. In Britain there were too many other things: a highly developed commercial press; perhaps the most popular system of organized sport in the world; the sheer business of earning a living.

Secondly, the British working-classes had not suffered active persecution, nor seen their Party driven underground, as the Germans had done. This was a political trauma that shaped the personality of the German labour movement. It welded the German working-classes together, probably heightened their political consciousness, and certainly made the S.P.D. the focus for emotional loyalties that the British Labour Party has never received.[26]

Finally, the Labour leaders mistakenly assumed that the unions and the Party would, of necessity, march together. But this was very much one of Henderson's personal obsessions; since his prestige was so high and his administrative skills so overwhelming he was able to force through policies (the reorganization of 1920 was one) in which the unions were only reluctant partners.[27] Yet the relationship between the two was an unequal one. The Labour Party always needed the unions; the unions did not always need the Labour Party. They had the alternatives of industrial action or of directly negotiating with the other side. Henderson, himself, was deeply disappointed at the unions' willingness to disregard the 'political wing'. In 1920, for example, looking back over a momentous year of actual and threatened industrial stoppages, he told the national executive that 'the political wing has been completely excluded from participation in the trade union consultations and conferences'. Only when 'there is a possibility of the venue being changed to the political arena [is] the political wing . . . invited to seek the co-operation of the industrial wing'.[28]

On the other hand, the Labour Party had no such freedom. As a popular institution it was nothing without the unions. Politically, Labour can choose to govern 'in the national interest', to treat the unions as just another pressure group. And it has done so, but always to its cost.

If the attempt to create a great unified movement foundered on a practical divergence of interests, so did the attempt to bribe into the Party all men of goodwill. That essay in breaking out of electoral dependence upon the industrial working-class was an inevitable failure.

[26] For this generally, see G. Ritter, *Die Arbeiterbewegung im Wilhelminischen Reich: die Sozialdemokratische Partei und die freien Gewerkschaften, 1890–1900* (Berlin, 1959).

[27] See above, pp. 212–13.

[28] In a commentary circulated to members of the N.E.C., dated ?20 Sept. 1920, and filed as 'LPLF: JSM Uncat. Misc.'.

But much time and some money was wasted on trying to win rural seats that could not be won and were not necessary for victory anyway. Above all, the 1918 constitution did not work in the way both its protagonists and its opponents assumed that it would. The socialist and managerial middle-classes, if they existed at all outside the Fabian imagination, did not support the Labour Party in any significant numbers. The post-1918 constituency parties were, of course, even more union-dominated than they had been before. Anything else would have been cause for alarm, though it did not suit the curious ideology of the Labour leadership to say so. In a nation profoundly divided by class, the Labour Party could expect no real support outside the class that had given it life.

The result was paradoxical: one of the most highly class-conscious working-classes in the world produced a Party whose appeal was specifically intended to be classless. Accepting the Labour Party meant accepting not socialism but an intricate network of loyalties. In return, the Labour Party accepted its members as long as they understood its disciplines and conventions. MacDonald was rejected in 1931 not because he lost his principles but because he lost his loyalties. This was a trade-union code of behaviour; so were the political aims of the Labour Party essentially trade-union ones. Commending the new constitution to the June 1918 conference, the Party chairman, F. W. Purdy of the Shipwrights, said that

... the broadening of the Constitution to include the worker by hand or brain (a step necessary if Labour is to take its rightful position in national life) will bring into our Party all those who are willing to give of their best in the social service of the community and place our claim to be a National Party in its broadest and widest sense before the country ... Our aim is not to serve sectional interests alone, or to set class against class, but rather to secure that all classes as far as possible, shall come together to make this country a place in which every man, woman and child will have ample opportunities to live and enjoy a happier and better life than has hitherto been possible.[29]

Within these limited terms the Labour Party has had reasonable success. If it is objected that it has not served the cause of socialism or even the 'true' interests of the working-classes the answer is that it was never designed to do so.

[29] *Conference Report*, June 1918, p. 25.

BIBLIOGRAPHY

All printed matter is published in London unless otherwise indicated.

I. ARCHIVAL SOURCES

At Transport House, London:

Labour Party Letter Files
(Note on Cataloguing. When this book was begun none of the Labour Party Letter Files was catalogued in any numerical or systematic way; other than giving the name of such boxes as had originally been classified, there was no useful way of referring to the Files. Recently, much of the Party correspondence has been catalogued and this process is continuing. If, therefore, a letter has been catalogued I have given the reference number. If the letter is not catalogued, or was not catalogued before the completion of this book, but has a recognizable box name, I have given that—for example, 'Affiliations 1917'. Since I, myself, reboxed a lot of correspondence as 'Middleton Papers', I have used the notation 'JSM: Uncat.' for such letters. Similarly, if any correspondence is boxed as 'MacDonald', but not otherwise catalogued, I have provided the notation 'JRM: Uncat.'. If, to my knowledge, correspondence is not classified in any helpful way, I have simply called it 'Uncat.'.)
Minutes of the National Executive Committee of the Labour Party
Minutes of the National Joint Council of the Labour Party and the Trade Union Congress
Minutes of the Scottish Executive Committee of the Labour Party
Daily Herald Files
Minutes of the Executive Committee of the Women's Labour League

At Congress House, London:

Minutes of the Parliamentary Committee of the Trades Union Congress
Minutes of the General Council of the Trades Union Congress

At Nuffield College, Oxford:

Fabian Historical Documents (Archives of the Fabian Society)

Local Labour Party Archival Sources:

Minutes of the Glasgow Central Labour Party
Minutes of the Glasgow Trades Council
(Both in the Mitchell Library, Glasgow)

Minutes of the Liverpool Labour Representation Committee
(Liverpool City Library)

II. PRIVATE PAPERS
At the London School of Economics:
Herbert Bryan Papers
Dalton Papers
Lansbury Papers
Morel Papers
Passfield Papers

At the Beaverbrook Library:
Lloyd George Papers

At Nuffield College, Oxford:
J. A. Pease Papers

III. PRINTED DOCUMENTARY SOURCES
Labour Party, *Reports of the Annual Conference*
Scottish Council of the Labour Party, *Reports of the Annual Conference*
Trades Union Congress, *Reports of the Annual Congress*
Co-operative Union, *Reports of the Annual Congress*
Independent Labour Party, *Annual Conference Reports*
Labour Research Department, *Annual Reports*
Barrow-in-Furness L.R.C., *Reports*
Clitheroe Labour Party, *Agent's Annual Reports*
Dundee L.R.C., *Annual Reports*
Edinburgh Labour Party, *Reports*
Ince Division Labour Party, *Rules*
Leeds L.R.C., *Year Books*
London Labour Party, *Report of the Executive*
Manchester and Salford L.R.C., *Annual Reports*

Printed Diaries:

COLE, MARGARET (ed.), *Beatrice Webb's Diaries, 1912–1924* (1952).
MIDDLEMAS, R. K. (ed.), *Thomas Jones, Whitehall Diaries* (Oxford, 1969).
WILSON, T. (ed.), *The Political Diaries of C. P. Scott, 1911–1928*
(1970).

IV. NEWSPAPERS AND PERIODICALS
National:
The Times
Manchester Guardian
Daily Chronicle
Daily Citizen
Daily Herald

Daily Telegraph
Daily News
Co-operative News
Labour Leader
Liberal Magazine
Nation

Local:
Birmingham Post
Cheshire Daily Echo
Derby Daily Express
Derbyshire Courier
East Sussex News
Eastern Daily Press
Glasgow Herald
Holmfirth Express
Islington Daily Gazette and North London Tribune
Keighley News
Lanarkshire News
Liverpool Courier
Liverpool Echo
London Labour Party Circular
London Labour Party Chronicle
London News
Ludlow Advertiser
Motherwell Times
Newcastle Daily Courier
Newcastle Daily Journal
Norwich Mercury
Retford, Worksop, Isle of Axholme and Gainsborough News
Scotsman
Seaham Weekly News
Shepton Mallet Journal
South Wales Daily Post
Western Mail
Widnes Examiner
Woolwich Gazette and Plumstead News
Woolwich Herald
Yorkshire Post

V. OFFICIAL PRINTED SOURCES

Parliamentary Accounts and Papers, 1924 (2), xviii (Electoral Expenses of
   Parliamentary Candidates, 1922).
Parliamentary Accounts and Papers, 1924 (151), xviii (Electoral Expenses
   of Parliamentary Candidates, 1923).
Parliamentary Accounts and Papers, 1926 (1), xxii (Electoral Expenses of
   Parliamentary Candidates, 1924).

VI. THESES

ARDITTI, CYNTHIA I., 'The History of the Co-operative Party in the Manchester District' (Manchester M.A. thesis, 1953).

BATHER, L., 'A History of the Manchester and Salford Trades Council' (Manchester Ph.D. thesis, 1956).

BLEWETT, N., 'The British General Elections of 1910' (Oxford D.Phil. thesis, 1967). Since published as *The Peers, the Parties and the People* (1972).

Cox, D., 'The Rise of the Labour Party in Leicester' (Leicester M.A. thesis, 1959).

DOWSE, R. E., 'The Independent Labour Party, 1918–1932' (London Ph.D. thesis, 1957). Since published as *Left in the Centre* (1966).

GREGORY, R., 'The Miners and Politics in England and Wales, 1906–1914' (Oxford D.Phil. thesis, 1964). Since published as *The Miners and British Politics, 1906–1914* (Oxford, 1968).

HASTINGS, R. P., 'The Labour Movement in Birmingham, 1925–1957' (Birmingham Ph.D. thesis, 1959).

MACFARLANE, L. J., 'The Origins of the Communist Party in Great Britain and its Early History' (London Ph.D. thesis, 1961). Since published as *The British Communist Party* (1966).

McKIBBIN, R. I., 'The Evolution of a National Party: Labour's Political Organization, 1910–1924' (Oxford D.Phil. thesis, 1970).

McLEAN, I., 'The Labour Movement in Clydeside Politics, 1914–1922' (Oxford D.Phil. thesis, 1971).

MADDOCK, S., 'The Liverpool Trades Council and Politics, 1878–1918' (Liverpool M.A. thesis, 1959).

MARWICK, A. J. B., 'The Independent Labour Party, 1918–1932' (Oxford B.Litt. thesis, 1960).

THOMPSON, P., 'London Working Class Politics and the Formation of the London Labour Party, 1885–1914' (Oxford D.Phil. thesis, 1963). Since published as *Socialists, Liberals and Labour: the Struggle for London, 1885–1914* (1967).

WINTER, J. M., 'The Development of British Socialist Thought' (Cambridge Ph.D. dissertation, 1970).

VII. SELECTED SECONDARY WORKS

ALLEN, V. L., 'The Re-organization of the Trades Union Congress, 1918–1927', *British Journal of Sociology*, 2 (1960).

ARNOT, R. PAGE, *History of the Labour Research Department* (1926).
– – *The Miners: Years of Struggle* (1953).

BARNES, A., *The Political Aspect of Co-operation* (Manchester, 1922).

BEALEY, F., and PELLING, M. M., *Labour and Politics, 1900–1906* (1958).

BLEWETT, N., 'The Franchise in the United Kingdom, 1885–1914', *Past and Present*, 32 (1965).

BRIGGS, A., and SAVILLE, J. (eds.), *Essays in Labour History, 1886–1923* (1971).

BROCKWAY, A. F., *Inside the Left* (1942).
– – *Socialism over Sixty Years: the Life of Jowett of Bradford* (1946).

BUTLER, D. E., *The Electoral System in Britain* (Oxford, 1953).
CLARKE, P. F., 'British Politics and Blackburn Politics, 1900–1910', *Historical Journal*, 2 (1969).
— — *Lancashire and the New Liberalism* (Cambridge, 1971).
CLEGG, H., FOX, A., and THOMPSON, A. F., *A History of British Trade Unionism since 1889* (Oxford, 1964).
COLE, G. D. H., *A Century of Co-operation* (Manchester, 1944).
— — *A History of the Labour Party since 1914* (1947).
DALTON, H., *Call Back Yesterday* (London, 1953).
FYFE, H. H., *My Seven Selves* (1935).
FYRTH, H. J., and COLLINS, HENRY, *The Foundry Workers* (Manchester, 1959).
GWYN, W. B., *Democracy and the Cost of Politics* (1962).
HAMILTON, M. A., *Arthur Henderson* (1938).
JEFFERYS, J. B., *The Story of the Engineers* (1945).
KINNEAR, M., *The British Voter* (1968).
LANSBURY, G., *The Miracle of Fleet Street* (1925).
LOVELL, JOHN, and ROBERTS, B. C., *A Short History of the T.U.C.* (1968).
MCKENZIE, R. T., *British Political Parties* (1964).
MARWICK, A. J. B., 'The Impact of the First World War on British Society', *Journal of Contemporary History*, 1 (1968).
MATTHEW, H. C. G., *The Liberal Imperialists* (Oxford, 1973).
MIDDLEMAS, R. K., *The Clydesiders* (1965).
MORRISON, H., *An Autobiography* (1960).
PEASE, E. R., *The History of the Fabian Society* (1963).
PELLING, H. M., *Popular Politics and Society in Late Victorian Britain* (1968).
— — *Social Geography of British Elections, 1885–1910* (1967).
— — *The Origins of the Labour Party* (1965).
POIRIER, P. P., *The Advent of the Labour Party* (1958).
POSTGATE, R., *Life of George Lansbury* (1951).
ROBERTS, B. C., *The Trades Union Congress, 1868–1921* (1958).
SNELL, H., *Men, Movements and Myself* (1936).
SNOWDEN, P., *An Autobiography* (1932).
TRACEY, H. (ed.), *The Book of the Labour Party* (1926).
WEBB, S. and B., *A History of Trade Unionism, 1660–1920* (1920).
— — *The Consumers' Co-operative Movement* (1921).
WERTHEIMER, E., *Portrait of the Labour Party* (1929).
WILLIAMS, J. E., *The Derbyshire Miners* (1962).
WILSON, T., *The Downfall of the Liberal Party* (1966).
WINTER, J. M., 'Arthur Henderson, the Russian Revolution and the Reconstruction of the Labour Party', *Historical Journal*, 4 (1972).

INDEX